FROM EMPIRES TO IMPERIALISM

Translated from the original Russian, this book analyses the economic development of leading European empires and the United States of America. The author exposes the myths of the spontaneous emergence of the market economy and the role of government as a disincentive towards private initiative, when for centuries the state power has been carrying out a 'coercing to the market' with all its strength.

This book presents a somewhat epic depiction of the development of Western hegemonic powers within the capitalist world system, from the struggles of the late Middle Ages to the rise and crisis of the American Empire. It both develops and questions some of the traditional assumptions of the world-system theory, arguing that it was very much the political form of the state that shaped capitalism as we know it and that, though the existence of a hegemonic power results from the logic of the system, hegemony is often missing in reality.

A major work of historical Marxist theory, this book is essential reading for students of international political economy, globalisation and the crisis of capitalism. This book is also ideal for students of politics, history, economics and international relations.

Boris Kagarlitsky is Director of the Institute of Globalization and Social Movements in Moscow, a Fellow at the Institute for Comparative Political Studies, the Russian Academy of Sciences and a Coordinator of the Postglobalization Initiative, Moscow. He was a political prisoner under Brezhnev and latterly has been an adviser to the Chair of the Federation of Independent Trade Unions of Russia.

Rethinking Globalizations
Edited by Barry K. Gills

NEWCASTLE UNIVERSITY, UK

This series is designed to break new ground in the literature on globalization and its academic and popular understanding. Rather than perpetuating or simply reacting to the economic understanding of globalization, this series seeks to capture the term and broaden its meaning to encompass a wide range of issues and disciplines and convey a sense of alternative possibilities for the future.

FROM EMPIRES TO IMPERIALISM

The state and the rise of bourgeois civilisation

Boris Kagarlitsky

Translated by Renfrey Clarke

Translation sponsored by the Postglobalization Initiative, www.pglobal.org

LONDON AND NEW YORK

First published 2014
by Routledge
2 Park Square, Milton Park, Abingdon, Oxon OX14 4RN

and by Routledge
711 Third Avenue, New York, NY 10017

Routledge is an imprint of the Taylor & Francis Group, an informa business

British Library Cataloguing in Publication Data
A catalogue record for this book is available from the British Library

Library of Congress Cataloging in Publication Data
Kagarlitsky, Boris, 1958–
[Ot imperii--k imperializmu. English]
From empires to imperialism : the state and the rise of bourgeois
civilisation / Boris Kagarlitsky ; translated by Renfrey Clarke.
pages cm. -- (Rethinking globalizations)
Includes bibliographical references and index.
1. Civilization, Western--History. 2. Imperialism--History. I. Title.
CB451.K3413 2014
909'.09821--dc23
2013049427

ISBN: 978-1-138-77884-9 (hbk)
ISBN: 978-1-138-77885-6 (pbk)
ISBN: 978-1-315-76919-6 (ebk)

Typeset in Bembo
by Taylor & Francis Books

Printed and bound in the United States of America by Edwards Brothers Malloy on sustainably sourced paper

CONTENTS

FOREWORD TO THE ENGLISH EDITION

The English edition of this book is an abridged version of the Russian original. I have to confess that, indulging my curiosity in the libraries of Europe and America, I came up with a work so voluminous that taking it on was beyond the possibilities either of the translator or of a publisher. For anyone who would like to delve more deeply into the sources and arguments I employed, I have retained most of the footnotes. Readers if they wish can thus retrace my path independently, or if they know Russian, can read the unabridged version that appeared in 2010 under the imprint of the publishing house of the Moscow Higher School of Economics.

I began work on this book in a comparatively peaceful period, but as the text developed, the social situation changed as well. The latest crisis of capitalism, which broke out in 2008, provided additional material for research and brought with it an obvious need to analyse the sources of the system whose death agony we can now observe in the course of everyday life. Studying these well-springs of capitalism is essential if we are to understand the innermost mechanisms of its functioning, the logic of its transformation, and the prospects and chances for social change. In other words, theoretical analysis is itself becoming a key factor determining the success of political action.

As in the past, historical analysis of capitalism is weighed down, even in Marxist literature, with mythical concepts of the dominating role of the market in the origins of the bourgeois system, of private entrepreneurship developing somehow of its own accord and spontaneously reconstructing society, which had then only to follow the path laid down by the needs of the market economy. Accordingly, the critique of capitalism in left-wing circles has been transformed at every step into a monotonous critique of the market, at the same time as this 'critique' itself has often been reduced to a stream of lamentations, or else to a spiteful yet banal irony. Within such narratives, and notwithstanding the efforts of historical sociologists, the military-political and socio-economic histories of states have too often remained simply as backgrounds for one another, intersecting solely in moments of revolutionary cataclysm.

In actual history, meanwhile, the 'Western' state has continuously acted, in relation both to its own subjects and to the outside world, as a consistent and implacable force *compelling participation in the market*. This was the case even before the state itself became fully bourgeois. Writing the history of the real interrelationship between the state and capital is not a task for a single author, or for just one book. I acknowledge, however, that in this case I was motivated by curiosity. I was trying as far as possible to discover, to understand and to formulate for myself the history of the state and capital, which have persistently appeared as two parallel subjects, needing to be combined into a unified whole.

Of course, I am far from being the first person to have been struck by such a thought. If this book is in any way superior to other works, it is only in the respect that I have tried to deal with this question systematically, turning a dry historico-economic analysis into a consistent narrative encompassing the events of several centuries. Unifying and bringing order to this vast material required an overriding theme, provided in this case by the notion of empire. Fortunately for me, this concept suddenly became fashionable toward the beginning of the present century.

Boris Kagarlitsky
May 2013

INTRODUCTION

The theme of 'empire' has always occupied the attention of historians. Some of these have worked to the order of the authorities and have celebrated the feats of conquerors, seeking to prove the immutability of state borders while in various ways depicting the loyalty and gratitude of the subjects – speakers of diverse tongues united beneath the sceptre of a single dynasty, a single flag, a single ideology or religion. Other historians have unmasked injustice and oppression, attempting to rewrite history from the standpoint of the defeated and subjugated. This has been done more or less successfully, but only for those peoples that have survived, retaining their culture and social cohesion while often also developing them under the sway of empire. Paradoxically, the most detailed narratives of imperial oppression have been left by the ideologues of peoples whose oppression was comparatively light. The nationalist traditions in Ireland and India, in the countries of Eastern Europe that found themselves under the rule of the Habsburgs, and in the Baltic lands seized by Russia have left us an abundant list of complaints against various empires. But we know of the conquest of Africa by Europeans, and of the enslavement of Africans, mainly through the open-hearted confessions and through the archives of the oppressors themselves. From many peoples, not even a list of complaints has remained. These peoples have disappeared from the face of the planet.

The peoples who have been fortunate enough to obtain their own 'national' state have acquired along with it their own 'national' history, serving the interests of the state just as earlier history served the interests of the empire. Lenin in his time called for a distinction to be drawn between the nationalism of rulers and that of oppressed peoples, but in the area of history anti-imperial nationalism is no more trustworthy than the imperial variety. At the basis of anti-imperial nationalism lies the same demand for the legitimation of the exclusive rights of one's own nation or state. In the second half of the twentieth century the most blatant example of such an approach was Zionism; within the framework provided by this ideology the tragic story of pogroms, of anti-semitic mockery of Jews, and ultimately, the appalling history of the holocaust are no more than arguments used to help explain why the Israeli state can allow itself to ignore international law and the interests of the Arab population of Palestine. In the politics of the Baltic countries an analogous role is played by the history of their conquest by Russia, with the narrative transformed into an incessant ideological self-justification for the new national elites.

For history as a science there is no difference between the myths kindled by one nationalism or another, since they are constructed on the same basis. In these myths the political and ideological outcome of development is projected into the past, and events are interpreted according to the logic of state interests, even if at the time of the events depicted the state itself did not exist. Any uprising is now presented to us as a struggle for national rights, even if its real causes had nothing to do with this, and any conflict between the local elites and the imperial capital is explained in terms of discrimination and a clash of cultures.

By the end of the twentieth century arguments to the effect that 'the age of empires is past' had become generally accepted. The great monarchies were now to be found only in the history books, colonial powers had ceased to exist, and the collapse of the Soviet Union in 1991 was perceived by liberal opinion as 'the inevitable fall of the last empire'. The map of the world was now a motley of colours as national states, energetically constructing borders and strengthening their tariff barriers, sought studiously to ensure that their new subjects should not show the slightest sympathy for the foreign neighbours who only recently had been their fellow citizens.

Theoreticians of globalisation set out to prove that not only empires, but national states as well were archaic features of a bygone epoch that would soon give way to some new order in which the might of state functionaries would be replaced by the 'natural laws of the market', and by decisions of huge corporations.

In the early twenty-first century, however, the theme of empire has once again come into fashion. Nationalist ideologues in Russia have shed an ocean of tears while expending tons of paper and wasting some incalculable amount of electrical energy on propagating nostalgic tales of a great imperial past. In Britain books have begun appearing one after another explaining to the reader that there is no need to be ashamed of the former colonial empire.[1] As one historian put it, the politics of empire initiated globalisation by unifying the world, and no-one but British gentlemen could have done this so quickly, effectively, elegantly and humanely.[2] In transforming the world, the British empire acted as 'an agency for imposing free markets', implanting the rule of law, defending investors and in sum, installing incorruptible rule over approximately a quarter of the earth's land surface. The empire also did its utmost to support analogous tendencies outside its own territory through the use of its economic influence; this was an 'imperialism of free trade'. Ultimately we are supposed to recognise that through conducing to the growth of global well-being, the empire on the whole was 'a Good Thing'.[3]

It may be noted, as an example of an instructive 'Freudian slip', that Niall Ferguson as the author of this passage never once mentions democracy or human rights – perhaps because intellectual honesty does not allow him to present the empire as the bearer of these values, and perhaps for the reason that in speaking of such really important things as free markets and the defence of investor interests, he simply forgot about such trifles. But however scandalous Ferguson's argumentation might seem at first glance, it is not to be summarily dismissed, at least for the reason that even so irreconcilable a critic of capitalism as Marx recognised that the spread of the bourgeois order across the planet was a part of human progress.

Taking over from Britain as leader of the capitalist world, the United States' ruling class refused initially to recognise America as an empire. By the beginning of the twenty-first century, however, their rhetoric had changed. They were now open in discussing ancient Rome and the new role of American power as its legitimate heir on a global scale. On their left flank the fashionable thinkers Michael Hardt and Tony Negri constructed their theories with no less enthusiasm, depicting a sort of utopian-fantastical Empire, omnipresent, all-penetrating and all-encompassing, but somehow quite invisible.[4] This Empire (invariably with a capital letter) amounted in their words to an already total and fully-fledged reality, but at the same time was still at the stage of birth and formation.

At the basis of all these theoretical constructs is not so much knowledge or analysis as a sense, a social intuition, telling the authors that the age of empires is far from over. The imperial principle, however, has clearly found its realisation not in the shape of a monarchic state, seeking the loyalty of its subjects, but in a different guise that has escaped the understanding of these writers. The worse they have perceived what is occurring, the less clearly they have understood obvious phenomena, and the more mystical and hence also attractive is the image of Empire in their writings.

In the mid-twentieth century the critique of imperialism was reduced, to a significant degree, to a list of possible excesses and to a moral judgement on them. But in our present century the obligatory recognition of colonial crimes has turned into a sort of alibi for conservative historians, who after lamenting this cruelty have shifted to discussions of the civilising role of empires. Meanwhile, it must be recognised that throughout history crimes and barbarities have been perpetrated constantly, in the name of empires and of national liberation, in the name of revolutions and of counter-revolutions. The task of the researcher is not to complain about this situation, or to try to justify what has occurred, but to try to understand the complex historical mechanisms that underlie the drama being depicted.

Empires, though a state form created by the ancient world, have proven to be a requirement of capitalism, and moreover, of global capitalism. For many years the origins of capitalism went largely unquestioned. To Marx and other writers of the second half of the nineteenth century there was nothing mysterious about the fact that Western Europe had subjugated India and China, forcing the countries of Asia to follow in the tracks laid down by the world economy that the Europeans had constructed. The productive forces of the West were significantly more developed, and as a result, it was in the West that more advanced productive relations – and thus a more dynamic and effective society – had become established.

The picture changed completely once it became clear to historians how greatly the countries of the East in the fifteenth and sixteenth centuries had outstripped Western Europe in their level of economic development. But while forcing us to reject nineteenth-century political economy, this research did not provide us with new explanations for the processes being described. Or more precisely, the explanations that were ventured seemed highly unconvincing and superficial, beginning with the presumption that the culture of the West was unique and superior, and extending to the desperate conclusion of Andre Gunder Frank in his later years that the West was simply lucky that Columbus had chanced to discover America.

Over a decade and a half this discussion revealed that Marx's original theory, for all its shortcomings, was both more logical and more firmly based in scholarly terms than all the conceptions that had been advanced in an effort to supplant it. An apparently insoluble contradiction had arisen: Marx's theory rested on a series of clearly mistaken premises, and thus was 'factually' untrue, but all the other theories were even more incorrect! The only possible answer was that Marx's theory was true after all, but not complete. There was some missing link that had not been analysed fully by the author of *Capital,* and that lay behind the disjunctures in the historical schema. This missing link was most likely the institutional role of the state. 'Right up until the industrial revolution of the nineteenth century,' Fernand Braudel considers,

> until the moment when capitalism appropriated industrial production and made it the source of vast profits, the system felt itself at home primarily in the sphere of circulation, even if it did not disdain to carry out something greater than simple raiding operations when the chance arose in other areas.[5]

With characteristic intellectual caution, Braudel in this quotation leaves himself a path of retreat, recognising that by no means all of the development of capitalism can be reduced to trade, but that it was in this sphere that the system's development proceeded in its purest form. The penetration of capital into the sphere of production began long before the industrial revolution, and involved not only the urban manufacturing establishments of Western Europe, but also agriculture. There is no doubt, however, that commercial capital expanded more quickly and aggressively, and acquired political influence earlier, than the capital that arose in the area of industrial production. The American sociologist Charles Tilly is much more categorical. Neither the emergence of capital nor the use of hired labour was in itself enough to create the bourgeois system. All that took shape was a certain economic formation, developing and functioning within a society that as a whole operated according to different rules. Commercial capital in its turn was in no hurry to combine itself with hired labour in productive activity. This combination only occurred on a large scale toward the end of the seventeenth century in Western Europe, at the direct instigation of the state. Prior to this, Tilly states, the owners of capital had flourished for thousands of years without involving themselves directly in production. Capitalism as a system appeared at a late stage in the development of capital.[6]

The aim of a capitalist economy is the accumulation of capital, and the means is the exploitation of free, hired labour. Capital, however, can also be accumulated through other means. Historically, neither commercial nor financial capital has had any requirement for hired labour as a necessary condition for its existence, or else has needed it only to a limited degree (employing the labour of bailiffs, sailors and clerks). Commercial and financial capitalists have been able to carry out accumulation on the basis of production organised along non-bourgeois lines.

Things are different in the case of industrial (or in the broader sense, productive) capital, which properly speaking also embodies the bourgeois mode of production. The great Russian historian Mikhail Pokrovsky examined the evolution of the bourgeois system from the point of view of the interaction and antagonism between commercial and industrial capital, showing that it was commercial capital, not the feudalism that had vanished into the past, that was the key element underpinning the *ancien régime* in Russia. But was this the case in Russia alone?

If we extend Pokrovsky's concept to Western Europe and to the colonial world in the modern era, numerous problems and mysteries can be resolved.

While stressing the importance of hired labour as the basis for bourgeois productive relations, Marx in *Capital* pointed simultaneously to the fact that in the sixteenth century world trade and the global market opened up a new history of capital.[7] Hence capital, along with the market economy, not only existed long before capitalism, developing and strengthening themselves above all in the sphere of trade, but also rested on production that was by no means organised as yet in accordance with the new bourgeois principles. The peasant and the artisan suffered expropriation, lost their petty property, and were transformed into hired workers. But this did not occur immediately, and took place after the bourgeoisie had already acquired economic and political influence. In other words, capital first arose outside of production, then took control of production, and only after that created its own production on a massive scale, based on the use of hired labour.

Even the bourgeoisie themselves did not immediately become capitalists in the sense which this word had acquired by the late nineteenth century. Accumulation of capital took place on a substantial scale prior to the beginning of the industrial revolution, primarily outside the productive sphere. As Marx himself testified in *Capital,* primitive accumulation on the whole has little in common with production. Even in the sixteenth century, not to speak of the fourteenth and fifteenth, it was far easier to make a fortune in trade (often accompanied by war and plunder) than by investing money in the production of handicraft goods. As early as the fifteenth and sixteenth centuries some manufacturing enterprises had become large, flourishing undertakings. Nevertheless, the capital holdings of merchants and of the owners of industrial workshops were not remotely comparable. Trade required substantially greater investments, but yielded dazzling profits; otherwise, distant sea voyages and trading caravans would simply have been impossible. This situation arose not just from the opportunity to obtain super-profits from the sale of exotic and sorely needed goods or luxury items, but also from the very nature of commercial capitalism. As Pokrovsky noted, the accumulation of trading capital was bound up closely with the preservation of the old pre-capitalist, feudal and even more primitive modes of production. As the capitalist system came into being, all the costs remained (and were absorbed) within the pre-capitalist sector, while the profits were concentrated in the hands of the commercial bourgeoisie.

Nevertheless, it is only possible to talk seriously of the triumph of capitalism once capitalist principles have affirmed themselves in a massive way within *production,* and when as a result the social division of labour and the structure of society have become fully bourgeois.

Supporters of the orthodox interpretation of Marxism have viewed trade merely as a form of the organisation of exchange, and as a result have stripped it of its system-forming function within the economy. Meanwhile trade, as Immanuel Wallerstein has repeatedly observed, can have a range of economic functions. In one instance we are dealing with an exchange of surpluses between countries and regions. This exchange, aiding the development of the economy, of commodity–money relations, and eventually the accumulation of capital, does not alter the social system or the mode of production in radical fashion. But trade takes on a completely different character if it serves to bring about an inter-regional and international division of labour. What we have here is not simply world-systemic ties of a new type, replacing the earlier exchange of surpluses. The function of trade changes; it directly subordinates production to itself, and dictates not only what will be produced, but often how, through what means, this commodity will come into being.

The American Marxist Paul Sweezy noted that international trade transformed feudal production into a new, market system.[8] From the moment when it first arose, world trade acted not only as a factor in the accumulation of capital, but also as a factor in the organisation of production. The bourgeoisie established plantations to grow African coffee in the Americas, turned Chinese tea into a crucially important product in the agriculture of India, and made sugar cane the basis for the development of the Caribbean islands. All this was done for the sake of supplying European markets. The spread of slave labour in the plantations of Virginia and the triumph of freely hired labour in the industrial enterprises of Britain were linked closely one to the other, and this connection came into being precisely through commercial mediation. In other words, the bourgeois mode of production (or more accurately, its global triumph) would have been impossible without capitalist trade. But would organised international trade have been possible without the state which defended, organised and supported it?

In the sixteenth and seventeenth centuries the importance of trade and of the conflicts associated with it was so great that the question arises: why was it that by the end of the seventeenth century commercial capital in the West was increasingly being invested in production, while long-distance trade was being transformed from an instrument of accumulation into one of redistribution – that is, from the patriarchal economy of the 'periphery' to the economy of the 'centre', with its roots in freely hired labour? Bonded labour on the 'periphery' no longer served exclusively to enrich the commercial bourgeoisie, but also subsidised the use of free labour in Europe and in the protestant colonies of North America.

The Soviet historians who located the beginning of the modern era not in the great geographical discoveries and in the Reformation, but in the English bourgeois revolution, were correct in the sense that it was from the late seventeenth century that the nature of economic development gradually began to change. This was true not only with regard to the supplanting by capitalism of pre-bourgeois forms of social organisation in the West, but also to the immanent character of the developing capitalism itself. This process, however, went ahead slowly and painfully, reaching its completion only in the epoch of the industrial revolution. It is only from this point that one can speak of the rise of the British empire as an effective, fully-formed hegemon within the world-system.

From a certain point, the logic of behaviour of the bourgeoisie changed as well; from accumulating wealth, the members of the class made the shift to accumulating capital, subordinating their economic activity to the investment cycle. Also playing a considerable role here were the famous protestant ethic extolled by Max Weber and the needs of the new urban production, which unlike agriculture and traditional trade was no longer bound up with the cycles of nature. The reproduction of industry depends on the scale and effectiveness of investment, not on the changing seasons, and the greater the volume of industrial production, the greater the importance of the investment cycle.

How was it, though, that this turning-point in the seventeenth and eighteenth centuries determined the new vector of development? Neither qualitatively new technologies nor a new organisation of labour were to appear for a considerable period, until steam engines were installed on a large scale. But a division of labour between 'centre' and 'periphery' was gradually taking shape on a global level. Immanuel Wallerstein sees this division as existing already in the sixteenth and seventeenth centuries, when resources from overseas countries were beginning to flow into Western Europe, stimulating the development there of new social and productive relations. But while the early bourgeois economy of the sixteenth century was subject to the logic of accumulation of commercial capital, by the eighteenth century we can observe industrial capital coming gradually to the forefront in the West, while in the countries of the 'periphery' the domination of commercial capital continued and was even strengthened.

Periods when free trade policies have predominated have unfailingly and regularly been replaced by periods of active state intervention and government regulation. On the level of ideology Manchester free trade might have been replaced by French mercantilism, and Keynesianism by neoliberalism, but one way or another the alternation of these two tendencies has characterised the entire history of the bourgeois economy. The liberal ideologies that were dominant from the late eighteenth century of course presented the matter as a clash between 'natural market laws' and a wide range of 'obstacles' put in the way of these laws by the state and by a society that failed to understand its own advantage. But the repeated rise of these 'obstacles' and the economic gains achieved in the corresponding periods showed that for capitalism, state intervention is no less organic and essential than private property and the market.

The alternation of these phases corresponds to the changing relationship of forces between the different forms in which capital can exist: commercial-financial 'mobile' capital (as Max Weber termed it) is dominant during epochs of the free market, while industrial capital achieves its greatest successes during periods when the economic role of the state is activated, either through necessity or conscious choice. Here, of course, we are dealing only with general tendencies which are very rarely expressed in their pure form. Governments are compelled at times to increase their economic role despite their ideology, and sometimes, while not renouncing a desire to impose regulation, have been forced in practice to curtail it because of pressure from dominant business groups. Hence British governments, which from the mid-eighteenth century until the Great Depression of the 1930s invariably professed to adhere to the principles of free trade, in practice often took active steps to stimulate industrial development, out of military or political necessity.

Free-market policies often presuppose no less activity by the state, and at times even more, than periods when governments regulate the economy. This activity takes different forms, often appearing as military aggression or as crackdowns on popular liberties. Even if a government assigns itself the role exclusively of a 'night watchman', it must be remembered that this watchman needs to maintain a constant vigilance.

Free trade requires defence by the state. The existence of an empire-hegemon has proven to be an indispensable condition for the functioning of the world market, at least as an important factor in its stabilisation. The world market, however, has always coexisted with local markets whose development has by no means always or in every respect coincided with global trends. These contradictions have posed the main problem which any global hegemony and any world empire in general has had to confront. But at the same time, resolving them has been a crucial task for this hegemony, a task for which, properly speaking, hegemony has also been essential.

In the view of Immanuel Wallerstein, the rise of capitalism saw numerous independent world-economies and world-empires combine themselves into an integral world economy which gradually came to encompass the entire planet. The form of organisation of the world space that corresponds to capitalism is that of national states that establish themselves at the 'centre' of the system, while the system's 'periphery' to an important degree remains subject to the power of various empires. The leading world power acts as hegemon, organising the system as a whole and enforcing the general rules, while forced at the same time to defend its position against the encroachments of other powers that from time to time lay claim to hegemony.

Other researchers from the school of world-system analysis, including Andre Gunder Frank, Samir Amin and Giovanni Arrighi, have put forward their own versions of the history of capitalism. One of the most notable results of this work is Arrighi's book *The Long Twentieth Century*. The particular service rendered by Arrighi lies in the fact that to a greater extent than any other theoretician of the world-system school he has revealed the link between the development of the world-system and the cycles of accumulation of capital. Ultimately, it is not the political dominance or economic success of particular countries that has brought about the dividing of the world-system into centre and periphery, but the logic of the accumulation of capital. For accumulation to be effective, this process has to be concentrated in a limited number of centres. These may compete with and replace one another, but unless there is centralisation, a dispersal occurs that blocks the entire process or sends it into reverse. This approach, however, led Arrighi to the mechanistic proposition that every cycle of accumulation must not only have its own hegemon, but that this hegemon itself must conform more or less to one and the same 'standard'.

By contrast, Samir Amin and a number of other writers object categorically to the schema that reduces history to a series of 'successive hegemonies'. There have been lengthy periods when it has been impossible to demonstrate convincingly the presence in the world-system of any single power successfully fulfilling this role. At times, several rival states at once have laid claim consciously or unconsciously to this status (instances include the conflict of Holland with Spain and Portugal in the sixteenth and seventeenth centuries, the English struggle with Holland in the late seventeenth century, and the clash between Britain and France in the eighteenth and nineteenth centuries). World empires that lay claim to a global role have also needed constantly to take account of regional powers and their challenges, and to maintain a balance of forces between them, especially where European politics have been concerned.

To liberal commentators in the late twentieth century, it was self-evident that the concept of empire needed to be viewed in contradistinction to that of the national state. Just as axiomatic was the thesis of the eternal conflict between state institutions and the free market, which supposedly developed only when government intervention in the economy ceased.

Both these ideas are comparatively new. While the idea of the national state arose largely in the nineteenth century, and became widely current only during the Europe-wide revolution of 1848, the concept of the state as a force restraining the market economy first appeared in the propaganda of the British Whigs in the eighteenth century, assuming its final shape only in the nineteenth century at the very time when the labouring classes and their allies among the intelligentsia and petty bourgeoisie made their first timid efforts to use political institutions to limit exploitation.

To the bourgeois of the sixteenth century such ideas would undoubtedly have seemed not just absurd but extremely dangerous. After all, bourgeois economic development was in practice closely tied up with the development and transformation of state institutions, while nations in the modern sense of the word arose in the process of constructing empires (whether successfully or unsuccessfully). We are, of course, concerned here with empires of the modern era – bourgeois empires, radically different from the empires of antiquity.

Nations are a comparatively recent invention. For the most part, the numerous peoples and tribes of antiquity and of the Middle Ages did not identify themselves with any particular state, and did not associate their civil status with their ethnic origin. The state, as a rule, was either greater or lesser than 'the people'. For the Greeks the state was limited by the territory of the *polis,* which has mistakenly been termed a 'city' – the original *polis* may simply have been a collection of villages.

To the Egyptians and Assyrians the homeland was the expanse over which the authority of the Pharaoh or emperor held sway. The Romans, of course, described themselves as the 'people of Rome'. But this 'people' did not at first include even the whole population of Latium, who spoke the same language, while by the final years of the empire Hellenised Jews, civilised Gauls and unfailingly loyal Greeks were viewed as among its inalienable parts.

The essence of the national idea lies in the organic confluence and indivisibility of a people and a state.

The ancient Greeks were a people, but could not be a nation, since they had no unified state. The Romans were citizens who had a single state, but this state was their own only for citizens who enjoyed full rights. Slaves did not feel themselves to belong to the state, and not even the strictest law-maker and patriot of Rome would have demanded this of them.

Empires created not only a political, civic and legal space, but also an economic one; without this latter, the growth and development of markets would have been inconceivable. The functions of empires included simplifying exchange and devising a unified system of taxation, often burdensome, but essential for concentrating the resources without which the growth of production would have been impossible.

From the time of Adam Smith, the idea prevailed in Europe of a self-regulating market economy, so much more efficient than any other form of economic organisation that through the operation of 'natural' laws it would make its own way provided only that 'artificial' barriers, created by the state, religion or tradition, were cleared from its path. Imperial forays, campaigns of conquest and colonial adventures were in turn condemned regularly by economists as completely unnecessary excesses, arising either from human weaknesses or from the desire of the state to meddle constantly in anything and everything. In other words, rather than perceiving the aggressive policies of the European powers as an essential condition for the development of the bourgeois economic order, eighteenth-century economists viewed these policies as a relic of the Middle Ages or a deviation from the norm, and as an obstacle on the road to progress.

In numerous accounts of the development of the market economy we find tales of enterprising trading ventures, and of travelling merchants penetrating into the most remote corners of the known world, forging links between isolated economic units and in the process, forming markets. These narratives, sometimes diverting, anecdotal or even comic, and recorded in thousands of memoirs and archival documents, have mesmerised not only liberal historians, but also such critical-minded scholars as Fernand Braudel, who moreover, avoids drawing any straightforward conclusions.[9] Even Marx and Engels in the *Communist Manifesto* wrote of the bourgeoisie that its main weapon consisted of cheap goods, and that it expanded its civilisation thanks to its rapid perfecting of the tools of production.[10]

If this were always so, why was there any need for the heroic campaigns of British redcoats in India and Africa, and why did the United States have to resort to 'gunboat diplomacy', while Russian Cossacks and government agents built forts throughout Siberia?

On this point, the founders of capitalism were far more open and insightful. In 1619 Jan Pieterszoon Coen, founder of Batavia (now Jakarta) and one of the leaders of the legendary Dutch East India Company, coined a phrase that became one of the mottoes of European politics throughout the following centuries: 'We cannot carry on trade without war, nor war without trade.'[11]

For the exchange of commodities to take on a truly massive character, and for it to be augmented by technical collaboration between regions and a division of labour between them, economic integration was needed on a scale that could never have been ensured by the efforts of wandering traders and entrepreneur-adventurers. The integration of the world economy was carried out by the state, resorting to violence whenever obstacles arose and could not be overcome through other methods.

The counterposing of local and global development, so attractive to provincial romantic traditionalists who idealise the independent patriarchal life of 'small peoples', has no validity. Global processes are impossible without local resources. Local resources, meanwhile, have not found a use (and often, have not even been 'resources' at all in the economic sense) until the whirlpool of political events has united the everyday life of the places involved with broader processes. In all this, the decisive role has been played by the state.

More than four hundred years of world history, from the sixteenth century to the early twenty-first, have unrolled before us a broad picture of the global process. This is the construction of capitalism, often spontaneous, sometimes conscious, occurring frequently as a side effect of other processes and conflicts, but continuing without pause and invariably requiring the efforts of the state, or more precisely, of the whole system of states.

According to Max Weber, states since the time of the Renaissance have competed for 'mobile capital'. This competition has determined both the character of international politics, and also many internal processes that have affected the development of European countries; it led, in Weber's view, 'to that unforgettable union between rising states and prosperous, privileged capitalist forces that was the main factor behind the founding of modern capitalism.'[12] In other words, capital at this time through its demands and interests was already an important factor shaping government policies and the state itself. This approach, however, treats capital as something existing prior to, separate from and independent of the state. Meanwhile, capital has not by any means been immutable and 'external' in relation to the state power. It has evolved in close connection with the policies pursued by governments, with established mechanisms of rule, with laws, customs and the dominant political ideology.

In contrast to Weber, Fernand Braudel maintains that capitalism is created by the state, with the bourgeois economic order arising when and as the bourgeoisie itself becomes the state: 'Capitalism does not triumph until it identifies itself with the state, until it becomes the state.'[13]

Commodity exchange and the market have existed since remote times, but in earlier periods they were secondary in relationship to production and did not play a decisive role in reproducing the village communities, and at times even towns, that acted as administrative and religious centres. For production to be made subject to the tasks of exchange, for labour to be alienated from consumption, and for the market to become the fundamental economic regulator required not only the efforts of merchants and entrepreneurs, but also a fair helping of state compulsion. The market developed where the authorities favoured it, and achieved ever-greater scale thanks to the unremitting efforts of officials, of rulers, and of military and punitive organs.

The incorporation of new peoples into the world market, along with their inclusion in the international division of labour, was accompanied by incessant violence. The power of the conquerors and of the rulers themselves compelled millions of people to take part in new economic and social relations of which, shortly before, they had not had the slightest conception. Colonial expeditions and plunder played the decisive role in 'economic integration', which proceeded according to the scenario worked out by the leading powers of the West. By the end of the sixteenth century the superiority of European military organisation had become an obvious factor defining the character of the emerging world economy and deciding its hierarchical structure. But this military strength that made it possible to impose new rules on the peoples of the future capitalist periphery, and to regulate the relationships within European society itself, did not arise spontaneously either; it was the outcome of a complex process of political and social development.

Within this system, unstable, exploding constantly in conflicts and wars, and resting on contrary interests and unreliable alliances, a certain order, logic and predictability were nevertheless essential; without them, progress would have been unthinkable. The system required a hegemon, a guiding force, by no means always declaring itself publicly, not necessarily recognised by all parties or conscious of its own mission, but nonetheless moving into action whenever equilibrium was disturbed.

Maintaining the world-systemic order presupposed a constant need to struggle with and wage war on someone, to defend someone or on the other hand to put them in their place. Each new stage in technological and economic development brought with it another breach of equilibrium, fresh clashes and crises which had to be concluded through the establishing of a new state of order. This role of political hegemon of the emerging world-system fell throughout most of its history to the British empire, though for a brief period it seemed as though the part might be played by Holland. With the twentieth century, it passed to the United States of America.

The role of hegemon has never been officially recognised, or made the subject of generally accepted rules. As a result hegemony itself, its limits and the methods of its exercise have constantly been the topics of doubts, disputes and struggles, not only between rival powers but also within the state exercising hegemony.

Of course, the predominance of a single leading power has not always been obvious. The system periodically has been in a state of chaos. Sooner or later, however, the chaos and the accompanying shocks, crises, wars and social cataclysms have culminated in the restoring of the old hegemony or the installation of a new one.

Empires that lay claim to hegemony have not been able to remain aloof from regional conflicts. In such local struggles they have constantly had to choose one side or the other. The larger the scale and effectiveness of the hegemony, the harder it has been for the hegemons to restrain themselves and remain uninvolved. The British empire at certain stages achieved this (it is enough to recall its 'splendid isolation' in the nineteenth century), but the United States has almost never managed it. To try to satisfy everyone at once means seriously weakening the overall system of global hegemony.

Regional powers in turn have always been ready – on certain terms – not just to accept the compromises advocated by the hegemon, but also to give the leading power direct support, above all defending hegemonic interests against the claims of other regional powers. The price of such support, though, has often been so high as to alter the long-term relationship of global forces and to place the whole system of hegemony in doubt.

It would be unjust, meanwhile, to try to present the entire history of bourgeois states as consisting uniformly of conflict and resistance. Often, world-empires have acted in partnership, with yesterday's enemies routinely transforming themselves into strategic allies. Defeated in its struggles against England, Holland became for many years a British ally. After the Napoleonic wars, the same happened with France.

Finally, an important element in the system ever since the seventeenth century has been 'empires of the periphery' – Russia, Turkey, and until its collapse the *Rzeczpospolita*, the Polish-Lithuanian Commonwealth of 1569 to 1795. Economically part of the periphery, and organising what was essentially the colonial exploitation of their own populations, these states managed not just to preserve their independence but often to lay claim to the role of great powers, at times entering into conflict with leading countries of the bourgeois 'centre'. The interests of imperial development compelled actions which constantly exceeded the bounds of regional politics, turning Istanbul, Moscow, St Petersburg and in the early period Warsaw as well into important centres which more advanced bourgeois countries had to take into account.

From the first day of its existence, the world capitalist economy had need of political organisation. It required a more or less durable structure, a system of laws supported by power, not merely on a local but also on an international level. Capital needed order. The evolving capitalist state not only conquered ever new expanses, turning them into 'new markets', and not only acquired millions of new subjects, training them to be hired workers and consumers, but also and incessantly expanded beyond the boundaries of its territory. The world economy appeared with the rise of the Spanish and Portuguese global empires. It was transformed under the impacts of the successes of Holland, and in the course of the Anglo-French conflict. The outcome of the global development of capitalism in the late nineteenth century was imperialism, which doomed humanity to two world wars. The Russian Revolution, the Great Depression and the Second World War shook the system to such an extent that a substantial part of the population of the planet was torn from capitalism's grasp. But by the end of the century the countries that had experienced an anti-bourgeois revolution were returning one by one to the bosom of the capitalist order. Following the dissolution of the Soviet Union the elites of the 'new Russia' dreamed only of a worthy place in the ranks of the world capitalist oligarchy, a status to which the leaders of China, still formally true to communist ideology, also aspired. Despite the granting of independence to former colonies, recognition of the equality of nations and the practising of political correctness, imperial domination remained a crucial tool for maintaining control within the system, and erstwhile national liberation movements one after another put the countries they controlled at the disposal of foreign capital. But very soon, the triumph of the bourgeois world order turned into a new catastrophe, the global economic crisis. Now, as time passes, the mechanisms of control are working less and less well. The capitalist order itself is moving inescapably toward its end. Only the rise of a new global civilisation, built on qualitatively different foundations from capitalism – in other words, a socialist society – can put an end to this process.

Notes

1 For an example of neoimperial apologetics in English, see: N. Ferguson, *Empire: How Britain Made the Modern World*, London: Allen Lane, 2003. See also: V. Davis Hanson, *Why the West has Won: Carnage and Culture from Salamis to Vietnam*, London: Faber, 2001.

2 A. Herman, *To Rule the Waves. How the British Navy Shaped the Modern World*, London: Hodder & Stoughton, 2004, p. xvii.

3 Ferguson, *Empire*, p. xx.

4 See M. Hardt and A. Negri, *Empire*, Harvard University Press, 2000.

5 F. Brodel', *Material'naya tsivilizatsiya, ekonomika i kapitalizm, XV-XVII vv.* [Material civilisation, the economy and capitalism, 15th-17th centuries], Vol. 2, Moscow: Ves' Mir, 2006, p. 230.

6 Charles Tilly, *Coercion, Capital and European States AD 990-1992*, Malden, MA: Blackwell Publishers, 1990, p. 17.

7 K. Marx and F. Engel's, *Sochineniya* [Works], 2nd edition, Vol. 23, p. 157.

8 R. Hilton (ed.), *The Transition from Feudalism to Capitalism*, London: Verso, 1978, p. 42.

9 See Brodel', *Material'naya tsivilizatsiya, ekonomika i kapitalizm, XV-XVII vv.*, Vol. 2, pp. 126–51.

10 See K. Marx and F. Engel's, 'Kommunisticheskiy manifest', *Sochineniya* [The Communist Manifesto. Works], Vol. 4, p. 428.

11 Quoted in N. Robins, *The Corporation That Changed the World: How the East India Company Shaped the Modern Multinational*, London: Pluto Press, 2006, p. 40.

12 M. Weber, *Economy and Society*, Berkeley, CA: California University Press, 1978, p. 353.

13 F. Braudel, *La dynamique du capitalisme*, Paris: Flammarion, 1985, p. 68.

1

WORLD-EMPIRES

In the last years of the twentieth century, when confidence in the Marxist historical tradition had been undermined – not so much by scholarly criticism as by the political collapse of regimes that appealed to Marxist ideas – the 'civilisational approach' came into fashion. Instead of analysing the development of social relations, researchers were supposed to study the specifics of self-contained and essentially unchanging 'civilisations' that were in irresistible, inexplicable conflict with one another.

Originating in Germany and Russia in the nineteenth century, this tradition remained for many years on the periphery of historical thought, since it stood plainly counterposed to the dominant progressivist tradition. The conservative Russian thinker N. Ya. Danilevsky formulated this opposition precisely, setting forward the theory of 'cultural-historical types' even before Spengler and Toynbee. In Danilevsky's book *Russia and Europe,* the clash of Western and Russian civilisations is perceived as something age-old and fundamental, self-explanatory and insuperable. A hundred years before the publication of Samuel Huntington's book *The Clash of Civilizations,* Danilevsky argued that Russia, as the bearer of the ideas of discipline and order, needed to crush the West, the bearer of the destructive idea of freedom.

The collapse of the West was also predicted by Oswald Spengler in *The Decline of the West* (Der Untergang des Abendlandes). Entranced by the way civilisations 'appear, mature, fade and are never repeated', he presented history as a process unfolding 'with sublime aimlessness'.[1] The same ideas were developed and systematised by Arnold Toynbee in his treatise *A Study of History*; Toynbee was the only member of this school who clearly sought to distance himself from the racist, nationalist and authoritarian conclusions which other writers of this persuasion reached with astonishing but natural inevitability. Late in the twentieth century the link between civilisational theory and the conservative political agenda was restored in full: the work of Samuel Huntington on the 'clash of civilisations' provided the ideological foundation for a new crusade by American right-wingers against the 'islamic threat'.[2]

Underlying the civilisational approach is a clearly expressed denial of any common human history, or even of the potential for it. Attempting to summarise the ideas of the numerous supporters of the 'civilisational approach', who disagree with one another on almost everything, the Moldavian historian L.A. Mosionzhnik writes that a civilisation is a 'complex hierarchical community of people, on scales from an *ethnos* and greater, which is capable of prolonged autonomous existence and self-development on the basis of its own specific laws'. At the basis of its existence lies 'a unity of subconscious, archetypal conceptions of the world and humanity'; this complex of conceptions, accessible only to intuitive understanding and feeling, 'cannot be adequately expressed in words', and is 'most readily discovered in symbols and mythology'.[3]

Where, though, do these enduring 'subconscious conceptions' come from? Why do some civilisations exhaust themselves, while others survive for millennia? How and why do the 'specific laws' of one civilisation differ from those of another? Paradoxically, the only clear answer to these questions is to be found in the Marxist tradition. Examining the early stages of human history, Immanuel Wallerstein concluded that although there could not be a global economy in pre-capitalist times, there did exist what could be called world-economies.[4] The political form which such a world-economy assumes is mostly that of a 'world-empire'. In each of these worlds a more or less durable market has taken shape, with its own system of economic ties; on the basis of these, a common system of cultural norms and symbols has developed. From this, a similarity of artistic tastes has ultimately grown, along with a unity of political, religious and aesthetic concepts and of rules of everyday life. The world-economies of Wallerstein are the civilisations of Spengler and Toynbee.

As the economy develops, an enduring system is established of the institutions, rules, cultural traditions and even aesthetic tastes that are essential for maintaining stability and continuity in the socio-economic structure, in the predictability of the market, and in reliable productive cooperation. The common technological culture rests on traditional society, where the main basis of production remains human physical strength; on shared religious concepts and similar norms of social life; and on similar conceptions of duty, obligation and hierarchy. Needless to say, these concepts, embedded in culture and everyday behaviour, become self-sufficient to a degree, reproducing themselves on an unconscious level. But if the material basis of civilisation is destroyed or changes radically, the corresponding norms and concepts disappear or are forced to evolve. In the time of Max Weber the conservative Chinese tradition dating back to Confucius was considered one of the causes of the country's backwardness, but by the turn of the twenty-first century the same tradition was being invoked to explain the rapid progress of the states of East Asia.

The more a world-empire is isolated, and the more it is economically and technologically self-sufficient, the more individual its civilisation appears. To the extent that local markets and economies merge into a single capitalist world market, 'civilisational self-sufficiency' comes to an end.

In the early stages of human history we observe everywhere the formation of local world-economies, developing in parallel with one another and more or less independently. Of course, this parallel and independent development does not mean there was no interaction – Chinese artifacts were already to be found in Rome in the imperial epoch, not to speak of goods from India, whose ties to the Eastern Mediterranean were maintained over the centuries. But this exchange of commodities did not play a decisive role in local production; unlike the situation in later times, it was not a factor determining the social relations and institutions that were coming into being.

The crisis of 'world-system theory' in the early years of the new century led to the appearance of new works by Andre Gunder Frank and Giovanni Arrighi, depicting a single world economy as having existed since time immemorial, as something eternal and in essence extra-historical. To the initiators of such theories, capitalism appeared at best to be a particular episode in world economic history, and the suggestion at times was that capitalism had never existed as a specific, qualitatively new system; all that had occurred was a temporary predominance of West over East. On a methodological level the point of this 'revisionism' was to break the link between the 'world-system school' and the Marxist tradition, returning to the principles of the liberal political economy of Adam Smith.

As the main argument underpinning their views, Frank and Arrighi cited the existence back in antiquity of powerful flows of commodities from Asia to Europe, and of an analogous flow of silver in the opposite direction. Consequently, the West was said to be no more than a periphery of the great Asian economy whose centre was China.

The existence of commodity exchange between Europe and Asia does not yet prove the existence of a world-system, which presupposes a global division of labour. Long before Frank and Arrighi, Immanuel Wallerstein had pointed to the existence of such trade, stressing that what was involved was an exchange of surplus goods which in itself did not exercise any decisive influence on the social or economic structures of East or West. Strictly speaking, this exchange had a decisive, systemic role only in relation to the 'transit economy' of Iran and Central Asia, in which the 'revisionists' of the world-system school showed least interest of all.

We can speak of a single world economic system only to the extent that we are dealing with an international division of labour in which whole sectors of production (and the corresponding social relations) in certain countries are oriented toward producing goods for sale in the markets of other countries. An international division of labour was only just beginning to take shape in the late seventeenth century. Classic examples of such development are the coffee plantations of America (coffee bushes were brought from Africa to America and planted there solely in order that coffee could be sold in Europe); the mass production of hemp in Russia in serf-holding times so as to supply the British and Dutch fleets; and the development by the British of tea plantations in India and later in Kenya.

A peculiarity of the Asian economies of antiquity and of the Middle Ages was that despite the constant flow of silver from the West, no active process of capital accumulation took place. The fact that capitalist structures did not develop despite the presence of a developed market economy, relatively advanced technologies and rich resources is one of the key mysteries of Asia, and without unravelling it one is hard put to identify the reasons for the success of the West. The world-system established itself and developed together with capitalism, just as capitalism triumphed thanks to the fact that it burst onto the world arena and found at its disposal the rich resources of America and Africa. But the bourgeois order itself did not arise in Europe automatically as a result of economic development; otherwise, it would have appeared much earlier in China or India, and in much more developed forms.

Civilisation-empires

Every narrative about the history of Western civilisation and the market economy begins with Ancient Greece and Rome. Antiquity is considered to have provided the cultural and historical foundation for the West. But which antiquity was involved here? Are we talking about the society and culture that existed in Athens, in Rome or in the Alexandria of the first century BC, or the antiquity that people discovered for themselves and reconstructed during the epoch of the Renaissance? This reconstruction, that underlies modern European culture, differs from actual history just as the white marble statues studied by Winckelmann differ from the brightly painted sculptures that really decorated the cities of Ancient Greece. Antiquity, thoroughly forgotten for centuries in Europe, was unexpectedly reclaimed and reconstructed to fulfil the historical tasks of the modern era. By contrast, the ancient tradition that had played an important role in the world of medieval Arab Islam, was almost completely forgotten in Ottoman Turkey.

The fact that the triumph of the bourgeois mode of production occurred in the West ensured both the universal spread of Western culture, which was dominant within the framework of the world-system, and also a readiness to identify the power of capital with the hegemony of the West; liberation, accordingly, came to signify escaping from this hegemony. But European bourgeois society arose in the eighteenth century, and bourgeois relations in the fourteenth and fifteenth centuries; meanwhile, the 'Western civilisation' to which the ideologues of the bourgeoisie appeal rests on the heritage of antiquity and Christianity – in other words, has its origins in the ancient past. Here, of course, we are confronted with the profoundly ideological demands of the ruling class as it seeks to present its institutions, principles and needs as eternal or at least ancient, and as sanctified by history and tradition.

The fact remains, however, that most of the institutions that now provide the basis for the market economy did not arise in the West. Their roots have to be sought not in Greco-Roman antiquity, but in the history of the Eastern empires.

As Immanuel Wallerstein stresses, the world-economies of antiquity tended to transform themselves into world-empires.[5] This was a logical result of economic integration. In order for production and markets to function as a unified whole, it was desirable for a single political and legal order, and single systems of weights and measures and of money, to exist throughout their common space. But like any general scheme, Wallerstein's concept breaks down if we try to apply it as a universal master-key. The process through which ancient civilisations fashioned states in the form of world-empires occurred unevenly, by way of acute social conflicts, and was by no means always successful. The outcomes of political struggles in turn influenced nascent economic institutions, the norms of administration and the mode of production.

The scholar of far eastern civilisations Marcel Granet noted that China came into being as a unified geographic and economic space as a result of irrigation works undertaken in ancient times by local rulers.[6] On this basis, the system later to be known as the 'Asiatic mode of production' took shape. Looking back, European historians and commentators have almost invariably depicted this system in negative terms; from the mid-nineteenth century onward, numerous Western and Russian writers have drawn attention to its rigidity and conservatism, its crushing of individuality, its bureaucratic centralisation and resistance to innovation. But it should not be forgotten that for many centuries the centralised Chinese empire had the largest and most advanced economy in the world, and was the birthplace of vitally important discoveries – gunpowder, silk, porcelain, ventilation systems, paper and the compass – without which the modernisation of Europe would have been unthinkable. As Granet observed, at the basis of the Chinese social order lay 'not a rigid logic of subordination, but a flexible logic of hierarchy';[7] in other words, not just the subjection of the low by the high, but also a clear division of powers. Thanks to this understanding of administration, the authoritarian structure of the bureaucratic empire did not lead necessarily to formalism and the suppression of initiative.

For its time, the bureaucratic system of the Celestial Empire was extremely advanced and effective.[8] The formation of a rational bureaucracy was a key task, without whose solving Europe could hardly have become what it did by the eighteenth century. China not only dealt with this crucial task of the state many centuries earlier. The bureaucratic system constructed in the country was linked inextricably with an entire system of culture and education which reproduced itself spontaneously even when the political institutions themselves were undermined or even destroyed. The Confucian tradition proclaims: 'Good order depends to an important degree on correct language.'[9] In its turn, language – or more precisely, the system of knowledge and of social concepts – reproduces order.

The 'Asian' type of state, embodied most consistently in the Chinese empire, was by no means the norm for the entire continent (Mesopotamia, for example, developed along a quite different path). On the other hand, we find the 'Asiatic' type of state in many parts of the world that were in no way subject to Chinese influence – in pre-Columbian America and in ancient Egypt. It is in pre-Columbian America that we find the most consistent expression of the Asiatic mode of production.

In all these cases, and despite 'civilisational' differences, a common element was the need to coordinate people's economic efforts across significant territories. Dispersed communities were united by an outside power that organised their interaction and mutual aid on scales unattainable through 'network coordination' between neighbours and relatives. Collaboration can be voluntary or forced, and it can manifest itself in the form of direct productive cooperation or in that of exchange. But the greater its scale, the more important the role of a central government.

Because of the regular floods of the Nile, the building of irrigation systems was just as essential in Egypt as was the taming of the rivers in China. The unpredictability of agriculture, with the alternation of abundant harvests with years of 'lean cows' placed a further task on the agenda: creating strategic reserves, and redistributing resources between communities. This role of the state was understood by the members of these communities, and accepted by them without any special coercion.

Describing the rise of the state, Engels stressed that lying at the basis of power are violence and coercion, which in turn become indispensable to the degree that antagonism exists between classes. But the experience of the ancient powers of the East (which in chronological terms were much older than those in the West) bears witness to the fact that state structures began taking shape long before the formation of social classes. Meanwhile, a social division of labour already exists in one form or another, and it leads inevitably to the formation of social classes, representing as it does a starting-point for social differentiation. The need for a division of labour gives rise both to classes and to the state simultaneously. The rise of a state apparatus provides an important stimulus for social stratification. Even if cooperation is voluntary, an alienation of powers is essential, with the assigning of authority to some organ located outside the communities and above them. Privileges and a social division of labour emerge; closed castes take shape, appropriating not just political authority but also ideological status, securing for themselves a monopoly on a particular type of knowledge.

It was enough for the state to be established for it to become in itself an important catalyst for the development of social and class differences. Little by little, the elite made the shift from administration to oppression. But it was precisely this exploitative character of the new elite that made possible expanded reproduction, the concentration of resources and outside expansion.

The new political order disrupted and weakened the bonds between people, bonds which earlier had been founded on kinship, replacing these ties with a commonality based on the territory over which the ruler exercised control. The main principles of bureaucracy are accounting and control. But these in turn require the development of a written language and of mathematics. It is thus no accident that humanity is indebted to the bureaucratised societies of antiquity for these two crucially important acquisitions.

The ancient societies of the East gave birth not only to bureaucracy, with its achievements in terms of civilisation, but also to numerous other structures that later came to be considered 'discoveries' of the European West. Phoenicia and Babylon created the trading state significantly earlier than the Greek cities, which to an important degree retraced this prior experience. In a society that concentrates on trade, the functions of power are altered; they become primarily the maintenance of order, the observance of rules, and the defence of commerce.

It was the trading state that shifted the coercive function to the forefront. The state was required not simply to organise life on its own not-very-significant territory, but also to be capable of defending the interests of its merchants far beyond its boundaries. The territorial expansion of the bureaucratic empires of the East was slow and not particularly aggressive. The Egyptian wars of conquest began only when the development of the merchant centres of the Eastern Mediterranean transformed the whole local economy, drawing the pharaohs and their subjects into a struggle for trade routes and supplies of raw materials. Egypt's military weakness became evident relatively quickly, in clashes with the Hyksos nomads, the Assyrians and the Persians. China was always a state with a powerful bureaucracy, but an extremely weak coercive component. The Celestial Empire was not so much a conqueror of its neighbours as it was itself, and constantly, a victim of conquests.

Having become politically independent, the trading cities took on a new role and acquired possibilities which the urban centres of the ancient empires had not possessed. Those centres had fulfilled administrative functions, and the development within them of trade and production had occurred only as a side effect. Such cities had possessed little economic significance in the later European sense. They were, of course, hubs of commodity exchange, but in the first instance were military-political, religious and, as we would now say, scientific centres (the present-day distinction between religion and science would have greatly amused the Incas and Aztecs).

From the moment a trading city becomes politically independent, its relations with its rural hinterland change as well. Unequal exchange with the countryside becomes the norm, maintained over centuries; the growth of cities requires additional extraction of surplus product from the villages. This might be effected through compulsion or through trade, but one way or another the countryside finishes up subordinated to the town.

The cities of antiquity and of the Middle Ages needed the countryside far more than the countryside needed them. To an important degree, the rural population was self-sufficient. Of course, it required goods from the city, but if the growth of cities had been predicated exclusively on the need of the villages for urban products, the flourishing of commercial centres would hardly have been possible. Hence from the very beginning extra-economic compulsion was a vital factor and condition for the rise of markets. The development of the latter is hard to imagine without the extraction of surplus product. The redistribution of resources between the masses and the elite was augmented by another redistributive current – from the countryside to the city.

Political power was concentrated in the cities, and provided them with resources. Trading cities and the agrarian (irrigation) state developed to a significant degree in parallel. From a certain point, however, they began to need one another. After acquiring its independence, the trading city remained extremely vulnerable. It needed to maintain and defend links with its 'internal territories' (sales markets and sources of raw materials); it needed an administrative mechanism for ensuring the flow of resources from rural regions. The urban economy in turn created new opportunities for the rulers of the agrarian empires to enrich themselves.[10] So it was that the 'mixed economy' of antiquity began to take shape.

The states of Mesopotamia and of the Eastern Mediterranean were among the first to exhibit a mixed model of authority, a characteristic combining of commercial tasks with productive economic ones. Here we find a mixture of the elements of economic and social organisation out of which the 'antique' and 'Asiatic' modes of production would later evolve. The two paths of development were finally to branch off, it appears, only in the Dark Ages, when trading and cultural ties were broken and when the Greek 'West' and Asiatic 'East' for a time supplied their own needs. The only exception is Egypt, where the structures of the Asiatic mode of production had not only established themselves and achieved full development during the period of the Old Empire, but also showed themselves to be remarkably durable, surviving Hellenism and preserving themselves without serious change even under the Ptolemies.

The pioneers of the market economy in the Mediterranean were not the Greeks, but the Phoenicians.

After a brief period when the ancient civilisations in Mycenae and on Crete flourished, a new period of decline, described by historians as 'dark ages', settled on these localities. It was at this moment that the first shoots of civilisation began bursting out in the West. But there too an important role was played by the influence of the East. To the Phoenicians, Oskar Jäger notes, belonged 'the honour of transplanting the cultural acquisitions of the Eastern world to the West.'[11] With the East in economic decline, the trade of the Phoenicians could survive only through the appearance of new markets. In searching for them, the Phoenicians penetrated to the most remote corners of the European continent, offering the wares of more developed peoples to the still-barbaric tribes of the North, and in the process spreading the experience of the most advanced civilisations of their time.

It was not only money, credit and many other basic elements of the market economy that arose in the East. Sharing the same origins were the imperial state, bureaucracy and the 'European type' of alphabet, not to speak of 'Arabic' numerals, brought to Europe from India by Jewish merchants. The *polis,* which became the earliest form of democratic state, did not have its origins in Greece as often supposed. City-states of the *polis* type already existed in ancient Sumeria, and later among the Phoenicians, long before the beginnings of Greek history. As in Greece, the origins of the *polis* lay in a number of village communities that united for military, economic or religious reasons. Babylon too began as a city-state, not all that different from those of the later Greeks. Of course, these Sumerian cities were not democracies, but this was not true of the early Greek states either.

Although the cities of Mesopotamia had kings, the position of the latter was not any stronger than that of their counterparts in the early Greek cities. The monarchy in Phoenicia was weaker still: 'Also beneath the unremitting control of the large slaveholders was the king, who in the commercial city-states of Phoenicia did not have the despotic power of the kings of Egypt and Babylonia.'[12]

The strengthening of monarchic power occurred in line with the territorial expansion of the state, something which applies to Greco-Roman history as well. Like Athenian democracy, the republican system in Rome was more an exception than the rule in the ancient world, where monarchies and oligarchies predominated.

If the history of democratic Athens ended with the collapse of the state, that of the Roman republic culminated with the founding of a great Mediterranean empire. Politically, however, the outcomes of the Roman victory and the Athenian defeat were strikingly similar: in each case the democratic order came to an end, and the citizens fell beneath the power of monarchs. The large territorial units of antiquity simply could not be managed according to the rules of *polis* democracy, which to a significant degree was a relic of the communal order, though transformed under the impact of new conditions. This democracy differed fundamentally from the estates-based representation that was practised in medieval Europe, and that became a prototype of bourgeois parliamentarism. The first of these, moreover, was far from providing fertile soil for the development of the latter. Democracy of the *polis* type, when it arose (or more precisely, was refounded) in the cities of Europe between the tenth and twelfth centuries, held back the establishing of a unified state. Florence, Novgorod and Lübeck did not give birth to parliaments, land assemblies or *états-généraux*. These forms of class representation were established by monarchies that suppressed the political independence of the cities.

The classic example of a republican oligarchy was, of course, Carthage. But in an even earlier period the republican form of rule was known to the Phoenicians; a surviving item of diplomatic correspondence 'in relation to a number of cities such, for example, as Arvad speaks only of "the people of Arvad", never mentioning a king of Arvad'.[13] During the era of Persian rule the form of internal government of the Phoenician cities beneath the Persian protectorate was republican. Monarchic rule also gradually disappeared in the cities of Etruria.

Most of the information on the political system of the Phoenician colonies that is available to modern historians comes from Greek and Roman sources, which depict appalling corruption and universal venality, in contrast to the republican virtues of the Romans. Such accounts undoubtedly bear the stamp of political propaganda. Throughout the history of Carthage we observe the same struggle between the traditional oligarchy and democrats as we find in the Greek cities and in Rome itself, and by the time of the Third Punic War the democrats were clearly starting to prevail.

The coining of money, the evidence suggests, was an invention of the Asiatic state of Lydia. This was a kingdom that flourished thanks to possessing its own deposits of gold, in the mines of Tmol and the gold-bearing sands of the River Pactolus. It was here that the idea seems to have arisen of cutting a gold wire into small pieces, placing a stamp on them, and then using the precious metal for small and medium-sized trade dealings.

It was the multinational and culturally diverse societies of the East, not the ethnically more homogeneous West, that acted as a constant source of innovations, technical, economic and cultural. Archaeologists and historians are united in speaking of the 'backwardness of Europe' at the end of the Bronze Age.[14] This backwardness is evident in the simultaneous weakness of central state authority and the lack of development of the market economy. At least at this stage of history a strong government, characteristic of the ancient powers of Asia and the Eastern Mediterranean, was a factor conducing to the development of the market.

In the area of military tradition, the West is indebted to Assyria no less than to ancient Greece and Rome. As one historian noted ironically, 'Assyria gave the world nothing apart from the idea of empire and the organising of a military machine.'[15] Unlike the bureaucratic or theocratic states that had arisen in China and Egypt, the rulers of Assyria succeeded in founding a large territorial state on the basis primarily of organised military force. In 745 BC King Tiglatpalasar III established history's first professional army, maintained at the expense of the treasury. It had something like a single uniform; standardised armaments stored in the royal arsenals; and standards (two galloping buffaloes on the background of a disk attached to a pole). The forces were divided into units of various kinds; alongside the cavalry and infantry there were also engineering divisions, and an intelligence service customarily headed by the heir to the throne. The army also had its 'political commissars' – priests attached to the military units – and even military musicians. In battle such an army could keep tight formation and discipline, and could be effectively controlled by its commander. As the historian L.A. Mosionzhnik observed, 'such an army changed the whole character of the society'.[16] To an important degree, military organisation became the basis of the political system. Maintaining a powerful military machine on a permanent basis required large resources that could be obtained either through military pillage and constant expansion of the state, or through harsh exploitation of the subjugated territories. Meanwhile, this exploitation could only be effective if it was in a financial form; paradoxically, the militarist regime within the empire aided the development of the money economy, since no other form of economy could satisfy the need of the empire to maintain a regular army.

The Assyrian state eventually collapsed, after encountering the problem of the limited nature of its resources. The military machine devoured the entire Assyrian people, and the ranks of the army were filled up with ill-assorted riff-raff from all ends of the empire.

After the collapse of the Assyrian empire, a new state – Persia – arose in the same historic region. The expansion of the Persian empire to the west was a natural result of the strengthening ties between the trading cities and the agrarian empires. The Phoenicians, especially the inhabitants of Sidon, resisted the conquerors far more actively than the Greeks, since the Phoenician cities were oriented to global maritime trade. The cities of Mesopotamia, though, were loyal to the Persians, while the Ionic Greeks, despite their contempt for barbarians, displayed no striving for freedom whatever. It was they who drew the Persians into war with Athens and Sparta!

History records numerous cases in which Greeks crossed over to the Persians – on this list we find not only Alcibiades, but even Themistocles himself, who by defeating the Persians at Salamis saved Greek freedom. Slandered by his compatriots, he fled after lengthy wanderings to the Persian King Artaxerxes I, and was given the governorship of a number of Greek cities of Asia Minor. Greek troops and ships were permanent elements in the Persian military machine. The Persian state contained an influential Greek 'segment' with its specific interests, which the kings not only took into account but often allowed to determine their policies.

Greece in its early period lay on the border of the cultural zone of the 'Middle West', which extended from the Eastern Mediterranean to Mesopotamia (the region now called the Middle East). The Ancient Greeks were not the first to make use of the market economy or even to establish the institutions of popular rights. The historical service they performed was to impart their own forms to the ideas and experience they obtained from the East, forms so refined, well-reasoned and consistent that their culture spread in short order throughout the entire Mediterranean, having become a model for imitation.

Far more significant were the innovations made by the Greeks in warfare. The disciplined militia was transformed into phalanxes of heavily armed hoplites. Earlier, it had only been possible to form such elite units in the capacity of royal guards; now, the democratisation of the military system carried out by the Greeks allowed mass mobilisation of the citizens of the *polis,* and their provision at the same time with good weapons.

On the sea, the Greek cities created a permanent navy. The Phoenicians, while skilled seafarers, did not make sea-borne war a distinct art. Neither Tyre nor Sidon, despite their being large commercial centres, was a naval power in the military-political sense. They sent warships out to sea as required by the defence of their own interests or as demanded by the current land empire that was ruling them. Failing to create their own military strength, at least at sea, the trading cities with the exception of Carthage did not become serious political centres. By contrast, Athens in the course of its wars against the Persians not only built a powerful fleet, but also turned it into a permanent, active force, taking to sea not only during wars but also in peacetime. This continuing maintenance of the fleet was pivotal to the Athenian maritime alliance; the lesser partners had regularly to sacrifice money to keep this strength up. Having concentrated naval power in its hands, Athens unexpectedly found itself a centre of financial accumulation.

Phoenicia and Greece can be seen as the 'Holland' and 'England' of antiquity. Like the Dutch in the seventeenth century, the Phoenicians were the sea transport specialists of the ancient world, concentrating in their hands the intermediary commerce of the entire Mediterranean and even beyond. As Mosionzhnik observes,

> all of sea trade from Britain to Somalia was conducted on their ships, so that until the epoch of Alexander the Great all the great powers of south-west Asia hired Tyrians and their ships instead of acquiring their own fleets. But the trade of the Phoenicians was precisely and exclusively intermediary in character. Both in the kingdom of Tyre and Sidon and in Carthage, the Phoenicians' own handicraft manufacturing was weakly developed, and in essence served the needs only of these cities, which traded in goods produced by others.[17]

The Greeks, like the British in the modern era, were different – not just traders but also producers.

> Unlike the Phoenicians, the Greeks did not restrict themselves to transport-ing the wares of others in their ships, but traded mainly in their own

products: artisan ware, wine, olives and so forth. It was this that ensured the Greeks victory over the Phoenicians in their competitive struggles. The Greeks retained their importance as world traders even when the political liberty of Greece had finally vanished into the past.[18]

A struggle between oligarchic and democratic parties was typical of most states of the *polis* type not just in Greece, but also further afield. The revolution of the seventh and sixth centuries in Athens, however, led to the oligarchy suffering an unprecedented defeat. In this context an enduring democratic system, maintaining itself over a prolonged historical period, was really an exception. This was true not only in relation to the East, but also to most of Greece.

The spread of Greek culture to neighbouring countries, however, had nothing in common with the spread of the institutions of democracy. To the contrary, the defeat of the democratic forces in Athens and other city-states marked the beginning of a new epoch when Hellenism was transformed into a cultural instrument of the short-lived but brilliant Macedonian empire.

The Hellenisation of the East was under way long before Alexander the Great, just as the Hellenic world in earlier times had been under the strong influence of the societies that had become established in Egypt and south-west Asia. The Greek colonies in the East interacted constantly with the 'barbarians', who seized actively on everything they found useful, including artistic styles and philosophical knowledge. The Greeks in the cities of Asia Minor were subjects of the Persian kings, and émigré Greeks were royal advisors, sometimes even acquiring the rank of satrap, while Greek mercenaries made up the shock troops of the Persian army. Most crucial was the fact that by incorporating the Greek cities and Phoenicia in their empire, the Persian monarchs united continental Asia with the Mediterranean economically long before Alexander the Great united these regions culturally and politically. This is why Alexander's campaigns of conquest were astonishingly quick and successful, why Hellenisation proceeded thereafter with striking speed and ease, and why the Greek dynasties of the diadochi stayed firmly on their thrones despite the initially small numbers of Greeks and Macedonians in the subjugated societies. It also helps explain why India, which had not earlier been affected by the process of economic and cultural integration with the Mediterranean, proved mostly beyond Alexander's grasp.

Ancient Greece in the sixth and fifth centuries BC played the role of economic and cultural hegemon in relation to the 'semi-barbaric' Epirus and Macedonia, but it was the Macedonians who managed to transform Greek economic and cultural influence into political ascendancy. The Macedonian kings of the Temenid dynasty, before expanding their influence to Greece, had learnt to employ Greek cultural hegemony as a political tool in their own realm. The Greek tongue of the ruling dynasty (which traced its descent from Argos in the Peloponnesus) was made the state language, allowing the diverse tribes of Illyrian or Thracian origin to be united into a single whole.[19]

Although the cultural assimilation of 'barbarians' proceeded spontaneously over a prolonged historical period, the Greeks themselves had not only failed to promote this process consciously, but on the contrary, had sought to restrict it in every way possible, making a strict distinction between Greek-speaking barbarians and Greeks proper. The Macedonians, themselves Hellenised barbarians, sharply transformed the situation, putting cultural rather than ethnic identity in first place. This policy, aimed at the cultural assimilation of newly conquered subjects and enacted in Macedonia itself, was later imposed on the Greeks, along with the overcoming of the city-state parochialism that viewed even Greeks from the neighbouring *polis* as foreigners without rights. Subsequently, it became a norm that has influenced the cultural practice of all successful empires.

In the geographical sense, the Persian empire represented a land bridge between the world-economies of the Eastern Mediterranean on the one side and south and east Asia on the other. Alexander the Great, who conquered this empire, extended this 'bridge' to include the Greek world in the West and the banks of the Indus in the East (in other words, achieving what had eluded the Persian kings Xerxes and Darius in their wars against Athens and Sparta). But the conquests of the Macedonians, despite the accompanying cultural and ethnic changes in the East, not only failed to impose unity and forge mutual ties between the subject territories, but on the contrary, brought about the collapse of this 'bridge'. Moreover, the Seleucid state, which inherited most of the Persian empire, itself disintegrated quite rapidly.

This outcome cannot be explained solely by the early death of the conqueror and by the subsequent rivalry of his successors, the diadochi. Obviously, the economic and cultural integration of the Persian domains was insufficient to maintain a unified state, and moreover, the integration grew steadily weaker. The conquest of the vast Persian empire by the modest forces of Alexander the Great has been viewed as a military-political miracle, and the longer the period that has elapsed since the Macedonian campaigns, the more astonishing and miraculous their results have seemed. Hypnotised by the image of the powerful Macedonian phalanx, historians have repeated that 'it was the phalanx that won the victories that brought glory to Alexander'.[20] The Eurocentric historical tradition has seen in this proof of both the spiritual and organisational superiority of the 'West' over 'Asia'.[21]

The Macedonian phalanx was indeed a very powerful military machine. But it was invincible only so long as its flanks were reliably covered, and while its opponents were unable to manoeuvre actively. Those who confronted the Macedonians were by no means hordes of wild barbarians, and often were the same Greek phalanxes, made up of mercenaries in the service of the Persians. Aware of the merits of Greek hoplites, the Persian kings made these units the basic fighting force of their army. Alexander's most effective victories were gained thanks to the actions of his cavalry, or more precisely, thanks to the effective combining of forces of different types. The superiority of the Macedonian army over those of the Persians was not so much a reflection of the superiority of Western over Eastern organisation, as of the superiority of the Macedonian phalanx over the Greek. Compared to the Greek spear the Macedonian *sarissa,* 14 elbows (6.3 metres) in length, was like the British rifle compared to the smooth-bore Russian musket at the Battle of Alma. By the time of Alexander's campaign, both the Greek city-states and the Persian empire were in steep decline. Philip II, the father of Alexander, was thoroughly conscious of this when he began preparing a big campaign in the East immediately after sub-jugating Greece. But the same factors that had ensured the ease of the Macedonian victories also made certain that the empire that was founded would be unstable. Instead of subjecting Persia to their own rule, the Macedonian conquerors merely hastened its collapse. The weakness of the link and the lack of reciprocal economic demand between the Mediterranean world and the societies of India, China and South Asia made the great Macedonian empire unnecessary and impossible. As the notion of the absolute cultural superiority of the West retreats into the past, we find that the victories of Alexander the Great were more the culminating stage in the collapse of the Persian state than the foundation for a new world empire.[22] The campaigns by the Greco-Macedonian army were accompanied by a significant destruction of the productive forces in Central Asia, and even the economic recovery that followed, associated with Greek colonisation and the establishing of city-states, did not lead to the creation of a unified economic space on the vast territory from the Indus to the Nile that had come under the authority first of Alexander and then of the diadochi. The disintegration of the Macedonian state testifies eloquently against the 'revisionist' version of world-system theory that seeks to present the world economy as already a unified whole even in antiquity. In order to develop, the Mediterranean economic world also required a consolidation of the territories of South-West Asia, Egypt and Anatolia. This was achieved through the conquests of Alexander. It is not surprising that it was on these territories that the cultural and political heritage of Hellenism proved to be robust and long-lived, preparing the way for state unification under the power of Rome, while in more easterly regions this heritage dwindled to nothing. The reason lies not in geographical remoteness, but in the weakness of the economic links. Following the disintegration of Alexander's empire, the Greek presence remained very strong in Bactria, but objective cir-cumstances forced the Bactrian rulers to interest themselves more in Indian affairs than in those of Greece or even Babylon. The existence of Hellenist Greco-Indian states is an obvious refutation of the idea of closed, self-sufficient civilisations living their own isolated lives. The realm of the Greek King Menander, who entered Indian tradition under the name of Milinda, became one of the centres of the development of Buddhism.[23] Menander is depicted in Buddhist texts as 'the wise and attentive confidant of the Buddhist monk Nagasena'.[24] To thinkers in the early twenty-first century Aristotelian logic and the mentality of the East might seem two diametrically opposed approaches to life, but for people in the Hellenist epoch they were merely two complementary sources of wisdom.

The collapse of the Hellenistic states in the Middle East shows, however, that despite the development of inter-regional trade no unified economy or firmly established division of labour existed, and that there were no indissoluble links between regions. The trading ties between East and West were never broken, but they were not essential to the survival of either system. A few successful borrowings survived; thus, the Attic coinage standard persisted in India and Central Asia for many years after all other traces of Greek civilisation had disappeared. Similarly, the

Greek alphabet remained in use in these regions for a full thousand years, until it was replaced by Arabic script.

While the unified political and economic space in the East was coming apart, in the West a consolidation was under way. The struggle between Rome and Carthage for control of the Western Mediterranean formed a prologue to the rise of a new empire, uniting Italy and North Africa, Spain and Egypt, Britain and Syria beneath the power of a single state. If anyone in the Western Mediterranean tried to lay the basis in antiquity for a future world empire, it was not the Romans but the Carthaginians. They not only mastered new trade routes, but also drew into regular exchange resources that had earlier been inaccessible and peoples who had been outside the frontiers of the usual trading community. In exchange for goods from the Mediterranean, the inhabitants of other lands provided gold, which in the view of later historians had been brought 'from the Western Sudan, by a route known later in the era of Arab trade'.[25] This was the same gold in search of which the Portuguese, a millennium and a half later, undertook their voyages along the west coast of Africa.

According to historians, Carthage initially 'was more preoccupied with forming trade networks than with founding an empire'.[26] But the logic of commercial expansion inevitably brought political expansion with it.

The political structures of the two rival states were extremely similar. Just as the Roman state in Italy in its early stages consisted of an unequal federation of cities and territories, in which the only citizens with full rights were the inhabitants of Rome, the Carthaginian state as well combined the citizens of the city-state with allies and subjects who were of lower status. In both cases we find struggles between parties, revolts by the urban masses and rule by an oligarchy through a Senate. The two Carthaginian *shofets* corresponded precisely to the two Roman consuls.

The Roman republic was more democratic, which allowed it to form its army on the basis of a universal obligation of citizens to perform military service. In Carthage, where the level of social stratification and accordingly, the sharpness of the conflicts between high and low were significantly greater, the ruling layers could not allow such a thing, and went to war with a mercenary army. In itself this merely demonstrates that Carthaginian society had outstripped that of Rome in its development. The Roman state was to encounter such problems only later; this was, however, at a time when the empire already possessed enough resources to solve them. Carthage, riven by social contradictions, did not survive its struggle with the relatively consolidated society of Rome.

The collapse and rebirth of the West

The Roman epoch was marked by the rapid development of the market economy. Some scholars have even claimed to detect in ancient Rome a sort of antique capitalism. But this was a market economy with limited accumulation of capital, and most importantly, without the free hiring of labour power.

Needless to say, workers were hired in Rome, and abundant testimonies to this practice are to be found in Latin texts. Hired labour, however, was not the basis on which the bulk of production was performed. A fully realised market economy requires labour power to be turned into a commodity, but it was only European capitalism that managed to solve this problem without turning human beings themselves into commodities. The ancient market in labour power was a market in slaves. The ending of offensive wars and stabilisation of the empire meant a simultaneous decline in the flow of slaves and a gradual weakening of the economic basis of the state. But neither was there any possibility of waging endless offensive wars. The territory of the empire had reached its natural limit when it united the entire Mediterranean space with Gaul and Britain – already linked with it in Phoenician times through shipments of raw materials – and with the Black Sea coastal region, a supplier of foodstuffs. The economic integration of the single space was achieved within the widest possible boundaries (for a short time the Romans even controlled Babylon), but it was precisely this fact that made further expansion, extending beyond the borders of the then-familiar world, extremely difficult and expensive.

Although a gradual barbarisation of Rome was to be observed in the third and fourth centuries AD, ancient civilisation was simultaneously spreading to the barbarian tribes outside the borders of the empire. By the end of the fourth century, however, the situation was changing. Rome was still being barbarised, but the barbarian world itself was also becoming more savage. This was connected both with the degradation of Roman civilisation and society and also with the powerful onslaught of the Huns and other nomadic peoples from the East, who destroyed the society of the Goths and threw the entire barbarian world to the east of the empire into a state of catastrophic instability.

The results included an obvious decay of barbarian society. Tribes that had lived by trade and agriculture were transformed into nomads or semi-nomads. State systems collapsed, giving way to the military organisation of bands and tribes. By the fourth century the barbarians in many respects had reached the same level as the Romans and Greeks had attained on the threshold of their classical history. The Goths, for example, had possessed a well-administered state, but it was destroyed by the Huns.

The degradation of the civic institutions of Rome led, as we know, to the barbarisation of the army. Meanwhile, it is noteworthy that the Romans recruited to their legions and auxiliary units the fiercest and most savage barbarians (these same Huns, for example). The upshot was that the 'Roman' army was no longer especially Roman, and in many ways was closer to the barbarian society on the other side of the frontier than to 'its own' society. Second, a breach opened up between the military organisation, which had become openly barbarian, and the civilian organisation, which remained Roman. Barbarians were permitted to attain high posts in the military hierarchy, but they were categorically excluded from the civilian institutions of the empire. At the same time, the civilian institutions were growing steadily weaker, and the importance of the military organisation was being strengthened. Eventually it remained only to finish constructing the system politically by subordinating the civilian to the military institutions, which occurred under Odoacer and Theodoric. Meanwhile the same system of dual administration remained, only under the political control of the barbarian chiefs who had replaced the Western Roman emperors. By the end of the fifth century the same system had been reproduced in other barbarian kingdoms and in Gaul. In other words, the emergence of the barbarian kingdoms was as much the outcome of a gradual evolution of the Roman state, and even of an internal military revolution, as it was the result of conquest.

The final collapse of Roman civilisation occurred not during the period of the invasions but during the 50 to 70 years that followed, when the disintegration of the empire resulted in the breaking of economic ties between regions and in the economic decline of the west. The final blow was dealt by the 'liberating' wars of Justinian, who despite the gifts of Belisarius as a military leader, was unable to conquer Italy in short order and subjected it to many years of ruinous warfare. The outcome was the definitive decline not just of Italy, but also of the other regions of the West linked to it. Earlier, Italy had represented the principal market and centre of exchange for the Western provinces. The effect of its ruination was that even relatively peaceful territories were unable to develop. Deprived of outside markets, their economies were ravaged, production collapsed, and the cities fell into decline.

Barbarian rule

The decline of the West that set in after the fall of the Roman empire was not the result of wartime devastation. The barbarian chiefs and their entourages were thoroughly familiar with Latin civilisation, and sought to make use of its customs and institutions. Some of these rulers, like Theodoric the Great, even made deliberate efforts to restore its former lustre. The main reason for the decline was the disintegration of the economic links between the provinces of the former empire that followed the destruction of its political unity. In the words of the British historian Chris Wickham, what occurred in the Western Roman empire in many ways resembled the fall of the Soviet Union. After the unified state disintegrated into its component parts, each part retained elements of Roman social, economic and political structures, but developed them in its own fashion.[27] The German kings who had taken possession of Roman territories imitated the style of rule of the later Russian emperors, and often based themselves on remnants of the old bureaucracy. But with their diminished extent, the new states could not maintain economic life on the former level. Once the imperial centralisation had vanished and government revenues had declined, the resources were lacking for maintaining a developed infrastructure. Roads fell into disrepair, and the ties between neighbouring provinces weakened. In proportion with the decline in trade, the cities sickened as well. Society became increasingly agrarian, and the transition gradually took place to a natural economy.

The period of economic decline and political chaos ended with the rise of the Frankish state of Charlemagne. Taking the title of emperor, the king of the Franks not only imposed his rights of overlordship on the peoples and tribes he had subjugated, but also declared his empire the successor to Rome. The rebirth of the empire was closely associated with the idea of restoring order, tradition and culture. The wave of economic and cultural revival in Western Europe rested on the internal resources of the region that had been consolidated politically under Charlemagne's rule. The Carolingian renascence signified the end of the 'Dark Ages' and the beginning of a new period in the history of the West, which during the centuries that followed the collapse of Rome had become still more backward in its development, lagging not just behind Byzantium and the Arab societies that had arisen in the Near East, but even behind the state of Kievan Rus that had arisen on the eastern margins of Europe.

The Carolingian system proved unstable since it did not have a professional bureaucracy, relying instead on collaboration between regional elites that combined the performing of administrative functions with ruling their own feudal estates. As the French historian Lucien Musset notes,

> [S]o long as progress continued, the imperial power still had the opportunity to obtain results. But it was incapable of dealing easily with serious setbacks and unexpected dangers. It had neither a standing army, nor a fleet, nor strong fortifications, nor finances worthy of the name, and probably even lacked real support among the population. There is nothing convincing about the idea that a few hundred families who enjoyed the benefits of the regime were capable of winning the support of society, at least while they lacked estates that could be distributed among their most devoted friends. There is no doubt that almost until 840 the imperial elite were capable of responding to the new tasks that confronted them. But later, this capacity for renewal was quickly extinguished. Within the splintered empire the ruling class, totally immersed in internal conflicts, lost its power of warding off major problems of external politics.[28]

A new wave of barbarian invasions, consisting of Vikings from the North, Saracens from the South and Hungarians from the East, shook the political and social system of the West to its foundations, making possible a partial replacement of the elites and the rise to power of new non-Carolingian dynasties (the Capetians in France and the Ottonians in Germany). By the eleventh century, however, a certain calm had settled on the West, mainly because the new waves of barbarians had integrated themselves more or less successfully into the European system, strengthening it with their own military–political institutions.

A new burst of social development began in the second half of the eleventh century. In Western Europe, processes were under way that would alter the appearance of the continent in revolutionary fashion. Construction technologies now made it possible to erect stone fortresses, and to do this relatively quickly, in three to five years. A process began that was to earn the name *castellazione*, from the Italian *castello*, a castle. Log palisades were replaced by strong stone walls and high towers within which retinues and bodyguards, food stores and arsenals could be accommodated. Strengthened control over the peasants and greater exploitation made it possible to increase the amount of surplus product going to maintain the ruling class; now, not only more powerful armed detachments could be maintained, but also minstrels, book copyists, and court artisans. Around well-constructed castles on trade routes, towns quickly became established.

The growth of local centres, at once military and economic, nevertheless led to a still greater weakening of the state, which remained neither strong nor efficient. England following the victory of William the Conqueror was in some ways an exception. After avenging himself on the Anglo-Saxon nobility, the former Norman duke concentrated much of the land in his own possession, refusing to allow the formation of large feudal estates. It was this that lay behind many of the later successes of the English monarchy. In the north of the country, near the border with Scotland, local lords established near-independent domains onto which the central government heaped the burden of defending the country from dangerous and warlike neighbours, with whom conflict was almost incessant. But the southern areas of the kingdom were under the firm control of the central authority.

The England of William the Conqueror and his successors, however, was an obvious exception. The state in the early Middle Ages was unquestionably weak. It possessed neither the resources nor the institutions to effectively control its territory and population. But paradoxically, this weak state was far more centralised, or at any rate more unified, than the kingdoms and empires of the twelfth and thirteenth centuries.

The initial result of the economic development that by the end of the eleventh century had radically altered the face of Europe was precisely the disintegration of the unified state – the process which in Soviet historiography was to receive the name of 'feudal atomisation'. This process did not occur at the beginning of medieval history, but at the moment when Europe finally emerged from the gloom of the Dark Ages, when cities were growing rich and the first universities were being founded.

The natural economy of the early Middle Ages, in which money was almost unknown, ruled out any possibility of establishing strong governments, resting on a professional bureaucracy and a regular army. But it also made impossible the appearance of local centres of power, hotbeds of development with their own interests that often contradicted those of the monarchy or of neighbouring regions. The isolated communities had no particular need of a state, while not being hostile to it either. The rise of early forms of the market economy, by contrast, gave rise to a new situation in which conflicts of interest were inevitable, in which the possibility and need appeared for intervention by a central authority. At the same time, the need for independence arose as well. The result was that a strengthening of political authority took place on the local level – as a rule, in opposition to the 'centre'. Regional leaders assumed new functions; the princes, dukes and barons transformed themselves from local representatives of the central authority into independent rulers. The state grew weaker at its centre, but took shape and consolidated itself on a regional level.

Overall, the period from the eleventh to the thirteenth centuries was a time of dynamic economic, social and cultural development. The Mongol invasion that shook Eastern and Central Europe in the first half of the thirteenth century not only failed to stop the continent's economic development, but by mid-century had lent it a new impulse. 'The vast Mongol empire united the whole of the Great Steppe,' writes the historian S.A. Nefedov,

> and this made it possible to forge a new route for the Great Silk Road – directly across the steppe from Karakorum through Sarai to the ports of Crimea. Thousands of huge carts harnessed to camels and laden with silks, porcelain and other goods moved along this route from one caravanserai to another. In the port of Caffa the goods were loaded onto Italian ships which conveyed them throughout the entire Mediterranean.[29]

The trade routes became safe and well organised, and the flow of goods was accompanied by the transmission of technology and information from east to west. With the establishing of firm trade ties, the cultural achievements of Chinese civilisation began spreading about Europe. The discoveries that became available to Europeans included gunpowder, the smelting of cast iron, and much else.

The population of Western Europe grew noticeably, and the increase in the number of people outstripped growth in the productivity of agricultural labour. The vacant lands in Western Europe were almost all ploughed up. But the 'demographic explosion' affected not only the lower orders of society. Feudal families now contained substantial numbers of younger brothers with no chance of obtaining either titles or land by inheritance. As yet there was no apparatus of central government in which this mass of young people seeking careers might install themselves. The only chance of winning status and land lay in 'taking to the sword'. Internecine wars, however, were made more difficult by the advent of stone castles. The forces of a feudal detachment were insufficient to seize even the small castle of a neighbour. Local princes were becoming the rulers of mini-states, between which an unstable equilibrium arose.

Within its former borders, Western Europe was now becoming crowded. Its expansion proceeded in three directions. To the south-west, the *Reconquista* unfolded in Spain. The Eastern Mediterranean saw the beginning of the era of the crusades. To the north-east, German feudal armies crushed the resistance of the Slavs on the Baltic coast and extended German territory eastward. By the beginning of the thirteenth century the Danes and Swedes were organising crusades to the north-east.[30]

The expansion of the West

The success of the First Crusade was stunning. In the space of a few years the richest and most densely populated provinces of the Near East were conquered, along with leading commercial cities. The crusader states not only seized almost all of the trading centres of the region, but also a substantial portion of its fertile lands – the narrow coastal strips of Palestine, the Levant and Syria had far greater value than the sands of the Arabian desert. The very success of the crusaders, however, brought with it their subsequent difficulties. Later historians have repeatedly noted the inability of the crusader rulers to manage relations on the territory of their kingdoms not only with their Muslim and Jewish subjects, but even with the Orthodox (Eastern) Christians. The historians have sought to explain this on the basis of religious fanaticism and feudal haughtiness. Both were undoubtedly present, but there was also a far more profound cause at work. Western Europe required new lands for feudal, peasant and commercial colonisation. Without this factor, the Christian rulers in the Near East would not have enjoyed the support of Western Europe. But the more these rulers encouraged colonisation, and the more they relied on a narrow and slowly growing layer of settlers, forcing out the native inhabitants, the more they came into conflict with the local population – numerous, well organised, and more cultured than the interlopers from the still-backward countries of the West. In this situation the collapse of the crusader states was inevitable, despite their initial military superiority. By the end of the thirteenth century, when the demographic pressure from Europe had weakened, the position of the crusaders in the East had become desperate.

This by no means signifies that the expansion of the West came to an end. Quite the reverse. By familiarising Europeans with new technologies, and providing a stimulus to trade and artisanry, the crusades rendered this expansion still more massive. Now, however, this Western European expansion proceeded in several directions simultaneously. Germany grew by conquering the lands of the Western Slavs, and then through the crusades organised by the Teutonic and Livonian knights in the Baltic region. The kings of Denmark and Sweden subdued Estonia and Finland (the landholdings of the Danes in Estonia passed later to the Livonian order). The Castilian, Aragonese and Portuguese kings drove the Arabs out of Spain. Meanwhile, the cities continued to grow and the royal bureaucracies to take shape. More and more often, ambitious feudal leaders preferred state service to waging campaigns in the remote East, and vows to take part in crusades remained unfulfilled. Crusading expeditions came to be of interest mainly to Rome and to some degree to the French aristocracy, linked by kinship and feudal ties to the noble houses that maintained a stake in the Holy Land. The material and demographic base of the crusader movement narrowed rapidly. The powerful order of the Knights Templar preferred to occupy itself with financial operations in the West (as a result of which it was ultimately dissolved by the French king, who coveted its profits). The order of the Hospitallers continued waging war in the East until the 1520s, but its main concern came to be defending the sea routes for European trade.

An important motivating force for the crusades and the *Reconquista* was the land hunger of the petty nobility. In the fourteenth century, however, the changed demographic situation in Europe saw the outward expansion of the Western world draw to a close. An epidemic of plague definitively altered the population map of the West. In the new situation the collapse of the crusader states in the Holy Land became inevitable, while in Spain the *Reconquista* halted until the late fifteenth century, allowing Arab rule to persist in Granada for a whole further epoch. In the Baltic region, where all the 'heathen' lands had already been conquered, a relative calm prevailed. The knights of the Livonian Order made the shift from armed clashes with Novgorod to a policy of peaceful coexistence. The same applied to relations between Novgorod and the Swedes. The onslaught of the German knights against Lithuania, which was gradually being Christianised, grew weaker, and after being defeated in battle at Grünwald the knights were themselves forced onto the defensive, ultimately becoming vassals of the Polish-Lithuanian kingdom.

The knightly orders also fell into decline. The retribution dealt out to the Templars in France is usually explained as resulting mainly from the greed of the monarchy. This was indeed a factor, but the defeat of the Templars was only part of a more general process that saw the strengthening of the territorial state, gradually overcoming the resistance of the extra-territorial institutions of the Middle Ages. The Templars were an obstacle not only to the royal authority, but also to the urban bourgeoisie; creating their own feudal financial networks, the knights competed with the developing commercial-financial capital of the cities. At the same time as Templars were being accused of heresy and burnt at the stake in France, the Castilian and Aragonese kings were waging a drawn-out struggle to subject the knightly orders to their control. This struggle was to be successful in the fifteenth century. By contrast, the German knights transformed themselves into a typical territorial state under the protection of the Holy Roman Empire.

In the late fourteenth century agitation around the crusades gave rise to a final burst of knightly enthusiasm. But since the epidemic of plague had radically altered the social and demographic situation in Europe, crusading expeditions had become hopeless endeavours, despite appeals from the papacy as it sought to revive the crusader movement for the struggle against Ottoman Turkey. At the very end of the fourteenth century European feudal armies set off for the last time to the East, responding to appeals from the Holy See and from the Italian merchant cities. The outcome of this campaign was the Nicopolis catastrophe of 25 September 1396.

The situation in Eastern Europe evolved quite differently. The population density here had been lower to start with, and the amount of unused land significantly greater. In technical and political respects the Finno-Ugrian, Slavic and Baltic tribes against whom the offensive was waged were a whole epoch behind the crusaders. It is not surprising that even the relatively small forces of the conquerors here managed far more enduring results. The closeness to the metropolis, meanwhile, created favourable conditions for a growing stream of colonists. The members of the German feudal nobility showed less and less interest in Palestine, to which the popes called on them desperately to make their way, but instead campaigned increasingly actively in the north-east as their successes there grew.

During the thirteenth century a genuine revolution in sea navigation took place in the Baltic, radically altering the general relationship of forces. The place of the Slavic-Viking *ladya* sailing vessel was taken by the broad-beamed German *Kogge*. The importance these latter ships held for their human contemporaries, and the striking impression they made, can be judged by the coats of arms and seals of the seacoast cities. Almost everywhere, these feature depictions of such ships.

The displacement of the vessels on the Baltic sea routes, and along with it their carrying capacity, was sharply increased. The *ladyi* of the Novgorodians and Vikings were excellent ships; the sagas tell of distant voyages by the Vikings to the coasts of Iceland, Greenland and even North America. But such long voyages needed a store of provisions and fresh water, which could be carried only at the expense of reducing the amount of freight carried. The *ladyi* could not venture far from shore with trading goods. By contrast, the cogs could choose the optimal routes, steering by the sun and stars in the well-studied Baltic seaway.

The alliance of cities that has entered history as the German Hansa was founded on the initiative of merchants from Lübeck – a city built on lands conquered from the Western Slavs.

In 1241 the port cities of Hamburg and Lübeck concluded an alliance that lay at the basis of the German Hansa. Six years later they were joined by Braunschweig, and then by Bremen. Lübeck became the capital of the Hansa, and it was there that the councils of the alliance gathered every three years and the archives were kept. By the beginning of the fourteenth century the alliance had expanded to include 85 cities, grouped in four regions. Hanseatic trading houses had been opened in London, Brugge, Bergen and Novgorod, corresponding to the main markets where the foreign trade of the alliance was conducted.

Directing themselves to the East, the German merchants quickly drove their Scandinavian rivals from the Baltic (before long, a substantial number of the trading houses in the merchant cities of Sweden, Denmark and Norway belonged to Germans) and entered into conflict with Novgorod.

The Russian merchants lost out to the Germans not only in technological terms, but geographically as well. The Russians could, of course, build ships analogous to the cogs, and the later ships of the Russian *pomory* people of the northern seacoast differed little from the German ships of the Middle Ages. But to service a new fleet, maritime harbours were needed, and the Russian trading cities stood on the banks of rivers. During the times when the fleet had consisted of *ladyi*, this had even been an advantage. But now everything had changed. The draught of the German ships still allowed them to enter rivers, but a good port required a large harbour and suitable roadstead, allowing a large number of ships to be serviced in a short time. Neither Novgorod nor Pskov had such possibilities.

Even at the summit of their power, the Hanseatic cities needed the support of territorial states. Competing with the Danes, they established close ties with the Swedish kings. Meanwhile, on the southern shores of the Baltic the knights of the Teutonic and Livonian orders, who under the patronage of the German emperor and the pope had established their own military-religious state on the lands they had conquered from local pagans, were prepared to defend Hanseatic interests.

The Germans and Danes occupied all the suitable sites on the Baltic, erecting not only port structures but also strong stone fortresses. The independent sea trade of the Novgorodians lost any purpose; all that remained to them was to use their river *ladyi* to transport goods to Revel, Narva, the Swedish city of Vyborg or at the furthest, Riga, and there to hand them over to German merchants. The Germans gained most of the profits when the goods were resold in the West. After a few decades of competition, Novgorod was transformed into a trading partner of the Hansa and a peaceful neighbour of the German knights.

The birth of a new order

In its economic growth, Europe was supported not only by the development of technology, but also by an increase in available resources. The silver mines of Bohemia met the need of Germany and other countries for good coinage. The development of the money economy allowed the kings to establish their own paid administrative apparatus, while the need of the treasuries for money transformed life both in the cities and in the countryside. The division of labour between the two again became the motive force of economic development, aiding technological innovation and the spread of money.

The desire to improve the castles created a need for the development of architecture, and not only in the area of fortifications – the feudal rulers wanted their residences to be more comfortable. The growth of consumption and accumulation of wealth continued, along with increases in the demand for luxury items. Doing business became more complex; it was necessary to conduct correspondence and maintain account books. An entire staff of servants, assistants, experts and administrators appeared. Often, property-owning noblemen, feeling the need for money, would hire themselves out as advisors and administrators to feudal rulers of somewhat higher degree.

The cities grew richer. In the twelfth century the first, initially tentative efforts were made to improve roads. At any rate, far more attention was now paid to them, especially in Lombardy, the Venetian republic and Tuscany.[31] River and sea transport was far better suited to moving heavy loads, but required constant military protection; it was for this reason that for such states as Venice and Genoa or for the German Hansa, commercial and military-naval power went hand in hand.

From the late thirteenth century a new architectural style, the French Gothic, spread across Europe. The master-builders erected mighty cathedrals, striking in their combination of delicacy and monumentality. Like any long-term project, building a cathedral required accurate organisation and planning, including on a financial level. In the cities the first, initially timid efforts were made to provide public amenities; wooden bridges were replaced with stone, and streets were paved.

The state now became able to maintain not only permanent military detachments – their size, at first almost insignificant during times of peace, gradually expanding – but also increasing numbers of bureaucrats.

The first model for European bureaucracy was the Catholic Church, organised around a single spiritual-political centre in Rome.[32] But in the twelfth and thirteenth centuries the kings not only began appropriating the experience of the church (among other ways, by appointing clerics to key government posts), but also sought to develop their own culture of administration.

The transformation of the state proceeded in most dynamic fashion in England, where the conflict between the royal power and the feudal nobility ended with the founding of new political institutions. The outcomes of this struggle were invariably imposed through institutional compromise and through the acceptance by the two sides of mutual obligations. The first victory of this type was the Magna Carta, which the unfortunate King John (John Lackland) was forced to sign in 1215. The adoption of the Magna Carta, however, was not the culmination but merely the beginning of the conflict. New steps to transform the English state were taken in the mid-thirteenth century by Simon de Montfort. It is significant that de Montfort, despite entering history as the founder of the English parliament, began with attempts to strengthen the centralised administration – and not in England, but in the French domains of the Plantagenets.[33]

British Whig historians have a major problem with de Montfort: the 'founder of British freedom' was a Frenchman. He did not serve England, but the dynastic state of the Plantagenets, of which Gascony was a no less organic part than Yorkshire. His conflict with the royal authority stemmed from the fact that having been appointed to represent the centre in Gascony, and while trying to put an end to the arbitrary power of the feudal nobility and to bring order to the cities, he not only failed to obtain the expected support from London, but was in essence betrayed by the court. Loyalty to the dynastic principle ultimately spelt de Montfort's defeat. Having in practice become dictator of England, he could not bring himself to encroach on the prerogatives of the monarchy. This was not simply because he was unable, as a man of the Middle Ages, to imagine a large state except as monarchic, but also for the reason that even a change of dynasty was impossible for him. Together with the Plantagenets, the state which he served would have disappeared.

Notes

1 O. Shpengler, *Zakat Evropy. Ocherki morfologii mirovoy istorii* [The sunset of Europe. Sketches in the morphology of world history], Vol. 1, Moscow: Mysl', 1993, p. 151.
2 See S. Huntington, *The Clash of Civilizations and the Remaking of World Order,* New York: Simon & Schuster, 1996.
3 L.A. Mosionzhnik, *Antropologiya tsivilizatsiy* [The anthropology of civilisations], Kishinev: VASh, 2000, p. 47.
4 See I. Wallerstein, *World-Systems Analysis: An Introduction.* Durham, NC: Duke University Press, 2004.
5 See I. Wallerstein, *The Modern World-System I. Capitalist Agriculture and the Origins of the European World-Economy in the Sixteenth Century,* San Diego, CA: Academic Press, 1974, p. 16.
6 M. Grane, *Kitayskaya tsivilizatsiya* [Chinese civilisation], Moscow: Algoritm, 2008, p. 63.
7 M. Grane, *Kitayskaya mysl' ot Konfutsiya do Laotszy* [Chinese thought from Confucius to Laozi], Moscow: Algoritm, 2008, p. 397.
8 G.V. Scammell, *The First Imperial Age: European Overseas Expansion c. 1400–1715,* London: Unwin Hyman, 1989, p. 2.
9 M. Grane, *Kitayskaya mysl' ot Konfutsiya do Laotszy* [Chinese thought from Confucius to Laozi], p. 301. Spreading beyond the bounds of the Celestial Empire proper, this social system was reproduced to one degree or another almost everywhere Chinese cultural influence prevailed. An exception was Japan, which developed a different social order approximating to European feudalism.

10 The city-states of Asia, except for Babylon, were continually under the control of foreign rulers, and were not unhappy with this subjection. Even the Greeks of Asia Minor were for long periods loyal subjects of Persia, providing it with troops and ships for use against their fellow Greeks to the west. The cities did not suffer under the dominance of the Asian monarchs, and derived significant advantages from collaborating with them.

11 O. Eger, *Vsemirnaya istoriya* [World history], Vol. 1, *Drevniy mir* [The ancient world], St Petersburg: Poligon; Moscow: AST, 2001, p. 36.

12 *Vsemirnaya istoriya* [World history]. Moscow: Akademiya nauk SSSR, Politizdat, 1956, Vol. 1, p. 389.

13 Ibid.

14 See ibid., p. 86.

15 Mosionzhnik, *Antropologiya tsivilizatsiy*, p. 103.

16 Ibid., p. 97.

17 Mosionzhnik, *Antropologiya tsivilizatsiy*, p. 128.

18 Ibid., p. 388.

19 See *The Cambridge Ancient History* (2nd edition), Cambridge University Press, vol. 3, p. 3, ch. 40.

20 S.A. Nefedov, *Voyna i obshchestvo. Faktornyy analiz istoricheskogo protsessa. Istoriya Vostoka* [War and society. A factor analysis of the historical process. The History of the East], Moscow: Izdatel'skiy dom 'Territoriya budushchego', 2008, p. 31.

21 See V. Davis Hanson, *Why the West has Won: Carnage and Culture from Salamis to Vietnam*, London: Faber, 2001.

22 A.A. Popov, *Greko-Baktriyskoe tsarstvo* [The Greco-Bactrian monarchy], St Petersburg: Izdatel'stvo Senkt-Peterburgskogo universiteta, 2008, p. 223.

23 *Istoriya mira. Drevniy mir* [The history of the world. The ancient world], p. 376.

24 Popov, *Greko-Baktriyskoe tsarstvo*, p. 96.

25 *Istoriya, sotsiologiya, kul'tura narodov Afriki. Stat'i pol'skikh uchenykh* [The history, sociology and culture of the peoples of Africa. Articles by Polish scholars], Moscow: Nauka, 1974, p. 47.

26 E. Dridi, *Karfagen i Punicheskiy mir* [Carthage and the Punic world], Moscow: Veche, 2009, p. 76.

27 C. Wickham, *Framing the Early Middle Ages: Europe and the Mediterranean, 400–800*, Oxford: Oxford University Press, 2005, p. 10.

28 L. Myusse, *Varvarskie nashestviya na Zapadnuyu Evropu: volna vtoraya* [The barbarian invasions of Western Europe: the second wave], St Petersburg: Evraziya, 2006, pp. 140–41.

29 S.A. Nefedov, *Istoriya Rossii. Faktornyy analiz* [The history of Russia: a factoral analysis], Ekaterinburg, 2009, vol. 1, p. 102.

30 The participants in these events understood perfectly the connection between what was occurring on the shores of the Baltic, in Spain and in Palestine. See *Krestonostsy i Rus'. Konets XII-1270g.* [The crusaders and Rus'. From the late twelfth century to 1270], Moscow: Indrik, 2002.

31 See G. Luzzatto, *Storia economica d'Italia. Il Medioevo* [Economic history of Italy. The Middle Ages], Florence: G.C. Sansoni Editore, 1963, p. 211.

32 On the church as the prototype for centralised imperial administration, see J.D. Tracy (ed.), *The Political Economy of Merchant Empires*, Cambridge: Cambridge University Press, 1991, p. 124.

33 B. Simms, *Three Victories and a Defeat. The Rise and Fall of the First British Empire, 1714–1783*, New York: Basic Books, 2007, p. 10.

2

CRISIS AND REVOLUTION IN MEDIEVAL EUROPE

Early in the fourteenth century, economic growth in Europe was replaced abruptly by crisis. Unfinished Gothic cathedrals provide a visible demonstration for us of the scope of the crisis and of society's unpreparedness for it.

The growth of feudal society had increased the demand for resources, which were clearly inadequate. Up to a certain point this problem could be solved by cultivating unused land or by external expansion. But increasingly, the formerly unexploited land was ploughed up, and the opportunities for external conquests were exhausted. There were now too many people for them to be fed adequately with the existing productivity of labour, and too few for the expansion of the 'Christian world' to continue through demographic pressure alone.

The crisis of the fourteenth century

The turning-point was a series of plague epidemics, the first of which swept across Europe in 1348. But indications of crisis had appeared much earlier, and by the 1330s the situation had become stark. Historians note that in France as early as the turn of the fourteenth century 'the numbers of the population had ceased growing, and even begun to decline'.[1] Between 1315 and 1317 the country was seized by a genuine famine. Compared to the beginning of the century the population of France – the largest state of Western Europe – had halved by mid-century, and according to some accounts had shrunk by two-thirds.[2]

The productivity of agricultural labour was insufficient to feed a growing population, and all the readily available land was already being cultivated. The feudal estate-holders, whose incomes had earlier risen in proportion to the number of their subjects, began to experience serious difficulties. They had more and more need of money, but money was now in short supply. Although the demographic decline that followed plague and famine stimulated the growth of production in the long term, it led initially to a simultaneous fall in the tax base of the state, in the incomes from feudal landholdings, and in demand for the goods produced and sold by the towns. For example, data for tax collection show that the population of England by 1376 had shrunk to 2.5 million people.[3]

The plague transformed landholding relations in Europe. Some members of the feudal elite, experiencing material difficulties, saw freeing their peasants in exchange for money as the only way they could quickly obtain ready cash and patch the holes in their budgets. Others, renouncing the old feudal bonds, sought to attract new settlers to the now-empty lands.[4] Finally, the estate-holders appealed to the state, hoping to use its might to tie the peasants forcibly to the land and strengthen feudal exploitation. This aroused the resistance of the peasants, and made the state the arbiter and main avenue of appeal for resolving numerous social conflicts. The ability of the state to cope with these tasks was not always great. The weakness of the governing apparatus, revealed during a period when the ruling class had particular need of an effective state power, impelled society toward reforms and revolutions.

With a growing need for money, both the monarchs and leading members of the nobility tried desperately to find new means of obtaining it – and increasingly, resorted to seizing assets from one another. But the financial crisis, which grew more acute after the epidemics of plague, had begun much earlier. The affair of the Templars in France was among the more scandalous instances in which monarchs employed large-scale judicial fraud in order to obtain funds that earlier had been inaccessible to them. Most of the monarchs resorted to debasing the coinage, trying in this way to cope with budgetary shortages. Both state and individual debts increased, while incomes fell, reducing the state's tax base. This occurred even in the most advanced areas of Europe, such as Italy, Bohemia and Flanders.[5]

By the beginning of the fourteenth century it had become clear that the most popular suzerain was the one who could regularly subsidise his vassals. More and more complicated weapons had to be acquired for money, and their price grew continually. The military-political role of a feudal landholder came to depend increasingly on his economic means. But whether a king or prince had money to spare depended in turn on his relations with the towns, and on his ability to collect taxes. In other words, it depended on the degree to which he could rely on the embryonic bourgeois economy, and on bureaucratic organisation.

It was the rulers who could base themselves to some degree on non-feudal relations who also became the most effective members of the feudal elite. The interconnection between bourgeois and non-bourgeois relations in this case appears as a mirror-image of the relations that existed on the periphery of capitalism in the eighteenth and nineteenth centuries. The only difference lies in the fact that from late in the eighteenth century capital made use of feudal structures to obtain resources, strengthening the bourgeois order worldwide, while in the Middle Ages everything was reversed.

The consolidation of the state that began in Western Europe in the thirteenth century, the establishing of a centralised apparatus of rule and the first attempts at organising permanent military forces were accompanied by a rapid growth in state expenditures, which the treasuries by the mid-fourteenth century could no longer sustain. In the late thirteenth century the increase in state budgets aided the flourishing of the first banks. If their activity at first had been limited to supplying credits to merchants at fairs, and to supporting long-distance sea trade, their clients quickly came to include kings and landholding seigneurs. The new financial capital developed most strongly in Italy, where Tuscan cities were transformed into international financial centres. Italian commercial companies began taking on a transnational character. In the mid-fourteenth century the Peruzzi trading house had 133 agencies in various countries, while by 1345 the Bardi company had 346 affiliates spread from London to Jerusalem.[6] In the same category were the Buonsignori of Siena, and the Agnioni of Florence.

Not far behind the Italian bankers were those of Spain and Portugal. By the late thirteenth century the banking houses of Barcelona, Valencia and Burgos were participating actively in European financial markets.[7] In Germany banking companies in the proper sense were established. Smaller-scale usury was left to Jewish money-lenders, arousing the spite and jealousy of respectable Christians.

The kings took out loans, which they used to help pay for wars and meet administrative expenses. But by the mid-fourteenth century not even the most brilliant military victories or efficient management yielded the funds needed to pay off creditors, as is shown by the case of the English King Edward III, who was forced to declare himself bankrupt. The defaults by the kings of England and Sicily, flowing closely one upon the other, led to a wave of bankruptcies in Italy. In the view of Florentine chronicler Giovanni Villani, this crisis resulted not only from the insolvency of the royal debtors who had borrowed from the Italian financiers, but also from the burdens placed on local business by the Florentine polity, which like other states was short of money. Villani describes these events as 'a great calamity and setback', the like of which Florence had never before experienced.[8] According to contemporary accounts, the bankruptcy of the Bardi and Peruzzi financial houses had the character of a 'genuine civic catastrophe', whose consequences were 'more grievous than a military defeat'.[9] The north Russian republics of Novgorod and Pskov also met with economic hardship. The plague, brought to them from Germany, did them no small damage. Meanwhile, the Moscow usurer-prince Ivan Kalita during the same years hatched the idea of turning the general European economic crisis to his advantage, seizing the lands of his neighbours as compensation for their non-payment of debts. He did not, however, have to bear the military expenses, being helped in extracting debt payments by the Khan of the Golden Horde.

In Russia the crisis of the fourteenth century coincided with the rule of the Tatars, whose domination was by no means uniformly destructive where the lands beneath their sway were concerned. The consequences of the 'Tatar Yoke' are still a topic of intense discussion among Russian historians. The rise of Moscow as the future capital would have been unthinkable without the involvement of the Tatars. But it would be strange to see the Golden Horde solely as a benefactor to the

Russian people, if only for the reason that the Khans were least of all interested in the well-being of their Orthodox Christian subjects. The productivity of agricultural labour in fourteenth- and fifteenth-century Russia was extremely low, and in these circumstances the 10 per cent tax paid to the Khans became a heavy burden. Meanwhile, the Tatars introduced a system of accounting whose principles they had borrowed from China, which they had conquered. The conditions now existed for establishing a workable state bureaucracy, and the 'Yamskoy chase', based on a regular changing of horses, ensured improved postal ties between the territories of the future Russian state. The business and trading centre of Russia shifted to the south, from the old trading republics on the shores of the Baltic to the more southerly regions that made up the core of the future Muscovite realm.

City and state

It would be a complete error to imagine the late Middle Ages as an era of conflict between an unchanged feudal system or a feudalism that was 'disintegrating under the impacts of the market' on one hand, and on the other, bourgeois relations that were developing in parallel with it. Nor can one speak of a clash between a conservative countryside and dynamically developing cities. The modernisation of European society in fact went ahead in a series of waves. Very often, the social relations and political forces that had been engendered by a previous wave of changes were themselves overturned by the waves of modernisation that followed.

Bourgeois productive relations took shape in Europe from the late fourteenth century, attaining an important degree of development in Italy, in the Netherlands, in England, and in some parts of France and Germany. Nowhere, however, did these relations succeed in implanting the critical mass of economic change that would have transformed bourgeois structures into the dominant mode of production, into the capitalist system.

In its initial formative stages, the bourgeoisie was in no sense antagonistic to feudalism; to the contrary, it aided feudalism by providing new stimuli for its development. It is a well-attested fact that the monarchies in Flanders and Castile, and later in England too, consolidated their positions through relying on the cities, which became sufficiently strong to act as a counterweight to the feudal elite. Embodying new social and economic relations, the bourgeoisie in turn required a strengthening of central authority – not only in order to defend its rights against the feudal seigneurs, but also for pursuing its quest to definitively reorient rural production away from the natural economy and toward the needs of the cities. Just as the trading cities of antiquity could not get by without support from the territorial empires that expedited their contacts with interior provinces, so now the strengthening of the state was a vital condition for bourgeois development. Finding their opportunities restricted within the framework of local markets, the merchants yearned to buy and sell goods on the scale of the entire continent. Striking as a manifestation of the new trading economy were the famous markets in Champagne, where Italian merchants and their commodities met with buyers from Northern

Europe. The economic crisis of the fourteenth century, however, sent the markets into decline.

The collaboration between the central authorities and the towns took on extremely varied forms depending on the social and economic situations of particular regions, and these forms were by no means always suited to the spread of new, more democratic social relations. A comparison of the two Spanish states, Castile and Aragon, shows clearly that the development of commercial capital did not of itself lead to an increase in the use of free, hired labour, or to the overcoming of feudalism. The cities of Castile were artisan centres, comparatively small and not especially wealthy, and were developing on the basis of exchanges of commodities with the surrounding countryside. The peasants in turn were for the most part free. Even if the communal peasant bodies, the *behetrías,* had established nominal relations with the seigneurs, they reserved the right to change their protectors 'even seven times in the space of a day'.[10]

In Aragon, where a powerful centre of international trade had appeared around Barcelona, far more conservative relations prevailed. The peasants remained in thrall to powerful aristocratic families who collaborated closely with the owners of merchant capital. The feudal elite helped the merchant oligarchs to conquer strongpoints in the Western Mediterranean, establishing political and economic outposts in the Balearic Islands, Sicily, Southern Italy and even Tunis. Meanwhile, the city elite which controlled community life in Barcelona or Palma de Majorca invariably acted alongside the aristocracy in resisting periodic peasant revolts. Urban society in Aragon was far more homogeneous and cohesive than in Castile; in Aragon social conflicts erupted regularly, which in turn strengthened the interest felt by the commercial oligarchs in collaborating with the feudal nobility.

The Italian, German and Russian city-republics, viewed by many authors as examples of early bourgeois states with advanced economies, in fact presented a far more complex picture. From the fourteenth century all of them, from Venice to Novgorod, tended to go into decline, though this was by no means always recognised by contemporary observers.

Between the twelfth and fourteenth centuries the Mediterranean trade turned Venice and Genoa into key economic centres whose importance was great not only for the West. The handbook *Practica della mercatura,* compiled in the fourteenth century for employees of the Florentine Bardi company, describes the markets of the entire Mediterranean and of other regions, including territories far beyond the boundaries of the ancient Roman Empire.

Sea voyages required not only serious preparation but also long periods of time. To sail from Venice to Beirut or Alexandria and back took six months, and a trading expedition to Bruges in Flanders a whole year. It is understandable that with technology as it was the turnover of funds was bound to be extremely slow, which in turn demanded a highly effective and developed banking system, which through its credits allowed merchants to maintain themselves in the intervals between commercial operations.

With a limited quantity of precious metals at their disposal, the Europeans would simply not have been able to carry out their commercial expansion had they not simultaneously been able to export their own products, for which there was a steady demand. Carrying on trade with the Arab ports of the Mediterranean, the Italians not only exchanged silver for goods from the East, but also offered their own wares.[11] To the Near East they exported cloth and metals, often weapons, glassware, paper, dyestuffs, jewellery, wine, and when harvests in those areas were poor, grain. In addition, the Venetians and Genoese carried on intermediary trade, delivering to the countries of the Maghreb spices from Asia and other goods they had acquired in the Levant. In their turn, the Italian trading enterprises through a system of fairs supplied products from the Mediterranean to various European countries. From the thirteenth century, the merchants furnished foreign markets not only with exotic and expensive commodities for the feudal elite, but also with 'goods of primary necessity, meant for the very broadest layers of society'.[12]

The development of international trade had a particularly direct effect on production, allowing it to expand and strengthening the control of capital over the immediate producers.

> It was the requirements of large-scale international trade [*grande commerzio internazionale*] that led to improvements in technical methods and also juridical institutions, to the appearance of more rationally organised and managed enterprises, and also to the development of the spirit of initiative and entrepreneurship without which the figure of the capitalist of the new era would have been unimaginable.[13]
>
> *(Luzzatto 1963: 230)*

Increasingly, production became divorced from local markets and oriented toward export, while in turn starting to depend on imports of raw materials. Italian textiles were sold in Germany, but the dyes for them came to the workshops of the peninsula from India, Egypt and Mesopotamia. Also dependent on foreign supplies was pharmaceutical production, which in its turn was oriented increasingly toward external markets. Here a direct dependency was to be observed: the possibility the merchants had of organising the export of goods to foreign markets enabled the use of more expensive raw materials and technologies. Trade in turn assisted the development of shipbuilding, the building and repairing of roads, and technical improvements.

Along with industrial production, Italian agriculture also became reoriented toward export markets. Wine and olive oil were supplied to Northern Europe, as well as salt and grain, which 'together with cloth and textile articles formed the basis of large-scale medieval commerce'.[14]

It was not only Italians who were engaged in trade, but also Catalans, Portuguese and merchants from Marseilles. Historians have reasons for considering that the commercial balance of these operations was by no means always negative for the Europeans. In Tunis, representatives of the Florentine banking houses of the Bardi, Peruzzi and Acciaioli had gained a foothold by the early fourteenth century. The crisis that followed saw these institutions bankrupt, but the business ties remained, and from the mid-fifteenth century began once again to expand.

Defending their political independence, the trading bourgeoisie of the Italian republics and the German Hanseatic cities turned the state into a tool for pursuing their commercial interests. But, as soon became apparent, this not only failed to stimulate the development of the economy and the establishing of new social relations, but from a certain point began acting as a brake on them.

Bourgeois relations took shape not only in the cities but in the countryside as well. Indeed, the spreading to rural areas of hired labour and market-oriented production played a decisive role in the development of the new social order.[15] One result was that city-states that had become cut off from the feudal countryside failed to become effective centres of social change. They went into hibernation, and stagnated on the social level. In remote regions of Europe, the establishing of strategic outposts on the seacoasts did not provide a substitute for ties with the rural economy. These ties grew weaker; in Novgorod, where the rural areas controlled by the city were substantial, these areas were sparsely settled, the productivity of labour was extremely low, and the merchant oligarchs purchased land not for the purpose of investing in production, but as a way of safeguarding their capital against commercial risks.

The development of politically independent cities had very little effect on life in the surrounding countryside, which remained completely feudal. The cities did not transform the society that surrounded them so much as divide themselves off from it, defending their right to live differently. Moreover, the territorial expansion of the cities in such circumstances led to a feudalisation of their ruling bourgeois elites. Both in Novgorod and in Venice, the bourgeois notables who bought rural estates did not transform them along the lines of capitalist enterprises (as occurred later in England), but became feudalised themselves. For example, the Venetian 'new colonies' that were seized in the Balkans and in the Eastern Mediterranean as the position of Byzantium weakened had a pre-eminently feudal character.[16] Thus the Venetians, after conquering Crete, distributed the best lands among their patricians, exploiting the dependent local population.

It was no accident that the evolution of the political systems of the city-states proceeded from democracy to oligarchy. The further a city rose in terms of power and influence, the more oligarchic its internal system became. This was equally true both of Novgorod and of Venice.

Describing the evolution of the state in the later Middle Ages, Giovanni Arrighi counterposes 'capitalism', regarded as embodied in Genoa and Venice, to 'territorialism', considered to have triumphed in France and England.[17] After the defeat of the city-states the struggle between these two principles culminated, in thoroughly Hegelian fashion, in a synthesis that took the shape of the 'national state', territorial in form and bourgeois in content.

It is not hard to see that Arrighi here compares the incommensurable. Capitalism as a mode of production and system of trade, together with the social relations that correspond to it, cannot conceivably be ranked alongside an abstract 'territorialism', by which the researcher understands the principle of organisation of large territorial states (strictly speaking, from Arrighi's reasoning on these states we understand only that they are large). In reality, city-states at times controlled extremely extensive territories. During the fifteenth century Novgorod in territorial terms was among the largest states in Europe. Venice too established a territorial empire of impressive dimensions. Genoa possessed extensive landholdings in Crimea. These territories were in various cases separated from the capitals by large expanses of sea, but that can also be said of the Portuguese empire of later times. Denmark, which became one of the leading states of the North, like Venice controlled lands scattered along various coasts. There is no basis whatever for regarding Venice or Novgorod as extraterritorial formations of some kind, structured solely around commercial and financial operations. They commanded armed forces of considerable dimensions; their elites invested profits from their trade in acquiring landed estates; they fought for control of strategically important territories; and they entered into political alliances and coalitions.

Charles Tilly links the decline of the city-states to a shortage of resources. The problem in fact lay not in the size of their territories (Venice and Novgorod had greater territories and populations under their power than many European kings), but in their structures, in the internal forms of organisation of these oligarchic republics. They simply failed to set themselves the tasks which the future national states of Europe confronted and solved.

The main problem was not the size of the territories under the control of Venice, of Florence, of the German Hansa cities or of Pskov and Novgorod, but the degree to which the type of oligarchic rule that had taken shape there corresponded to the imperatives of capitalist development. The dynastic states were in fact no less bourgeois than the trading republics, but while the city-states depended on the traditional 'international markets' of the Middle Ages, that were limited in extent, the dynastic states simultaneously *created their own internal markets and a new world market*. By virtue of this, they were also far more representative. Despite the views that became current in later times, the power of the monarchs was by no means unlimited; it presupposed deliberate interaction with people from various social strata and regions, while the politics of the city-states, for all the formal 'democratism' of the procedures involved, were founded on oligarchic control within the city walls and on harsh suppression of the subjects outside.

The transformation of the city into a commercial enterprise made it unsuited as a political tool for establishing capitalist society; indeed, it became an obstacle to such development. The formation of the capitalist system cannot be reduced to the pursuit of commercial profits (as also occurred long before the triumph of the bourgeois order), but in certain situations directly counteracts this goal. Capitalism requires integrated markets, and in the first instance, the creation of a sizeable labour market, without which an expansion of bourgeois production is inconceivable. Defending their commercial privileges and specific interests, the city-states were one of the most serious obstacles along this path. The inability of a centralised state to crush the resistance of the city-republics in Italy and Germany was a crucial impediment to modernisation and bourgeois development in these countries.

The markets of the city-states proved to be too narrow to allow the accumulation of capital, which in the late thirteenth century was already seeking broader territories and more powerful clients in the kings, who possessed a serious tax base. Moreover this tax base, still located in the agrarian economy, was far more resilient before the fluctuations of the market conjuncture which in the fourteenth century sent the largest Italian companies bankrupt.

The successes of the Hansa cities were impressive, which makes eliciting the reasons for their subsequent decline still more important. The economic and political degradation of the Italian city-states is usually linked with the fall of Constantinople, the discovery of America and the shifting of trade routes, but for the cities of the German Hansa the displacing of trade to the north-west was more of a favourable factor. Many of the German ports continued to develop vigorously, while the importance of the Baltic as a trade zone increased steadily throughout the sixteenth and seventeenth centuries. But this in no way strengthened the political positions of the old Hansa centres.

Nineteenth-century German historians tied the economic decline of the coastal cities to the events of the Thirty Years War, but the process involved began significantly earlier. The French historian Ernest Lavisse observes that by the beginning of the fifteenth century the Hansa was 'in a state of total decay'.[18] Under the Kalmar Union of 1389 the kings of Denmark, traditionally in conflict with the Hansa, annexed Norway and Sweden, which had a tradition of collaborating with the Hansa cities. Although Sweden by the mid-fifteenth century had effectively seceded from the union, and did so officially in 1523, the relationship of forces in the region had changed irrevocably.

During the sixteenth century trade in the North Sea and the Baltic developed rapidly, but it was not the Germans who succeeded in exploiting these new opportunities so much as the Dutch and to some degree the English. The problems of the city-states, in Italy as in Germany, had begun in the fifteenth century, even before the fall of Constantinople. The roots of these problems need to be sought in the social and political structures of the city-states, in the limited nature of their economic bases, in the narrowness of their internal markets and in the oligarchic character of their rule, which had damaging effects on their commercial policies.

By the beginning of the fifteenth century Venice was clearly outstripping its rivals, Florence and Genoa, both in sea power and in financial, political and territorial respects. For Genoa, in the west of Italy, the French market and political ties with the French kings were of great importance. The events of the Hundred Years War thus dealt the Genoese bourgeoisie a serious blow. A part of the capital that was now unused was redirected westward, to Spain and Portugal, where Genoese money played no small role in financing the seafaring expeditions and geographical discoveries. In the sixteenth century Genoese firms were still harvesting the fruits of their success, receiving substantial income from Spain and Portugal.[19]

The successes of the Italian trading cities were closely linked to the Byzantine empire. As historians have noted, the Italian seafaring republics were in a position to give Byzantium effective military support in exchange for commercial privileges.[20] The decline of Constantinople brought with it an inevitable weakening of the positions of Genoa and Venice. But the Italian entrepreneurs derived an important share of their profits from direct trade with Moslem countries. Despite almost incessant military conflict, these relations were never completely broken off. It should also be noted that the Venetians fought the Turks and traded with the Arabs; the political conflicts here did not coincide in any way with religious differences. In Crimea the Genoese colonies were *de facto* protectorates of the khans of the Golden Horde, though from time to time the two sides entered into conflict. Genoese infantry were among the Tatar forces in the battle against the Russians on the Kulikovo Field, and when Byzantium fell the Genoese not only refused to support the Greeks, but preferred to reach an agreement with the Turks.

In the late fourteenth and early fifteenth centuries more than 60 per cent of the ships that left the port of Beirut were bound for Genoa or Venice. From Alexandria every fifth, and at times every fourth vessel set sail for Genoa. Only Barcelona could compete with the Italian ports, receiving between a fifth and a quarter of the commercial traffic.[21] The strengthening of the position of Ottoman Turkey, and its later conquest of Syria and Egypt, dealt the interests of the Venetians no less a blow than the capture by the Turks of Constantinople.

The commercial influence of Venice extended not only to the Eastern Mediterranean but also to southern Germany, where local trading houses worked in close alliance with the Venetians. In the markets of the Netherlands Italian merchants exchanged goods with representatives of the German Hansa that dominated the Baltic. Investment had by now taken on an international character; money acquired through trade with the Levant went to develop mines in Bohemia and textile production in Flanders. English wool made its way to Florence, where high-quality cloth was produced for sale throughout Europe. The development of the economy was accompanied by a growth of class contradictions and of socio-political struggle. In Genoa alone between 1413 and 1453 there were 13 uprisings and revolutions. Venice appeared as an island of stability, mainly because authority was divided effectively between the dominant commercial groups. Nevertheless, as an Italian economic historian recognised, conflicts between property-owners and workers arose constantly, after 1400 'taking on the clear character of class struggle'.[22]

The main thing that distinguished Venice from Florence and many other Italian republics was that production (with the exception of shipbuilding) was not especially developed – the basis for the republic's wealth lay in trade. While the Florentines and Flemings produced goods for the growing urban population, the Venetians specialised in producing luxury items, or built ships in the state shipyards. The local industries in Venice did not suffer particularly from fluctuations in mass demand, but at the same time were among the most backward in the Adriatic.[23]

As in the case of all empires, the state played a very important role in the economy of Venice, not only acting as a wholesale customer (it needed to outfit the fleet and build fortresses), but also owning a large merchant fleet. The local maritime laws were the model for the British Navigation Acts, forbidding imports of spices except on ships belonging to the republic. Warships accompanied trading convoys, making navigation safer. The republic's economic policy was consistently protectionist.

The Venetian state rested on an effective fiscal system that allowed the treasury to obtain important sums in the form of taxes and customs duties. Even membership in the aristocracy depended not just on ancestry, but also on fulfilling one's financial obligations to the government.

Not only the tax system and various monopolies, but also important areas of transport were in government hands. Unlike the case in Genoa, the fleet of galleys belonged to the republic; from the fourteenth century all galleys passed gradually into government ownership.[24] In circumstances of economic crisis the concentration of resources in the hands of the government proved to be a vital condition for development, and did not arouse discontent among the bourgeoisie. The galleys could be used both for military and commercial purposes, in peacetime making regular voyages between Venice and the ports of the Eastern Mediterranean. As early as 1278 a system was established for dispatching convoys to the East. Schedules and rules were drawn up which had to be observed 'now and forever' (*d'ora in poi*).[25] In the early fourteenth century analogous routes, to England and Flanders, were added to the eastern convoys. Since the Venetian fleet had now to venture into the Atlantic Ocean new, sturdier galleys started to be built; later, these also came to be used on the traditional sea routes. Armed galleys transported the rarest and most precious cargoes (spices, perfumes, dyed fabrics, medicines, precious stones, and also Venetian wares to be exchanged in the East for these items).[26] The price of the goods loaded onto a single galley might come to 200,000 ducats or even more.[27] Cheaper goods were supplied to the consumer by 'sea tramps'.[28] These small ships belonged to joint stock companies of a distinctive type, set up by bourgeois families; management of the business was in the hands of the family that owned the largest share.

The actual productive base of the Italian city-republics was at first relatively narrow. Intermediary trade played the decisive role. Luxury goods brought from the East were exchanged in these cities for textiles from Flanders, or for silver and copper mined and smelted in Central Europe. It was only gradually that the quantities of goods produced by the city-states themselves increased, and its quality improved. Venice produced glass, ceramics, paper and jewellery, and Florence, textiles. Adopting Eastern technologies, the Venetians learned to grow sugar cane on Crete and Cyprus, whence it spread to Sicily and Malta, and then to Spain, Portugal and islands in the Atlantic. Demand for Italian wares increased gradually to the point where new centres of production had to be established in southern Germany, in Ulm, Augsburg and Nuremberg. The Italian technologies were imitated in Flanders and France. Exports of capital and technology came to replace exports of goods. Not only were the technical and organisational innovations of the Italians readily grasped in German and Flemish trading cities, but new institutions were devised, corresponding to the demands of the bourgeois economy. The first securities exchange appeared during the Middle Ages in the Flemish city of Bruges, next to the house of the noble Van den Börse family. This was the origin of the German word *Börse,* meaning a stock exchange.

'In the fifteenth century,' Antonio Gramsci states, 'the enterprise shown by the Italian merchants declined sharply; they preferred to invest the funds they had acquired in landed estates, and to receive a secure income from agriculture instead of again risking their money in expeditions and investments abroad.'[29] Agrarian production, however, did not so much become bourgeois as the bourgeoisie became feudalised. By the mid-fifteenth century the Italian cities had returned to the role of commercial and financial centres, while the centres of production shifted increasingly to the north. By the sixteenth century the Netherlands and England possessed a far more powerful productive base than the Italian city-states.

The European bankers of the fifteenth and sixteenth centuries (the Fuggers of Augsburg and others) had been active in providing credit to kings and emperors, and it was working with these large clients, rather than with entrepreneurs at one remove, that brought about the rapid development of private financial institutions. The city-states of the late Middle Ages, where similar banking houses had arisen, soon proved too small for these institutions to develop. As Gramsci notes, the impossibility of the effective development of capitalism was guaranteed by 'the very structure of the state-commune', which could not 'develop into a large territorial state'.[30]

The bankers needed large, powerful states; these guaranteed access to far more significant resources, while simultaneously providing defence across a large territory. Finally, it was within these kingdoms that the opportunity arose for employing credit not only in trade, but also in agriculture, which despite all the changes that had occurred remained the basis of every economy. As a rule, of course, it was not a matter of agrarian credit as such. The landowning aristocracy resorted to borrowing in order to finance its growing consumption, to rebuild castles and country houses, and to maintain numerous servants as well as their retinues of other employees. To pay off their creditors, the aristocracy intensified the exploitation of the peasants and redirected the countryside toward producing for the market. The technical and organisational improvements were more often side effects of these efforts than the result of thought-out strategies and investments.

Between the feudal elite and the urban oligarchs, a *rapprochement* took place. Feudal families moved to the cities (at times, they were even compelled to do so), and invested money in commercial undertakings. Meanwhile, prominent bourgeois clans were purchasing country estates on the urban fringes, and acquiring titles and feudal privileges. This picture was to be seen equally in medieval Italy and in the Russia of Novgorod and Pskov.

The seigneurs who came to power in the cities toward the end of the fifteenth or in the early sixteenth century were themselves offspring of the bourgeoisie. The emergence of 'new feudals' from the milieu of the urban oligarchy was a result precisely of the political triumph of the city. In Germany the picture was similar. After defending their independence in the fourteenth and fifteenth centuries, the free cities by the sixteenth century were in crisis; as a German historian observes, 'the entire social system of the city-republics was collapsing, not only under pressure from outside, but also from within.'[31] Adding to social struggles by the lower orders were divisions within the elite, the rivalry of oligarchic groups and the rise to power in this setting of 'urban despots' (*Stadttyrannen*), who ignored the traditional republican institutions.

The subsequent development of protestant trading centres did nothing to stimulate the development of Germany as a whole, since the cities were not prepared to share their resources with backward regions in the name of creating a national market. Meanwhile, the creation of a unified market is of fundamental importance for the development of capitalism, especially at the stage of the transition from the hegemony of commercial capital to the development of industry. The final disintegration of Germany into independent mini-states reinforced its backwardness, just as the unification of the country in the mid-nineteenth century was a crucial precondition for its industrialisation. The same can justly be said of Italy, except that the backwardness in that case had its own specific causes. By the sixteenth century it had been discovered that the merchants from the city-states could not compete with traders from the new centralised states.[32] The same trend is apparent in Western Europe, in Asia and in Russia.

As the Czech historian Josef Macek noted, the fourteenth century unfolded 'no longer beneath the insignia of struggle between the feudal elite and the cities, but of a stormy conflict between the burghers in the patriciate'.[33] The growth of foreign trade, as the Belgian historian Henri Pirenne observes, resulted in producers losing their direct contact with consumers, and in goods being sold through intermediaries. This in turn led to the proletarianisation of artisans, who now worked not for themselves but for merchants, who in practice hired them to fill export orders. Consequently, 'a sharp division appeared between the merchant and the producer: the former was a capitalist, the latter a hired worker.'[34]

In the more developed parts of Western Europe in the first half of the fourteenth century hired labour was widespread, and not only in the large cities. Flanders, northern Italy, and some areas of France, England and Germany underwent a rapid process of urbanisation. By the mid-fourteenth century the largest cities of Flanders had as many as 50,000 residents.[35] 'The worker masses of the large cities evidently lived in conditions relatively close to the conditions of life of modern proletarians,' Pirenne stated early in the twentieth century.[36] The numbers of the proletariat had increased thanks to the economic expansion that had continued throughout a century and a half. The crisis that replaced the era of growth was accompanied by an increase in unemployment and by acts of protest. Already in the thirteenth century, the heresies spreading about Europe were not only anti-feudal but also anti-bourgeois.

In the Italian republics toward the end of the fourteenth century the class struggle reached white heat. The key questions were those of wages and of the right of hired workers to establish their own guilds. The urban revolts of the fourteenth century in Florence and Siena displayed the same political and ideological characteristics as the later Hussite movement in Bohemia. The revolts by the *ciompi* in Florence showed that attempts to transfer the burdens of the economic crisis onto the labouring masses were fraught with the danger of serious social upheavals. During this period the *ciompi* – wool-combers and other hired workers in the textile industry of Florence and other Italian cities – staged repeated uprisings.

Through terror and corruption, the oligarchies of the city-republics managed to hold onto power, but they lacked the resources to achieve a social compromise acceptable to most of the population, and without this, no long-term development was possible. The invasion of Italy by the French in 1494 showed the military and political impotence of the city-states. The French armies made their way throughout the whole country without encountering serious opposition. Niccolò Machiavelli and other thinkers of the period, who not long before had considered Italy the most important centre of world politics, were shaken. The only way of stopping the French was through the formation of a league which included not just Venice, Milan and the pope, but also Spain. Once the Spanish had set foot on Italian territory, however, they showed no inclination to leave, and in the sixteenth century Spanish and French armies moved freely about the country fighting one another. To the degree that victory swung in the direction of the Spanish forces, hegemony in Italy passed into the hands of the 'Catholic monarchs' of Spain and of their Habsburg descendants. Only Venice and Genoa retained their independence and the traditional institutions of the oligarchic republics. Naples became a possession of the Spanish crown, and the northern dukedoms became *de facto* protectorates of the Habsburgs for several centuries. In a humbled political condition, the Italian cities and their oligarchic elites carried on reproducing their social structures for a further century and a half, priding themselves on their cultural achievements and heroic pasts.

The victory of the Portuguese over the Egyptians in the Indian Ocean, and the subsequent conquest of Egypt by the Turks, had catastrophic consequences for Venetian commerce. To the Venetians, Alexandria had been crucially important. In a context of reduced commercial activity private financial capital fell into decline throughout the countries of the Mediterranean region, though it continued to develop in Northern Europe. 'Throughout Italy, with the exception of Genoa,' Luzzatto states, 'private banking houses had ceased to flourish by the beginning of the sixteenth century, their place being taken by public banks.'[37] With Catalonia as a model, such banks were established in Sicily, Naples, Rome, Milan, Venice, and finally Genoa.

As various historians have noted, the 'fatal turning point'[38] for the Italian trading cities was the Thirty Years War. The loss of German markets caused the Venetian economy to collapse, while the Genoese bankers, tied closely to the Spanish Habsburgs, suffered defeat along with them. The financial bankruptcy of Spain – evident as early as 1627, long before the country's final military defeat – signified the end of the Genoese financial empire.

Uncompleted revolutions

'Obedience is dead, justice is suffering, and good order does not exist anywhere,' said the anonymous author of the tract *Reformatio Sigismundi,* written in the mid-fifteenth century.[39] This was a period that might best be characterised using the words of Stalin, uttered in reference to another time and different circumstances: an epoch of wars and revolutions.

The British historian Thomas A. Brady describes the period of the late fourteenth and early fifteenth centuries as a 'political Golden Age of the Common Man', which gave the masses the elements of self-rule, but which was simultaneously 'stagnant, troubled and disrupted'.[40] This characterisation might be applied to virtually any revolutionary epoch. The popular revolts of the late Middle Ages did not lead, and could not have led, to the creation of a democratic system. While objectively representing early attempts at bourgeois revolution, they could not have established a new bourgeois society, and nor could they have satisfied the demands of the masses for real popular power. The crisis of late feudalism was ultimately overcome by regimes of a 'Caesarist' or even 'Bonapartist' type. A new absolutist state could come to power through a process of social transformation which society itself was incapable of implementing. But a new monarchic system could not fully overcome the crisis either, so long as additional resources, able to drive the process of development forward, were not at its disposal.

The epicentres of change turned out to be in England, Bohemia and Flanders, where fierce political and ideological conflicts opened the way for new social relations, undermining an old and seemingly natural order that had been established for centuries.

In terms of its level of economic development and its traditions of civic freedoms, fourteenth-century Flanders might seem to rank with Italy. But in fact, it presents a more complex political picture. Describing the ideological evolution of Flemish society, Henri Pirenne noted that among city dwellers, 'a republican ideal, as in almost all commercial and industrial states', was widespread.[41] While attaining a significant degree of independence, the Flemish cities could not rid themselves completely of feudal dependency. As a result, they found themselves drawn into a much larger-scale social and political process, not only defending their own interests, but also acting on the surrounding society as a transformative force. This was the case not just in Flanders and Brabant, but also in England and France, and to some extent in Germany.

In the early fourteenth century the Flemish cities experienced a fierce outburst of social strife, culminating in a French intervention which proved catastrophic for the invading army. As Pirenne notes, the Franco-Flemish war was the outcome 'not only of political conflict, but also of class struggle'.[42]

The cities of Flanders became the setting for a powerful social movement. In 1280 uprisings took place among the urban popular masses, accompanied by fighting on street barricades. Fear of the masses drove the patricians to turn for help to the French king, drawing Paris into local political life. Such was the spiral of events that led eventually to the Battle of Courtrai and the Hundred Years War. The Battle of Courtrai not only saw the first decisive victory of infantry over cavalry, marking the beginning of a revolution in military strategy, but was also the model for a whole series of revolutionary clashes, such as the Battle of Valmy, in the course of which the insurgent masses showed their superiority over professional armies.

A civil war, interspersed with French interventions, continued in Flanders for two decades, culminating eventually in the restoration of the feudal regime and in nominal French sovereignty over the local cities. The large bourgeoisie, frightened by the growing political influence of the urban masses, preferred to make concessions in the name of order and stability, and the uprising died away. At the battle of Cassel, 26 years after Courtrai, the French knights succeeded in taking their revenge, emerging victorious over the Flemish volunteers. Large-scale repression followed, and it appeared that the rebellious spirit of Flanders had been broken. But the conflict soon flared anew, this time in the form of an international confrontation into which England was drawn alongside France.

The notion of 'international conflict' can be used only conditionally with relation to this epoch. Since no such thing as a national state yet existed, the borders of one or another 'society' remained extremely diffuse. It is, though, possible to speak of Bohemia and England as societies whose physical limits more or less coincided with their state boundaries. Consequently, it was here that political and social processes were to be observed at their most intense. Seizing broad masses of the population, the changes left no-one on the sidelines, and inevitably resulted in ideological and political crises. The interaction of city and countryside was so profound that the crisis of the feudal order affected all aspects of life, and a political struggle that had begun with a single local conflict would grow and spread throughout the entire country, involving not only different regions but also diverse groups of the population. In the course of these conflicts, people came to feel that they were participants in what was occurring throughout the country as a whole, and the national state thus came into being.

In England and Bohemia, the social conflicts quickly took on the dimensions of a revolutionary crisis. The impulse to social renovation in the two countries acquired a similar ideological basis in the teachings of Wyclif and Hus, who were obvious predecessors and in essence, early representatives of the religious Reformation. In France, by contrast, the crisis of the fourteenth century was accompanied rather by a strengthening of the position of the traditional feudal elite; the tumultuous changes that followed were to an important degree the result of external influences and challenges.

The centralisation carried out in the thirteenth century by the kings of England and France had the unexpected effect of altering the political structure and system of interests of the feudal class. While in earlier times individual princes had fought against the kings for their independence, defending the interests of the provinces against the capitals, in the late fourteenth and in the fifteenth century the feudal magnates fought among themselves for influence at court, trying, as Édouard Perroy writes, 'to dominate the administration, to control the state'.[43] In no way, however, did they loosen their ties with the provinces. Modernising the bureaucratic apparatus in their own domains, they copied the structures of the central administration, turning their courts into 'real nurseries of functionaries'.[44] The task they now set themselves was not to defend their political independence, but by making use of the royal bureaucracy and finances, to redistribute general state revenues to their own advantage.

In England, it seemed by the beginning of the fifteenth century that with the establishing in power of the Lancaster dynasty the centralised state bureaucracy, supported by the bourgeoisie and petty nobility, had crushed the feudal magnates, who had been weaker here to begin with than on the continent. But in France the magnates were increasingly gaining the upper hand, and the bourgeois leaders were reduced to trying to defend their interests by forming a compact with one or another competing aristocratic faction. To a significant degree, this refeudalisation of France was a result of the earlier policy of centralisation. In the thirteenth century almost all the large vassal domains on the territory of the kingdom had been annulled or made strictly subordinate to the monarchy (the exceptions were Brittany and Gascony, the latter belonging to the English Plantagenets). In the fourteenth century, however, the royal power began granting new landholdings to relatives and clients of the ruling dynasty. Unlike the magnates of the previous epoch the holders of these estates enjoyed only limited rights; inheritance of the estates was not automatic, and Paris could resume or confiscate them at any time. But as the economic and political crisis deepened, the ability of the centre to control the situation diminished. The Hundred Years War was the outcome of these internal contradictions of French society. It was not so much a struggle between English and French as a series of civil wars fought within France itself, accompanied by a series of English interventions.

The war began with the simultaneous flaring up of two smouldering conflicts which had emerged a good while earlier. Gascony, which was part of the domains of the English monarch (remaining from the territories held by the Plantagenets in France), was a constant topic of discord between Paris and London. Meanwhile the Flemish cities, defending their independence both against the local seigneurs and the French king, were seeking support from England. Exports of wool to Flanders were a key component of the English economy. Dependent on them to a large extent were the royal budget, the incomes of the merchants, and the flow of money into agriculture. Meanwhile, the permanent financial crisis that afflicted the French royal government drove it to act in ways that aggravated both problems at once. The French pressure on the wealthy Flemish lands was intensified, while in Paris a decision was once again made to confiscate the Plantagenet domain in Gascony (Guyenne). Such attempts had already been made several times, ending regularly with the conclusion of treaties. But this time, the patience of the English court gave way. Rendering the situation still more fraught was the fact that the English ruler King Edward III had no worse a claim to the French crown, and perhaps even a better one, than the new Valois dynasty that had recently been enthroned in Paris. It is true that no-one for the time being was touching Gascony, and that Edward had not claimed his entitlement, even doing homage to the French king in respect of the territory. But once Paris had announced the confiscation, London for its part remembered the hereditary rights.

The Plantagenets were always ready to renounce their rights, obtaining a guarantee of peace in exchange for territory. Describing the policy of Edward III on the eve of the peace negotiated at Brétigny, Perroy concluded:

> Dynastic claims, so far as he was concerned, were merely small change. Here it was made clear what he really wanted: the return of Guyenne, within the

broadest possible boundaries. For the moment, the boundaries concerned were those of the dukedom in the time of good King Louis the Pious, but with the successes of English arms, appetites would grow. For this enlarged Guyenne, moreover, he was intent on demanding full sovereignty: no more ties of vassalage, no interference by French bureaucrats in its affairs, no appeals to the Parisian parliament, and no threats of confiscation. If Guyenne ceased to be part of the French kingdom, the Plantagenets would finally come to own it, and the very cause of the war would disappear.[45]

It may be noted that the new sovereign princedom of Aquitaine, created on the basis of the old Guyenne, would also be outside the control of the London parliament, having been transformed into the personal property of the dynasty.

If, however, the Plantagenets defended their dynastic rights, then the traders and artisans of Flanders, who had urged Edward to go to war with France, had an interest of their own at stake. In 1339 Flanders and Brabant concluded an anti-French treaty, justifying their joint action on the basis that 'these two countries are full of people who cannot exist without trade'.[46] Even before the alliance with England had been formally concluded, Holland joined in the pact. Then in 1340 Edward III, on the urging of the Flemish leaders, swore an oath at the Friday market in Ghent in the capacity of the new king of France, promising to observe the rights and independence of the cities of Flanders. It is not hard to see where the initiative for this move had originated. The English king had been wavering, but the Flemings impelled him to take irreversible steps, seeing in the struggle between the two kingdoms their only defence against the depredations of the French feudal power.

Even before the first English soldiers had set foot on the continent, it had been made clear in London that this war would be quite unlike all its predecessors. It laid the basis for a crucially important institution without which the state of later times would be difficult to imagine: mass propaganda.

Of course, a certain system of ideological domination is a characteristic of any class society. But earlier the leading ideological role had been played by the church. Moreover, the kings and princes had given little thought to the question of how they might inform their subjects and ensure popular support on questions of current politics, let alone addressing international public opinion. Now everything was different.

> Apart from sending official letters to the Pope, to the cardinals and to secular rulers, King Edward made a whole series of appeals to his subjects, and to the subjects of the French kingdom and other states. These appeals and proclamations, attached to the doors of churches in all large cities and even read aloud by clerics and royal officials in places where people gathered, regaled the population with important items of news, informing them of the causes of the war, attacks by the enemy, victories, truces and so forth.[47]

Some of the arguments used are strikingly reminiscent of the political propaganda of the late twentieth century. Seeking to establish his right to the French throne by the female line of inheritance (for lack of a direct male heir), Edward, completely in the spirit of modern feminism, accused his French rival Philippe of Valois of 'trampling on the rights of women, against the law of nature (*jus naturae*)', while sowing hatred 'person against person' and 'sex against sex'.[48]

The English also resorted to economic warfare. For the first time, a trade blockade was used as a means of struggle between states. Trying to destabilise the situation in Flanders, Edward forbade the exporting of English wool, on which the Flemish weaving industry depended. The embargo struck a blow against the Flemish textile industry and aided the development of the sector in England itself, especially since many Flemish weavers crossed over to the island. The main aim of the blockade, however, was to exacerbate the class conflict, well understood in London, between the bourgeoisie and the feudal elite in Flanders. A cause of social conflict that had been closed off for several decades by the victory of the French at Cassel in 1328 came into operation once again.

In the middle of the century, the city of Ghent came to figure as the epicentre of protests by the common people. Social peace had been ensured there by concessions and compromises which led gradually to a strengthening of the positions of the democratic party. Mass unemployment was accompanied by an explosion of hatred for the government that had permitted the conflict with England and the shutting-down of the cloth industry. As Henri Pirenne wrote, 'The patricians who had long ruled the city united with the very same weavers, all of whose efforts to revolt they had pitilessly crushed not long before.'[49] Early in January 1338 a revolutionary government took power in the city; it was composed of five 'captains' (*hooftmannen*) and three master artisans representing respectively the weavers, fullers and small guild associations. This compromise opened the road to power for the legendary Jacob van Artevelde, who as head of the democratic party managed to unite the cities of Flanders around Ghent and in alliance with the English, to deal a severe blow to the French monarchy.

Artevelde, whom conservative historians depict as a bloodthirsty tyrant (like all revolutionaries), became the hero of Flemish folk songs and of works by left-wing historians in later times. An insightful politician, he put his stake on the rising wave of the democratic movement, reacting keenly to the pressures and demands of the masses. He had entered the government of Ghent as one of the three captains representing the interests of the privileged layers, but having become one of the city's leaders, threw in his lot with the democratic forces.

Following successful negotiations with the English, wool once again began reaching the fulling-mills of Ghent and other Flemish cities. But after the unsuccessful siege of Tournai, Artevelde's position became precarious. Just as insecure was the Flemish alliance with Brabant, whose patricians were fearful of any spread in the influence of the democratic party. Conflicts broke out in Ghent between artisan guilds that had supported Artevelde, with weavers and fullers engaging in armed clashes. Before long new disturbances flared up in Ghent, and in the course of these Artevelde was killed. In the words of Pirenne, this political figure was doomed inescapably to failure. His career was based on class compromise, but the interests of these classes were too directly counterposed for agreement between them to be lasting. Because of the contradiction between the interests of rich and poor, merchants and workers, small guilds and those engaged in the processing of wool; because of the later contradictions within these same guilds; and finally because of the rivalry between weavers and fullers, the harmony of the first days was quickly replaced by clashes and civil strife.[50]

The new social contradictions were already too developed for the possibility to remain of an effective politics built on the representation of estates, on agreements between guilds and dynastic factions. But these contradictions were still too weak to permit the rise of a new politics resting on settled and durable interests of the leading classes. Here lay the drama not only of Artevelde, but of his whole epoch, and in this was to be found one of the most important causes for the failure of the attempts at revolution and reform engendered by the 'crisis of the fourteenth century'.

The common people on the field of battle

The military historian Alfred Burne noted that the armed formations of the English King Edward III that landed on the continent in 1339 were the first army of the modern type in Western Europe. The king was not only a brilliant tactician, but also 'a master of strategy'.[51] Burne pointed to 'some surprisingly modern features about Edward's campaigns, such as his carrying on operations in the winter seasons'.[52] Most European armies were not able to do this even in the eighteenth century.

Especially important were a degree of organisation of supply and transport quite unknown to previous feudal armies, and organisational methods and devices for mobilisation that had been developed by the English as early as the latter decades of the thirteenth century. The soldiers and knights served not on the basis of feudal obligation, but of individual or collective recruitment. From 1277 soldiers in England had been paid a wage for serving the king, and from 1338 formalised their relations with the crown by signing written contracts when they joined up.

In England, something like a system of universal military readiness was instituted. All grown men, including even clerics, were made to assemble and to train at shooting with bow and arrow. The famous Welsh longbow was a fearsome weapon, which the traditional knightly armour could not withstand. But guaranteeing the military effectiveness of the longbow was the ability of the soldiers to maintain a fast and concerted fire, carrying out commands with precision.

For the creation of a mass army, not even such universal military preparedness was sufficient. The main problem was not the presence or absence of people; the population of Europe in the early fourteenth century was approximately the same as in the mid-sixteenth century, when quite substantial armies were gathered beneath the military banners. But the productivity of labour was so low that even a highly effective system of military conscription, such as existed in England under Edward III, allowed only a maximum of 2 or 3 per cent of the male population to be taken from their work; this was already a general mobilisation.[53] The superiority of the English system lay not in its ability to mobilise large masses of recruits, but in the fact that there were always people in England who were ready for military service, with no need for additional training. The army gradually lost its class character; poor gentlemen who did not have the money for armour enlisted as archers, while foot-soldiers were taught to ride. The English bowman of the period of the Hundred Years War shifted onto horseback, and hastened into battle. The knights in turn were trained to wage battle together with the archers in the line of foot-soldiers.[54] The distinction between cavalry and infantry ceased to be a mark of class division, and was transformed into a purely tactical difference. In this respect the archers of Edward III resembled the later dragoons, or even the motorised infantry of the twentieth century. The speed with which they could move came as a complete surprise to their adversaries. In its social respects, this was an army whose capacity for coordinated action was ensured by a degree of social and cultural homogeneity that was high by medieval standards.

Engels noted that the battles fought by the English army in the period of the Hundred Years War had a mainly defensive character, combined with offensive counter-attacks, in this respect resembling Wellington's battles in Spain and Belgium.[55] A successful defence, however, depended on whether the previous manoeuvring had allowed the army to choose the location in which it could give battle on the most favourable terms, and to seize the dominant positions on the field. The superiority of a regular army lay not just in the fact that it fought more effectively once battle had been joined, but in its ability, as a more homogeneous and disciplined force, to move more rapidly. During the victorious campaigns of Edward III and Henry V the English, with relatively insignificant forces, repeatedly defeated French armies many times larger, due to their speed of manoeuvre. Holding the initiative, the English detachments appeared where they were not expected, and dealt sudden blows. Or, they were able to choose more suitable terrain on which to fight. The small size of these detachments was even an advantage; at LaRoche-Derrien Sir Thomas Dagworth, and at Auberoche the Earl of Derby, achieved brilliant victories precisely because the forces they commanded were small.[56]

Even if Edward III had succeeded in mobilising more soldiers for his campaigns, the extreme backwardness of European naval technology at that time would not have allowed him to transport a large army to the continent. Meanwhile the Breton, Gascon and, later, Norman contingents that supported the English fought mainly on their own feudal lands, and, except for the Battle of Poitiers, did not participate in campaigns that penetrated deep into hostile territory.

The French kings tried to balance quality with quantity. Their armies assembled slowly, letting the initiative slip. The narrow battlefields of medieval times did not allow whole forces to be used at once, and they had to be sent into battle in lines, meaning that the effect of numerical superiority was lessened. Directing forces once battle had been joined was virtually impossible. Huge, awkward columns entered the fight too early or too late, creating chaos. Quantity was transformed into quality, but not in the way the Valois monarchs had hoped. In all the famous battles of the Hundred Years War the numerical superiority of the French worked against them. Undisciplined groups of knights and poorly marshalled crowds of foot-soldiers constantly impeded and crushed one another, became mixed up, and got out of control.[57]

The most famous military campaigns that ended in the rout of the French forces developed according to a similar scenario. The English retreated under the pressure of the Valois armies, many times larger. Then, after the pursuers had succeeded in overtaking them, the general battle ensued, and turned into the destruction of the French knights. At Crecy the French knights experienced for the first time the might of the longbow. Having dealt with the French field army Edward III proceeded to Calais, answering the appeal of Artevelde, by this time already dead, to put an end to this 'nest of bandits, those who have robbed and killed merchants'.[58] The port city was compelled to capitulate. Those of the population who refused to swear an oath to the Plantagenets were banished from the city and replaced with English settlers, who were followed by the commercial capital of merchants from London and Dover. After that, Calais remained for 300 years not only a military but also a trading outpost of England on the continent. Through Calais, wool was transported to Flanders and Brabant.

After an interval due to the plague epidemic, military actions resumed. This time, an Anglo-Gascon army headed by the 'Black Prince', the son of Edward III, moved from south to north. Near Poitiers the pursuing French forces, under the leadership of King John II, were crushed. The Battle of Poitiers was not only a success for the English archers, but also a triumph of the Gascon knights, who in the words of Perroy were 'the creators of victory'.[59] With a cavalry attack on its flank they shattered the last French column, and took King John prisoner. Later, at Orléans, the forces that went into battle against Joan of Arc included not only Englishmen but also Parisians, as well as detachments of Picards and Normans.

The first Anglo-French war ended with the Peace of Brétigny, under which the Plantagenets received their own sovereign princedom in Aquitaine, while renouncing their claim to the French crown. The now-sovereign Aquitaine was not an English possession, even if in military terms it remained a protectorate of the English. Juridically, it was a new independent state, connected with England through a shared monarch.

France was now in a deplorable condition. The previously effective bureaucratic model of government collapsed before people's eyes. Peasants, angered by the feudal exactions, rose in revolt, and their movement, which acquired the name *Jacquerie*, in its initial stage aroused the sympathy of the Parisian bourgeoisie, who demanded a less expensive administration and an end to corruption.

Assembled in the capital, the Estates-General demanded reforms, while the provost of the merchants of Paris, Étienne Marcel, headed the revolt. A crowd broke into the chambers of the Dauphin, slew courtiers before his eyes, killed the Marshals of Normandy and Champagne, and then draped the heir to the throne in a blue and red hood – the colours of the Parisian townsfolk.

The German historian Winfried Eberhard observes that the Marcel uprising was in fact the 'first revolution' of the French bourgeoisie.[60] Authority in Paris, Eberhard notes, was in the hands of 'informal assemblies' of the people. These assemblies 'acquired almost as much importance as official institutions', taking key decisions and sanctioning 'acts of revolutionary violence'.[61] People gathered in churches, in graveyards, and on the Place de Grève and other squares of the capital. Free discussions ended in collective decisions. Figures of authority, including the Dauphin and later, his rival Charles of Navarre (Charles the Bad) were forced at these gatherings to appeal to the people to approve their actions. A classic picture of revolutionary dual power was opening up, with the official authorities impotent and the power of the people without legal status.

Sensing that his power was becoming more precarious by the day, the Dauphin fled from the capital.

As Perroy puts it, Étienne Marcel 'saw himself as having been called upon to enact great schemes. He considered himself the defender of civic freedoms against the incompetent and despotic power of the monarch. He wrote to the Flemish cities and reminded them of Artevelde, designating himself the latter's spiritual heir.'[62] The moderate section of the bourgeoisie, however, had little liking for the power of the urban masses who supported the 'dictatorship' of Marcel, who, moreover, had spoken out in support of the peasants. Conspiracies followed one upon another. The movement of the *Jacques* was drowned in blood. At the request of the Parisians an Anglo-Navarran garrison entered the city. Charles the Bad, the ruler of Navarre and Normandy who enjoyed the support of the English king, was named captain of the city. But the 'moderates' succeeded nevertheless in staging a coup. Étienne Marcel was killed, and Charles the Bad abandoned the city. The movement was crushed, but the terror experienced by the aristocrats and official functionaries during the Marcel revolt remained in the class memory of the French elite, long determining their fearful and suspicious attitude to their own capital and its population.

The new war that broke out between the Valois and the Plantagenets turned into an unexpected defeat for the latter. Military historians have expressed puzzlement at the ease with which the English conquests in Aquitaine were lost after the peace of Brétigny. A state possessing a victorious army that had not lost a single large battle in 20 years yielded up city after city to an enemy that had not even resolved to engage in open battle. British authors explain the failure of their compatriots on the basis that 'the command of the sea passed to the French and their Spanish allies'.[63] And indeed, the Franco–Castilian fleet blockaded the coast of Aquitaine, stopping English reinforcements from landing. But this did not prevent John of Gaunt and a 15,000-strong army from carrying out a 'great march' in 1373, crossing all of France from Calais to Bordeaux without encountering resistance.

Lawrence James puts forward a much more prosaic reason for the catastrophe suffered by the Aquitainian domain of the Plantagenets in the 1370s. The English king had simply run out of money.[64] Lack of funds forced Edward III to declare himself bankrupt, and this sovereign default ruined the Lombard bankers who had given him credit. It is true that he subsequently managed to find financiers on the continent who were prepared to lend him money, but these ventures for the most part ended badly for the creditors. Not even the huge ransom obtained after Poitiers for the captured French King John II could remedy the situation, though it is true that the agreed sum was never paid in full.

Fourteenth- and fifteenth-century England could assemble an army of a new type, but it still relied on a medieval financial system. The country could not maintain such armed forces for long. Consequently, each victorious battle was followed not by a furthering of the success, but by a withdrawal and a breathing-space. While scoring triumphs on the battlefield, Edward could almost never develop these victories in strategic terms.

The later Plantagenets made use of their regular army and modernised state to achieve goals that remained completely within the framework of feudal politics. The resources and capabilities of the English state were mobilised in order to defend the dynastic interests of one of the French feudal rulers who was simultaneously King of England. For the English bourgeoisie, which through parliament kept a watchful eye on how funds were apportioned, the sole really valuable acquisition at Brétigny was the port of Calais. This city remained in English hands not only after the lost war for Aquitaine, but even after the Hundred Years War ended in 1453 with victory for the French.

A regular army could not be maintained under conditions of peace. Trying to find a use for his soldiers, left idle and unpaid, the Black Prince intervened in the struggle between the rival claimants to the throne of Castile. Although the English archers again proved invincible, this adventure had catastrophic consequences. The costs of the Castilian campaign were not repaid. Castile finished up an ally of France against the Plantagenets. Meanwhile the Black Prince, as ruler of Aquitaine, tried to recoup his expenses by levying additional taxes. This provoked discontent among the local aristocracy, who responded by addressing appeals to Paris.

The territories that had been seized had to be defended by English garrisons, for whose upkeep the parliament was less and less willing to provide money. The same applied to naval expeditions to the Bay of Biscay. The discipline of the regular army became a thing of the past, with the English military leaders turning into field commanders fighting often for their own personal and pecuniary interests. Gascony was made to defend itself, while lacking both the necessary resources and the type of military-political organisation that existed in England. In their French domains, the Plantagenets had preserved the traditional feudal order; meanwhile, the strength of the English consisted precisely in their success in gradually overcoming these institutions. The hopes the Plantagenets placed in the loyalty of the Gascon nobles proved exaggerated. Although the bourgeoisie of the large cities and most of the aristocracy stayed faithful to them, important feudal rulers wavered, adhering to whichever side seemed stronger at a particular moment.

Before long the Plantagenets retained none of their recent conquests, failing even to keep all of the old province of Guyenne under their control. Only Bordeaux and a few small territories surrounding it now remained subject to the English king. The defeats suffered by the English in the 1370s represented a continuation of the same political logic that had seen them victorious in the 1340s. The essence of this logic lay in the weakening of the military organisation of feudalism, which was destined to be replaced by a new state.

The Hussites: revolution from below

While the kings of England and France were contending for power in the Hundred Years War, even more radical developments were under way in Bohemia. Historians in recent centuries have described the Hussite movement variously as a social protest, as a national uprising by the Czechs against German domination, and as a religious struggle. But the great significance of the movement lies in the fact that it amounted to a full-scale revolution that convulsed society and attempted to change it.

The revolution of the Hussites was the earliest of the well-known revolutions of history, and remains the least studied. Here we are not, of course, talking about the vagaries of the political and military struggle, described in detail in numerous accounts, or about the military tactics of the Hussite army, but about analysis and understanding of the specific nature of the revolutionary process.

The Czech historian Josef Macek states: 'The nationalist myth reduces the complex picture of the Hussite movement to a simple tale of a victorious struggle by Czechs against Germans.'[65] The ideologues and leaders of the popular uprisings Jan Hus and Jan Žižka are presented to us as patriots, fighters for independence. Their movement, however, never defined itself as national.

> The program of the Hussites was based on Christian universalism. The movement was joined by German priests and Polish nobles, while its proclamations were spread in Flanders and Hungary (in Hungarian Transylvania in 1438 there even took place a mass uprising of peasants headed by Hussite preachers). All this bears more than ample witness to the internationalism of the Hussite revolution.[66]

Hussite Bohemia was in its way a model for all later revolutionary upheavals right up to the twentieth century. The Taborites and cup-bearers were prototypes of later revolutionary parties, of puritans and independents in England, Jacobins and Girondistes in France, and of Mensheviks and Bolsheviks in Russia. The Hussite revolution had its 'Thermidor', the battle of Lipany, and its own 'Bonaparte' in the Hussite King Jiři z Poděbrad.

The developments in Bohemia in the early fifteenth century were linked closely to broader European processes, just as the 'heretical' ideas for which the Prague theologian Jan Hus was burnt were closely associated with the theories advanced by John Wyclif in England. After Wyclif's death his followers, the Lollards, came to be persecuted in their homeland; many of them moved to Bohemia, where they exerted a considerable influence on supporters of Hus, despite some of their ideas seeming to Hus himself to be excessively radical.[67]

By the end of the fourteenth century Bohemia was one of the most developed countries in Europe, in the same rank with Northern Italy and Flanders. Silver from the local mines played an important role in the economy of the entire continent. In mid-century the yields of silver had been worth approximately 100 thousand marks per year, a vast sum for those times.[68] From 1348 Prague was the seat of the largest, and for some time the only, university in Central Europe.

In the mid-fourteenth century the imperial crown was on the head of the Bohemian King Charles of Luxembourg, who as a skilled diplomat used his position as formal leader of the German empire to expand his own domains and increase the wealth of Bohemia. Beneath his power were lands in the Upper Palatinate, Thuringia and Saxony, and even the margravate of Brandenburg. Unlike his father John the Blind, who had used Bohemia as a source of funds for incessant and as a rule, unsuccessful adventures, Charles saw the development of the Czech lands as a guarantee of his influence within the empire, and was thus careful to ensure their prosperity. Other parts of the empire benefited much less from his rule; it was Charles who, with his Golden Bull of 1356, reinforced the division of Germany into numerous small principalities.

The plague and the economic crisis affected the lands of the Czech crown much less than neighbouring countries. Output of silver, tin and iron steadily increased, while various technological improvements were introduced – new hearths for iron-smelting, and the water-driven mechanical hammer. Foundries were established, to be used later for the casting of artillery weapons. Weaving and cloth manufacturing were also developed. Hired labour was already employed on a large scale in the local factories and mines, with historians dating to 1399 the first reports of strikes, accompanied by demands for improvements in working conditions and increases in wages. In the same year Prague apprentices established something resembling a trade union. A further large strike took place in Prague in 1410.

The growth of production, however, also had a negative side. The Czech economy was being stimulated by 'a sudden outpouring of silver from the mines of Kutná Hora, which bore with it all the consequences of inflation'.[69] The purchasing power of money declined. Merchants were discontented at the reduction in profits. The rapid growth was replaced by stagnation. Significant numbers of the population sank into debt.[70] Grain prices increased, as did rents.[71] Artisans were angered by the competition they encountered from monastery workshops that were not subject to taxation. The masses were outraged at the growing cost of living. The bourgeoisie as a whole demanded equality before the law for all social strata, along with a 'cheap church'.

In the countryside, social differentiation in the villages increased, as did the need for money. A section of the nobility fell on hard times, and as a result 'the situation of a rich peasant was at times better than that of a poor landowner'.[72] The impoverished nobles hoped to improve their position by seizing the lands of the church.

The social tension was superimposed on conflicts between German and Czech members of the bourgeoisie. Germans made up the urban patriciate, along with the top layers of the church and monasterial hierarchies. Meanwhile, the majority of the urban bourgeoisie and of the petty landed gentry, like the peasants, spoke Czech. It is not surprising that the criticism by the townsfolk of the official church became overlaid on anti-German sentiment, and the translation by Jan Hus of the

Bible from Latin into the vernacular language – that is, Czech – took on a far more acute political significance than in England, where Wyclif had done the same.

The landholdings of the Catholic church by the mid-fourteenth century had become enormous, with the Archbishop of Prague alone controlling 900 villages, 14 towns and five castles. This aroused not only the envy of the local nobility, but also the hostility of the crown. At the Bohemian court, appeals by radical preachers for the nationalisation of church lands found interested listeners.

In Prague in 1391 the Bethlehem Chapel was established; there, sermons were preached in the Czech language, and in 1409 the German professors were ousted from Prague University in favour of Czechs. The outraged Germans made their way to Leipzig, where they founded a new university, while Hus, already famed for his preaching in the Bethlehem Chapel, was elected as rector in Prague.

King Václav encouraged Hus in his activity, and events at first followed the course of reform from above; discussions on similar moves also took place within ruling circles in England, where Wyclif had been received favourably. Meanwhile Václav, like many unsuccessful reformers, was inconsistent, vacillating between supporters of Hus and the conservatives. Václav's death, and the succession to the throne of Sigismund, equally inconsistent but influenced by conservatives, furthered the development of the revolutionary crisis.

The critical preaching of Hus and his sympathisers went unpunished in circumstances where the Catholic church itself was in a state of anarchy, with the right to the papal throne disputed by two, or even three, rival pontiffs. But in 1414 the unity of the church hierarchy was restored, and the Council of Constance addressed the problem of how to deal with Hus. The Czech reformer travelled to the German city protected by a charter of immunity issued by the emperor, Sigismund of Luxembourg, but this did not prevent the organisers of the council from throwing the preacher into prison. The question of his fate was decided by an inquest in which the delegates to the council, after brief discussion, decided that the simplest course was to have Hus burnt. This was done on 6 July 1415.

Even before Hus was executed, Bohemian and Moravian nobles had begun drawing up petitions to Emperor Sigismund declaring that they 'regarded the accusations against Hus as accusations against and affronts to the Czech nation and the Bohemian Crown'.[73]

Along with the purely religious demand for lay people to take part in the eucharist, specific economic slogans were advanced: for the abolition of church tithes, and for the expropriation of estates held by the church. Spontaneous seizures of church and monastery properties began to occur, with significant elements of the middle strata of society and even of the Czech aristocracy taking part. From the point of view of later history, the slogan that called for lay people to receive communion from the chalice might seem purely symbolic, but for people in the fifteenth century it had a definite political meaning. Arguing in favour of the same ritual entitlements for everyone, the Hussite movement laid the basis for civil equality. The chalice on the banners of the Czech insurgents thus became a particularly clear and attractive symbol.

The peasants refused to make their obligatory payments to the church, and the rural priests supported them in this. Monasteries began to be ransacked. In July 1419 some 42,000 peasants and members of their families assembled on the hill of Tabor, joined by significant numbers of impoverished knights, Czech priests and members of the urban lower classes. The new city which they founded became the political centre of the radical wing of the Hussite movement, fulfilling the same role in the Czech revolution as the Jacobin Club played in the revolution in France. 'In the Hussite revolution,' writes Robert Kalivoda, 'we thus encounter for the first time the radical left wing of the bourgeois revolution and its program.'[74]

On 30 July 1419 the common people of Prague, headed by the preacher and leader of the plebeian masses Jan Želivský, rose in revolt. The popular classes began to threaten churches, and the homes of German patricians. The uprising spread to Pilsen and other cities. The political platform of the revolution came to be summed up in the 'Four Prague Articles', and later, in the more radical 'Twelve Tabor Articles'. The death of King Václav IV the same year deepened the situation of anarchy, since the candidate for the imperial throne Sigismund of Luxembourg, who had the greatest claim to the Bohemian crown, was unacceptable to Czech society, which could not forgive him for the death of Jan Hus.

At the heart of the ideology of the Taborites lay a sort of communism, which 'was the ideal inspiring the masses and the basis which united their democratic community (*Volksgemeinschaft*)'.[75] In the camp of the Taborites were adherents of all the future left currents, from moderate socialists to anarcho-communists, and many leaders of the Taborites took an extremely disapproving attitude to the propaganda of the radicals. Productive activity was not collectivised in Tabor; this was a 'communism of consumption'.[76]

Ultimately, the nobility and the large bourgeoisie gained from participating in the Hussite movement, increasing their fortunes out of the confiscated property of the church, but this was a gamble whose outcome was not obvious right up until the battle of Lipany. The 'left wing' of the Hussites, united around Tabor, came periodically into conflict with the moderate Prague townsfolk, known as cup-bearers or Utraquists. It is thus not surprising that in Germany, Hungary and Italy the embryonic middle class placed its hopes not on revolution but on reforms.

In the words of Robert Kalivoda, we 'find in the Hussite revolution a classic embodiment of the mechanism and dialectic of left and right wings that is characteristic of the course and culmination of a revolution of the bourgeois type'.[77] The external threat did not permit a consolidation of the gains of the 'moderates', while fighting off the Crusades organised against rebel Bohemia by emperors and popes would have been impossible without the support of the masses, and thus 'required the hegemony of leftism throughout almost the entire fifteen-year period of revolutionary clashes'.[78]

The radical wing of the Hussites even had its own concept of Permanent Revolution:

The starting-point for the Taborites was their doctrine of the world overturn that had already begun, and that would end with the victory of good people over evil ones. The Taborites conceived of their revolution as involving the forcible elimination of 'sinners and enemies of the law of God'; among such people, they surmised, were the feudal elite, the higher clergy and functionaries of the feudal state.[79]

This overturn, so pleasing to God, needed to be carried out under the leadership of a politico-religious 'vanguard' made up of the 'faithful' and of zealots for 'God's work' who were ready to 'personally spill the blood of the enemies of the law of Christ'.[80]

The revolution that overthrew the power of the House of Luxembourg was incapable for a prolonged period of organising stable state structures. This was not just because the idea of a republic was as yet little disseminated or understood in society, but above all for the reason that the movement had arisen from below, and as something completely new for its time, lacked ready-made political forms for its expression. A future king would have had to recognise the 'four Prague articles', but no European monarch was ready to obtain the Bohemian crown at such a price, since this would have meant an open break with the pope.

As in later epochs, the export of revolution became a major international question. Describing the shift made by the Hussites in 1427 from defensive to offensive military operations, Delbrück correctly states: 'This development was analogous to that which world history later witnessed during the English and French revolutions.'[81] But the spread of the political influence of the Hussites did not by any means rest solely on the superiority of the armed forces their revolution created.

In France, funds were collected to support the Bohemian combatants, and in Flanders supporters of the Hussites carried on open agitation, which the official church managed to crush only through harsh repression. From Poland and Hungary, volunteers made their way to Prague.

The Hussite movement received strong support in Poland.[82] But the nobility in Germany and other neighbouring countries, despite the stake they held in the prospective dividing-up of church lands, nevertheless sensed too keenly the anti-feudal essence of the revolution.[83] As a result, the ideas of the Hussite revolution found an echo primarily among the common people.[84]

The growth of national consciousness in the Czech lands was more a consequence of the revolution and of the successful liberation wars than it was a cause. As with subsequent bourgeois revolutions, the nation took shape under the influence of the social overturn. The German patricians who supported the Catholic party were driven out of the large cities, and as Josef Macek correctly notes, this resulted above all in 'the triumph of the Czech bourgeoisie'.[85] Taking control of the cities, this bourgeoisie was now able to exert cultural hegemony. The Czech language was one of the first of the new European languages to take the place of Latin.

The response by Rome to the Hussite movement was to call for a crusade. The first clash between the Hussites and the crusaders of Emperor Sigismund took place near Vitkov. The Hussite army was barely a tenth the size of the imperial forces. But seizing the dominant high ground, the Taborites put the knights of the opposing cavalry at a disadvantage. A pointless assault on fortified positions ended badly for the crusaders, and they were forced to retreat.[86]

One after the other, subsequent battles ended in defeat for the crusaders. Changed social and economic conditions had also allowed changes in the relationship of forces due to new tactics and equipment. The Hussites were not just a peasant militia, but a revolutionary army. In contrast to similar militias not long before, they did not flee under the impact of a cavalry charge, but applied a new urban technology. For the first time, the Hussites made effective use of firearms on the field of battle, creating a high density of fire that was able to hold off and scatter a head-on cavalry attack. As military historians have noted, the Hussite tactics were based on the fact that fifteenth-century Bohemia was among the most developed industrial regions of Europe, while the forces of Taborite leader Jan Žižka 'were mainly peasant infantry with no tradition of pike warfare.'[87] In Tabor, therefore, new armaments were fashioned on the basis of the peasants' work implements – axes, chains, forks and so on. This infantry made active use of firearms, not only heavy bombards but all possible types of hand guns, still a novelty on the field of battle. The infantry fought beneath covering fire from mobile fortresses, consisting of heavy carts with armoured sides. This *Wagenburg* was not an invention of the Czech rebels, but the Hussites turned it into a central tactical element of their military organisation. Like the English army of Henry V, the Hussites combined the use of defensive tactics in battle with high mobility and an ability to appear quickly where needed. To repel the Crusaders, the Utraquists and Taborites were forced to unite, and the Tabor infantrymen were strengthened by the Utraquists' heavy cavalry.

The victories over the crusaders were accompanied by a sharpening of the struggle between various parties in the Hussite camp. In 1424 armed conflict broke out between the Utraquists and the Taborites. On 7 June 1424, at the city of Malešov, Žižka smashed the Utraquists. For some time after this victory he was *de facto* ruler of the Czech lands, but on 11 October 1424 he died amid a sudden outbreak of the plague.

Until 1436 the Czech lands were without a king. In 1433 the Catholic clergy, gathered in the Council of Basel, reached a compromise with the Utraquists. The document that set down the conditions of that agreement has gone down in history as the Compacts of Prague. The council accepted that members of the laity should receive communion from the chalice, and agreed to the secularisation of church property that had been carried out in the Czech lands. The new owners acquired legal status. This was the 'Thermidor' of the Hussite revolution. The moderate Utraquists, supported by the Catholic party, defeated the Taborites at the Battle of Lipany on 30 May 1434. Tabor was not captured; it was occupied only many years later by the Hussite king Jiři z Poděbrad. The country had grown tired of wars, of revolutionary shocks and anarchy. It dreamed of peace and order, as promised by the policy of compromises the Utraquists were pursuing.

Medieval Bonapartes

Bonapartist or 'Caesarist' regimes arise amid the decline of a revolution, when the new elite is attempting to normalise the situation by bringing the angry masses under control while at the same time securing some of the results of the revolutionary overturn. In the words of Antonio Gramsci, 'Caesarism is a reflection of a situation in which the forces struggling against one another are in a state of catastrophic equilibrium, that is, balanced in such a way that a continuation of the struggle can have only one outcome: the mutual annihilation of the contending forces.'[88]

The political situation that existed in England in the early fifteenth century, and to an even greater degree in the Czech lands toward the end of the Hussite wars, fits this definition precisely. There was, of course, no revolution in England, but the social shocks had nevertheless been massive. The old feudal order had suffered a serious blow. In this sense it is possible, making use of Gramsci's terminology, to speak of a 'passive revolution', or of a 'revolution from above'.

As described by Gramsci, a 'passive revolution' is carried out by a section of the elite in response to growing pressure from below. Elements of the revolutionary programme are enacted from above by the ruling groups themselves. In these circumstances the state leader enjoys a relative freedom of action, with the opportunity to manoeuvre between classes. For this reason, a 'Caesarist regime' is able as a rule to lay claim to great victories; a politician who knows how to exploit the opportunities that have opened up may come to occupy a far stronger position than rivals tied to traditional interests.

The epidemic of plague that swept across Europe in the mid-fourteenth century was at the same time the culmination of a crisis, and a turning-point after which the decay of the old feudal economy began to be accompanied by the rise of new relations of production.

The plague reached England late in the summer of 1348. After it had exacted an enormous death toll, there was no-one left to work on the feudal estates; the villeins had simply perished. If the main problem earlier had been a shortage of land, it was now a shortage of labour power.

The crops of 1348 were good, and grain prices at first dropped sharply; after all, the number of consumers had fallen catastrophically. Sheep and cattle, which often remained without owners, could also be had cheaply. But in the following year prices rose just as abruptly, since production had declined. Complaining of the 'evil intent' of workers, who refused to hire themselves out on the earlier conditions, landowners demanded that the state intervene. This 'evil intent', the Soviet historian D.M. Petrushevsky observed, 'was not just displayed by agricultural workers. No less "insolent and refractory" (*elati et contrariosi*) were artisans who raised the price of their labour, and also sellers of foodstuffs who demanded more for items of primary necessity.'[89] State intervention followed in the form of a royal ordinance of 18 July 1349, obliging all hired workers to labour for the same payment that had been customary in the corresponding localities during the five or six years before the plague epidemic. In other words, while prices were freed, wages were frozen (as may be seen, state regulation of the market did not begin in the twentieth or even the nineteenth century).

The ordinance of 1349 sharply inflamed the social situation, creating the conditions for a politicisation of social discontent. The contradiction between particular hired workers and their landlords became transformed into a conflict between the nascent class of hired workers and the royal authority. This conflict reached its culmination during the peasant revolt of Wat Tyler in 1381, when for several months the royal power in England hung by a thread. In 1399 Henry Bolingbroke, Duke of Lancaster, overthrew the Plantagenet King Richard II and with the support of parliament, became King Henry IV. On ascending the throne he promised a new order of responsible government and financial discipline, but remained a typical feudal ruler.

The Lancastrian kings laid the basis for a modern bureaucratic state in England, to a significant degree against their own will. For two centuries, since the signing of the Magna Carta, a certain balance of forces had been maintained in the kingdom. Monarchs tried to strengthen their power, manipulating the major feudal clans, inciting them them to fight one another or satisfying their growing ambitions through external expansion in Wales, Scotland, Ireland and France. The aristocracy in turn, together with the most important cities and relying on the growing influence of parliament, sought to limit the power of the kings. Each time a king exceeded the bounds of his authority another feudal revolt began, with support from the townsfolk. Then followed a reconciliation, and the power of the monarch returned to the limits set out in the Magna Carta. Social order was shaken in the fourteenth century by the plague, which altered the economic structure of the countryside, and then by the revolt of Wat Tyler. But despite the sharpening of class struggle in the later years of the century, the political regime endured for some time yet. The rise to power of the House of Lancaster, however, dramatically altered the rules of the game.

The reign of Henry IV saw a rapid succession of feudal revolts, and unlike the case in the previous epoch, the antagonisms could not be reconciled. The throne had completely lost the support of the feudal aristocracy. The Lancastrian kings had no choice but to seek support from the cities and parliament, making one concession to them after another. The alliance between wealthy bourgeois elements and the feudal barons that had been traditional in the previous epoch was destroyed.

Earlier, the government had been made up of members of aristocratic families, but now their place was taken by professional administrators. Most of these administrators, of course, came from the same aristocracy, but the system through which the system was formed had changed radically. In the past, the most important criterion for selecting functionaries and the basis of political influence had been ties to one's clan, as membership of one or another party would later become. But from this time on, people would be chosen on the basis of their personal qualities. The less the bond one or another administrator felt to his feudal kinsfolk, the better.

For putting down aristocratic revolts and suppressing the guerrilla struggle that had broken out in Wales, a troop of feudal body-guards was quite unsuited. Nor was it possible to feed an army through plundering the local population; after several years of counter-insurgency operations in Wales, there was nothing left to plunder. What was required was a disciplined, reliable army, made up of soldiers who would not disperse to their homes when the mood seized them.

The military reform that had begun as early as the end of the thirteenth century, and that had continued under Edward III, received a new stimulus. For a long time to come the principle on which the troops were recruited remained feudal, but the organisation and command began to change. Soldiers could now be reassigned to different companies, and the commanders of units replaced, something inconceivable in a feudal army. Within the armed forces specialised engineering and artillery units appeared, reconnaissance was organised, and field surgeons were appointed. The organisation of a medical service was a special preoccupation of the heir to the throne, Prince Harry, who had received an arrow-wound in the face while putting down one of the revolts in England.

Supplied with food and regularly paid, Harry's army while campaigning in Normandy in later times did not rob the peaceful population and did not set fire to villages except when specifically ordered to. In these respects it compared favourably with the French forces, who terrorised their compatriots.

During his Welsh campaign, Prince Harry came to understand that war was above all a question of money. From this time onward, no serious undertaking was begun without basic financial preparation and an agreement with parliament. The aims and rationale of war were changing; the interests of the bourgeoisie were replacing the traditional feudal motives.

To the end of his life Henry IV remained strictly a feudal magnate, who had seized the throne, was preoccupied with retaining his booty, and was tormented periodically by pangs of conscience. The promise of a new order materialised under Henry V, who as prince had divided his time between crushing feudal rebellions and discussing financial questions with parliamentary commissions. This warrior monarch devoted as much time to financial book-keeping as to military operations, personally read the account-books, made notes and checked calculations. It is not surprising that parliament readily entrusted money to such a king; the revenues of the treasury doubled as a result of strictly supervising the work of local crown representatives, rooting out corruption and abolishing feudal sinecures. The royal fleet, in the intervals between military campaigns, made commercial voyages transporting wine from Bordeaux.

Contemporaries remarked on the deep religious faith of Henry V.[90] His speeches and letters are striking for their extreme religious exaltation.[91] The same traits, in the same proportions, were to be observed in the leading figures of the English and Dutch revolutions a century and a half later.

Adding to the image was Henry's studiously modest ('not royal', in the opinion of contemporaries) manner of dress, which may make us recall the clothing of the puritans in the seventeenth century. This appeared particularly strange against the background of the refined 'Burgundian fashion' of the aristocracy of the period, but it impressed the common people and the bourgeoisie.

The king's religious views were clearly influenced by Wyclif and the Lollards. Wyclif himself went no further than to criticise clerical feudalism, considering that relations between 'masters' and 'servants' should be conducted on a basis of strict fulfilment of mutual obligations. Among the Lollards, as later among the Bohemian Hussites, a 'left' and 'right' took shape. The ideology of the Lancastrian party might be described as a sort of 'soft Lollardism'. Here we see an example of a typical Bonapartist tactic. While sympathising with the idea of reform, the king and his entourage not only refused to break with Rome, but showed no hesitation in sacrificing Wyclif's radical supporters to the cause of stability. Accused of preparing a plot, the leaders of the Lollards were repressed, and several of them were executed.[92]

Later English historians were to argue at length over what might have been if Henry V with his administrative abilities had renounced his foreign campaigns and stayed in his homeland. This question, however, makes no sense; for Henry, as for Bonaparte in later times, war was an essential element in his state project, a condition of the consolidation of the nation and of the legitimation of the established regime.

Henry V decisively rejected the feudal strategy of the earlier Plantagenets, showing little interest in forcing the return of family domains. The task he set himself was a new one: establishing a commercial power on both shores of the English Channel. For this, he did not need Aquitaine but Normandy. This approach was understood immediately not only by English trading interests but by the French bourgeoisie as well. English raw materials, Flemish manufacturing and the Parisian market had to be combined. Military actions needed to be subject to a clear plan that included the concentrating of forces, the securing of the rear, and the goal of totally destroying the enemy's main forces.

Henry's military campaigns ended in brilliant victories that overshadowed the achievements of Edward III and the Black Prince. The battle of Agincourt turned into a slaughter of the French knights, including many prominent members of the aristocratic elite. In essence, the opposing military formations represented two different epochs: on one side was a regular army, and on the other an aristocratic militia. The English detachment of 60,000 easily overcame an opponent which by the most modest calculation had a three-to-one numerical advantage (most sources, including French historians, speak of the Valois army outnumbering Henry's forces by six to one).

The catastrophe suffered by the French forces was so massive that some historians have simply refused to believe in the numerical superiority of the defeated side.[93]

In reality, it was the excessive numbers of the French that determined the unprecedented scale of the rout. Crammed into a confined space, the masses of mounted and dismounted knights were impossible to control. The small but precisely commanded army of Henry V, subject to orders and discipline, turned the numerical superiority of its opponents to its own advantage.

Henry's military victories yielded the predictable result that the French bourgeois of Paris and Normandy put their stake on an English victory. After the murder of John the Fearless, Duke of Burgundy – a crime committed with the obvious connivance if not personal participation of the French Dauphin Charles – the political struggle in France sharpened dramatically. Burgundy, whose influence also encompassed the cities of Flanders, broke with the Valois and officially took the side of the House of Lancaster. The authority of the French ruling dynasty fell to minimal levels, with the population more fearful of 'their own' feudal bands than of the foreign forces. After the army of the Valois, headed by the party of the Armagnacs (supporters of the House of Orléans) had been smashed at Agincourt, many people in France regarded Henry of Lancaster as the only figure capable of restoring order in the country. A coup d'état in Paris brought to power supporters of the Burgundian party, who together with Queen Isabella prepared a peace treaty in Troyes. The treaty declared Henry heir to the French throne and regent of the kingdom due to the madness of the reigning monarch. The marriage of the English king to the French princess Catherine was meant to unite the two contending dynasties, and the son born to this marriage, later Henry VI of England, seemed fully acceptable as successor to the throne of France. Perroy notes that Henry of Lancaster entered Paris 'to the welcoming cries of the townsfolk'.[94] The Estates of Languedoeuil (Northern France) supported the agreement with enthusiasm. 'It appeared that the nightmare of the civil war that had raged for thirteen years, and the nightmare of the foreign war which for the previous five years had been added to the first, had finally dissipated.'[95] But Henry died before he could be crowned officially as King of France.

If Henry V was a political exponent of 'passive revolution', his younger contemporary Jiří z Poděbrad was obliged for his success to a genuine revolutionary movement coming from below.

Jiří's father, Viktorín z Poděbrad, was one of the leaders of the Taborites, the radical wing of the Hussites, but after a time crossed to the camp of the moderates. Jiří quickly distinguished himself as a military leader and as a member of the party of the Utraquists. In 1434, at the age of 14, he took part in the Battle of Lipany, and was later a militia commander in the eastern provinces of Bohemia.

After the battle of Lipany the Hussites, and to some degree even the Catholic aristocracy, strengthened their hold on the property they had seized in the course of the crisis, but the situation of the victors remained unstable and ambiguous. The death of Albrecht von Habsburg in 1439 overturned the plans of those who had hoped that the restoration of the monarchy in the Czech lands would bring about a consolidation of political reaction. The struggle between the Catholic and Hussite parties resumed with new force, and for Jiří z Poděbrad, opened the road to power. In 1448 Jiří's troops seized Prague, driving out the local authorities who had consisted of Catholics and moderate Utraquists. This coup made Jiří *de facto* ruler of the country, but he did not take the throne and initially did not seek to become king. From 1452 he was considered the official ruler of the Czech lands. The Taborites met these developments without enthusiasm, but nevertheless recognised the new ruler and opened their gates to him.

After a time, the monarchy was again restored. With an inclination to compromise, Poděbrad agreed to the crowning of Ladislaus I. The boy king Ladislaus von Habsburg was elected to the Bohemian throne in 1453, while Jiří z Poděbrad as regent remained in effective control of the country. Despite the presence in Prague of a legitimate king, Jiří continued confidently determining state policies. Ladislaus did not survive for long, dying in 1457. After his death the Czech lands were again without a monarch, until in 1458 the Sejm, convoked by Jiři, elected him king. In neighbouring Hungary Mátyás Corvin, from the Hunyadi family, was chosen for the throne in analogous fashion; like Jiři, Mátyás was not of royal birth.

When Jiři was finally crowned King of Bohemia on 2 March 1458, he became the first official leader of the European West who did not profess the Catholic faith. Despite a clear shift to the 'left', connected with the restoration of the Hussite ideology and a strengthening of the central authority resting on the Prague burghers, the Bonapartist order which Jiři installed was built on compromises. The landed aristocrats took a contradictory attitude to the new regime. They did not like Jiři's administration, but in many respects it met their requirements. It was relatively strong and effective, and most importantly, had legal status, allowing the results of the land redistribution that had occurred in the course of the revolution to be legitimised.

The work of the tax system was improved, and the state could now rely on a constant flow of revenues into the treasury. The coinage ceased to be debased. To provide help in solving economic problems, advisors from Germany and Italy were invited to the court. The judicial authority was put in order and began working properly. Public order, the lack of which had so clearly undermined the power of every regime during the preceding years, was also restored. The Czech armed forces were reorganised on the basis of local militias (*Landfrieden*). Peace agreements were concluded with all major political and military groups. The city of Tabor supported the king, and successful economic development turned the former stronghold of plebeian communism into a 'normal' bourgeois centre, in which an acute struggle unfolded between contending classes. In 1452 the leaders of the radicals were arrested by the Taborites themselves and handed over to Jiři, who had them imprisoned in his native Poděbrady.

For practical purposes, power in Bohemia passed into the hands of the bourgeoisie and petty nobility. It was on the basis of these layers that the new administration was formed, with burghers who were appointed to state posts being automatically ennobled.

As a typical leader of the Bonapartist type, Jiři was forced to strike a balance between conflicting social forces, periodically arousing the displeasure of the nobility, but keeping the democratic lower orders of society under control. The task of the authorities was to consolidate the outcomes of the Hussite movement, in a form that suited the middle layers of the society of the time.

The *Cambridge Medieval History* extols Jiři z Poděbrad as one of the most progressive figures of his age. The amicable relations that were established between the heretic Jiři and a number of Catholic rulers had an 'almost revolutionary significance'.[96] A line was drawn between the religious and the political, and long before the peace treaties of Augsburg and Versailles, the principle of state sovereignty was asserted. Jiři's political partners in the Czech lands and further afield were forced to recognise that religious differences did not affect 'matters touching government and administration'.[97]

For all the arts of compromise he had mastered as the 'Hussite Bonaparte', Jiři was forced to wage war almost without let-up. Headed by Zdeněk ze Šternberg, the aristocratic opposition formed the League of Zelená Hora, which mounted first a political and then also a military struggle against the king.

Jiří's growing influence in German and European affairs set him to dreaming of the imperial crown, but here the hostility of Rome was an insurmountable obstacle. For a time the Bohemian king was able to reassure the pope with discussions on church unity between the Hussites and the Catholic church, regularly postponing the fulfilment of his promises with references to the complex internal political situation. But these diplomatic games aroused discontent among the Utraquists, who forced the king to make a solemn commitment to preserving the Hussite rites. This was followed by a new flaring-up of the conflict with Rome, and fresh crusades. The Czech forces routed the crusaders, but now Jiří was forced to contend with Rome, with the emperor, and even with his son-in-law, the Hungarian king Mátyás Corvin, whose quest for the throne had benefited significantly from Czech help. With the help of diplomacy Jiří again managed to prevail, calling for assistance from Poland. To receive the latter he was forced to put a resolution through the Czech Sejm to the effect that after his death the throne of Bohemia would pass to the Polish king. Dynastic interests, it seemed, did not exist for Jiří; he was already a politician of a new type, far more preoccupied with party and national questions (and in this respect comparing favourably not only with his contemporaries but also with Napoleon Bonaparte, who dreamt persistently of becoming a 'real' monarch and the founder of a dynasty). Mátyás Corvin was captured and imprisoned, and in 1469 was forced to sign a truce. But in 1471 Jiří z Poděbrad died, without completing the task he had begun. Two of his sons, Viktorín and Hynek z Poděbrad a Minstrberka, later served the Czech crown as ordinary subjects. Despite all his successes Jiří, like the other 'medieval Bonaparte' Henry V of Lancaster, was something of a failure; the state he had founded began quickly to disintegrate.

The Hussite wars prepared the way for the later Reformation not only ideologically, but also on the level of collective social experience, creating a basis on which the dramatis personae of the bourgeois revolutions that followed could rest. The political successes of the European bourgeoisie over a period of two centuries were prepared by the class battles of the late Middle Ages. The effect of these conflicts was to ensure that the new state and social order with which the rising capitalism would have to contend was no longer completely feudal.

The 'passive revolution' in France

In France in the mid-fifteenth century we see the same signs of passive revolution and of a Caesarist regime manoeuvring between feudal and bourgeois interests. But the modernisation of the French state proceeded with great difficulty, and in response to pressures from below rather than initiatives from above.

The royal power came increasingly under the influence of the aristocratic party of the Armagnacs, headed by the dukes of the House of Orléans. The bourgeois strata in Paris and other cities coalesced around the Burgundian party.

The economic and cultural development of Burgundy was relatively dynamic, especially since the commercial and industrial centres of Flanders were under its sway. Like the Lancasters, the Burgundian dukes sought in their politics to take account of the interests of the local bourgeoisie, and the latter in turn ensured them a stable financial base. The bourgeois of Paris and other French cities saw in Burgundy a model of the well-governed state, in contrast to the French monarchy which was controlled by aristocratic cliques. When the Parisian bourgeoisie supported the Burgundians against the Armagnacs, they acted in perfect awareness that behind the Duke of Burgundy stood the Flemish trading cities. Paris supported the Burgundians steadfastly not only against the Armagnacs, but also, later on, against Joan of Arc.

In 1413 the Parisian artisans and traders rose in revolt, headed by the butcher Simon Caboche. The reprisals against the aristocrats that followed caused the later English historian Janet Barker to draw an apt analogy with the 'mob violence, which would be a hallmark of the French Revolution in the 1790s'.[98] The rebels demanded that power be transferred to the Burgundian party. Invading the palace, they once again, as in 1358, forced the king to don the emblem of the rebellious common people – this time, a white cap. The Caboche uprising was in many ways a re-make of the Etienne Marcel revolt, but this time its outcome was a decree on administrative reform prepared by a commission whose members included Pierre Cauchon, later to be defamed by historians for his role in the trial of Joan of Arc.

After several weeks of disturbances the aristocracy managed to regain their hold on power, relying on the moderate faction of the bourgeoisie, who had been frightened by the excesses of the revolt. Once order had been restored, a campaign of repression followed against Caboche and his supporters, many of whom were saved by taking shelter in the Flemish cities belonging to the Duke of Burgundy.

In 1419 the Armagnacs murdered the Burgundian duke John the Fearless, and his successor Philippe resolved to collaborate openly with the English. This decision was not dictated simply by feelings of revenge or by the feudal ambitions of the dukedom. The Flemish cities that were controlled by the Burgundians were exerting a powerful influence on the policies of both the English and Burgundian courts.

Until 1420 Burgundy, while not really taking part in the war against England, retained a formal loyalty to the Parisian dynasty of the Valois. Answering the summons of the French king many Burgundian knights had gone to Agincourt, moved not by national feeling but by ideas of feudal honour. The knights were welcomed, and their loyalty was not doubted. Meanwhile, the Parisian militia were not allowed onto the battlefield, for fear they would stab the knights in the back. The 'foreign' Lancastrians were closer to the Parisian bourgeois than 'their own' Orléans and Valois families.

The events of 1420 were interpreted in hindsight as an attempt by the English to conquer France. In reality, the question of annexing France to England, or of establishing a unified Anglo-French state, never arose at any point during the Hundred Years War: 'For the English kings the lands of the Plantagenets always had a separate existence from the patrimony of the Capetians. The two crowns had to coexist, not to be combined.'[99] At the very beginning of the war Edward III was forced by pressure from parliament to issue the Statute of 1340 on the separate existence of the two states if he were to succeed in gaining the crown of France. The concern of parliament was understandable, since unification of the two kingdoms could have threatened English liberties. A fusion of England with the still pro-foundly feudal France would have meant the loss of the political conquests of the bourgeoisie. In 1420, after the concluding of the Peace of Troyes, parliament demanded that Henry V reaffirm this statute, which he accordingly did.

The peace treaty concerned was considered to represent a victory for England, but a careful reading reveals something quite different. While proclaiming the personal union of the two kingdoms, the treaty compelled the English to return to France all conquered territories, including Aquitaine. The law and administration of the French kingdom remained unchanged, and there was no talk of any merger of the states. In agreeing to the treaty, Henry V sacrificed the interests of England in the name of dynastic interests. We are left to guess whether this meant that the French won back on the field of diplomacy everything they had lost on the field of battle, or that in the English king the feudal lord had triumphed over the politician of the new epoch.

At the height of his popularity and success, the victor of Agincourt could allow himself a great deal, but sooner or later English society was bound to express discontent. Henry and his heirs needed the French crown, but the English bourgeoisie was indifferent to the heritage of the Plantagenets. It needed ports in Normandy, a safe sea route through the English Channel, and open doors for trade on the continent. It was for the sake of this that the merchants of London had financed Henry's expeditions.

Since the official goals of the war were acknowledged by everyone in England and not disputed, criticising the Treaty of Troyes was impossible. Henry V had formally achieved the goal of many years for which the war had been fought, had fulfilled the ideological programme of the war, but at the same time had brought to nothing the economic and political results of the conflict. The bourgeoisie expressed its attitude to the outcome of the war in line with its own concerns: parliament drastically limited spending on military and political affairs in France, explaining this on the basis that the French should finance their new government themselves.

The essence of the Treaty of Troyes was that whoever was victorious, Valois or Lancaster, the English would have to evacuate Normandy and Aquitaine. A refusal by the English to fulfil the terms of the treaty would always remain legal cause for the aggrieved party to renew the war at whichever moment was most convenient. The Treaty of Troyes was perhaps the first great triumph of French diplomacy, a triumph that remained uncelebrated only because the ideological priorities of the French state in the subsequent period required a different interpretation of history.

Henry V was obliged to return to England, leaving matters unresolved on the continent, in order to calm public opinion and to restore his relations with parliament. After his death the Duke of Bedford, who had become regent in both kingdoms, fell short of funds and had to feed his troops at the expense of the French territories. Taxes to maintain the army had to be levied on the French, a situation which naturally evoked resistance. Unlike the case in England, taxes in France did not have to be agreed with parliament, but attempts to gather them were nevertheless unsuccessful. Receiving pay only irregularly, the army more and more often resorted to plunder, and discipline declined. Worse still, Bedford was forced by his lack of money to resort to the traditional feudal means of 'material stimulation', rewarding English noblemen for their service by giving them grants of French lands. This allowed him to strengthen his control over the French territories, but aroused new conflicts.

Even with relatively few troops, the English forces in France were capable of holding off the French army over a lengthy period. But money was catastrophically short, and the government had to resort to loans. No-one, however, wanted to lend money to the crown in the 1440s, and it was quite clear that so long as the war lasted, interest would not be paid on any capital extended.[100] Holding Paris and Rheims, the English demonstratively delayed the coronation of the underage Henry VI as king of France; many in London hoped to end the war by striking a deal with the Dauphin in which renunciation of the French crown would be exchanged for unification of Normandy with England. Winning over the supporters of the Dauphin to such a deal would not have been especially difficult. But the English ruling circles were not united on this question; the interests of the bourgeoisie were in contradiction with feudal claims. Meanwhile, the Burgundian party in Paris were not prepared to yield to the Armagnacs.

In military respects as well, the situation had reached a grim pass. Bedford, who was receiving almost no support from his homeland, lacked the resources to advance southward. But an attempt by the supporters of the Dauphin to advance to the north with an army whose main striking force consisted of Italian mercenaries and Scots allies of France ended for them in further catastrophe in a battle at Verneuil.

The bourgeoisie and clergy of northern France actively supported the Lancastrian regime. In the countryside the situation was more complex. As the English historian Colin Mooers notes, for significant numbers of the peasantry the second half of the Hundred Years War was 'a period of significant prosperity and economic advance'.[101] But the earlier aristocratic estates in the north of the country had passed gradually into the hands of English knights and urban bourgeois, who sought to extract the maximum gain from their new property. Taken in perspective, the change of owners did not mean a weakening of oppression but an intensification. The disappearance of the large feudal domains saw the owners of the estates seeking to make a commercial profit from them, and if these owners were bourgeois, the feudal rents were required to be paid in natural form. Only now, the purpose was not to feed the owner of the estate along with his family and retainers, but to supply the market with goods for which a demand existed.

Relying on support from the cities, the authorities were hostage to the objective contradiction between the interests of the urban bourgeoisie and the peasants. From the English, the bourgeoisie obtained what the French government could not provide them with: effective administration that supported industry and trade, and that was, moreover, cheap. But even a cheap government had to be paid for, and the more the more the royal administration sought the support of the bourgeoisie, the more it was compelled to load financial burdens onto the village, where the struggle between peasants and estate owners was in any case growing more acute.

Meanwhile Charles of Valois, who had chosen the city of Bourges as his capital, held an important advantage: he had more money. The southern provinces that had suffered least from the war remained in the hands of the Dauphin's supporters. The relationship in terms of income between the 'Bourges kingdom' and 'Lancastrian France' was clearly not in favour of the latter. As calculated by Perroy, the flow of money into the treasury of Charles VII was 'a full five to six times greater than the sum that Bedford could expect to collect from his domains'.[102] Even in less successful years, the Valois received no fewer than 500,000 livres compared to the 100,000 or 200,000 obtained by the Lancastrian administration. If it took no less than a quarter-century for this gap in finances to tell on the course of the war, this was only because the custom in the Bourges kingdom was to steal and waste treasury funds instead of using them, in the English fashion, to create a regular army and an efficient administration.

Historical tradition depicts Charles VII as a feeble-willed ruler, weak of character and apathetic, but crafty. Strangely enough, he was among the most successful monarchs in the history of France. Almost all his initiatives ended in success. During his reign the country was unified, and returned to the arena of European politics as a leading power. The economy was restored, and Charles's personnel policy aroused the admiration of contemporaries; it was no accident that while still alive he was given the nick-name 'Charles the well-served' (*Charles le Bien Servi*).[103] He had a remarkable talent for finding the most fortunate moment to act, and a rare gift for biding his time, for preparing his blows at length, and for holding off when a premature move could have brought his downfall.

Charles managed to seize the chance that befell him when the fanatical Joan of Arc appeared at his court, and when the Maid began to pose a danger, succeeded in ridding himself of her. He was persuaded readily enough to mount an expedition against Rheims, but did not allow himself to be drawn into the new offensive campaign which Joan and her comrades in arms undertook following their successes at Reims and Orléans.

At Orléans the English forces laying siege to the city were seriously inferior to the defenders in numbers and armaments even before Joan and her army appeared, and with such a relationship of forces, only hugely superior morale can explain the fact that they could conduct offensive operations at all. A fundamental task for Charles VII was to raise the fighting spirit of his troops, and the young heroine proved an ideal propaganda weapon. Her appearance on the scene marked a psychological turning-point in the war. Meanwhile, the expedition to Rheims which Joan had organised was a brilliant move on the strategic level. Politically, the coronation in Rheims served to legitimise Charles, who prior to this had been only the unrecognised Dauphin. By moving in that direction, the forces of the Bourges king had driven a wedge between the positions of the English and the Burgundians. Finally, they had seized the wealthy trading cities of Champagne, where there were no English garrisons or where the English presence was merely symbolic.

The campaign against Rheims not only marked the beginning of the rise of Charles VII to power in France, but also the beginning of the end for Joan of Arc. While the Maid and the captains surrounding her were inclined to attribute the successes they achieved to their own military prowess, the king understood perfectly that the victories had been possible because the English had been taken by surprise. Once the shock caused by the defeat at Orléans and a chance setback at Patay had passed, the military-administrative machine of Lancastrian France would again be set in motion. Since Verneuil the king had come to realise that his army was simply incapable of defeating the English on the battlefield, and that strategically he had no chance of winning the war until the Anglo–Burgundian alliance was broken. In the summer of 1431 the French forces suffered one defeat after another, surrendering the positions they had occupied in Champagne, and in 1432 a crowd of townsfolk in Rouen literally tore to pieces a group of French saboteurs who had broken into the town's citadel. When Joan and her army reached Paris, where there were almost no English forces, they were repulsed by the city's residents themselves.

Not limiting herself to plans to capture Paris, Joan dreamt of a new crusade against the Hussites in the Czech lands. She addressed the inhabitants of Bohemia in a haughty letter demanding that they lay down their arms and submit to legitimate authority and the church, 'threatening to wage war on them with her army'.[104]

After his failure at Paris Charles VII did everything he could to rid himself of the Maid, who was now far more useful to France as a martyr than in the role of a military leader. The French king did nothing to save her when she was taken captive and put on trial in Rouen. Later, during the process of her rehabilitation, he was to go to extraordinary lengths to create an effective legend that would become one of the key national myths of France.

The newly strengthened French state needed its own ideology. The second trial of Joan of Arc was intended to rehabilitate her, and was charged with setting in place a new, ideologically correct version of events. The creators of the myth of the Maid of Orléans not only achieved their goals, but in a sense were over-zealous; other figures of the epoch, including Charles VII himself, finished up overshadowed by Joan. While hundreds of works of history and art were devoted to her, the name of the French king who won the Hundred Years War is recalled only dimly, and few know anything of Arthur de Richemont, who founded a new French army and drove the English out of Normandy. Charles VII was ultimately to appear before his descendants not as a brilliant administrator, a successful reformer, a diplomat and an effective politician – all of which he unquestionably was – but as a coward and traitor, indirectly guilty of the death of the national heroine. Also remaining unnoticed are the roles played by other figures of the epoch such as Jean and Gaspard Bureau, the creators of the most advanced artillery of their epoch, to whom France was indebted for its victories in the really decisive battles of the 1440s and 1450s.

The shift in the course of the Hundred Years War resulted not from the miraculous appearance of the Maid of Orléans, but from the reforms of Charles VII, who oriented himself increasingly toward the interests of the bourgeoisie. Although the policies of the Lancastrians ended ultimately in defeat, the presence of the English in Paris had a considerable influence on the development of France. It was no accident that almost all the figures who played decisive roles in the rebirth of the French state under Charles VII had begun their careers in the administrative and military structures created by the Lancastrians.

The treaty between the Burgundians and the French crown that was concluded in Arras in 1435 brought an end to the Anglo-Burgundian alliance, at the price of very serious concessions on the part of the king. Not only did Charles VII repent of the murder of John the Fearless and undertake to punish those guilty of it, but he conceded to the duke lands and towns on the Somme, while retaining the right to redeem them for the sum of 400,000 écus. More important, however, was the reconciliation of the Valois with the bourgeois elements of the Burgundian party, the people who controlled the country's capital and various other cities.

In 1436 the Burgundian commander Jean de Villiers de l'Isle-Adam captured Paris and placed it under the control of the French king. The English garrison abandoned the city without a fight, 'to the catcalls of those very citizens who had once joyfully welcomed it'.[105] Following the departure of the English from Paris active military operations virtually ceased for a time. The English remained in control of Normandy and Aquitaine – a situation that accorded, on the whole, with their original plan.

During the second half of the 1430s the English forces won a series of important victories, and despite their break with the Burgundians, were able periodically to expand the territory under their control. English military units reached the suburbs of the French capital without encountering opposition. The drawn-out nature of the war, which lasted for 14 years even after the ending of the Anglo-Burgundian alliance, was connected with the fact that the fighting capacity of the French remained significantly less than that of their adversaries.

The compromise between the Valois and Burgundian parties, however, had far greater weight than any battles in determining the outcome of the war. It not only represented an agreement between Charles VII and the Duke of Burgundy, but also signified the final defeat of the Armagnacs in the internal political struggle. Charles put his stake on the bourgeois faction within the Burgundian party. It was not the French victories on the battlefield that led people to make the shift from the Lancastrians to the Valois, but the fact that influential people transferred their allegiances that led to the turning-point in the struggle between the two dynasties.

While the Lancastrian regime in England was growing weaker, undermined by feudal strife and financial difficulties, in France reforms were going ahead, destined not only to alter the system of rule but also to broaden the social base of the monarchic power. The post of royal treasurer was assumed by Jacques Coeur, who from humble origins as the son of a Bourges furrier had become one of the founders of French silk manufacturing. Coeur was the initiator of a whole tradition, that of the members of the French bourgeoisie who accumulated capital and acquired influence through working with the treasury, which they systematically subsidised but just as systematically robbed. Admitted to the nobility, Coeur became a fully-fledged member of the ruling stratum, in the process laying the basis for the integration over the next two centuries of the financial elite into the feudal hierarchy. Unlike the English model, which stressed transparency and rigorous accounting, French absolutism was prepared to farm out its financial affairs to members of the bourgeoisie, though not through the establishing of representative institutions, but on the basis of private compacts between the court and particular entrepreneurs. This system, which endured until the French Revolution, allowed the rapid rise of a whole series of financiers who were talented but not always scrupulous, and who achieved not just wealth, but also power and fame. These histories, however, ended just as systematically in similarly rapid and catastrophic declines, since these financial geniuses (unlike their far milder English colleagues) lacked the solid support of the bourgeois class as a whole. Jacques Coeur was the first to follow this trajectory; once the English had been driven from France, he found the king no longer needed his services. Corruption scandals, to which no-one had paid any attention shortly before, were now revealed publicly. In 1451 Coeur was dismissed, then arrested, and two years later was banished from the country.

While in England the bourgeoisie systematically expanded its influence, forcing rights from the aristocrats and the monarchy or bargaining for concessions, on the continent the royal power played a more determined game, enacting modernisation in the degree and form, and at the pace, which it itself thought necessary. The French model of integration of the bourgeoisie into the state was one such example, directly counterposed to English practice. Instead of the bourgeois class limiting feudal plunder through establishing a system of political control, its members were given the opportunity to share in the pillage.

For all their limited nature, the reforms of Charles VII by the early 1440s had created a quite new situation. The estates-general had come to play a definite role in shaping tax policy, though a portion of taxes was collected without their sanction. The ending of military operations aided economic revival, and lands abandoned earlier began once more to be cultivated. Most important was the fact that the monarchy reached a compromise with the sector of French society that in the early fifteenth century had supported the Burgundians and English. The institutions of power that were functioning in Paris and in the provinces that had been under Anglo-Burgundian control were integrated with the administration which Charles VII had organised in Bourges and Poitiers. Under a decree of 1447, new landholders who had received their property from the Anglo-Burgundian administration after the expulsion of the old feudal families were guaranteed against the return of the former owners.

This decree sanctioned the spontaneous redivision of lands which had occurred during the war, mainly in areas occupied by the English. In practice, this opened the road to Normandy for the French forces. In place of the old feudal elite, new landholders had gradually appeared, people who no longer needed the support of

London to defend the lawfulness of their rights. Even Englishmen who had received landed property in Normandy were ready to make their peace with the new regime on the condition that it guaranteed they would retain their holdings. In the words of a present-day historian, 'the speed with which the English were assimilated and became rooted in the territory of the French province' was so great that it forces one 'to ponder the conditional nature of national identity in the period under examination'.[106]

The political turn carried out by Charles VII aroused discontent among his recent allies. In 1440 the king managed to suppress the outrage of the feudal elite, but the year 1442 saw the discovery of a conspiracy instigated by the Count of Armagnac. The count's landholdings were confiscated, to the benefit of the king. The party of the Armagnacs, who had been responsible for the catastrophe at Agincourt, lost their positions, and the feudal elite, who had been devastated by the English archers and ruined in the course of the land redistribution in northern France, now lost their economic positions in the south as well.

By this time, the bourgeois of Paris and other large cities were quite satisfied with the relations they enjoyed with the royal administration, and had no need of protection from the Duke of Burgundy. The lower orders of society, meanwhile, could expect nothing good from the English, or from the Burgundians, or from their 'own' king. But it was in these circumstances that the national idea took on a particular value, allowing the social base of the regime to be expanded to the maximum.

In Tours in 1444 the English and French agreed on a five-year truce. This halt in the fighting was used by Charles VII to continue his reforms, above all in the area of the military. The decisive element here was the appearance of 'ordinance companies', intended to replace the feudal cavalry. These units, expanded through the inclusion of people who did not have noble rank, came to serve as the basis for a new professional army subject to orders and observing discipline. Men of bourgeois origin could now form the backbone of the heavy cavalry, equipping themselves with expensive and reliable armour. Though not mercenaries, they served for payment, receiving a quite respectable salary. In peacetime the companies were quartered in various provinces of the kingdom, with the costs of maintaining them levied on the local authorities. The inducement to serve was no longer the prospect of booty, but a military career and enhanced social status. At the same time the ideology of patriotism, destined to consolidate the kingdom, began to be developed and propagandised.

When the war resumed after the truce of Tours, the English faced a quite different France. Unaware of this, they provoked a new spiral of conflict by seizing Fougères. Under the young King Henry VI the English royal power had grown weaker, while the moderate politicians in London failed to monitor the situation. As often happens in military affairs, the English relied on the experience of earlier campaigns, failing to realise how the situation had changed. The French army unleashed a counter-attack, and were soon in Rouen.

This campaign, however, was not seen as liberating by everyone whom it affected. In rural areas the arrival of the French forces was perceived as the end of a ruinous war, but the feelings of townsfolk were mixed at best. When the army of Charles VII was already standing before the walls of Rouen, a delegation from the Norman capital arrived in London, demanding that an army be sent urgently to defend the city from the French. But the small detachment that landed in Normandy after Rouen had already capitulated was caught between two French armies, and was defeated at Formigny.

Then came the turn of Gascony. Despite the lack of any help from London, the Gascons resisted stubbornly. Even the capture of Bordeaux by a royal army failed to put an end to the resistance. In 1452 the city revolted, with the uprising followed by rebellions in other cities. Nevertheless, the province could not defend itself through its own efforts. In response to appeals from the Gascons another landing-force was sent from England, small in numbers as before but headed by the legendary John Talbot. Since the opposing forces were unequal, Talbot anticipated the tactical methods of later times and sought to defeat the French columns, which were advancing from various directions, one at a time before they could combine against him. But at Castillon the Anglo-Gascon forces were defeated, and Talbot was killed. By 1453 the resistance of Gascony had been broken. Only the port of Calais remained in English hands, to be lost by the English Queen 'Bloody Mary' in 1558.

After the English had been expelled from France the transfer of feudal property to the bourgeoisie did not come to a halt, but gathered strength. The recognition of the rights of the new owners had been a crucial decision by Charles VII, and to a significant degree ensured his victory. In the view of British historian Colin Mooers, this process was connected indissolubly with the strengthening of the political regime of the first Valois kings. The arrival in the countryside of the 'bourgeois parvenu landlords' radically altered the situation.[107] The new owners of the estates, unlike the old aristocracy, possessed neither moral and ideological authority hallowed by tradition, nor their own armed retainers for use in compelling the submission of the peasants. Hence they needed a strong state, which in turn put its stake on them as a counterbalance to the old aristocracy.

Consequently, the rebirth of feudalism that occurred in the French countryside in the mid-fifteenth century did not result from the weakness of the bourgeoisie, but paradoxically, from its strength. Or more precisely, from the fact that the socio-political strength of the bourgeoisie was accompanied by a weakness of bourgeois productive relations. The upshot was the adoption of a strategy for the accumulation of capital that did not rest on a renovation of production, but on exploitation of the traditional sector.

The end of a revolutionary epoch

The political order that had been established in England under the rule of the Lancaster dynasty did not prove durable. Defeat in France deepened the crisis of the regime. The quality of government steadily declined. The decay of the Lancastrian regime meant the loss of the common interests shared by the bourgeoisie and the aristocratic administrative elite. The bourgeoisie did not rise up against the government, but simply stopped paying, leading the state into a deepening financial crisis. In its turn, the administrative aristocracy that controlled the key government posts became increasingly inclined, as in France a few decades earlier, to make use of its positions to solve its own problems. The administrative aristocracy and its feudal-landed counterpart fought for their interests with an air of demonstrative indifference to other social strata. An epoch of feudal reaction set in, to go down in history eventually under the name of the Wars of the Roses. The feudal groups that assembled beneath the banners of the rival Lancaster and York dynasties tore the country apart. Ultimately it was the Tudors, a cadet branch of the House of Lancaster, who established themselves on the throne. The founder of the new dynasty, the cautious and deliberate Henry VII, succeeded in winning the trust of the bourgeoisie, restoring the conditions of the earlier Lancastrian compromise.

While the outcome in England of the Hundred Years War was the collapse of the Lancastrian regime, the French state by contrast emerged from the war substantially modernised. The kings of the Valois dynasty not only set about establishing a regular army on the English model, but were also forced to make use of estate representation to ensure a dependable flow of money into the treasury. The Estates-General became an effective instrument for organising taxation and maintaining financial discipline within the government, while most importantly, participation by representatives of the various estates made certain that social stability would not be violated. Both the English and the French bourgeoisies strengthened their positions in society not through conflict with the monarchical state, but on the contrary, through close collaboration with it. The strategies of collaboration they followed, though, were fundamentally different, and this helped to determine subsequent events. In England the bourgeois class pursued its goals through a system of political institutions in which its collective interests were legally represented, while in France after the defeat of the popular movements of the late fourteenth century, members of the bourgeoisie sought to incorporate themselves into the feudal system, resolving their problems on the level of personal relationships with the court and with representatives of the authorities. Paradoxically, however, the weakness of the representative institutions that were charged with ensuring something like a consensus required the establishing of an effective working bureaucracy. Corruption at the top was by no means necessarily accompanied by thievery and bribe-taking at the local level. In this respect, the model of the French bureaucracy finished up by the eighteenth century a mirror image of its Russian counterpart, in which the topmost dignitaries observed the rules of a sort of aristocratic ethic and were not always corrupt, while at the lower and middle levels embezzlement reigned.

It is an irony of history that the success of the English intervention brought about a radical transformation of French society and the French state, and as a consequence of this, the eventual defeat of the English in France and the collapse of the Lancaster regime in England itself. Although the revolutionary shocks of the fourteenth and fifteenth centuries did not lead to the overturning of the feudal system and its replacement by a bourgeois order, the social and political set-up in Western Europe changed substantially. The main result of the changes was the rise of a new type of state.

This state was not yet bourgeois, but was no longer feudal either. Representing the result of a compromise between the old elites and the 'third estate' that was in the process of transforming itself into a bourgeoisie, the new state created optimal conditions for the development of capitalism, and proved an ideal instrument for the expansion of European economic interests throughout the world. Despite receiving the name of 'absolutism', the new system did not presuppose that the monarch held 'absolute' power. Over the next two centuries, kings had to wage a constant struggle to expand their powers. But the new state was distinguished categorically from the old by the fact that it constituted a system of orderly rule and bureaucratic administration that rested on members of the 'third estate', even if the people concerned had nominally been awarded titles of nobility. Such a system was ideally suited to the bourgeois elites and commercial capital of the period, but the rapid development of the world economy that began after the discovery of America and of the sea route to India altered the relationship of forces and gave rise to new contradictions, which in their turn called forth a new wave of bourgeois revolutions.

In various parts of Europe during the class battles of the fourteenth and of the first half of the fifteenth centuries radical plebeian movements, supported by the small landholding nobility and initially by a section of the bourgeoisie, threw down a challenge to the feudal order, but met with defeat – to a significant degree at the hands of the large and middle bourgeoisie, frightened by democratic chaos. The movements of Jacob van Artevelde, Étienne Marcel, Jan Žižka and Wat Tyler were crushed, but the feudal order sustained such severe damage that restoring it in its earlier form was no longer possible. The impulse of modernisation was picked up by the monarchic regimes that came to power amid the ruins of Europe after the crisis. Absolutism to a significant degree continued the work of revolution, but now from above, using authoritarian methods, without the democratic 'excesses' that had so terrified the commercial bourgeoisie. It carried out the same tasks with relation to medieval society that the Bonapartist regimes in France and other European countries fulfilled in the modern epoch.

The first attempt at radical democracy in Europe met with defeat, but the development of a new society, breaking through the bounds of feudalism, continued within the forms of the authoritarian centralised state. It was this development that gave rise to the system that later received the name of capitalism.

Notes

1 Zh. Karpantye (ed.), *Istoriya Frantsii* [A History of France] St Petersburg: Evraziya, 2008, p. 174.
2 See ibid., p. 175.
3 See L. James, *Warrior Race. A History of the British at war from Roman times to the present*, London: Abacus, 2002, p. 141.
4 J.M. Klassen, 'The Nobility and the Making of the Hussite Revolution', *Eastern European Quarterly*, Boulder, 1978. Eastern European Monographs, no. XLVII, p. 11.
5 Ibid., p. 21.
6 G. Luzzatto, *Storia economica d'Italia. Il Medioevo* [Economic history of Italy. The Middle Ages], Florence: G. Sansoni Editore, 1963, pp. 238, 239.

7 A. Ryukua, *Srednevekovaya Ispaniya* [Medieval Spain], Moscow: Veche, 2006, p. 155.
8 See Dzh. Villani, *Novaya Khronika ili Istoriya Florentsii* [The New Chronicle or the History of Florence], Moscow: Nauka, 1997.
9 Luzzatto, *Storia economica*, pp. 238, 250.
10 Cited in: A.E. Kudryavtsev, *Ispaniya v Srednie veka* [Spain in the Middle Ages], Moscow: URSS, 2007, p. 105.
11 *Istoriya, sotsiologiya, kul'tura narodov Afriki. Stat'i pol'skikh uchenikh* [History, sociology and culture of the peoples of Africa. Articles by Polish scholars], Moscow: Nauka, 1974, p. 131.
12 Luzzatto, *Storia economica*, p. 230.
13 Ibid., p. 209.
14 Ibid., p. 227.
15 The rise of agrarian capitalism, along with the role of this process in the development of the bourgeois mode of production, is analysed in great detail in the works of the American historian Robert Brenner. See R. Brenner, 'Bourgeois revolution and transition to capitalism' in *The First Modern Society*, Cambridge: Cambridge University Press, 1989; 'The Brenner Debate' in T.H. Aston and C.H.E. Philpin (eds), *The Brenner Debate: Agrarian Class Structure and Economic Development in Pre-Industrial Europe*, Cambridge: Cambridge University Press, 1988.
16 Luzzatto, *Storia economica*, p. 36. In the view of Richard Lachmann, both the rise and flourishing of the city-states and their subsequent decline resulted from the geopolitical conjuncture and general relationship of forces in Europe (R. Lachmann, *Capitalists in Spite of Themselves. Elite Conflict and Economic Transitions in Early Modern Europe*, Oxford: Oxford University Press, 2000). But the fact that the urban oligarchies of Italy and Germany chose a strategy of refeudalisation was due primarily to the limited nature of their resources and the narrow productive and economic basis of their rule.
17 See G. Arrighi, *The Long Twentieth Century*, London/New York: Verso, 1999, pp. 43–6.
18 E. Laviss, *Ocherki po istorii Prussii* [Essays on the history of Prussia]. Moscow: URSS, 2003, p. 181. To commercial decline was added a change in the migration routes of the herring, which shifted to the coast of Holland, helping Amsterdam to prosper.
19 Giovanni Arrighi in his book *The Long Twentieth Century* describes Genoa as a hegemon that not only controlled Mediterranean trade, but also acted as the political and economic centre for the entire process of capital accumulation. The reader, however, soon discovers with surprise that the author cannot convincingly demonstrate the role of Genoa as a hegemon in the commercial, military, productive or even financial field. The city's role is not substantiated, and does not even appear in the course of the narrative; it is simply declared. The only reason for Arrighi to draw his conclusion of 'Genoese hegemony' is that according to his logic the system by definition must have had a hegemon, and from his point of view Genoa was best suited to play this part. The possibility that the system as such might not yet have taken shape, or that at a particular stage it might have got by without a hegemon, is consciously excluded.
20 James D. Tracy (ed.), *The Rise of Merchant Empires: Long Distance Trade in the Early Modern World 1350–1750*, Cambridge: Cambridge University Press, 1993, p. 16.
21 See ibid., p. 19.
22 G. Luzzatto, *Storia economica di Venezia dall' XI al XVI secolo* [Economic history of Venice from the eleventh to the sixteenth century], Venice: Centro internazionale delle arte e del costume, 1961, p. 194.
23 Ibid., p. 67.
24 Luzzatto, *Storia economica*, p. 222.
25 Luzzatto, *Storia economica di Venezia*, p. 42.
26 Ibid., p. 46.
27 Ibid., p. 47.
28 Luzzatto. *Storia economica*, p. 222.
29 A. Gramshi, *Izbrannye proizvedeniya* [Selected works], Moscow: Izdatel'stvo instrannoy literatury, 1959, vol. 3, p. 268.

30 Ibid.

31 H. Schilling, *Aufbruch und Krise. Deutschland 1517–1642* [Break-up and Crisis: Germany 1517–1642], Berlin: Siedler Verlag, 1988, p. 171.

32 J.D. Tracy (ed.), *The Political Economy of Merchant Empires*, Cambridge: Cambridge University Press, 1991, p. 75.

33 J. Macek, *Tabor v gusitskom revolyutsionnom dvizhenii* [Tabor in the Hussite revolutionary movement], Moscow: Inostrannaya literatura, 1956, Vol. 1, p. 69.

34 A. Pirenn, *Srednevekovye goroda Bel'gii* [The medieval cities of Belgium], St Petersburg: Evroaziya, 2001, p. 222.

35 Ibid., p. 227.

36 Ibid., p. 224.

37 G. Luzzatto, *Storia economica*, pp. 238, 300.

38 Tracy, *Rise of Merchant Empires*, p. 33.

39 Quoted in Ya. Al'bert, *Gusitstvo i evropeyskoe obshchestvo* [Hussism and European society], Prague: Obris, 1946, p. 3.

40 Tracy, *Political Economy of Merchant Empires*, p. 137.

41 Pirenne, *Srednevekovye goroda Bel'gii*, p. 259.

42 Ibid., p. 331.

43 E. Perrua, *Stoletnyaya voyna* [The Hundred Years War], Moscow: Veche, 2006, p. 271.

44 Ibid., p. 273.

45 Ibid., p. 127.

46 Quoted in A. Pirenn, *Srednevekovye goroda Bel'gii*, p. 436.

47 *Iskusstvo vlasti* [The art of power]. Collection of articles in honour of Professor N.A. Khachaturyan. St Petersburg: Aleteyya, 2007, p. 137.

48 Ibid., p. 139.

49 Pirenn, *Srednevekovye goroda Bel'gii*, p. 427.

50 Ibid., p. 445.

51 A. Burne, *The Crecy War: A Military History of the Hundred Years War from 1337 to the Peace of Brétigny, 1360,* Oxford: Oxford University Press, 1955, p. 10.

52 Burne, *The Crecy War*, p. 40.

53 See James, *Warrior Race*, p. 141.

54 H. Delbrück, *Istoriya voennogo iskusstva v ramkakh politichiskoy istorii* [A history of the art of war in the context of political history], St Petersburg: Nauka, 2001, vol. 3, p. 297.

55 K. Marx and F. Engel's, *Sochineniya* [Works], Vol. 21, p. 414.

56 Perroy was one of the first historians to deduce that Edward III was victorious because 'his army was smaller' (Perrua, *Stoletnyaya voyna*, p. 131).

57 In the nineteenth and early twentieth centuries historians took a sceptical attitude to the figures cited in the chronicles for the numbers of medieval armies. But the more intently researchers have studied archival documents, the more they have concluded that the counts provided by the chroniclers were not greatly exaggerated.

58 Quoted in Pirenn, *Srednevekovye goroda Bel'gii*, p. 437.

59 Perrua, *Stoletnyaya voyna*, p. 148.

60 *Husitství – Reformace – Renesance* [Hussism – Reformation – Renaissance]. Prague: Historicky ústav, 1994, s. 86.

61 Ibid., p. 88.

62 Perrua, *Stoletnyaya voyna*, p. 154.

63 T.F. Tout, *The Political History of England*, London, 1906, p. 164; A.H. Burne, *The Agincourt War. A Military history of the latter part of the Hundred Years War from 1369 to 1453,* London: Greenhill Books, 1956, p. 25.

64 See James, *Warrior Race*, pp. 105–6.

65 J. Macek, *Histoire de la Bohème des origines à 1918* [History of Bohemia from its origins to 1918], Paris: Fayard, 1984, p. 123.

66 Ibid., p. 120. See also R. Kalivoda, *Husitská ideologie* [Hussite ideology], Prague: Nakladatelství Československé akademie věd, 1961, s. 496.

67 *The Cambridge Medieval History*, Vol. VIII, *The Close of the Middle Ages*, Cambridge: Cambridge University Press, 1936, p. 76.
68 See *Istoriya Srednykh Vekov* [History of the Middle Ages], Vol. 1, p. 445.
69 Ibid.
70 Ibid., p. 22.
71 J. Macek, *Die Hussitische Revolutionäre Bewegung* [The Hussite Revolutionary Movement], Berlin: Deutsche Verlag der Wissenschaften, 1958, p. 17.
72 J. Macek, *Tabor v gusistskom revolyutsionnom dvizhenii* [Tabor in the Hussite revolutionary movement], Moscow: Inostrannaya literatura, 1956, Vol. 1, p. 165.
73 *The Cambridge Medieval History*, Vol. VIII, p. 65.
74 R. Kalivoda, *Husitská ideologie*, Moscow: Politiadat, 1952, p. 497.
75 K. Kreibich, *Tabor. Eine halbjahrtausend-feier des Kommunismus* [Tabor. A five-hundred-year Celebration of Communism], Reichenberg: Verlag Volksbuchhandlung Runge & Co, 1920, p. 15.
76 Ibid., p. 14.
77 Kalivoda, *Husitská ideologie*, p. 498.
78 Ibid., p. 497.
79 *Vsemirnaya istoriya* [World history], Vol. 3, p. 702.
80 Ibid., p. 703.
81 H. Delbrück, *Istoriya voennogo iskusstva v ramkakh politicheskoy istorii* [The history of the art of war in the context of political history], Vol. 3, St Petersburg: Nauka, 2001, p. 309.
82 Th. Wotschke, *Das Hussitentum in Grosspolen* [Hussism in Great Poland], Posen: Oskar Eulitz Verlag, 1911, p. 42.
83 Ya. Al'bert, *Gusitstvo*, p. 15
84 Cited in ibid., p. 8.
85 J. Macek, *Le mouvement Hussite en Bohème* [The Hussite movement in Bohemia], Prague: Orbis, 1965, p. 91.
86 S. Zharkov, *Srednevekovaya pekhota v boyu* [Medieval infantry in battle], Moscow: Yauza—EKSMO, 2008, pp. 352–3.
87 M. Bennett, J. Bradbury, K. DeVries, I. Dickie and Ph. Jestice, *Fighting Techniques of the Medieval World, AD 500 – AD 1500*, London: Spellemount, 2005, pp. 63–4.
88 Gramshi, *Izbrannye proizvedeniya*, vol. 3, p. 185.
89 D.M. Petrushevsky, *Vosstaniye Watta Taylera. Ocherki iz istorii razlozheniya feodal'nogo stroya v anglii* [Rebellion of Wat Tyler], Moscow/Leningrad: OGIZ, 1927, p. 202
90 See P. Earle, *The Life and Times of Henry V*, London: Weidenfeld and Nicolson, 1972.
91 J. Barker, *Agincourt. The King, the Campaign, the Battle*, London: Abacus, 2006, p. 263.
92 T. Walsingham, *Historia Anglicana*, Vol. 2, p. 312.
93 See H. Delbrück, *Istoriya voennogo iskusstva v ramkakh politicheskoy istorii*, Vol. 3, p. 293.
94 Perrua, *Stoletnyaya voyna*, p. 307.
95 Ibid.
96 *The Cambridge Medieval History*, Vol. VIII, p. 102.
97 Ibid.
98 Barker, *Agincourt*, p. 54.
99 *Frantsuzskiy ezhegodnik 2008. Angliya i Frantsiya – sosedi i konkurenty XIV-XIX vv* [French annual 2008. England and France – neighbours and rivals from the fourteenth to the nineteenth century, Institute of World History (Institut vseobshey istorii) of Russian Academy of Sciences, Moscow: URSS, 2008, p. 16.
100 James, *Warrior Race*, p. 106.
101 C. Mooers, *The Making of Bourgeois Europe. Absolutism, Revolution, and the Rise of Capitalism in England, France and Germany*, London: Verso, 1991, p. 47.
102 Ibid., p. 333.

103 See ibid., p. 381.
104 Macek, *Histoire de la Bohème*, p. 108.
105 Perrua, *Stoletnyaya voyna*, p. 378.
106 *Frantsuzskiy ezhegodnik 2008* [French annual 2008], p. 24.
107 See Mooers, *Making of Bourgeois Europe*, p. 47.

3

REFORMATION AND EXPANSION

The social and economic order that had come to prevail in Europe by the beginning of the fifteenth century differed so profoundly from the classical models of feudalism that some historians have expressed doubts as to how the social system at that time should be described. Feudalism in Western Europe in the early fifteenth century was already dying if not dead, but capitalism had not yet been born, and the dominant order was 'neither feudal, nor capitalist'.[1] The necessity for social changes became a new political reality only in the sixteenth and seventeenth centuries, when the internal social evolution of the West received a powerful outside stimulus in the form of the new resources and new economic opportunities that had appeared as a result of the new geographical discoveries.

The British historian Neil Davidson links the defeat of the anti-feudal movements of the fifteenth century to their military and political weakness. But it was precisely in their military respects that the revolutionary and Bonapartist regimes of the late Middle Ages surpassed their adversaries. The Lancastrian regime in England did not fall as a result of its defeat in France; to the contrary, this defeat was a consequence of the internal trauma and degradation of the regime. Nor is it possible to talk of the Hussites suffering military defeat.[2] The failures of the early bourgeois movements were not the result of political but of economic circumstances. The economic base for the development of capitalism was still too narrow. This was evident above all in the small size of the market, the insufficient integration of the world economy, and the lack of a global division of labour.

For Europe, the resources needed for another forward sprint could only appear when the geographical discoveries by the Spanish and Portuguese had yielded a stream of precious metals and spices, along with fresh opportunities for military-political and commercial expansion. In the view of later historians, the trigger that set off this process was represented by the Turkish seizure of Constantinople and the crisis of European trade in the Eastern Mediterranean. But it was not only external events that impelled the kings and entrepreneurs of the West to seek new lands. The preconditions for expansion were created by the economic growth that had resumed following the crisis of the fourteenth century.

Adam Smith stressed that the discoveries of America and of the sea route to India represented 'the two greatest events in the history of mankind'.[3] If the benefits of these remarkable successes accrued only to Western Europe, the reason for this was the superior strength of the Europeans, a superiority that was just one of the 'attendant circumstances' accompanying the great discoveries. The military advantage enjoyed by the West gave rise to every possible kind of violence and injustice. It was because of this, the Scottish economist considered, that the native populations had not been able to benefit from the development of the new markets.[4]

An Aztec chieftain or an Inca peasant appeared to Smith as an analogue of an English bourgeois or Dutch farmer – that is, as someone who at the first suitable opportunity would exploit the newly emerged commercial opportunities and make haste to seize the new overseas markets, but for the unfortunate fact that the Europeans, driven by their own greed, had denied them the chance. The idea that the economic relations in the Americas prior to the arrival of the Europeans might have been structured on a fundamentally different basis was beyond the grasp of the liberal theoretician, who was certain that the laws of the bourgeois market were just as absolute as the laws of nature. Meanwhile, the Western merchants and soldiers who conquered the Americas two centuries before Adam Smith set to work writing his tome understood perfectly the reality they had encountered, and acted accordingly.

In the sixteenth and seventeenth centuries relatively small groups of people, without significant resources, managed to take possession of extensive territories and subjugate huge numbers of the inhabitants. The accepted explanation for these successes used to be the superiority of European weapons, or a moral superiority imparted by the Renaissance and Reformation. But whatever the material and moral factors that ensured the victories of the Europeans, their achievements would have been inconceivable but for the social and political organisation that allowed these factors to be successfully exploited.

Gunpowder and gold

From the late fifteenth century, and throughout the century that followed, Europe was constantly at war. Christians fought Turks, supporters of the Reformation fought its opponents, and the French monarchy fought with Spain to dominate the continent. At the same time, Spanish and Portuguese detachments were imposing their power on the lands which the geographical discoveries had opened up.

Forming a backdrop to the incessant armed conflicts was a process that historians would later designate the 'military revolution'. This was associated above all with the increasing use of gunpowder. 'The military revolution robbed the aristocracy of its weapons,' a Russian historian declared.[5] The feudal militias disappeared, to be replaced by paid armies. These changes are usually ascribed to progress in the development of firearms, which made knightly armour useless. But the facts show that changes in organisation not only preceded the technical ones, but also instigated and predetermined them.

As Engels noted, the longbow of the English yeoman at Crécy shot just as far as the smooth-bored musket at Waterloo, and perhaps even more accurately.[6] Siege artillery was extremely effective, but in technical terms it was just as capable of being combined with a feudal army as with a force of later type. The rise of the new army and the new tactics was not linked to technical innovations, but to the fact that kings everywhere sought to free themselves from the feudal militias and to establish their own armies.[7] It was these new armies that created the demand for technical innovations in the field of armaments.

The medieval knight was not only a heavily armed horseman. The knightly company amounted to a corporation, membership in which was not hereditary. Neither a title nor a rank made one automatically a knight; individual services were needed.

A key element in knighthood as a corporation was a system of orders that to a significant degree duplicated the structure of monastic orders, and that had been established in the course of the crusades.

Already in the fifteenth century complaints were encountered frequently of a deterioration in the knightly ethic, and in the sixteenth century the decline of the knighthood was obvious. The development in literature of the knightly myth, including the efforts of individual knights to maintain the myth on the level of personal conduct (as depicted with a note of tragic irony in Cervantes' *Don Quixote*) was a result of this process. Was this decline connected to the change in military technology? The ordinance companies of Charles VII struck the institution of knighthood a far greater blow than the first bombards and arquebusses, though the *gendarmes* of the ordinance companies did not differ in the least from the knights in their weapons and tactics.

Knightly service as a mark of vassal devotion lost its meaning as the feudal militia was replaced by a regular army, even if the weapons remained the same.

Heavy cavalry remained a powerful force on the battlefield. The appearance of the longbow, and later of firearms, did not yet make armour useless. Full (or 'white') armour appeared around the years from 1390 to 1410. Chain mail and breastplates were replaced by full suits that transformed the horseman into a real military machine, analogous to the much later tank. Progress in metal-working techniques had made possible the appearance of new cannon and culverins, but also allowed the production of armour which at least at a certain distance and at certain angles could not be penetrated either by the arrows of English archers or even by a firearm. For a long time the most serious danger to the horseman, encased in steel plate, remained as before a crossbow bolt, which flew to its target with improbable force and accuracy. But the crossbow did not allow of rapid fire.

Firearms were known in the West from 1330, but required almost two centuries to become the dominant weapon. The problem lay not only in the technical difficulties which the master gunsmiths needed to solve, but also in the changed military organisation which in turn arose from the evolving social and state system. The new forms of military-political organisation required new weaponry, and this stimulated technical innovation.

At first, firearms were less effective than the longbow and crossbow. The fire from a hand bombard or even an arquebus was less accurate than shooting from a crossbow, and for all the penetrative power of these weapons, reloading them was extremely slow. For this reason, many armies retained detachments of archers right up until the time of the Thirty Years War. Until the end of the war, heavy infantrymen continued to wear metal armour.

The Hussite armies, using firearms, of course regularly inflicted defeats on the German knights. But the Hussites also used crossbows, and their victories were achieved less through superiority in armaments than through organisation and tactics. At Vítkov, Sigismund of Luxembourg had marvellous bombards, but this did not help him.

The appearance of firearms on the field of battle served at first to increase the vulnerability of the infantry. At the battle of Crécy a volley from the English bombards disorganised and threw into disarray the Genoese crossbowmen who were advancing in the forefront of the cavalry. The dense ranks of English archers or Swiss pikemen became the perfect target for artillery. In the later period of the Hundred Years War the French army continually strengthened its artillery forces, which were to become a counterweight to the bows of the English.

Initially, the development of artillery increased the role of the city militias which were alone capable of using this new type of weapon. The importance of castles, meanwhile, declined. The problem did not lie in the vulnerability of stone walls. The catapult weapons of ancient times had been capable of doing damage fully comparable to the artillery-fire of the late Middle Ages, and some medieval fortifications kept their military significance right up until the Napoleonic wars. The superiority of the city over the castle was a complex matter. Factors of importance were the size, since a large perimeter was more difficult to blockade; the numbers of men in the garrisons; and the technical capability, including whether a 'repair base' was present for increasingly complicated artillery equipment.

Artillery required a more developed organisation of production, since producing cannon in artisan conditions was impossible. 'In 1356 most large cities, mainly those of the German empire – Nuremburg, Augsburg, Lübeck, Ulm, Speyer and others – already had their own cannon and stores of powder,' Hermann Weiss reports in his *History of Culture*. 'In the Flemish city of Louvain in that year twelve mortars were sold. Supplies of powder in the cities were sometimes so large that they caused destruction; in 1360 the Rathaus in Lübeck was blown up when powder stored in it exploded.'[8] The new weapons spread most rapidly in Italy and Germany; somewhat later, the casting of cannon was mastered widely in northern Europe, including in Denmark, Sweden and Muscovy.

To use modern-day language, artillery was a municipal undertaking, with the city authorities controlling not only the production of cannon but also their use. Often, the master foundrymen who were responsible for the casting of cannon also directed their 'exploitation'.

The advent of firearms, and their steady improvement, led to an arms race similar to the one that accompanied the development of armoured warships in the late nineteenth century or tank armour in the twentieth century. The artillerymen increased the penetrative power of the shot, and the makers of armour, its protective qualities. The advantage did not always lie with the projectiles. In the sixteenth century, experts note, high-quality armour underwent an obligatory testing with 'the most powerful hand-weapon of the day'.[9] The breastplate of a horseman had to withstand a musket or pistol-shot, just as the frontal armour of a twentieth-century tank had to protect its crew. Even in documents from the late sixteenth century we find armour described as 'pistol, caliver and musket-proof'.[10] The improvement of armour did not always come at the expense of making it heavier. The process of technical innovation that allowed better-quality firearms to be produced also ensured the production of more reliable armour.

The most effective weapons against cavalry in the fifteenth and sixteenth centuries were not the hand-held firearms of the time, but the pike and halberd. Without the protection of pikes, musketeers could not fight against cavalry even in the seventeenth century.

The struggle of the Swiss cantons for independence from the Austrian Habsburgs gave rise to a new armed force that became famous throughout Europe. As Delbrück observes, the basis for the military discipline of the Swiss lay in their ties to the civic authorities and in their strong communal organisation.[11]

Prevailing over the Austrians, Milanese, French and Burgundians, the Swiss were not only famed throughout Europe, but also turned their military art into a form of export business. By the early sixteenth century Swiss infantry were the shock troops of several European armies at once.

The victories of infantry over cavalry in the late Middle Ages were victories of the embryonic bourgeois system and of the bureaucratic state over the feudal order, but were in no way victories of new military technology over old. The common characteristic that united the Swiss and English infantry, the Flemish pikemen and even the Hussites was not tactics or weaponry, but their new 'democratic' form of social organisation, in which members of the 'elite' fought alongside the infantry. The fact that the change in the social system made new military tactics possible was another matter entirely.

High cost made armour a luxury that a large-scale military organisation could not afford. Meanwhile, the larger size of armies made heavy cavalry a less and less important factor on the battlefield. Quantity won out over quality. The superiority of infantry lay not in its armaments, but in its cheapness and its mass scale. This was not a tactical military superiority, but in the first instance an economic one; the new economics of war also radically altered the tactics employed in the fighting. It was not new military technologies that changed warfare, but changes in agriculture and artisanry that altered society, including its military structure.

In the armies, the individual demands made of a professional soldier were reduced, but new demands were made: of discipline, of an ability to carry out coordinated action, of precisely carrying out a general manoeuvre, and so forth. On the battle-field, a lone shot from a musket rarely hit its target. But soldiers armed with muskets had fearsome potential when they were assembled in companies and firing volleys. In other words, the musket was a weapon that could only be used effectively by a well-organised and comparatively large army.

With cavalry, the cohesion of a company and the precision of its actions were achieved through personal training of the riders and their horses. In the case of infantry the same effect was achieved through simple collective exercises, without any requirement for lengthy individual training.

The role of infantry was increased even at the cost of rendering armies less manoeuverable, and of reducing their mobility. The result of this evolution was the relatively static linear tactics of the eighteenth century. But infantry met the needs of the new armies, above all because it cost less. It won out in terms of the relationship of price and quality.

Replacing the longbow with the musket was also of social significance in relation to the lower orders of society. At first glance it might seem that as the infantryman became more important on the battlefield than the horseman, warfare would cease to be a matter for a professional, hereditary elite, and would be democratised. But the army was at the same time becoming alienated from the population; regular units, either paid or formed on some other principle, were supplanting militia, and the masses were losing their skill in the use of arms. A longbow, though not perhaps of the highest quality, could be prepared in domestic conditions or by village weapons-smiths. It was employed constantly for hunting. Any man could use it, though the ability to shoot accurately needed constant practice, which in England, for example, was compulsory for the entire male population, not excluding even the clergy. The longbow, in other words, was an ideal weapon for popular warfare, or an optimal form of armament for a popular army formed on a basis of mobilisation. Swords, halberds and pikes could also be produced in the countryside, even if their quality did not match that of the products of urban weapons-smiths. A musket was a different matter; it could be produced only in specialised workshops. Learning to load and shoot it required training, but there was no point in conducting this training in isolation from drill and tactical instruction. As a hunting weapon a musket was next to useless, since it was expensive to buy, and fired slowly and inaccurately. An army that was equipped with firearms allowed the state to wage war not just independently of feudal seigneurs, but also without the participation of the people. The main thing a government needed was not the support of its subjects, but money.

The new basis on which forces were organised inevitably meant that armies became larger. Researchers have calculated that between 1530 and 1710 the size of European armies grew approximately ten-fold.[12] This process can be traced with particular clarity using the example of France. In 1494, when Charles VIII invaded Italy and initiated a lengthy period of wars between France and Spain, he was leading a powerful army of 20,000 men. When the warring countries concluded the Peace of Cateau-Cambrésis in 1559, both sides had armies of 50–60,000, excluding their naval forces. France entered the Thirty Years War with 125,000 soldiers, while Louis XIV had as many as 400,000 men under arms.[13] For comparison, the Russian army of Peter the Great reached 200,000 men during this period, the Austrian forces numbered around 100,000, and even little Holland could put roughly the same number on the battlefield.[14] But the military efforts that reached their peak during the War of the Spanish Succession proved ruinous for France, and this contributed no less to the defeat of the Sun King than the military genius of the Duke of Marlborough and Prince Eugene of Savoy.

A still greater burden on the state budget was the naval fleet. In the Middle Ages even such future sea powers as England and Denmark were incapable of maintaining a strong fleet in peacetime. The only states to possess serious navies were the trading republics of northern Italy and the Hansa, which simply could not exist without them. Henry V's navy fell into decline after his death, and was reborn only under the Tudors, but by the beginning of the Stuart era it had again been sharply reduced. The epoch of geographical discoveries and of sea-borne commercial expansion required the creation of a fleet. But a navy was expensive, and had to be kept in good condition in peacetime, unlike an army which could be reduced in size or disbanded. The reverse side of military reform was an increase in the state debt.[15] The dependence of the monarchy on the bourgeoisie grew in proportion to the acuteness of the state's financial dilemmas. But even where state finances were relatively healthy, their administration was in the hands of members of the 'third estate' who were capable of dealing with such matters in professional fashion.

Without the bourgeoisie and its funds, war became impossible. But without wars, there was no possibility of meeting the challenges with which the bourgeoisie was confronted; appropriating new resources and establishing markets were tasks that were accomplished through conquering new countries.

The discovery of a new world

With a good deal of luck, people born in 1442 could still be alive in 1527. During this time, ideas of the dimensions of the planet and of the nature of the solar system were transformed. Instead of being copied by hand, books began to be printed using the printing press of Johann Gutenberg, in previously unimaginable print-runs of hundreds of copies. The Byzantine empire that had stood for a thousand years collapsed, and Turkish armies poured into Hungary. The pope was no longer recognised as the sole head of Western Christianity. Heresies became transformed into religious doctrines supported by secular authorities. People could now read the Bible in their native language. Peasants rose up against their masters. Castile and Aragon united to form a single Spanish state which not only completed the *Reconquista* by subduing Granada, the last Arab possession on the peninsula, but also founded an unparalleled empire on the other side of the earth. The small kingdom of Portugal established another world empire.

Ocean voyages aided technical progress, forcing the West to assimilate the knowledge and experience of Asian civilisations. The Mediterranean navigation of the period between the eleventh and the fourteenth centuries had not required the complex measuring instruments and other maritime technologies essential for ocean seafaring. It was only in the sixteenth century, when they faced the need to ensure continual access to lands beyond the oceans, that European navigators quickly began to study these questions, and to borrow technologies from Asia.

The expansion of the West was not the result of individual enterprise or a natural consequence of market competition, but the outcome of deliberate state moves, first by the kings of Portugal and Spain and then by the governments of Holland, England, France and Denmark. Conscious government efforts, the measures consistently implemented by Henry the Navigator, led to the Portuguese breakthrough into the South Atlantic and later, the Indian Ocean. Once the Europeans had arrived in Asia and America, they established new markets and created a new entrepreneurial culture, but the motivating force of the unfolding global process was not private initiative. More correctly, private initiative became a decisive factor in the changes thanks to the fact that it was steadily and systematically encouraged by the continually growing power of the state.

The impulse behind the search for new sea routes is usually regarded as having come from the Turkish capture of Constantinople in 1453. But the Portuguese Prince Henry the Navigator had begun organising expeditions into the Atlantic long before the fall of Byzantium. The Polish historian Marian Malowist reminds us that by 1453, when Byzantium fell, 'a Portuguese trading station had already existed for five years on the coast of West Africa, on the island of Arguin, and long before these events the Genoese had considered the possibility of economic expansion not only to the Iberian peninsula but also to the islands of the Atlantic.'[16]

The Portuguese exploration of the west coast of Africa was not at first aimed at finding a sea route to India, a route which many thought impossible (according to the geography of Ptolemy, there was no connection between the Atlantic and Indian oceans). Instead, the goal was to win access to African gold. The trade in gold, which from the eleventh century had been exchanged for salt and other commodities, was the basis for the flourishing of the African empires of Mali and Ghana. In the fifteenth century the place of these empires was taken by the Songhai state in the valley of the River Niger. Gold and slaves were exported to the countries of the Maghreb along caravan routes controlled by Arab merchants. The transit centres that were established there turned into wealthy trading cities with their own merchant oligarchies, recalling those of Venice and Genoa. The Soviet scholar L.E. Kubbel noted that the key starting points for the trans-Saharan trade 'lay as close as possible to the Niger, to the water-borne route by which the main regions of West Africa could be reached more easily and quickly, while also running less risk from the nomads of the southern Sahara fringe'.[17]

After the military-political might of Ghana had vanished into the past, the centre of commercial operations shifted to the region of Timbuktu. Most of the gold that was furnished in exchange for salt was sent to the Arab countries of the Near East, but a substantial part also reached Europe. The quantities were enough to allow these countries, which did not have their own supplies, to mint their own gold coins – in the case of England, of good quality. One result was that the buying power of gold in Europe declined. In France in the late thirteenth century the relationship of gold to silver had been 1:14, but in the fourteenth century it fluctuated between 1:12 and 1:6.6. In Tunis during the same period the rate of silver to gold varied between 1:11.6 and 1:9.3.[18] In the Western Sudan itself the abundance of gold led to high inflation long before the European 'price revolution'; in terms of Western coins, goods in that region cost far more than in Cairo or Venice. An Arab traveller noted that in Jenne 'large fortunes, which Allah alone could count', had been accumulated.[19] The social status of the commercial elite was so great that wealthy merchants married the daughters of local kings.

It was not only the Portuguese who sailed to the coasts of gold-bearing Africa. In 1421 the Chinese empire organised large-scale exploring expeditions whose participants traversed the Indian Ocean from east to west, while also studying many other lands. Between 1405 and 1433 the voyages led by Cheng Ho substantially exceeded anything of which Europe was capable, not only at that time but in the sixteenth century as well. Sixty-two ships and 28,000 people took part in the expeditions.[20] Compared to the Chinese expeditions of the early fifteenth century, the efforts of the Portuguese seafarers might at first seem trivial.[21] But no less striking than the scale of the Chinese expeditions is the fact that they had no practical result. As M.N. Pearson notes, these ventures were 'totally different in character' compared with those undertaken by the Portuguese, 'let alone as compared with the later Dutch and English'.[22] The government of the celestial empire soon ended its naval expeditions. Responding to historians who wondered why China should have acted in such fashion, Giovanni Arrighi notes that the discovery of a new sea route between east and west was less advantageous for China than for Portugal. But why were these expeditions mounted?

The Chinese leaders had their own needs and aims, which might or might not have coincided with those of the Europeans. The point, however, is that China and Western Europe in the fifteenth century were two quite different societies, living according to a different logic. China brought its exploration to a close because the purpose of this activity had nothing to do with developing trade.

In China, foreign trade was an imperial monopoly, and the bureaucrats neither knew how to conduct such trade nor wanted to do so. The Portuguese, who reached East Africa soon after the Chinese, also held to the principle of state commerce, but this did not prevent them from taking a dominant position on the shores of the Indian Ocean. With regard to the Chinese empire, some scholars also speak of a 'command economy'. Western researchers write of the 'anticommercial nature of the Confucian state',[23] but this by no means signifies that the celestial empire was fundamentally hostile to trade. The Chinese bureaucracy could be a difficult partner for foreign merchants, but it at least guaranteed safety and predictability in commercial relations. Ocean voyages consumed vast resources while yielding China almost nothing; it was simpler and cheaper to conduct trade through foreigners. A ban was placed on Chinese subjects travelling beyond the borders of the empire. The ships were dismantled, and soon afterward the building of large sea-going vessels was forbidden as well.

Meanwhile, by the end of the fifteenth century the Portuguese voyages along the coasts of Africa had yielded brilliant results. Rounding the Cape of Good Hope, the caravels entered the Indian Ocean, proving that the geography of Ptolemy had been wrong – there was indeed a sea route to India from the West. Soon Vasco da

Gama made his famous voyage to India. The kingdom of Spain, formed through the unification of Aragon with Castile, entered the race for discoveries, financing the expeditions of Christopher Columbus, who had promised to find a route to India by way of the Atlantic. Instead, Columbus discovered America.

The parallel discoveries ensured a division of spheres of influence – though one not without conflicts – between the two states of the Iberian peninsula. Spain received America and control over the Atlantic Ocean, while the Indian Ocean became the domain of Portugal. The Holy See sanctioned this division of the world. In 1493–4 Pope Alexander VI declared that from then onward Portugal would be 'the possessor of the navigation, conquest and trade from Ethiopia, Arabia, Persia and India'.[24] In other words, the Indian Ocean was recognised as Lisbon's sphere of influence.

It is true that Portugal's conquests were not limited to Africa and the coast of the Indian Ocean. One of the Portuguese expeditions was carried westward from the African coast by the wind, and discovered the shores of the future Brazil. From this moment the Portuguese empire, without ceasing its expansion in the direction of Africa and India, began colonising the New World.

The first maritime empire: Portugal

The expeditions into the Atlantic that were begun by Henry the Navigator in the fifteenth century continued, and yielded impressive results. In the countries where the Portuguese made landfall, they did not meet with significant resistance. Local inhabitants collaborated with them willingly, and the rulers of the local land empires did not see them as a serious threat.[25]

The undertakings mounted by the Portuguese were aimed against the Venetian monopoly even more than against the Turks. Just as the later trade mediation of the Dutch became more and more burdensome to the rest of Europe, the commercial monopoly of Venice in the fifteenth century aroused wide discontent. The seizure of Constantinople by the Turks hindered the development of Venice's trade, making it more dangerous and expensive, but Alexandria remained as a major commercial port that was open to Italian merchants.

The Portuguese King Manuel I viewed expansion to the east as a continuation of the crusades. There is no reason to doubt the sincerity of his religious beliefs, since in 1496 it was he who ordered the burning of all Jewish prayer-books in Portugal, and that Jews should either convert to Catholicism or leave his kingdom. But commercial advantage was never far from the attention of the Portuguese. When Vasco da Gama's ships in 1498 pulled in to the shores of India, and two Arab merchants asked why they had come, the reply was unambiguous: 'We came in search of Christians and spices.'[26]

In West Africa the Portuguese had already discovered spices that could be exported to Europe. In India vast commercial opportunities opened up. The appearance of Portuguese ships in the Indian Ocean, however, led not only to a growth of commodity exchange between Europe and Asia, but also to immediate armed conflict with Arab and other Muslim merchants who had earlier controlled the exporting of spices to the West through Lebanon and Egypt. The difference in faith had not prevented the Egyptian and Venetian merchants from striking profitable deals. Now the arrival of the Portuguese changed everything; they did not incorporate themselves into the old system of relations but destroyed it, forming new markets and trade routes.

The first consequence of the geographical discoveries completed by Vasco da Gama was an intensified trade war with the Muslims. Both sides acted extremely aggressively, with the Arabs making the first armed attacks. But the Portuguese had an important advantage: their expeditions were organised and prepared by the state. They were equally capable of fighting and trading, and in the event were even more successful at the former than the latter. In the fifteenth century the pope blessed the Portuguese kings not only for their struggle against unbelievers, but also for their plunder. The first such bull, *Dum diversas,* was issued in 1452, to be followed in 1455 by *Romanus Pontifex,* and in 1456 by *Inter caetera.* As an English historian notes, papal bulls did not envisage any mercy where Muslims and heathens were concerned, calling on Christians 'to capture their goods and their territories, to reduce their persons to perpetual slavery'.[27]

Between 1502 and 1505 one expedition after another allowed the Europeans to create military-commercial beach-heads in Asia. In the disputes between the Christian trading stations and the Muslim commercial empires, the main argument proved to be Portuguese cannon. Trade turnover rose rapidly. Between 1497 and 1500 the Portuguese crown sent 17 ships into the Indian Ocean; in the period from 1501 to 1510 the figure was already 150.[28] Each of these flotillas was simultaneously a military and commercial enterprise, and their growing commercial success permitted increased military efforts. The trade of the Arabs and Venetians in the Levant went into decline. The export of spices through Alexandria, which had fluctuated between 480 and 630 tons per year in the late fifteenth century, fell in the early sixteenth century to 135 tons. The same occurred in Beirut. But each year in Lisbon as much as 42,000 tons was unloaded.[29]

It was only after some years that the Arabs managed to organise resistance on the state level. An expedition headed by Emir Hasain Mushrif al-Kurdi was sent from Egypt. The first clash between the Egyptian fleet and Portuguese ships took place in March 1508, and ended in victory for the Egyptians. But in February 1509, near the Indian port of Diu, a Portuguese squadron attacked a larger Arab fleet and destroyed it.

Having arrived in the Indian Ocean, the Portuguese discovered there a developed system of commodity exchange, 'a multiplicity of trades, both local and long distance'.[30] Moors from Africa reached Malaya, and Chinese sailed to Africa. In India European goods, brought there by Arabs and Armenians, were exchanged for spices and durable goods from South-East Asia. This system could function only by making use of transit ports that acted as cosmopolitan centres of cultural, informational and commodity exchange. The Portuguese conquerors tried as a matter of priority to control these nodal points. They seized key positions on the coast of East Africa, establishing fortified trading stations there that served military and strategic rather than commercial goals.[31] The result was to undermine the prosperity of the ancient Arab cities, which were transformed into impoverished settlements on the old trade route.[32]

Even before the outcome of the naval campaign was known, a governor was sent from Portugal to India to administer the new possessions. Don Alfonso de Albuquerque was the first European to be given the post of viceroy of India. The Indian empire founded by the Portuguese, the *Estado da India,* stretched from the shores of East Africa to Indonesia, and included port cities along most of the Indian Ocean coastline – Mombasa, Muscat, Goa, Mumbai, Malacca and Timor. Ceylon was turned into an important strongpoint on the route from the western to the eastern part of the ocean. Goa, seized in 1510, became the administrative centre of the empire. Making no effort to penetrate the interior beyond the coast, the Portuguese commercial empire ruled over the Indian Ocean. This allowed the new masters of the sea not just to trade on their own account, but also to gather customs duties on the trade of others, including the native merchants. The key element in the entire system was the *cartaz* – the pass without which trading in the local region was virtually impossible. Revenues collected from the sale of passes not only helped to fill the treasury in Lisbon, but also provided stable financing for the administration of Portuguese India, sparing the crown the burden of meeting the expenses of its empire.

Such a system could not possibly have been created and maintained through military victories alone. It was necessary to build fortresses and churches, to establish and rebuild port facilities, warehouses, barracks and administrative buildings. The Portuguese were the first to understand the advantage a strong fleet armed with powerful artillery gave them. Their land forces were augmented to a considerable degree with native units, something which became the norm for later European colonial armies in India.

Even in Brazil the Portuguese were at first interested only in the coast, only gradually advancing into the interior of the continent. From Mozambique to Macao, and from Goa to Ceylon the Portuguese *Estado da India* embraced ports, islands and small strips of coastline, between which stretched expanses of sea. The principle of this empire was not control over people or territories, but over trade routes, and not over production, but over exchange.

The Portuguese officials strictly regulated the functioning of their ports, introducing a royal monopoly on the sending of vessels to India. The exporting of precious metals from Portugal and the importing to Europe of pepper and spices were under strict government control. Some historians have seen in this empire the first example of state capitalism or, to use the phrase of Manuel Nunes Dias, 'Portuguese monarchic capitalism'.[33]

The Portuguese crown engaged directly in trade, organised military and commercial expeditions, built ships and equipped them with crews.[34] In 1506 the trade in spices provided the treasury with 27 per cent of its revenues, and in 1518 with 39 per cent. This substantially exceeded the income from the European holdings of the crown. It would be wrong, however, to suppose that the bourgeoisie did not enjoy a share of the profits. The sale of spices to the final consumer was carried out by numerous private traders not only in Portugal but throughout Europe. Even Jews who had just been banished from the country were drawn into the reselling of the royal commodity. Often, the government farmed out enterprises to private companies, invariably bringing them back under its control once the agreed period had elapsed. The weakness of the Portuguese bourgeoisie meant that many of the new opportunities were taken up by foreign entrepreneurs, with a substantial part of the Portuguese supplies being sold in Antwerp. Italian banking houses that financed the Portuguese expeditions gained handsomely, but the economies of the Italian cities lost out; the money earned was not returned to Italy, but was invested in new commercial projects in which the Portuguese crown held a share. Venice suffered serious losses; the flow of spices that earlier had been controlled by its merchants was now directed through Lisbon, while most of the capital employed in the Portuguese economy was from Genoa.

In the second half of the sixteenth century, as the Lisbon government gradually ceased conducting an active economic policy in Asia, the Portuguese bourgeoisie went into decline as well, with the gains from the eastern trade going increasingly to cosmopolitan companies which had few ties to the country. In the late 1560s the government began to liberalise the system, under the influence of Spain, where a more market-based approach to trade prevailed. At the same time, the Portuguese state concluded monopoly contracts with large merchant firms from Milan and Augsburg. From 1581, when the two Iberian kingdoms were united under the rule of a shared monarch, the economic policy of Portugal was almost identical to that of Spain. But once it had become clear that this system did not yield the expected gains, the state began a return to direct control over commercial operations.

The Portuguese empire laid the basis for a general approach that was characteristic of all Western states in Asia throughout the next 250 years. A combination of military-administrative and commercial activity became the norm. This combination was to be observed on all levels of government, and gave rise to universal corruption.[35] The same later occurred with the officials of the Dutch and British East India Companies.

In parallel with the development of its Asian trade, the Portuguese crown expanded its presence in the Americas. Brazil, the largest Portuguese colony, became the main supplier of sugar to European markets. Until the 1530s the American possessions were of less interest to Lisbon than the Asian and African trading stations. In Brazil the Portuguese began cutting the red *pau-brasil,* or brazilwood, used for dying fabrics in Europe,[36] but unlike Mexico and Peru, the colony was not at this time a source of gold or silver.

It was only the appearance of the first French expeditions on the shores of the Americas in the 1530s that forced the Portuguese crown to strengthen its hold on its American possession. Subsequently, the Portuguese administration in Brazil organised the production of sugar cane, which immediately began yielding huge profits. In 1549 the royal Governor-General Thome da Sousa arrived in the colony; his main task was to try to make Brazil economically profitable, like the *Estado da India.* The Indian population, which put up resistance to the colonisers, was exterminated or driven into the interior. But after the Indians had been wiped out, the problem arose of finding labour power. The dilemma was solved with shipments of African slaves. Plantations of sugar cane and tobacco became attractive economic propositions thanks to the use of slave labour on a massive scale. The expansion of production presupposed a similarly massive development of the slave trade, and the Portuguese possessions scattered along the opposing shores of the Atlantic made up just as mutually interrelated a system as in India. Of the Brazilian colonial population of 57,000 people in 1585, a quarter were slaves.[37]

The colonies on the African coast supplied water and provisions to the ships headed for the Indian Ocean, repaired them and provided additional crew members. But the main task of these colonies was now to obtain slaves from the interior of the 'dark continent'. In West Africa a new economy developed at breakneck pace, with its main sector the trade in people. At first the Portuguese acted through native kings who joined actively in the business. From being partners in the trade they were gradually transformed into allies, and then into vassals. Firearms were supplied by the Portuguese only to those African rulers who were not only their military allies, but who also accepted Catholicism and showed a readiness to convert their subjects to the new faith. A particular stake was put on the kingdom of Congo. But despite their *de facto* dependence on Portugal, the kings of Congo Diogo I and his son Don Álvare did not recognise themselves as vassals of Lisbon, while the Portuguese for their part did not restrict themselves to trading through the Congo ports. In the 1550s a rivalry arose between Congo and Ndongo over the question of who would be the main supplier of slaves to the Portuguese.[38] Political instability in Ndongo led to a series of crises that ended with Portuguese intervention and the creation in 1575 of a colony in Angola. Luanda quickly came to flourish as a slave-trading centre. As one of the local officials wrote, the supply of slaves to Brazil was now guaranteed 'until the end of the world'.[39]

The world-empire of Charles V

From the first years of his reign, the founder of the Spanish Habsburg state and simultaneous head of the Holy Roman Empire Charles V was undoubtedly the most powerful monarch in Europe. Uniting beneath a single sceptre possessions in Germany, Italy and the Netherlands, as well as the kingdom of Spain and its rapidly growing conquests in the New World, he was able to rely on a seemingly inexhaustible flow of gold and silver from the other side of the Atlantic. With probably the best army of the time under his banners, Charles succeeded in beating off the attempts by his French rival Francis I to claim the leading role in Europe. His alliance with Venice held out the prospect of a successful struggle against the Turks, who had grown stronger in the East, while good relations with neighbouring Portugal guaranteed that no-one would challenge the dominant position of his empire in the Atlantic.

In essence, the conflicts of the sixteenth and of the first half of the seventeenth centuries decided the fate of the new world-economy that was taking shape around its European centre. Immanuel Wallerstein argues that the struggle of Charles V with France represented an 'attempt to absorb the European world-economy into his imperium'.[40] Indeed, it seemed initially that the Habsburg state would become the centre of an unprecedented world empire, uniting both sides of the Atlantic. Resistance to the efforts of the emperor, however, grew steadily. Leaving the Spanish crown to his son Philip II, Charles charged him with continuing his policies, but despite all efforts the opponents of the Habsburgs kept increasing in number. The decision by Charles V to divide his empire between two branches of the Habsburg family amounted in essence to recognising the failure of attempts to build a world-empire, a 'transition from a universal empire to defence of the interests of the "Austrian family" (*austriacismo*), in other words, to a close alliance between two parts of the dynasty, aimed at guaranteeing the hegemony of Catholicism and of the dynasty within Europe'.[41]

The 'world-empire' policy of Charles V and his efforts to construct a 'global monarchy' met with resistance not only from other European states (above all from France), but also from within Spain itself, where serious uprisings raged in the years from 1520 to 1522. Throughout the 200 years during which Spain remained a world power, the ruling Habsburgs had to fight simultaneously on many fronts, against the Arabs and Turks in the Mediterranean, against France in Italy, and against Protestant princes in Germany. Later, the adversaries in the North included the rebellious Netherlands and the rising English state. The Habsburgs had practically no allies anywhere in Europe, except for the Catholic princes of Germany and for the mutual aid given to one another by the Spanish and Austrian branches of the dynasty, divided after CharlesV's abdication. Nevertheless, the resources available to the Habsburgs by the beginning of the seventeenth century were of such scope as to make possible the waging of a prolonged struggle.

At the end of the fifteenth century it was Spain that possessed the financial and military-political strength required for establishing an empire. The colonial epoch of the sixteenth century in the Americas represented a continuation of the *Reconquista*. It is symbolic that Christopher Columbus obtained the support of the 'Catholic monarchs' for his venture in the Atlantic beneath the walls of Granada and during the very days when the Spanish court was celebrating the capitulation of the last stronghold of the Moors. The offensive thrust also continued in the direction of Africa. The land hunger of the nobility was to be satisfied under the control of the absolutist state, which directed and organised foreign expansion, and with the active collaboration of the bourgeoisie, which financed and exploited this process. The main problem lay in maintaining control over the conquistadors and in preventing them from establishing their own feudal kingdoms on the conquered territories. The task of the central government was made easier by the fact that the new possessions needed people, without whom maintaining authority and carrying out administration there was impossible. These people could be obtained only from Europe.

Despite the mobilisation of human resources in the European countries under Spanish rule, there were not enough people for colonising the New World. Hence the need to integrate the native population, a need that would not be felt later by the protestant colonists of New England. The low productivity of labour in the empire of the Habsburgs ensured (though not everywhere, it is true) the natives' physical survival. The Indians in Spanish America were converted *en masse* to Christianity, after which the settlers interbred with them, creating a large population of mestizos.

As the American historian Henry Kamen notes, 'the empire was made possible not by Spain alone, but by the combined resources of the Western European and Asian Nations, who participated fully and legally in an enterprise, that is nominally thought of, even by professional historians, as being "Spanish".'[42] In relation to other European peoples, above all the Italians, the Spanish acted more as consumers of cultural and technical innovations than as creators of anything new. However, 'it was this passive Iberian culture that had the ability to produce world power.'[43] This cultural passivity of Spain was perhaps an advantage, making it possible to imbibe and assimilate foreign experience and knowledge, and to attract new people. In this sense, Kamen observes, the empire was created to no less a degree by Americans, Africans and Asians than by Europeans.[44] Ultimately, Spain did not create the empire, but 'the empire created Spain'.[45] The same can also be said of the British empire.

The Portuguese empire is usually considered to have been maritime, and the Spanish empire territorial. But the difference between Portuguese and Spanish colonial policies was not only the result of different initial principles, but also of differences in the social conditions of America and Asia. In the Americas the native empires collapsed like houses of cards at the beginning of the sixteenth century, leaving behind a political vacuum which not only allowed the Spanish to take possession of the territories concerned, but which also created an acute need for them to do this. In Asia, by contrast, the local states remained fully viable, but their sea-borne power was slight.

The expansion of the empire took place not only in the direction of the Americas. In the Pacific Ocean the Spanish strengthened their position with the conquest of the Philippines in the 1560s. In the imperial system, this archipelago acted as a transhipment point between the New World and China.[46] The riches of Asia were paid for using silver obtained from American mines. By the end of the seventeenth century as much as a quarter of all the silver obtained in the Americas was being sent to China.

Why, then, did this brilliant empire go into eclipse by the mid-seventeenth century? Usually, this is explained on the basis that the feudal system then holding sway in Spain could not withstand competition from the bourgeois societies of Holland, England and France. But bourgeois relations in the countries that challenged the Habsburgs had developed rapidly precisely as a result of the discovery and conquest of the Americas, in other words, directly or indirectly as a result of the successes of that very same Spanish empire.

The policies of the Spanish Habsburgs were by no means hostile to private enterprise. Of all the powers that were drawn into the global expansion of the sixteenth and seventeenth centuries, it was Spain that most of all handed its sea-borne trade over to private capital, and that did least to regulate its entrepreneurs.[47] Henry Kamen even notes that the Spanish empire had some features of a 'business empire', dominated by international capital.[48]

Of the silver supplied from the Americas, between a quarter and a third finished up in the royal treasury, with the rest going to diverse types of commercial and financial companies servicing the world-empire. These companies flourished and enriched themselves, which cannot be said of the Spanish economy. The government made a practice of handing over powers to private individuals who not only ran commercial enterprises, but at times even mounted military expeditions while acting in the name of the state. Others to resort to such methods included, for example, the Muscovite state in the conquest of Siberia, but it was the Habsburgs who pursued this line most consistently. Under Charles V the development of the empire was closely linked to the activity of the banking house of the Fuggers, whom Wallerstein describes as 'the most spectacular of all modern merchant-capitalists'.[49]

The Fuggers put their stake on the Habsburg dynasty, effectively buying the imperial crown for Charles V by financing his election campaign among the German princes. 'In the sixteenth century,' writes N.I. Kareev,

> the Fuggers, lending the Habsburgs substantial sums, exercised a direct influence on the course of the international politics of the epoch. Without financial help from the Fuggers, Maximilian I would have been completely unable to intervene in the Italian wars, while his grandson Charles V might not have been elected emperor, and the latter's brother Ferdinand I might not have been elected King of Rome (and thus designated in advance as heir-apparent to the imperial throne). The wars of both these Habsburgs against France, the Turks and the German protestants were also waged using money borrowed from the Fuggers, and various sudden shifts in the global policies of Charles V are to be explained by the generosity or miserliness shown to him at one moment or another by this famous banking house.[50]

Italian financial capital also supported the empire. The domination of Italy by the Spanish was maintained not only by force of arms, but also as a result of the shared interests of the conquerors and the local oligarchy.

Despite their global ambitions, the Habsburgs did not manage to establish a centralised bureaucratic empire. If the power of centralised bureaucracy is to be considered a factor impeding the development of capitalism and private initiative, then Spain should unquestionably have flourished. But the experience of the Habsburg empire is an obvious refutation of later liberal theories declaring that freedom of private entrepreneurship in and of itself ensures development. Comparing the empire of the Habsburgs with its more successful rivals, one discovers that the key difference between them lay not in any lack of state intervention in the economies of its rivals, but on the contrary, in the fact that in England and Holland, unlike Spain, the state intervened energetically in the interests of the bourgeoisie. The key problem of the Spanish state was not an inadequate reliance on the market, but the fact that the state, while relying on the market, was insufficiently bourgeois.

Spain consumed only a small fraction of the goods that reached Europe from its overseas possessions. In 1691, some 90 per cent of the goods brought from the Americas finished up outside the kingdom's borders.[51] The scale of the country's foreign trade did nothing to help expand the internal market. An interest in making profits did not translate into a desire for development, and trade did not stimulate the growth and modernisation of production. The lack of interest in the internal market also appeared in the harsh religious policy initiated by the 'Catholic monarchs' Ferdinand and Isabella. Accompanying the expulsion of Jews and Moors, and the persecution of Christianised Arabs (the *moriscos*), was the seizure of their property. Large sheep-grazing estates, which operated for export, were transferred to new Christian owners.

While the government provided protection for the sheep-graziers, who were engaged in the export of wool, other sectors of production suffered from this policy rather than benefiting. 'Agriculture and the rural economy as a whole were completely neglected,' a Soviet historian wrote,

> while stifling tutelage and strict regulation weighed on Spanish industry. The persecution of the Jews and Moors in particular dealt heavy blows to the country's industrial and commercial development. At the same time as enticing opportunities had opened up on the other side of the Atlantic Ocean, and an economic revolution had begun, ominous signs were ripening of an unavoidable decline.[52]

However much external ties expanded, the balance of Spain's foreign trade, of its exports and imports, was unfavourable. The textile industry was incapable even of satisfying the demand from the national market, let alone competing with its counterparts in Flanders or England. The government was in a permanent state of financial crisis. In Castile, the flow of tax revenues to the treasury increased between 1474 and 1504 from less than 900,000 to 26,000,000 *reales* per year,[53] but this was not enough to cover the still more rapid increase in state spending. The monarchy was forced to resort to loans, and the state debt grew exponentially. By 1543 no less than 65 per cent of the revenues flowing to the Spanish treasury was being spent to service loans. At the same time as the buying power of precious metals was declining, a decree of 25 May 1552 substantially reduced the silver content of newly issued coins. The reduction amounted to 21.43 per cent, which lowered both the weight of the coins and the nominal value of the currency accordingly.[54] Despite this, the government in 1557 was compelled to declare itself bankrupt.[55]

An important part of budget expenditure was associated with military operations. But the wars, at that point relatively successful, strengthened the economic position of the empire as well as costing money. The rapid increase in spending resulted from the need to carry out a general reorganisation and expansion of the state, creating a new bureaucratic apparatus; from the cost of maintaining ties with numerous territories; and from having to organise supplies of silver and other commodities from across the Atlantic and Pacific oceans – in short, from the requirements of a new political and economic system.

The empire depended more and more on tax revenues from Italy, and later from the Netherlands as well. For provoking the rise of the Netherlands national liberation movement, the tax demands of the Habsburgs were no less a factor than religious disagreements with the monarch. The practical-minded Flemish and Dutch burghers measured their loyalty to the crown against the profits they obtained as a result, and found the cost too high. This in turn led to resistance from the organs of estate representation. The Estates-General, in which the urban bourgeoisie was dominant, categorically refused to sanction new levies. 'After all, the representatives of the cities often were businessmen themselves,' a Dutch historian notes ironically in this connection.[56]

In 1568 the disagreements between the crown and the representatives of the Netherlands estates, superimposed on the religious conflict, provoked an open revolt. This led to the Eighty Years War between the Habsburgs and the United Provinces that were intent on seceding from their empire.

After the Dutch seized the 'silver fleet' in 1628 the Spanish government, chronically beset by financial difficulties in any case, fell into genuine crisis and sought desperately to raise funds to cover its budget deficit. New taxes introduced by the monarchy led in short order to revolts in Catalonia and Portugal, with the Portuguese using the demand from Madrid that they send troops to put down the Catalan uprising as a pretext for dissolving the union with Spain.

Protestantism, Catholicism and the spirit of capitalism

Max Weber's thesis concerning a link between the religious ideas of the Reformation and the formation of the capitalist system has become a commonplace of historical literature. Destroying traditional ideology and society, the protestant bourgeoisie frees itself from the fetters of religious interdictions. But at the same time, it subordinates its striving for profit to rational logic, restricting its consumption so that the acquisition of wealth is replaced by the accumulation of capital.

Although Weber places his accents differently from Marx, he agrees with Marx on the main point: capitalism is possible only on the basis of a corresponding organisation of labour in the process of production. It is here, however, that the key historical problem arises: the Reformation in its early period did not by any means give rise to rapid industrial development. It took a century and a half for the intellectual and moral energy of protestantism to turn into the general triumph of the new productive relations.

The history of Dutch and English colonialism, along with numerous examples from the history of the United States, shows that when protestant merchants and soldiers fell into a different cultural and political milieu they readily violated any and all moral norms. The practical accumulation of capital in the sixteenth and early seventeenth centuries was not by any means subordinated to the logic of rational investment, and nor was it tied to production. The rational principle which Weber esteems so highly was more likely to appear in the logical organisation of plunder, and in the effective use of armed force. Nor did the triumph of the Reformation in the eastern regions of Germany lead to the rapid development of capitalism; to the contrary, the regions east of the Elbe in the seventeenth century witnessed a 'second edition of serfdom'.

Protestantism was indeed a powerful ideological tool for accelerating bourgeois development, but primarily in places where the bourgeois revolution had already matured. Engels stressed that the Reformation was already a revolutionary act.[57] In the Scandinavian countries revolutionary revolt was replaced by reforms from above, but in each case the Reformation did not 'work' on its own, but only as part of a process of the corresponding transformation of society and the state.

The 'Reformation from above' implemented by the kings in England and the Scandinavian countries, and also by a number of German princes, had little to do with encouraging bourgeois entrepreneurialism or implanting market values. Its main goal was to strengthen the financial basis of the state. The English Tudors and the Swedish kings of the Vasa dynasty alike had an acute need for money. But even a significant flow of funds into the treasury from the seizure of church property did not solve the problem. Once the government had spent these funds, it faced the question of how to obtain still more money in order to maintain its activity on the new level reached thanks to the Reformation. Henry VIII's failed war with France from 1543 to 1551 led to a new financial crisis. The king was forced to borrow money from the banking house of the Fuggers and from Flemish merchants, to melt down confiscated church utensils into coins, and also to resort to debasing the currency. But his attempts to pay foreigners back with debased coins had dismal results. The government was forced to sell off monastery lands, leading to the rapid growth of a 'new gentry' which was not bound by the old feudal obligations and which actively reorganised its landholdings on a bourgeois basis. The development of capitalist relations in England was thus stimulated more by the financial crisis of the state than by the ideology or socio-cultural practice of Protestantism.

The owners of large-scale capital did not always make haste to associate themselves with the ideas of the Reformation. The Fuggers preferred the Catholic dynasty of the Habsburgs to Protestant rulers and merchants, though for a good rate of interest they were prepared to lend money to both. In the sixteenth century many wealthy French cities rejected the Huguenots, and the Italian merchants remained deaf to protestant propaganda. Where financial capital predominated, there was no particular striving for revolutionary change. The financiers found it more advantageous to work with the monarchs.

In the Austrian lands of the Habsburgs, historians have calculated, 'adherents of the new faith numbered around 70 per cent of the population'.[58] In the lands of the Czech king before the battle of Bílá Hora protestants made up 90 per cent of inhabitants. The Reformation spread quickly through the territory of Hungary, and also took hold of the Slavic population, for whom the translation of the Bible into their native languages was an important stage in the development of their national consciousness. The relationship of forces between Protestantism and Catholicism on the level of mass consciousness was thus approximately the same in the Austrian lands of the Habsburgs as it was in northern Europe where the Reformation triumphed. But the massive spread of Protestantism among the population did not make Hungary the centre of a rapid development of capitalism, or Austria a great commercial power.

Weber was unquestionably correct when he pointed to the link between protestant ideology and capitalism, but the decisive role in the triumph of the new economic system was not played by the Reformation itself, but by state support for it. Capitalism was not victorious wherever protestants appeared, but where the state made Protestantism its official ideology, serving the cause of economic and political transformation. Radical changes ensued when the new political order was combined with a new dominant world-view.

The needs of church reform went hand in hand with the needs of the changing state. The bureaucracy and army required a single cultural standard in order to act effectively. Unity of language was essential to ensure that documents sent from the capital would be understood without problems in any province. In the army, a new discipline of the troops would be impossible unless the entire mass of soldiers could clearly understand commands and fulfil them. Standardisation of the language now meant that military commanders could intermix contingents, combining men from different ends of the country in one formation. The standardisation of language undertaken by governments served to accelerate the formation of a single internal market, and was closely associated with other efforts to integrate society, such as the shift to uniform systems for taxation and for weights and measures, and to a single monetary system.

These innovations, though put into effect by protestant regimes, were of importance for all Europe. Of the capitalist countries, the one that was most active and consistent in implementing such measures was France, partly for the reason that at the end of the religious wars the former protestant Henry IV was on the throne.

In the early seventeenth century the economic position of France began improving rapidly. After the religious wars the kingdom was in ruinous condition, but thanks to the energetic efforts of the government of Henry IV and of his finance minister Sully, quickly began to recover. 'In the course of twenty years,' wrote the French historian Frédéric Ancillon, 'all sectors of the national economy were restored and the large cities of France came back to life, quickly achieving prosperity.'[59] Sully devoted particular attention to agriculture, abolishing or reducing a number of taxes and encouraging the export of grain. The Edict of Nantes, accepted by Henry IV on 13 April 1598, not only ensured a halt to armed conflict between protestants and Catholics, but also allowed the state to integrate members of the protestant party into the structure of government, along with their ideas, experience, and approaches to administrative and political work. Adding to the compromise between Catholicism and the Reformation in France was the political reform of the Catholic church itself, which became 'national'. The success of these measures was so great, and the spread of the new ideas so rapid and successful, that the royal power soon ceased to need the Huguenots. Under Richelieu their claims to enjoy special rights began to be viewed as an obstacle to national unity. The final outcome of the policies of centralisation enacted by Henry IV and his successors was the revocation in 1685 of the Edict of Nantes, after which French Huguenots who refused to change their faith were scattered throughout all of Europe from England to Russia, becoming, despite their rift with their native state, bearers of French cultural influence and traditions.

The French model of administrative centralisation and bureaucratic order spread throughout Europe, imitated both by protestant and Catholic countries, and from the time of Peter the Great by Orthodox Russia as well. Interest in the French bureaucracy was expressed even by Ottoman Turkey.

The key ideological question for the shaping of the bourgeois order was not overcoming Catholicism as such, but developing a new system of coordinates that would permit the religious tradition to be used for new social tasks, in the first instance for accumulating capital. During the shocks of the sixteenth and seventeenth centuries Catholicism was adapted to a changed economic reality. In the Catholic world, there was a compromise between religious and rational approaches to life. 'It worked in the Catholic world in a different way, but it was certainly no less effective. In every case, it created a new religious spirit, freed from dogma.'[60]

The Canadian scholar John Loughlin notes that the Reformation aided the rise of the national state by 'destroying the unity of the Catholic Church and laying the basis for national churches'.[61] Paradoxically, this was true not only of countries where Protestantism had triumphed, but also of states where the Counter-Reformation had been victorious. The link between church and state and the dependence of the religious on the political regime grew stronger throughout; governments took hold of a powerful ideological weapon, which the apparatus of power would at times use even more vigorously in Catholic than in protestant countries.

In 1555 the Augsburg religious peace proclaimed the principle *cuius regio, eius religio* – 'whoever rules, his (or hers) is the faith'. This principle not only provided a sort of preliminary summing-up of the Reformation period, but also laid the basis for the future of the national (sovereign) state. Religious politics, regardless of the dominant faith, became a tool for ideological control of the population and for mobilising loyalties with relation to the authorities. The concept of internal affairs took on a definite meaning, clearly associated with that of sovereignty and with the idea of a single ideology that might be more or less tolerant, but that was not therefore any less obligatory. What historical hindsight has termed the 'Westphalia system' should in fact have been called the 'Augsburg system'; by the time the Peace of Westphalia was signed, this system had already existed for almost a century as a generally recognised norm.

In the second half of the sixteenth century the Catholic church, recovering from the shock delivered by the first successes of the Reformation, went on the counter-attack. The spiritual and structural refurbishing of the church was to lend it a new dynamism. The ideology of Catholicism became militant and aggressive, with a revived enthusiasm for spiritual service. Both branches of the Habsburg dynasty, the Spanish and Austrian, mobilised their resources in support of the Counter-Reformation, linking the struggle for the preservation of the faith to propaganda demanding respect for traditional values and institutions. Among these institutions was the imperial power, the monarchy, combining political might with spiritual authority. Historians nevertheless observe that throughout the sixteenth century the Habsburgs 'did not succeed in implementing the principle of the Augsburg peace of 1555' throughout their own territories.[62] The land belonged to the Habsburgs, but the souls of their subjects stubbornly resisted the implantation of the Catholic faith. The emperors in Vienna remained Catholic rulers who were condemned to tolerate a predominance, or at least widespread incidence, of Protestantism among their subjects. The constant threat of a Turkish invasion, especially in Hungary, forced religious tolerance on them. If the Habsburgs despite this managed not just to keep their subjects within the Catholic fold, but also to restore the Roman church to its dominant position, this was not by any means solely the result of state repression. By the middle of the seventeenth century the burghers of the city of Vienna, who initially had been united in support-ing the Reformation, were just as united in returning to the Roman faith once it had become clear that the Catholic Habsburg monarchs were protecting their orders and markets, and defending their interests. In identical fashion, the restoration of Catholi-cism in the Czech lands after the crushing of the protestant army in the battle of Bilá Hora cannot be explained solely on the basis of military events. The defence of the Czech protestants against Catholic Austria was the most important ideological principle underlying the Thirty Years War. But when the victorious Swedish forces entered Prague a quarter of a century after Bilá Hora, the local population was far from meeting them as liberators. The Charles Bridge was blocked by the city militia, and the Swedes, despite the absence of the imperial forces, were stopped.

The success of the Counter-Reformation in southern and south-eastern Europe was ensured by the economic policy of the state, which corresponded to the interests of the urban bourgeoisie no less than did the course pursued by the governments of the North. It is beside the point that the business interests and conditions of activity of the entrepreneurial class in this case were different from those in England and Holland. To the degree that the crisis of the seventeenth century revealed the problems and contradictions of the regime of free trade that had prevailed earlier, the need of the bourgeoisie for a strong state increased as well. In this situation, loyalty to the existing authorities proved stronger than religious preferences.

Loyalty to the Habsburgs gave the nascent bourgeois class the chance to expand to the south and to exploit the agrarian periphery in Hungary and the Balkans. The only difference was that the entire world with its riches and diverse opportunities was opening up before the Dutch merchants, while it was only the rural expanse of provincial south-eastern Europe that lay before their Austrian class brothers. Holland's 'new periphery' lay beyond the seas, while that of Austria lay close at hand on the lower Danube.

Absolutism

The state that arose from the crises and wars of the late Middle Ages differed strikingly from the political systems of the feudal epoch. The system that in France came to be known in hindsight as the *ancien régime* was to pass into history under the general name of absolutism. Arising in response to the crisis of the fourteenth century, it underwent a further severe crisis in the seventeenth century, after which the political institutions of the majority of European countries maintained a relative stability until the French Revolution.

The state ceased to be perceived as a large feudal estate, belonging to a particular family by right of inheritance, and gradually acquired the features of a modern nation. Local differences and specific rights, obligations and freedoms, attached to particular provinces and even families, were replaced by uniform legislation, its implementation controlled by a centralised bureaucracy and its security defended by a similarly unified and centralised army and police force, to which organs of political surveillance were gradually added. Ambassadorial missions sent abroad periodically were replaced by systematically organised diplomatic and intelligence services. The bureaucracy not only grew and took on strength, acquiring a rational form of organisation, but also came to represent an important condition for the future development of industry, a condition which the bourgeoisie itself in many cases could not meet spontaneously within the context of its own, often chaotic market activity.

Foreign observers noted that the French bourgeoisie 'preferred to buy offices rather than to invest in commercial and industrial activities'.[63] By the end of the rule of Charles VII the bureaucrats had come to represent a serious social force. Having strengthened the French state by taking over the precisely operating government apparatus that had been established in 'Lancastrian France', the Valois were not simply able to govern more effectively than before, but also obtained a new base of social support:

> There were enough of these functionaries for them to form a relatively individualised social class, holding an intermediate position between the city-dwellers [bourgeois – B.K.], from among whom they were mostly drawn, and the nobility, to which they aspired. Their cohesion at all levels strengthened family alliances; at the country's centre arose real parliamentary dynasties whose members were linked by marriage to the *messieurs de finances*; analogous alliances appeared at the local level, and among the lower echelons.[64]

Prosperous bourgeois functionaries acquired titles of nobility, but still remained distinct with relation to the old aristocracy and members of the military caste. In Normandy alone between 1550 and 1650 more than 1,000 families were elevated to noble rank.[65] Alongside the *noblesse d'épée* (nobility of the sword) there thus appeared the *noblesse de robe*, completely bourgeois in its origins, associations and mode of existence, but not in the least anxious to overturn the feudal order, not to speak of altering the state system. Turning itself into a crucial prop for the government, the *noblesse de robe* not only controlled numerous key posts and institutions, but also employed them in its interests. This bourgeoisie transformed society not by struggling against feudalism, but by adapting it to its own interests and goals.

A dynamic compromise, managed from above by the monarchy, was supported from below by a wide-ranging network of social ties.

The formation of new structures of power proceeded unevenly, and was not by any means successful in every country. While in Spain various states and regions had moved swiftly to unite themselves into a single powerful entity, in Italy and Germany the reverse was seen – instead of a single monarchy regional states took shape, with some of them capable of playing an important role in European politics.

The formation of absolute monarchy in Europe was not by any means limited to the largest states, gradually transforming themselves into nations. The same model of government began also to be adopted by regional princedoms, which strengthened their independence after the failure of attempts to unify Germany and Italy. Saxony, Prussia, Bavaria and Piedmont all in one way or another formed their own variants of absolute monarchy, despite their limited funds, territories and populations.

Throughout Europe, from Portugal to Russia, events took place that altered the nature and form of existence of the state. The bureaucratic system rested on an increasingly unified system of education, and local dialects were replaced by the dominance of a single literary language, which at times needed to be put in order through conscious work. The transformation of military force into a monopoly of the central government was finally achieved toward the end of the seventeenth century. This became possible thanks to a rapid increase in state revenues. Vast spending on the military was made possible by the flow of precious metals from the Americas and by the rapid economic expansion in Europe that was associated with it. The purchasing power of money declined, but the ability of governments to concentrate financial resources in their hands increased noticeably.

Though never regarded as sufficient, state incomes had increased to the point where they allowed governments to borrow money in significantly greater amounts. Even where the state was an unreliable and insolvent debtor, its constant need for credit in and of itself aided the expansion of the banking sector, while the requirement for funds, extorted from the rural population for the payment of debts, accelerated the development of the money economy.

As the size of armies grew, their structures and tactics were altered sharply. The social composition of the forces, and the principle on which they were recruited, underwent changes. The armies were prepared if necessary to wage war far from home, provided their wages were paid conscientiously. The problem, however, lay in finding military professionals. 'Peasants and the unemployed,' an English historian writes, 'might well be prepared to join the army as a form of subsistence when the alternative was starvation, but they could not provide a trained and experienced elite army.'[66] In the search for professionals to serve in elite units many governments were obliged to turn to foreigners, and it was from these people that strike forces were made up in France, Poland and Russia. Small German states, Scotland and Switzerland supplied recruits to the armies of larger powers. A sort of general European market took shape; during their military careers officers and often common soldiers as well repeatedly changed not just their place of service, but also the country beneath whose banners they fought.

The Swiss played a particular role in this market. Since the fifteenth century they had been famed as fearless and disciplined warriors. Hiring themselves out to foreign monarchs, they were sought after not just as experienced warriors, but also as bearers of definite tactical principles. To a degree, the Scots were able to compete with the Swiss in the market for mercenaries. Numerous impoverished members of the Scottish petty nobility, who had grown up in a country experiencing incessant internal conflicts and border clashes with neighbouring England, readily found a place for themselves in foreign armies. Between the Swiss and the Scots there was even a sort of division of markets; the former hired themselves out for service in Spain, France and the Italian states, and later in Austria, while the latter were more inclined to seek their fortunes in Eastern and Northern Europe.[67]

Nevertheless, elite detachments made up of foreigners were expensive. The solution for the countries involved lay in forming their own regiments, imbued with the training and tactics of the foreign mercenaries. During the sixteenth century the infantry in Spain, and later in other states as well, was reorganised on the Swiss model. The same occurred during the seventeenth century in Muscovy, where 'foreign formation' regiments were organised under the command of Germans and Scots.

In a certain sense the mercenary armies of the sixteenth and seventeenth centuries represented a step backward compared to the military formations of the late fifteenth century. The state had taken the road of creating regular armies to replace feudal militias, but the royal authorities preferred to recruit expensive contingents of mercenaries rather than putting peasants under arms – obvious proof that the authorities sensed the contradictions of society rather acutely. To the extent that the bond between the armed forces and the state strengthened, their alienation from society increased. Where the government was prepared to rely on its own rural population in forming an army, the possibility appeared of creating something like a national army, and the effects of this were immediately apparent on the battlefield; it was for this reason that the Spanish forces in the sixteenth century were invincible in Western Europe, while in the seventeenth century the Swedes became a threat to the whole European north-east. Later, the Russian and Prussian armies were built according to the Swedish military system, and became the most capable armed forces on the continent in the eighteenth century.

In Germany the recruiting of mercenary soldiers, which had flourished during the Thirty Years War, not only failed to stop once the war ended but turned into something like a sector of the economy, a variety of commercial service provided by petty princedoms to the more powerful states of Europe. The most blatant example of such activity was to be seen in the small state of Hesse, where by the middle of the eighteenth century fully 7 per cent of the population was under arms.[68] The main purchaser of Hessian soldiers was Britain, which made particular use of them in its war against the rebellious colonists during the American revolution.

Maintaining discipline among the troops remained a major problem, with which all military leaders were forced to deal with greater or lesser success. In the Middle Ages plunder had been considered a natural part of military operations. It was a form of economic warfare, playing the same role as the bombing of cities and industrial installations during the twentieth century. Often, it was deliberately organised and instigated by the commanders, who entrusted their units with laying waste to hostile territory. The expensive mercenary army of the early modern era stole more, and more systematically, than the armies of the Middle Ages, since it had a greater need of material support. If the state lacked money to pay its soldiers, it could ensure peace in the ranks by encouraging the pillage of alien territory. But this inevitably told on the morale of its forces, whose fighting qualities declined. Moreover, soldiers who received permission to plunder enemy territory were liable to act in the same way in friendly regions. For the peaceful population, the mercenary armies which by the end of the sixteenth century had replaced feudal militias in Europe represented an even greater danger than the troops of the past. Albrecht Wallenstein (Valdštejn), the victorious commander of the imperial armies early in the Thirty Years War, not only encouraged the systematic pillage of occupied lands, but also ran a sort of protection racket, allowing cities and territories to buy off the marauders for money. In 1625, when the emperor was short of funds for continuing the war, Wallenstein, who possessed a fortune of thirty millions, offered to create for him an army of 50,000 men at his own expense, on the condition of course that he himself would be its commander-in-chief. The imperial administration promised to pay off the debt and allowed Wallenstein to extract funds from enemy lands to maintain his forces. With this army the imperial commander-in-chief defeated the partisan detachments of Peter Ernst von Mansfeld, sacked Mecklenburg, Pomerania, Schleswig and Holstein, and with the help of another imperial general, Count Johann Tilly, defeated the Danes and forced them to conclude a peace treaty at Lübeck in 1629. Wallenstein's campaigns, accompanied by the ravaging of occupied territories, caused catastrophic damage to the German economy, but enriched him personally to such an extent that the emperor began to fear the powerful general. Making use of defeats suffered by Wallenstein's army in battle with the Swedes, the imperial administration accused him of treason and dismissed him from leadership of the army. Soon afterward, the disgraced general was assassinated in Eger Castle in Bohemia.

The organised marauding of hired armies testified to the inability of their commanders to solve the problem of logistics. An exception here was the well paid and disciplined Dutch army, which in Europe, however, did not fight outside the borders of its own territory; it was for this reason that the bourgeois of Amsterdam and other commercial cities did not begrudge money for the soldiers' wages. In other theatres of war the situation changed only when the regiments of the Swedish King Gustavus Adolphus arrived from the northern shores of the Baltic. These soldiers astonished their contemporaries not only with their courage and cool-headedness, but also with their completely unaccustomed behaviour: they neither raped nor pillaged.

The state and accumulation

Carrying out political unification, the absolute monarchy resolved a crucial economic task for capital, forming and expanding a unified internal market. Transferring goods and procuring the supplies essential for production became far simpler, as did organising ties between producers and consumers and settling legal disputes. Of course, absolutism almost never managed to carry out the task of bureaucratic unification to its fullest extent. The system had to take account of traditional feudal liberties, of holdovers from old relationships, of the traditional borders and statutes of provinces, of family privileges of the aristocracy and of other circumstances inherited from the Middle Ages. These were restrictions of which the state could not rid itself completely without putting in question its own legitimacy; the work of the state in putting the bureaucracy in order was to be completed only by the French Revolution and Napoleon Bonaparte, and even then, not in all parts of Europe.

Assessing the role played by absolutism in the history of the West, Marx and Engels stressed that the bureaucratic state was no longer completely feudal, representing more of a compromise between old and new ruling classes. Engels termed a balancing-act between the landed nobility and the bourgeoisie a 'basic condition' for absolute monarchy, stressing that due to this equilibrium real power lay in the hands of the bureaucracy, 'standing outside and, so to speak, above society'. This lent the state 'an appearance of independence in relation to society'.[69] This kind of state, autonomous in relation to the bourgeoisie, proved repeatedly to be a highly effective tool of capitalist modernisation, since it could impose decisions corresponding to the general strategic interests of capital on individual representatives of the bourgeoisie who might suffer from them in the short term.

Marx pointed out that the powerful bureaucratic mechanism of absolute monarchy prepared the way for the triumph of the bourgeoisie and hastened the decline of feudalism.[70] Mikhail Pokrovsky held a similar view. In his opinion it was not the nobility and aristocracy but the interests of commercial capital that determined the decisions taken by the imperial court in St Petersburg. From the 1930s, however, a different view triumphed in Soviet historical literature, and was later accepted without particular discussion by Western Marxists. Perry Anderson in his book *Lineages of the Absolutist State* refers to a 'consensus of a generation of Marxist historians, from England to Russia', rejecting the conclusions of the author of *Capital* and considering absolutism a form of feudal hegemony.[71] The main task of the absolutist state was seen as being 'to increase the efficacy of aristocratic rule in pinning down a non-servile peasantry into new forms of dependence and exploitation'.[72] The state was seen as having nothing to do with the formation and consolidation of capitalist relations: 'The Absolutist State was never an arbiter between the aristocracy and the bourgeoisie, still less an instrument of the nascent bourgeoisie against the aristocracy; it was the new political carapace of a threatened nobility.'[73]

The substantial service which Perry Anderson performed for historical science in Britain lay in his introduction, during the 1960s, of a series of Marxist ideas into the everyday usage of the academic mainstream. But Anderson propagated historical materialism in the ossified and dogmatic form which it acquired after the liquidation of the 'Pokrovsky school' and after the general ideological purge conducted in the Soviet Union between 1932 and 1937.

Like the official Soviet historians of the second half of the 1930s, Anderson proceeds from the presumption that feudalism and capitalism were politically incompatible, supposing that the interests of the aristocracy and the bourgeoisie were invariably opposed. If such an approach is taken, not only do the economic and political reforms in Russia become impossible to explain, but also most of the measures enacted by 'enlightened absolutism' in Prussia and Austria. These reforms are viewed by the writers in question as forced concessions to outside circumstances. Meanwhile, the fact is lost from view that in many cases these reforms were imposed on society from above, and governments had continually to overcome massive popular resistance, often resorting to violence.

The truth is that it needed a considerable intellectual effort not to notice the obvious connection, appearing at every step, between the policies of the state and the interests of capital, especially since Marx had pointed unambiguously to this connection and had provided arguments to back up his conclusion. Neither the bourgeoisie nor the old landed aristocracy remained unchanged throughout the process of transformation. While England and Holland in the sixteenth and seventeenth centuries might be thought of as examples of the 'democratic' rise of the bourgeoisie, in France the process took on quite different forms, especially after the absolute monarchy had established itself there, coping with the Fronde rebellions and crushing both aristocratic resistance and attempts at democratic change. But this does not in any way signify that the political influence of the bourgeoisie did not grow stronger in Paris, in parallel with its increased political weight in London.

On the continent the absolutist state represented not only a compromise between the feudal aristocracy, the bourgeoisie and the masses of the petty landed nobility, for whom integration into the military-political apparatus of power presented far greater opportunities than exploiting the impoverished peasants on their small estates. It was also an ideal tool for simultaneously resolving two tasks that were interlinked, but which pointed in different directions: forming nations, and creating military-commercial empires.

Assessing the changes that occurred in the course of the sixteenth and seventeenth centuries, Immanuel Wallerstein draws the conclusion: 'By 1650 the basic structures of historical capitalism as a viable social system had been established and consolidated.'[74] This is disputed categorically by Neil Davidson, who reminds us that the bourgeois classes and the corresponding social relations in Europe at that time were extremely weak, and that even the Dutch Republic earned money 'servicing the existing feudal regimes'.[75] It could, however, be said with equal justice that the feudal regimes of all Europe served the accumulation of capital in Holland. This thesis, in itself perfectly valid, paradoxically confirms Wallerstein's argument. Capitalism took shape initially as a world system, and it was only later that national 'models' of bourgeois society became consolidated on its basis.

The weakness of the bourgeoisie in each particular country was tied directly to the development of the world-system as a whole. It was only the state, holding the position of hegemon in the nascent system, that could allow itself the luxury of a rounded, fully-fledged bourgeois development. The world-system took shape through the redistribution of resources and the integration of economic processes occurring in diverse regions of the world. As a result, societies that were still feudal in their structure were drawn into the global process of capitalist accumulation. This logic has been extensively studied and proven by twentieth-century researchers with relation to the countries of the capitalist periphery. The greater the resources that are drawn into capitalist development, the more they are used for global redistribution, and the less the resources that remain available to local capitalism and the local bourgeoisie. But in the sixteenth and seventeenth centuries the system was still in its process of formation, and the division of roles between centre and periphery was far from having assumed its final shape. To a considerable degree, the redistribution of resources also took place between the countries of the centre, benefiting the state that was in the position of hegemon. For precisely this reason, the struggle for hegemony within the still only partially formed system immediately took on a furious character, involving conflicts first between England and Holland and then between England and France.

Meanwhile, in the seventeenth century the model on which the world economic system had been constructed during the preceding epoch itself entered into crisis. The flow of precious metals that poured into Europe after the discovery of the Americas led to accelerated economic development and made it possible to pay for rapidly growing imports from Asia. But this was not its whole impact; as with any rapid increase in the quantity of money, the appearance in the markets of the West of gold and silver in unprecedented quantities first stimulated inflation, and then destabilised the social system.

Prices rose throughout Europe, but unevenly. Naturally, they rose more rapidly in Spain than in other countries. The prices for wheat can be taken as an example. Researchers note that 'while in England its price rose during the sixteenth century by 155 per cent, in Spain it rose by 556 per cent.'[76] Accordingly, there was also a redistribution of real incomes. Under the conditions of a price revolution, the buying power of Spanish workers fell by approximately a third, while in some other countries living standards rose.

The importing of silver and gold from the Americas to Europe via the Spanish possessions reached a peak in the years from 1591 to 1595, after which it began steadily to decline. The diminishing flow of silver was one of the factors characterising the 'crisis of the seventeenth century'. The opportunities for development through the plunder of new colonies were being exhausted.

Nevertheless the 'price revolution', despite all the drawbacks associated with the devaluation of money, was a powerful factor in the accumulation of capital. A rapid redistribution of financial resources occurred, both between countries and regions and among social layers. The classes associated with the land, including both the feudal elite and the peasantry, could not increase their incomes abruptly, and as a result suffered from every new spiral of inflation. But commercial capital benefited, along with everyone who was linked in one way or another to the exploitation of the colonies.

The increased abundance of commercial capital could not fail to have a huge transformative influence on production. As the commercial sector developed and grew stronger, it brought about a continuing redistribution of resources. This was not solely, and by no means always, redistribution from the future countries of the 'periphery' to those of the 'centre', but occurred primarily between traditional production and the nascent capitalist sector. This redistribution took place both on a global scale, and also within the countries of the West, altering the relationship of forces there between the various economic structures and social groups.

Trade began to shape the international division of labour, and along with it, the new political map of the world. It was not by chance that Adam Smith in the first chapters of his book devoted such close attention to this matter. His *Inquiry into the Nature and Causes of the Wealth of Nations* begins with the chapter 'On the Division of Labour', in which the Scots economist not only demonstrates the need for the division of society into classes, but also shows, long before Marx and Lenin, the link between these classes and the distribution of productive functions. While the discussion at first concerns the distribution of tasks between the workers in an enterprise, Smith later turns his attention to the division of labour between economic sectors and regions.[77]

Describing the relationship between the capitalist and non-capitalist economies, Rosa Luxemburg wrote:

> In the first half of the nineteenth century surplus value in Britain emerged from the process of production mainly in the form of cotton fabrics. But the material elements of the capitalisation of surplus value – cotton from the slave states of North America or bread (the means of subsistence for English workers) from the granaries of serfholding Russia – despite representing a surplus product, were by no means surplus value. The degree to which capitalist accumulation depends on these means of production, themselves not produced in the capitalist manner, is shown by the cotton crisis in Britain, which was the result of the halting of work on plantations as a consequence of the Civil War, or by the crisis in the European linen industry, which was caused by the ending of shipments of flax from serf-holding Russia because of the Eastern War. One need only recall the role played by the shipping of peasant-produced grain – that is, of grain not produced in capitalist fashion – in feeding the masses of industrial workers of Europe (thus comprising an element of variable capital) in order to understand how strongly capitalist accumulation, thanks to its material elements, is in reality associated with non-capitalist social strata.[78]

Creating an international division of labour, commercial capital organises and reorganises the world in accordance with the demands of the bourgeois economy, and carries on production whose sole aim is the obtaining of surplus value.

Capitalism, however, is not just production based on the exploitation of hired labour, but also, and above all, production subordinated to the logic of the accumulation of capital. Meanwhile, the accumulation of capital in manufacturing industry in the sixteenth and seventeenth centuries, not to speak of the preceding period, was slow and weak. This impelled the American historian Robert Brenner to conclude that capitalism has an agrarian origin (as also discussed by Marx in the first volume of *Capital*).[79] Analysing English society on the eve of its revolution, Brenner notes that as well as the 'new nobility' that had arisen thanks to the seizure and apportioning of monastery lands during the Reformation under Henry VIII, the old landed aristocracy too had been drawn into the new bourgeois organisation of the economy. But the 'new nobility' and the old aristocracy had been drawn into the market in different fashion, and their modes of existence in the changing society were different. Otherwise, they would simply have merged into a single social group, as happened after the 'Glorious Revolution' of 1688.

Not only was English society to an important degree bourgeois by the beginning of the seventeenth century, but the state as well was no longer entirely feudal. Hence in the historical sense the English revolution was not so much a victory of the bourgeois over the feudal order, or a liberation of the bourgeoisie from a 'feudal' state, as a victory of industrial over commercial capitalism. Of course, the meaning of the change that was occurring remained impossible for those involved in the events to grasp fully, especially since commercial capital did not represent a monolithic social bloc. But one way or another, the system of commercial capitalism that had taken shape in the course of the fifteenth and sixteenth centuries suffered a collapse during the crisis of the seventeenth century, as a result of the shocks of the Thirty Years War, of the English revolution and of the Anglo-Dutch wars. The old model, dominated by bourgeois exploitation of the traditional economy, was replaced by a new one based on the direct exploitation of hired labour by capital. Imposed simultaneously was a division between the 'centre', where the new productive relations had triumphed, and the 'periphery', which remained the province of commercial capital. This, properly speaking, was also the basis for a new political compromise within the framework of the developing bourgeois class.

This transformation was not the result of a smooth social evolution or of a process of progressive economic development, but the outcome of an acute political crisis, accompanied by civil war, terror and dictatorship. Political crisis was experienced not only in England, where it took the ultimate form of a revolution, but also in France, beset by the chaos of the Fronde, and in Holland, where the republic was shaken by a series of uprisings and cataclysms. In Naples and Catalonia the old authorities were overthrown by popular revolts that were suppressed only with great difficulty. In the same category were the Time of Troubles, the Schism and other shocks of the 'age of rebellion' in Muscovy. In Germany, meanwhile, the Thirty Years War was something far greater than a military clash of protestant and Catholic princedoms.

The European disturbances of the seventeenth century, despite the presence of an aristocratic element, were inseparable from the history of the development of capitalism. The political crisis arose from economic causes, reflecting the difficulties encountered by bourgeois development across the vast expanse from England to Russia. The successes of commercial capitalism soon led to the exhaustion of the seemingly limitless resources that became accessible thanks to geographical discoveries.

The growing crisis could be overcome only through active intervention by the state, oriented toward the development of production. Military orders aided the development of industry, and royal factories were among the first examples of large, well organised productive enterprises. Governments spent money on new technologies and on training workers, counteracting the decline of the market that became increasingly evident as the stream of silver from the Americas began to dry up. At first, however, this was done unconsciously and haphazardly, and with the state failing to cope with the tasks confronting it, the result was that the economic crisis became a political one. In the absence of changes to the structures of the state, and a radical review of government policies, a transition to new forms of capital accumulation would have been impossible. It was due to the efforts and organising work of the state that the market was transformed into a system of private entrepreneurship, and private entrepreneurship into the dominant mode of production. The transformation of the bourgeois economic *structure* into an economic *system* took place as a result of prolonged, methodical and large-scale exertions by the state.

It was only toward the end of the seventeenth century, and through the efforts of Jean-Baptiste Colbert, that in France such measures took on the character of a systematic policy which in hindsight was given the name of mercantilism. The European state was not simply the product of economic and social development, but was itself an important factor in the changes. The state shaped capitalism through its own policies, and along with capitalism, transformed itself.

Pirates and monopolies

Marx repeatedly stressed the predatory nature of the primary accumulation of capital. The property of the peasants was expropriated by landowners as the latter made the shift from the feudal to the bourgeois mode of exploitation. In the countries where the Reformation had been victorious the royal authorities confiscated the property of the monasteries, in Catholic southern Europe the state at every step confiscated the assets of Jews and protestants, and revolutionary regimes seized the estates of vanquished aristocrats. In conquered America and in the countries of Asia, seizure of the property of the native population became an everyday practice, and in Africa the seizure as slaves of the people themselves occurred on a massive scale. Later, in the colonial countries and in Eastern Europe during the period of the restoration of capitalism such actions would be repeated, unrestricted by any consideration of law or morality. But the violence that was applied to gathering capital into the hands of new owners could be crowned with success only if it were supported by the state. Unless the results of plunder were legalised, *booty* would never become *capital*.

The decisive factor involved in primitive accumulation, therefore, was not individual initiative (whether in the form of 'constructive' entrepreneurial activity, or of robbery and violence), but state policy, which provided the ultimate sanction for the redistribution of resources and property that was taking place. Respect for property rights became a sacred principle only when the redistribution had finished, and capital had completely crushed, subordinated and digested all other economic systems. In the countries of the periphery, where a multi-system economy has persisted throughout bourgeois history, brute force and the violation of civil rights – property rights and those of the person – remain an everyday part of people's collective existence, not in spite of capitalism but because of it.

Capitalist trade not only needed to be defended militarily, but in the process of the accumulation of capital, was inseparable from offensive operations. In the course of these operations territory and resources required for the development of commercial enterprises were seized, political regimes impeding trade by European interests were overthrown, competition was suppressed, and social relations were forcibly transformed.

The combining of trade with war and pillage came easiest of all to the sea pirates of the sixteenth and seventeenth centuries, but it should not be forgotten that it was from pirate flotillas that both commercial enterprises and the naval forces of England and Holland later arose. The problem with pirates lay in the fact that the scale of their activity quickly ceased to correspond to the needs of the accumulation of capital. By the mid-seventeenth century the free enterprise of the pirates had proved uncompetitive compared to the organised trade defended and supported by the state. By the early eighteenth century piracy, organised with state support by the bourgeoisie in the sixteenth and seventeenth centuries as a variety of entrepreneurship, had been replaced by 'primitive' sea-borne brigandage, against which the Royal Navy, founded by former pirates, now mounted an active struggle. As historians note, the suppression of piracy carried out by the British Navy in the mid-eighteenth century became possible thanks to a 'change of relationship between merchant and state'.[80]

The economic reorganisation carried out by Western capital in Asia, and simultaneously in Europe itself, would have been impossible without political changes and armed force. Needless to say, it was not only Europeans who took part in this process. Asian commercial elites put up active resistance to European influence, competed with the Europeans, engaged in price-cutting, and without hesitation resorted to provocations and violence. But in the first place the Asian merchants were trying to defend the status quo, while the Europeans were seeking changes, and second, the Europeans were using violence far more systematically, skilfully, and for the most part effectively. The Europeans created a system in which, as later historians have noted, 'the use of violence was subordinated to the rational pursuit of profit'.[81] They posed precise goals, which were pursued through the simultaneous use of military and commercial means. It was this *combination of market methods with violence that created the capitalist world economy,* and achieving this would not have been possible without the coordinating role of the state. The latter not only subsidised, supported and organised trade, regulated and adjusted the workings of the market, invested money in new, expensive production and acted as a client and advisor for capital. The state was also unhesitating in employing violence in the interests of capital, in creating armies and navies, and in sending soldiers and bureaucrats to distant countries to protect the trading interests of the rising bourgeoisie and to defend the markets the bourgeoisie was creating.

Among the instruments used by the state for regulating the economy in absolutist Europe were monopoly companies, that received exclusive rights from the king to take over new markets and to establish new economic sectors. These companies were also armed organisations that had received from their governments the right to use force.

The most famous of these corporations were the Dutch and British East India Companies. The history of trading monopolies, however, begins well before this – with the Muscovy Company, founded in London in 1554 with the personal support of Elizabeth I of England and her close ally Ivan the Terrible. New companies followed: the Turkey Company in 1578; the Eastland Company, set up in 1579 to conduct trade in the Baltic; and the Levant Company, founded in 1581. It was only later that the East India and Africa Companies arose in England. The colonisation of America also required the establishing of state–private monopolies – the Bermuda Company, the Providence Island Company, and the Massachusetts Bay Company. It was only later under Cromwell that the colonies, originally founded on the basis of monopoly charters, were opened to all who wished to develop them.

The oldest English colony, that of Virginia, arose as a private–state joint venture and was founded in 1587. In the words of an early twentieth-century German historian, the Virginia Company from the legal point of view

> represented the most surprising institution ever to exist. Supreme rights over the colony lay with the company, which numbered among its members a large number of wealthy London merchants and influential persons … Virginia was not, therefore, a Crown colony. Nevertheless, the company's management was of such a type that it offered extremely wide scope for government interference.[82]

Such a complex and confused system of government might have seemed doomed to lead to catastrophic inefficiency and unending conflicts, but in practice, although disputes certainly arose, they were always resolved with relative ease. This ability to deal with problems quickly and comparatively painlessly can only be explained in one way: underlying the activity of everyone involved in the process was an obvious commonality of interests. This state of affairs compelled historians to conclude: 'The British Empire was primarily a product of private enterprise.'[83] But it is just as possible to draw the reverse conclusion: colonial entrepreneurship was linked in the closest fashion with the construction of empire.

The experience of the English was assimilated by the Dutch, who thanks to an energetic combination of private initiative and aggressive state policy achieved impressive successes. The year 1621 saw the founding of the Dutch West India Company (WIC). Initially, the company engaged mainly in piracy and smuggling. In 1674, under threat of bankruptcy, the WIC was reorganised into a company specialising in slave trading, though contraband in South America and sugar plantations in Surinam also brought it considerable profit. It devised the three-sided trade in the Atlantic that linked together European manufacturing, the supplying of slaves from Africa, and the plantation economy in America.[84]

As a base of support for the WIC in America, the settlement of New Amsterdam was established; later, it was captured by the English, and under a peace treaty concluded in Breda in 1667 became part of England's overseas empire under the name of New York. Following on the heels of the Dutch, the English and French merchants developed their own trading operations in the same Atlantic triangle. The Dutch East India Company – founded even earlier, in 1602 – served in its turn as a model for imitation in England and the countries of continental Europe.

Observing that competition between Dutch merchants was weakening their positions in relation to the English, the government of the United Provinces pushed for a merger of the rival enterprises into a single company. In 1598 numerous competing commercial firms were combined into the United East India Company (Vereenigde Ost-Indische Compagnie – VOC). In 1600 the Great Pensionary (chief minister) of the Province of Holland, Johan van Oldenbarneveldt, secured the formation of a special commission to study the problem. Talks were conducted at the highest level, with the direct participation of the later Prince of Orange, Maurits van Oranje-Nassau, who held the republic's highest post of *stadhouder*. The merger finally took place in 1602.

When the forthcoming founding of the East India Company was announced in Amsterdam, a Dutch historian records, 'real enthusiasm' seized the city.[85] Of more than 1,000 shareholders, only some 84 who had put up 10,000 guilders or more were genuinely large-scale investors in the firm.[86] Most of the shareholders were artisans, small shopkeepers and even wage workers who invested usually about 60 guilders.[87]

The company received the right not only to trade but also to wage war, to build fortressses, to found colonies, to coin money and to conclude agreements in the name of the Netherlands Republic. Initially, decisions of the company management (the *Heren XVII*) were confirmed by the Estates-General, but by the end of the seventeenth century the company and the state were so inseparable that there was felt to be no need of this. In essence, one historian notes, the VOC 'was identical with the state'.[88] The VOC represented one of the first joint-stock companies; its shares, like those of the British East India Company, were quoted on stock-exchanges. But both companies were founded through decisions of government bodies, on the basis of official charters endorsed by the respective parliaments. State functions were privatised and farmed out to contractors, but at the same time the official authorities were directly included in the administering and coordinating of entrepreneurial activity.

In 1648, taking advantage of the end of the Thirty Years War, the VOC hired a large number of soldiers who had lost their employment in Europe and unleashed an offensive against the Portuguese possessions in Asia. The conquest of Ceylon was completed, and the Malabar and Coromandel coasts in India were seized.

The historian G.J. Ames notes that the Dutch system 'became a mirror image of the *Estado da India* more than a capitalist rejection of it'.[89] It was this ability of the Dutch bourgeoisie to put the institutions and traditions forged by Portuguese absolutism to effective use that lay behind the Dutch political and economic success in Asia. The strong state did not exclude the development of private enterprise, but on the contrary, was an important condition for it.

The VOC 'conducted itself as a Prince in Asia, but its princely head was carried by the body of a merchant'.[90] Despite the company's quasi-state functions, its main activity was commerce. In the VOC's budget non-commercial income (from taxes, customs duties and tribute) never exceeded 10 per cent of its overall revenues from Asia.[91] Meanwhile, its commercial success was closely tied to its political and military strength.

Although the Dutch had followed the example of the English, it was the activity of the VOC that became the model for a large number of analogous enterprises founded during the seventeenth century. In 1627 Richelieu founded a company to exploit the riches of Canada (New France). In 1664 Colbert established two companies at the same time, the *Compagnie des Indes orientales* and the *Compagnie des Indes occidentales,* to operate in the East and West Indies respectively. Later came the founding of a number of smaller companies, and in 1723 the *Conseil des Indes,* the Council of the Indies, was formed to reorganise and coordinate their activities. Similar companies were established in Scotland, Denmark, Sweden, Prussia and Russia (in the case of the last two, without notable success). In Sweden in the course of the seventeenth century a whole series of trading companies were organised on the initiative of the central authorities. These firms included the West Indies Company in 1640 and the Levant Company in 1646. The Sugar Company was founded in 1647; the Guinea Company, known also as the Swedish African Company, in 1649 ; and the Tobacco Company in 1651.

The aim of each company was to limit competition between the merchants of its respective country in order to raise their collective competitiveness in relation to merchants from elsewhere. From the beginning, however, the role of the companies was not to be reduced to regulating trade and ending 'intra-national' competition. Founded with state support, the companies from the outset enjoyed political opportunities which private entrepreneurs did not, and bore a definite political responsibility to their governments. Even the Muscovy Company, which lacked a military-political organisation, engaged vigorously in diplomatic activity within Russia, provided credit for the external expansion of the Romanovs, and helped the tsar to recruit troops and buy weapons. In similar fashion, the heads of the Istanbul bureaus of the Levant Company and Turkey Company held the status not only of trade representatives but also of royal ambassadors. Nevertheless the powers of the English commercial companies, including even the East India Company, were not at first as extensive as those of the Dutch VOC, which could independently declare war and conclude peace.

The fact that the monopoly companies combined military with trading functions not only allowed the bourgeoisie to make direct use of armed force to carry out its commercial tasks, but also lightened the tasks of the government. The bourgeois enterprises beyond the seas appeared as attractive additions to the traditional sources of revenue. States protected the monopoly companies and gave them constant support, supplying them with technology, finance and information. The French navy, the *Marine de guerre,* not only took part in guaranteeing the safety of the new Atlantic colonies, but also in their organisation and even, together with the merchants of Dieppe and Le Havre, in their financing.[92]

It may be said that the state (itself still far from bourgeois) willingly entrusted its functions and powers to private business. But the private entrepreneurs in turn were most successful in achieving their goals when they acted in the name of the state and on its behalf, with the option in times of extreme need of attracting the government's military strength and financial resources to their side. This closeness to the authorities became a key condition for implementing ambitious commercial plans, which in turn were often inseparable from political strategies. Evaluating the role of states in the amassing of large fortunes in the sixteenth and seventeenth centuries, Robert Brenner speaks of 'political accumulation'.[93]

Governments protected the monopoly rights of companies not only within their own countries, but also on the international level. When Denmark in 1616 established its own East India Company and tried to attract foreign capital to the firm, England and Holland not only forbade their subjects to subscribe to the Danish shares, but also threatened Copenhagen with war.

The activity of the monopoly companies has been subjected in hindsight to withering criticism from economists and historians who since the late eighteenth century have presented them as obstacles to the development of competition, and as barriers on the road of innovation and private enterprise. Among the most furious critics of monopoly trading companies was Adam Smith. 'Such exclusive companies ... ,' the Scots economist argued, 'are nuisances in every respect; always more or less inconvenient to the countries in which they are established, and destructive to those which have the misfortune to fall under their government.'[94] As a conscientious economist Smith was of course forced to recognise that the risks and expenses associated with colonial trade were often so high that organising such commerce on the basis of a free competition of capitals, without the help of such companies, would simply be impossible. But from this, he drew only the conclusion that in such a case the venture should not go ahead. If the lack of a monopoly company meant that a particular country could not conduct trade directly with the East Indies, then the trade should be rejected. In other words, countries that did not have a sufficiently high level of capitalist development should reconcile themselves to a commercial monopoly of Britain and the Netherlands, with this monopoly exercised not by specific companies, but by the British and Dutch bourgeoisies as a whole.

It is easy enough to see that when Smith directed his invective against the East India Company the position of Europeans in the countries of the East was already strong, the political and military difficulties had been resolved, and the markets had been opened. In this regard the attitude to the activity of the East India Company expressed by another British bourgeois thinker, Edmund Burke, is significant. In the 1780s Burke was famed for his wrathful speeches against Warren Hastings, who headed the administration of the East India Company in Bengal. Burke unmasked the tyranny and abuses of the British functionaries, their venality and lawlessness.

Nevertheless, biographers of Burke cannot help but acknowledge a certain inconsistency in his speeches. One of these biographers remarks that until 1773 'we find Burke, again and again, defending the East India Company'.[95] When the government tried to raise the question of limiting the dividends paid to company shareholders, Burke protested furiously, declaring that 'there is nothing like this to be found in the Code of Laws in any Civilised Country upon Earth – you are going to cancel the great line which distinguishes free Government.'[96]

The evolution of Burke's views reflects the general development of the situation in India. In the 1760s the struggle for control of the subcontinent had still been under way, and the position of the British in Bengal was not yet entirely secure. But by the end of the century the situation had changed; British merchants could now conduct business freely in India under the protection of a strong army, and no less important, of their own ships, having secured recognition of European legal norms by their 'native' partners and competitors. The attitude to the Company had changed accordingly. The time had come when the fruits of its victories could be enjoyed not just by its shareholders but by the entire entrepreneurial class.

In the sixteenth and seventeenth centuries, and even in the early eighteenth century, the picture had been completely different. If the Europeans in Asia had acted in line with the recommendations published with hindsight by Adam Smith, trading with the East would have been beyond the capabilities not just of individual countries, but of the West as a whole. Smith's misconception reveals the overall problem which liberal economic thinkers confronted throughout the next two centuries: while laying bare the inept handling of various objectives under the conditions of state control and monopolism, they were forced to remain silent about the fact that in any other circumstances the objectives involved would simply not have been attained. To the degree that liberal thought from the mid-eighteenth century had been inclined to depict economic laws as natural, and as unrelated to forms of social organisation, to the mode of production or to the specific conditions of social existence, the thinkers consciously let slip from their view the historical evolution of the market, along with the real circumstances under which various structures had arisen. Remaining even further outside their field of interest were the political moves with whose help market relations had in practice become dominant.

Capitalism, meanwhile, is not a competition of goods but a competition of capitals. The player who is able to concentrate greater resources wins out in the competitive struggle regardless of how effective his or her actions might be from the economic and organisational points of view. State support is thus a crucially important requirement for any private corporation that encounters foreign competition on the world market.

Support may be provided either by the 'home' state or by the 'native' state on whose territory market competition occurs. Issuing government orders and guaranteeing the rights of corporations was also a common practice in the countries of the future periphery; an example is provided by the *firmans* of the Great Moguls, on which the same British East India Company constantly relied. Serving to incorporate foreign corporations into the system of local power and administration, these decrees not only strengthened the place held by these corporations in the societies of the East, but also placed in their hands legal and to a degree even administrative tools with whose help foreign capital began to transform the societies concerned.

The monopoly companies that had arisen within the framework of the feudal system continued to operate both in bourgeois Holland and in parliamentary England following the revolutions in these countries. The corporations concerned played a vital role in organising the market, carrying out functions with which tens and hundreds of independent entrepreneurs could not have coped. The monopoly firms ensured a concentration of capital, lowered commercial risk, imposed general rules of commerce, sorted out relations between suppliers and customers, and accepted losses which independent entrepreneurs could not have borne. Their armed forces imposed a uniform *compulsion to the market,* forcing native populations to produce and offer for sale precisely those goods which European consumers needed. The companies developed and maintained relations with the authorities not only in the countries where their origins lay, but also in the new markets which they appropriated. Here, receiving political support and monopoly rights was especially important, since trade might otherwise have proved impossible, or so risky that it would not have justified the expense.

It was only after the market had been established, and the conditions for economic activity had become more favourable and, importantly, predictable, that the government began to come under pressure from entrepreneurs who were not receiving state privileges. The corporate elite put up resistance in turn, but its position quickly grew weaker, since by this time the corporations were not defending the general interests of capital, but merely their own interests.

In the West Indies the English crown met with these problems as early as the first half of the seventeenth century, when the 'new merchants' entered into conflict with the Stuarts, who were protecting the monopoly companies. The discontent of these 'new merchants', both in London and the colonies, became one of the factors contributing to the anti-monarchic revolution.[97] But in the East Indies, where the position of British capital was much weaker, the situation was harder to control, and foreign competition was tougher, the monopoly corporation not only maintained its status for a prolonged period after the revolution, but was not subjected to serious criticism at least until the second half of the eighteenth century.

The slave trade

The economic appropriation of the New World was the result not just of the energetic efforts and entrepreneurialism of the European settlers, but also of the labour of millions of African slaves, without whom production in the American colonies could not have reached the levels required by the world market. 'Slavery and the slave trade,' writes the British historian Robin Blackburn, ' ... turned out to be crucial to the whole enterprise of colonization in the Atlantic world. Quite apart from the direct trade in African slaves there was their critical contribution to gold trading, the maintenance of the coastal *feitorias* and the success of sugar-making.'[98]

Cotton, coffee, tobacco and other such products, together with sugar, were spread throughout Europe thanks to the labour of black slaves.

The Brazilian scholar Antonio Carlos Mazzeo notes that the plantation economy, founded on slave labour, would have been impossible without the existence of the capitalist market in Europe and of the corresponding international division of labour. The slave-owning economy of the New World 'in no way represents a distinct mode of production, existing outside capitalism; to the contrary, we are faced with a specific type of capitalism.'[99] This allowed Andre Gunder Frank to speak of the plantation economy as 'capitalist slavery'.[100]

The fact that the development of a new slavery coincided with the epoch of the 'second serfdom' in Russia and Eastern Europe (and also in Germany to the east of the Elbe) was by no means accidental. The cheap products of slave and serf labour were essential for subsidising free labour in the West, and this situation in turn acted as a key condition for the investment of capital in production. Without this Russian, African, Eastern European and South American 'subsidy', capitalist production in the West could scarcely have come to exist in the form in which we know it.

The formation of the new world economy and the development of commercial capitalism aided the revival of slavery as a recognised social institution on both sides of the Atlantic. As the creation of a new free world and the formation of liberal capitalism proceeded, slavery and the slave trade by the eighteenth century had taken on far greater dimensions than in the Mediterranean world of antiquity. 'Just as capitalist production cannot limit itself to the natural treasures and productive forces of the temperate zone,' Rosa Luxemburg wrote,

> but needs for its development to be able to exploit all countries irrespective of climate, so it cannot make do with the labour power of the white race alone. In order to make use of the zones of the earth in which members of the white race become unfit for work, capital needs other races; in sum, it needs the unrestricted possibility of exploiting all the labour power of the globe, in order with its help to set in motion all the productive forces of the earth, to the degree that this is possible within the framework of the production of surplus value.[101]

The sale of slaves was an important sector of Africa's trade during the Middle Ages. When the Portuguese moved into Africa, they followed on the heels of the Arabs. They succeeded in forging relationships with local rulers and with the chiefs of coastal tribes, and also with their commercial agents. The tribal elites drew considerable benefits from their position as intermediaries. European goods were exchanged for gold and slaves that had come from the depths of the continent.

The dicovery of America created a new demand and new markets for this live commodity, and the appearance on the scene of European entrepreneurs allowed the business to be put on a broad footing. The Europeans quickly worked out how to make use of their global advantages in order to trade on local markets. Hence cowrie shells, which took the place of money in West Africa, were now brought by the ton from the shores of the Indian Ocean in European vessels, and were exchanged for slaves. The latter began to be used by the Spanish to replace the Indians who were dying out on the islands of the Caribbean. It was the Portuguese, however, who devised an effective supply system, establishing stable relations of partnership with the African rulers and tribal chiefs. A lively trade in people developed in Senegal, spreading later to Guinea, Sierra Leone and all of West Africa. The Portuguese traveller Duarte Pacheco Pereira wrote home that business in these places was proceeding superbly: 'When the trade of the country was well ordered, it yielded 3,500 slaves and more, many tusks of ivory, gold, fine cotton cloths and much other merchandise.'[102]

During the period from the discovery of America to the beginning of the eighteenth century around a million and a half black slaves were brought to the New World, and around six million more in the course of the century that followed.[103] Improvements in shipbuilding and the appearance of means for ventilating ships allowed sharp increases in the quantity of human cargo delivered to the American plantations. In the seventeenth century one in five had died en route, but by the beginning of the eighteenth century the death rate during transportation had been reduced to 10 per cent, and by the end of the century to 5 per cent. Another factor aiding the expansion of the slave trade was the shift from the dominance of monopoly companies to the regime of free enterprise that had come to prevail in the Atlantic by the middle of the eighteenth century.[104]

By the early years of the eighteenth century the trade in slaves had become a more important part of Africa's economy than exports of gold or elephant ivory. Asian textiles were brought to the more developed regions of the African coast, where they were exchanged for live human commodities. European writers of the time noted that the African customers 'became very knowledgeable about general European and Asian products'.[105] As well as for textiles, there was demand in African markets for furniture and weapons. From Brazil, the Portuguese brought rum and tobacco.

In Africa, the development of the slave trade aided the emergence of a new Europeanised elite, made up of local aristocrats and merchants, as well as of mulattos who acted as middlemen. The mastering by the Europeans of the sea route along the coast of West Africa changed the economic situation within the continent. The states that had maintained themselves through their control over the caravan routes from the depths of the continent to the Mediterranean fell into decline and collapsed. The African sellers of slaves gradually familiarised themselves with the market economy, learning to extract the maximum profit from the growing demand. Prices for their living merchandise rose steadily.[106]

According to various estimates, the Portuguese between 1576 and 1591 shipped some 40–50,000 slaves to Brazil, mainly from the Congo and Angola.[107] But by 1600 the black population of Brazil did not exceed 15,000, most of them working on the sugar plantations. This gap between the number of slaves imported and their numbers on the plantations, the British historian Hugh Thomas notes, was linked to the extremely harsh conditions to which they were subjected, which led to massive mortality. On average, a slave was 'calculated' to have a life-span of ten years in the

New World, after which his value for labour purposes was exhausted.[108] From an economic point of view, it was more profitable to import grown slaves and to work them to an early death than it was to raise black children, who would need to be fed by the plantation for years before they became fit for work.

Slavery in the Americas was not at first the lot of black Africans alone. In the early sixteenth century convicts were sent to the Spanish colonies to serve their sentences. During the rule of Oliver Cromwell, Irishmen taken prisoner during the suppression of revolts were shipped by the English government to the West Indies. The American historian Basil Davidson notes that the white slaves enjoyed no privileges compared to the black ones.[109]

In the Portuguese colonies, a royal edict of 1519 regulated the conditions in which slaves could be kept, and required their obligatory conversion to Christianity before they were shipped. The latter provision was connected with the high mortality during the voyage; it was desirable that the slaves should die as Christians. Concern for the souls of Black slaves remained a vitally important question for European rulers. Compulsory baptism of slaves was also foreseen in an Act of 1648 issued by the French King Louis XIII.

Following on from the Portuguese, the Spanish, French, Dutch and English also took part in the slave trade.

In the market for labour in the Spanish colonies, a situation arose that was strikingly different from the one in Brazil. This was the result of mass migration to the colonies from Spain and Italy, where birth rates were high, and also of the presence of a large Indian population. The Spanish slave trade thus never reached the scale of its Portuguese counterpart. In 1574 the Spanish royal authorities, desperately short of money, levied a tax on slave-owners in the Americas, forcing them to pay a tax on every slave in their possession. Meanwhile a number of Catholic priests spoke out in condemnation of slavery and demanded the freeing of slave Christians, rendering the question substantially more complex from an ideological point of view.[110] It was only in the 1580s, when Portugal had come under the rule of Phillip II, that the slave trade trade in Spain's overseas possessions was set going in earnest with the help of experienced Portuguese merchants, financed by Genoese bankers.

By the early seventeenth century the French had consolidated their position on the coasts of Senegal and the Gambia, while the English had begun trading actively with Guinea. After some hesitation the Portuguese, who needed supplies of slaves for Brazil, began taking a tolerant attitude to the presence of other Europeans in Africa, on the condition that their commercial influence did not translate into political control over the territories concerned. Relations with the Dutch, who after winning their independence from the Habsburgs were at war with Spain and Portugal, developed in far more dramatic fashion. The Dutch managed to organise shipments of slaves as contraband, bypassing the official authorities. An important role in this was played by Portuguese Jews who had settled in Holland to avoid religious persecution. They knew the language and the market, retained commercial connections in Brazil and were used to circumventing official bans.

In 1620 a Dutch ship delivered the first shipment of black slaves to Virginia.[111] The English government also tried sending convicted criminals to Virginia to work on the plantations, but this practice aroused discontent among the settlers, since the convicts, once their sentences had expired, were freed and began living among the respectable citizens. Black slaves, by contrast, remained in bondage for life, and thus presented no problems.

As the Portuguese and Spanish yielded their leading positions in world politics to the Dutch, and later to the English and French, the relationship of forces in the slave trade changed as well. In 1660 the Royal African Company obtained the monopoly right to trade in this market. Late in the seventeenth century, when Spain, Portugal and Holland had lost their former might, the English government under pressure from independent merchants decided to end the monopoly. In 1698 it was partially abolished, and 14 years later, completely. Merchants from Bristol and Liverpool rushed to take part in this lucrative business, supplying slaves to the plantations of the West Indies. By 1740 Great Britain had become the world leader in the transportation of live human goods.[112]

The development of the British and French possessions in the Caribbean proceeded in such a way that the demand for African slaves exceeded the need for European colonists to settle on the islands. 'The development of the British and French Caribbean meant that the numbers of African slaves landed in the New World certainly exceeded the number of European immigrants in the period 1650–1700,' Robin Blackburn reports. 'But it was not until the eighteenth century that a huge disparity opened up with some six million African captives arriving in the New World, five or six times the number of Europeans.'[113] According to calculations by historians, delivering 9,000,000 slaves over the period from 1700 to 1850 required seizing around 21,000,000 people in Africa. Of these, about 7,000,000 were employed in Africa itself, carrying out the work of the military and commercial apparatus engaged in the supplying of slaves.[114]

The existence of the European colonies in Africa was tied directly to the development of the plantation economy of the West Indies. In the mid-eighteenth century the London *Gentleman's Magazine* argued enthusiastically that the African trading bases were of fundamental importance for the future of the empire: 'If through ignorance, negligence, caprice, or injudicious parsimony, these settlements should be lost, our sugar colonies must be lost also; because from these alone they are supplied with negroes, and without negroes they cannot subsist.'[115]

The slave trade was a key element in the mechanism of capital accumulation not only where the direct exploitation of slave labour was concerned. Like any business, this one required investments, organisation and credit. The colonies of New England that were free of slavery grew rich from these operations no less than the southern colonies where slave labour was employed directly.[116] Slavery was not simply an important element in the colonial economy, but also part of the free-market system that was taking shape. In business circles, the supplying of slaves was discussed in exactly the same terms as the supplying of any other commodity. Hence the British *Gentleman's Magazine* in the mid-eighteenth century reminded its readers of the need to attend to the 'annual supply of Negroes,' which had to be 'increased in an arithmetical series from 160 to 2500 in one year.'[117]

A system based on slavery required a strong state. This was not only for keeping a mass of enslaved people in submission, but also for the transporting and guarding of the living merchandise. Hence even the weakened Spanish and Portuguese empires remained a crucial element in the Atlantic economy. Powerful imperial institutions were essential for maintaining such a system. On this level the processes taking place in Russia, Virginia and Brazil were not just similar, and did not just occur in parallel, but to a degree were identical.

Notes

1 P. Sweezy, R. Hilton, M. Dobb et al., *The Transition from Feudalism to Capitalism*, London: Verso, 1976, p. 49.
2 Davidson links the failure of the Hussite movement to the Counter-Reformation that triumphed at the beginning of the Thirty Years War (see N. Davidson, *Discovering the Scottish Revolution, 1692–1746*, London: Pluto Press, 2003, p. 73.) But the defeat of the Czechs at the battle of Bílá Hora occurred in 1618, and the Hussite movement had arisen 200 years before that point.
3 A. Smith, *The Wealth of Nations*, New York: Bantam Classics, 2003, p. 814.
4 Ibid.
5 S.A. Nefedov, *Voyna i obshchestvo* [War and society], p. 28. С.А. Нефедов. Война и общество. Факторный анализ исторического процесса. История Востока. М.: Издательский дом «Территория будущего», 2008.
6 K. Marx and F. Engel's, *Sochineniya* [Works], vol. 21, p. 415.
7 Ibid., p. 413.
8 G. Veys, *Istoriya kul'tury* [History of culture], Moscow: EKSMO, 2002, p. 784.
9 C. Blair, *European Armour*, London: B.T. Batsford Ltd, 1958, p. 143.
10 Ibid.
11 H. Delbrück, *Istoriya voennogo iskusstva v ramkakh politicheskoy istorii* [A history of the art of war in the context of political history], St Petersburg: Nauka, 2001, vol. 3, p. 347.
12 See J.D. Tracy (ed.),*The Political Economy of Merchant Empires*, Cambridge: Cambridge University Press, 1991, p. 144.
13 As the British historian Richard Bonney notes, the official figures for the size of armies in the sixteenth and seventeenth centuries were of course somewhat exaggerated. The figures concealed the number of deserters, and the regiments included 'dead souls' whose pay was appropriated by the commanders. See R. Bonney, *The European Dynastic States: 1494–1660*, Oxford: Oxford University Press, 1992, pp. 352–7.
14 See T. Blanning, *The Pursuit of Glory. The Five Revolutions that Made Modern Europe: 1648–1815*, London: Penguin Books, 2008, pp. 289–90.
15 Ibid., p. 357.
16 *Istoriya, sotsiologiya, kul'tura narodov Afriki* [History, sociology and culture of the peoples of Africa], Moscow: Nauka, 1974, p. 120.
17 L.E. Kubbel', *Songayskaya derzhava. Opyt issledovaniya sotsial'no-politicheskogo stroya* [The Songhai empire. Findings of research into a socio-political system], Moscow: Nauka, 1974, p. 86.
18 See ibid., pp. 139, 140, 142. In the Western Sudan itself the shortage was of silver, and the relationship between the values of the two metals in the fifteenth century fluctuated around the level of 1:3 or even 1:1. See also p. 138.
19 Cited in Kubbel', *Songayskaya derzhava*, p. 89.
20 See Tracy, *Political Economy of Merchant Empires*, p. 104.

21 See A. Gunder Frank, *ReOrient: Global Economy in the Asian Age*, Berkeley, CA: University of California Press, 1998; G. Menzies, *1421: The Year China Discovered the World*, London: Bantam Press, 2002.

22 Tracy, *Political Economy of Merchant Empires*, p. 105.

23 Ibid., p. 102.

24 E. Shmidt, *Indiya, Tseylon, Indokitay* [India, Ceylon, Incochina], St Petersburg: Poligon, 2003, p. 217.

25 G.V. Scammell, *The First Imperial Age: European Overseas Expansion c. 1400–1715*, London: Unwin Hyman, 1989, p. 12.

26 G.J. Ames, *The Globe Encompassed. The Age of European Discovery: 1500–1700*. Upper Saddle River, NJ: Pearson, 2008, p. 5.

27 C.R. Boxer, *The Portuguese Sea-borne Empire, 1415–1815*, London: Hutchinson, 1969, p. 21.

28 See Ames. *Globe Encompassed*, p. 31.

29 See ibid., pp. 31–2.

30 G.V. Scammell. *The World Encompassed. The First European Maritime Empires*, London/ New York: Methuen, 1981, p. 234.

31 Ames, *Globe Encompassed*, p. 33.

32 *Istoriya, sotsiologiya, kul'tura narodov Afriki*, p. 253.

33 Tracy, *Political Economy of Merchant Empires*, p. 301.

34 See ibid., p. 310.

35 C.R. Boxer (ed.), *Portuguese conquest and commerce in Southern Asia*, London: Variorum Reprints, 1985, p. 323.

36 Ames, *Globe Encompassed*, p. 41.

37 See ibid., p. 43.

38 H. Thomas, *The Slave Trade. The history of the Atlantic slave trade, 1440–1870*, London: Phoenix, 2006, p. 131.

39 Ibid., p. 133.

40 See I. Wallerstein, *The Modern World-System I. Capitalist Agriculture and the Origins of the European World-Economy in the Sixteenth Century*, San Diego, CA: Academic Press, 1974, p. 170.

41 J. Vicens-Vives (ed.), *Historia de España y America* [History of Spain and America], Barcelona: Editorial Vicens-Vives, 1961, Vol. III, p. 212.

42 H. Kamen, *Spain's Road to Empire, The Making of a World Power, 1492–1763*, London: Allen Lane, 2002, p. xxv.

43 Ibid., p. xxvi.

44 Ibid., p. xxvi.

45 See ibid., p. xxv.

46 Ames, *Globe Encompassed*, p. 81.

47 For a comparison of the free enterprise that was typical of Spain and of the 'state capitalist' policy of the Portuguese kings, see Tracy, *Political Economy of Merchant Empires* and *Rise of Merchant Empires*.

48 See Kamen, *Spain's Road to Empire*, p. xxiv.

49 Wallerstein, *Modern World-System I*, p. 174.

50 N. Kareev, *Zapadnoevropeyskaya absolyutnaya monarkhiya XVI, XVII i XVIII vekov* [Western European absolute monarchy in the sixteenth, seventeenth and eighteenth centuries], Moscow: Gosudarstvennaya publichnaya istoricheskaya biblioteka Rossii, 2009, p. 211.

51 See Tracy, *Political Economy of Merchant Empires*, p. 81.

52 A.E. Kudryavtsev, *Ispaniya v Srednie veka* [Spain in the Middle Ages], Moscow: URSS, 2007, pp. 166–7.

53 See Ch. Tilly, *Coercion, Capital and European States AD 990–1992*, Malden, MA: Blackwell Publishers, 1990, p. 125.

54 Vicens-Vives, *Historia de España y America*, Vol. III, p. 45.

55 See ibid., p. 126.
56 P.J.A.N. Rietbergen, *A Short History of the Netherlands,* Amersfoort: Bekking Publishers, 2004, p. 68.
57 Marx and Engels, *Sochineniya* [Works], Vol. 21, p. 417.
58 K. Votselka, *Istoria Avstrii* [History of Austria], Moscow: Ves' mir, 2007, p. 136.
59 F. Ancillon, *Tableau des révolutions du système politique de Europe, depuis la fin de quinzième siècle* [List of the revolutions in the political system of Europe from the end of the fifteenth century], Paris: Anselin et Pochard, 1823, vol. 2, p. 298.
60 S. Amin, *The Liberal Virus. Permanent War and the Americanization of the World,* New York: Monthly Review Press, 2004, p. 55.
61 A.-G. Gagnon, A. Lecours and G. Nootens (eds), *Les Nationalismes majoritaires contemporaines: identité, mémoire, pouvoir* [The contemporary majoritarian nationalisms: identity, memory, power], Montreal: Québec Amérique, 2007, p. 195.
62 Votselka, *Istoria Avstrii,* p. 141.
63 Bonney, *European Dynastic States,* p. 344.
64 E. Perrua, *Stoletnyaya voyna* [The Hundred Years War], Moscow: Veche, 2006, pp. 382–3.
65 See Bonney, *European Dynastic States,* p. 344.
66 Ibid., p. 351.
67 See *The Edinburgh Review,* 1856, CIV (211), p. 27.
68 See Tilly, *Coercion,* p. 129.
69 Marx and Engels, *Sochineniya* [Works], vol. 18, p. 254 (F. Engel's, *K zhilishchnomu voprosu* [On the housing question] – II).
70 See ibid., Vol. 8, p. 206.
71 P. Anderson, *Lineages of the Absolutist State,* London/New York: Verso, 1974, p. 18.
72 Ibid., p. 20
73 Ibid., p. 18.
74 I. Wallerstein, *Historical Capitalism.* London: Verso, 1984, p. 42.
75 N. Davidson, *Discovering the Scottish Revolution,* p. 74.
76 Kudryavtsev. *Ispaniya v Srednie,* p. 202.
77 See Smith, *Issledovanie,* p. 79.
78 R. Lyuksemburg, *Nakoplenie kapitala* [The accumulation of capital] (5th edition), Moscow and Leningrad: Sotsekgiz, 1934, p. 250.
79 See Marx and F. Engels, *Sochineniya,* Vol. 23, pp. 752–4.
80 Tracy, *Political Economy of Merchant Empires,* p. 218.
81 N. Steensgaard in *Dutch Capitalism and World Capitalism,* London, 1982, p. 255. Cited in Tracy, *Political Economy of Merchant Empires,* p. 1.
82 K. Gebler, *Amerika posle otkrytiya Kolumba* [America after its discovery by Columbus], St Petersburg: Poligon, 2003, p. 169.
83 G.L. Beer, *The Old Colonial System, 1660–1754,* Gloucester, MA: P. Smith, 1958. Part 1, Vol. 1, p. 54.
84 G. Arrighi and B.J. Silver (eds), *Chaos and Governance in the World System,* Minneapolis/ London: University of Minnesota Press, 1999, p. 100.
85 R. Roegholt, *Short History of Amsterdam,* Amersfoort: Bekking & Blitz Publishers, 2004, p. 40.
86 Ibid., p. 39.
87 Ibid., p. 40.
88 Tracy, *Political Economy of Merchant Empires,* p. 86.
89 Ames, *Globe Encompassed,* p. 175.
90 J. De Vries and A. Van Der Woude, *The First Modern Economy: Success, Failure and Perseverance of the Dutch Economy, 1500–1815,* Cambridge: Cambridge University Press, 1997, p. 442.
91 Ibid., p. 431
92 R. Blackburn, *The Making of New World Slavery. From Baroque to the Modern, 1492–1800,* London/New York: Verso, 1997, p. 281.

93 See T.H. Aston and C.H.E. Philpin (eds), *The Brenner Debate: Agrarian Class Structure and Economic Development in Pre-Industrial Europe*, Cambridge: Cambridge University Press, 1988.
94 Smith, *Wealth of Nations*, p. 814.
95 C.C. O'Brien, *The Great Melody. A Thematic Biography and Commented Anthology of Edmund Burke*, Chicago/London: University of Chicago Press, 1992, p. 257.
96 Cited in ibid., p. 260.
97 See R. Brenner, *Merchants and Revolution*, London: Verso, 2003.
98 Blackburn, *New World Slavery*, p. 117.
99 A.C. Mazzeo, *Burguesia e capitalismo no Brasil* [The bourgeoisie and capitalism in Brazil], S. Paulo: Editora Arica S.A., 1988, p. 11.
100 A. Gunder Frank, *On capitalist underdevelopment*, Bombay: OUP, 1976, p. 27.
101 Luxemburg, *Nakoplenie kapitala*, p. 255.
102 Cited in: B. Davidson, *The African Slave Trade*, Boston/Toronto: Atlantic Monthly Press, 1980, p. 59.
103 See Tracy, *Rise of Merchant Empires*, p. 288. According to the calculations of later historians, this made up 63 per cent of the overall number of people transported from the Old World to the New.
104 See ibid.
105 Ibid., p. 291.
106 Ibid., p. 294.
107 See Thomas, *Slave Trade*, p. 134.
108 Ibid., p. 134.
109 Davidson, *African Slave Trade*, p. 64.
110 See Thomas, *Slave Trade*, p. 147.
111 Gebler, *Amerika posle otkrytiya Kolumba*, p. 171.
112 M. Radiker, *Between the Devil and the Deep Blue Sea. Merchant Seamen, Pirates and the Anglo-American Maritime World, 1700–1750*, Cambridge: Cambridge University Press, 1990, p. 45.
113 R. Blackburn, *The Overthrow of Colonial Slavery, 1776–1848*, London/New York: Verso, 1988, p. 12.
114 Blackburn. *New World Slavery*, p. 388.
115 *Gentleman's Magazine*, vol. XXVII, April 1757, p. 147.
116 R. Peet, *Geography of Power*, London/New York: Zed Books, 2007, p. 59.
117 *Gentleman's Magazine*, vol. XXXI, August 1761, p. 343.

4

THE CRISIS OF THE
SEVENTEENTH CENTURY

By the middle decades of the seventeenth century the free-trade economy whose development in Europe had received a powerful stimulus from earlier geographical discoveries had exhausted itself. The precious metals that had come from across the ocean had been devalued. The American mines were yielding less and less, or needed additional investments. The bulk of the population, who had by no means grown rich during the period of rapid economic expansion, exercised only a limited demand for goods. The countries of Eastern Europe had begun to lag behind the quickly developing West. They were prepared to sell raw materials, but could not provide an adequate sales market either for manufactured products or for the commodities that were coming from overseas. Political conflicts, which had never ceased, broke out with new force, superimposing themselves on internal civil disputes and internecine strife.

Initially, the struggle unfolded between traditional political and ideological blocs – Catholics, united around the Habsburg dynasty, and protestants, to whom for reasons of state interest Catholic France and Orthodox Russia also attached themselves. The clash of these blocs took on the form of an all-European war, unprecedented in its scale, in the size of the armies involved, and in the destruction it caused. Thirty years of uninterrupted military campaigns, unfolding most intensively on the territory of Germany, brought that country to economic catastrophe. But the ending of the Thirty Years War did not bring a return to conditions of peace, merely signifying the start of a new series of conflicts in which the recent victors took to fighting among themselves. Brandenburg went to war on Sweden, and England and France on Holland. Later, wars broke out between France and England. Dutch commercial hegemony was replaced by British. The Austrian and Spanish Habsburgs continued their struggle against the French Bourbons, but dynastic and religious conflicts gave way to the principles of state interest, formulated by the governing French Cardinal Richelieu, the Spanish Prime Minister Count Olivarez, and the Swedish Chancellor Oxenstierna. The national state gradually took shape, replacing dynastic monarchies, and together with it there also arose empires of a new type, actively defending the interests of their own bourgeoisies throughout Europe and on the expanses of the oceans. Belief in freedom of trade was replaced by an orientation toward state protectionism within the framework of the mercantilist system.

Dutch hegemony

By the mid-seventeenth century the commercial hegemony of Holland was an indisputable fact. After the death of Queen Elizabeth and the installing of the Stuart dynasty in London the English monarchy increasingly became immersed in internal discord, with contention between parties and factions, struggles between kings and parliament, and insoluble social conflicts holding back foreign expansion. Holland, which had already undergone its revolution, was by contrast able to concentrate its resources on goals corresponding to the interests of the victorious bourgeoisie. In this respect the history of the Dutch East India Company is significant. Arising after its English counterpart and using the latter's experience as a model, the Dutch company quickly took the lead, forcing all other European merchants to imitiate it.

The Dutch revolution resulted not so much from religious disagreements as from the desire of the Habsburgs to exploit the financial resources of the Netherlands in order to pursue their imperial policies, from which the Dutch bourgeoisie itself derived insufficient profit. For the Netherlands to use the same resources independently to create its own maritime empire was cheaper and made more sense.

Dutch trade in the seventeenth century rested on the experience, contacts and knowledge of markets accumulated by Netherlands merchants, who for several centuries had worked with Hanseatic and Italian entrepreneurs. As early as the fourteenth and fifteenth centuries the strategic location of the Netherlands, where collaboration and exchange took place between the commercial capital of the Baltic and Mediterranean-Atlantic trade zones, had given the Dutch merchants enormous advantages. The opportunities expanded dramatically following the discovery of the Americas and the increase in the importance of Atlantic trade. During the sixteenth century the Dutch, following on the English, mastered the northern trade route to Russia, where the port of Arkhangelsk was established on their initiative. Asian spices and Persian silks, rounding the Cape of Good Hope where the United Provinces had founded a colony, reached the further ends of Europe by way of Dutch ships. Goods bought in diverse parts of the world were resold by the Dutch in other regions. Becoming international commercial intermediaries, the Netherlands merchants swiftly seized competitive positions of unprecedented strength.

As the world market developed, Dutch entrepreneurs quickly assimilated new information, forged ties and pioneered new trade routes. The experience of entrepôt trade they had acquired in Europe proved very important for them in Asia, where Western manufactures attracted little demand. Initially, the redistribution of resources in the world economy was uniformly to the advantage of Asian countries, where European demand stimulated a rapid rise in production. The flow of silver from Europe reached such dimensions that it forced a Portuguese author to remark: 'This induces many people to say that it was India which discovered Portugal.'[1]

As the American historian Glenn Ames notes, the inability of the Europeans to sell their goods in Asia led them to expand their intermediary trade between Asian ports.[2] This was especially important for the English and Dutch, who did not have deposits of silver and gold in their own colonies (the Portuguese discovered precious metals in Brazil late in the seventeenth century). This situation remained until the mid-nineteenth century, when the London *Economist* stated without particular enthusiasm that trade ties with India and China were 'so intimately connected with each other' that developing one set of links was impossible without expanding the other as well.[3]

In the seventeenth century the Dutch learnt that the answer lay in carrying on trade between Asian ports. Indian textiles could readily be exchanged for spices in Indonesia, and Chinese goods could be supplied to West Asia. By the end of the century the Dutch VOC alone bought up 30 per cent of the refined saltpetre produced in Bengal. Ten per cent of the employment in the local textile industry went to meet European demand. Already in the sixteenth century output of spices and pepper in Asia doubled.[4]

Although the Dutch were primarily traders, they were traders who were armed and ready to use force without hesitation. The uprising against the Habsburg authorities, and the almost constant border warfare with Spain that followed, allowed the United Provinces to form an effective military organisation not only at sea but also on land. At first, the German military historian Hans Delbrück stated, the Netherlands 'held fast only to the principle that fortified cities should lock their gates to the Spaniards'.[5] The insurgents were more successful in operations at sea, or in using partisan methods. But the task of creating a field army capable of resisting the Habsburg military machine was posed and carried out with the efficiency and thoroughness always characteristic of the Dutch bourgeoisie.

In the first years of the seventeenth century Maurits van Nassau, Prince of Orange, carried out a profound reform that made possible the effective use of the relatively limited human resources the republic had at its disposal. Historians note that these measures can be considered 'a turning point in the history of soldiering and military organisation'.[6] With English regiments fighting under the command of Prince Maurits, the 'Dutch school' was well studied and understood in England, and during the English revolution influenced the formation of the New Model Army of Oliver Cromwell. Other forces to show the influence of the 'Dutch school' included the Swedish army of King Gustavus Adophus, and later, the Prussian army.

Approaching matters with a thoroughly bourgeois practicality, Maurits began with the question of logistical and technical organisation. Since plunder and insubordination by mercenary troops was harming the cause of the republic, the task was to create an army that was disciplined and well paid, while at the same time not too expensive. Feeding soldiers on the proceeds of wartime pillage was in practice impossible, especially since the military operations were at first conducted on the republic's own territory. The number of officers was increased, and non-commissioned officers made their appearance; this command staff 'had to be paid almost as much each month as all the soldiers of the entire company'.[7] But thanks to the innovations in military organisation, overall expenses diminished. As Jonathan Israel notes in his history of the Dutch republic, after 1585 society had to adapt to a situation without precedent in Europe, with large masses of soldiers needing to be supported for years, and garrisons maintained in densely populated cities.[8] For the local population, however, this turned out to have unexpected advantages; the forces were paid regularly and generously, and for everything they consumed, the troops were obliged to pay the residents among whom they were quartered.

Underlying Prince Maurits's tactical thinking was an intensive study of the writings of ancient authors. In 1607 Jacob de Gheyn published a famous textbook that was widely translated into other European languages. On its basis, numerous German princes prepared manuals for their own armies. Friedrich Wilhelm, Elector of Brandenburg, made a special study of military affairs at the court of the Dutch stadtholders. Officers now required professional training as well, and the first military academy was founded in Siegen in 1616.

The Dutch musketeers learned to draw themselves up quickly and effectively. Their weapons began to be standardised, which was not only important for organising their fire, but also advantageous for the owners of the weapons factories that supplied the army with muskets and munitions in large consignments.

From constant drill, the Dutch gained the ability not just to draw up their infantry in large squares but also to form small columns. The forces became more mobile. A linear order of battle was developed that allowed the possibilities of firearms to be exploited to the maximum.

Prince Maurits, like other military and political leaders of the United Provinces, was marked by caution and pragmatism, avoiding risky undertakings and in no hurry to seize the strategic initiative. He preferred to make a stand in fortified cities rather than to fight in the open field.[9] But in the year 1600, when avoiding a decisive battle proved impossible, he succeeded in inflicting a decisive defeat on the Spanish army near the town of Nieuwpoort in Flanders. As the military strength of the United Provinces grew, so too did the readiness to use it. In parallel with the defensive war in Europe, Holland pursued offensive wars in America and Asia.

Fighting for control over the spice market, the Amsterdam oligarchs clashed with the no less ruthless merchant oligarchy of the Banda Islands. The Moslem merchants, who dominated the waters of the Indian Ocean, saw the Europeans not just as competitors but as enemies of the faith. European accounts put constant stress on the aggressiveness and treachery of the local rulers, along with the unreliability and corruption of the merchants, not least with a view to justifying the actions of the Europeans themselves. Indeed, the Europeans in this regard conceded nothing to their Asian teachers. The Bandanese War began in 1609 after the local oligarchs killed a number of Dutch representatives. The struggle took on a drawn-out character, and in 1615 an expedition was sent to the islands with orders to exterminate the Bandanese Muslims and to 'repopulate the country with pagans'.[10] Appointed governor of the Dutch possessions in the East Indies, Jan Pieterszoon Coen fulfilled these instructions so precisely and conscientiously that in 1617 the *Heren* of the Amsterdam oligarchy themselves experienced something like pangs of conscience: 'We would have wished for matters to be taken care of with more moderate measures.'[11] At the height of their success in 1619 the Dutch seized Jakarta, transforming it under the name of Batavia into their long-term commercial centre and military strongpoint in the region.

From its inception the VOC mounted an offensive against the positions of its European competitors, above all the English, employing armed force in doing so. English merchants came under attack, their trading posts were seized and destroyed, and the defenders were slaughtered. Later, an offensive was mounted against the positions of Portugal, and in 1638 Dutch forces landed in Ceylon.

The separation of Portugal from Spain did not bring an end to Dutch military actions against the Portuguese. To the contrary, the United Provinces dramatically stepped up their pressure on the weakened kingdom. The Dutch reached an agreement with the kings of the Congo, who had grown tired of the Portuguese protectorate, and in 1641 seized Luanda. A substantial part of Brazil passed under their control. The scale of the slave trade could now be sharply increased, with control over the markets now combined with military and commercial dominance at sea. Business prospered; while in 1642 the Dutch had shipped off and sold in their possessions some 2,000 slaves, in 1644 the total was already 5,565.[12]

By the mid-seventeenth century the Dutch had managed to seize substantial parts of the Portuguese empire in Asia, Africa and the Americas. The Netherlands held Angola, Ceylon, Malabar and Malacca, and Dutch forces had landed in Brazil. The increasingly weak Portuguese realm was under attack from all sides. In 1622 a joint expedition of Persians and English captured Hormuz. Muscat was conquered by the Sultan of Oman. In Morocco, the Arabs had Portuguese positions under pressure. But by the 1670s, when Holland itself was under attack from England and France, the Portuguese kings had managed to take back some of their possessions. Understanding that it was impossible to win back everything, the government in Lisbon concentrated on the struggle for the Atlantic. In Brazil, Dutch rule was far more effective, and consequently more harsh, than that of the Portuguese crown had been; it thus aroused resistance, not only among white colonists but also among the Indian and black populations. A revolt ended with the expulsion of the newcomers, and combined Portuguese and Brazilian forces then drove the Dutch from Angola as well.

Ultimately, Holland was to retain control of most of Portugal's former Indies empire. Under the Dutch, commerce remained the key priority, but instead of controlling trade in the interests of the treasury the VOC sought to encourage it in the interests of the bourgeoisie. The difference between Portuguese and Dutch colonialism lay in the fact that the Portuguese had turned their state into a commercial enterprise, while with the arrival of the Dutch, commercial companies started taking on the functions of the state. Inheriting the political structures of the

Portuguese East Indies, the Dutch filled them with a new class content. The VOC, which was itself to a certain extent a private enterprise, sought to exercise monopoly control no less than had the Portuguese government, but the fruits of this monopolism were gathered in by its shareholders, who in another capacity were still the ruling oligarchy in the United Provinces. What had changed was not so much the relationship of the state to private enterprise, as the meaning and structure of the state itself.

Holding a dominant position on the island of Java, the colonisers forced the peasants to massively expand the growing of crops for which there was demand in Europe, and then as a form of tax in kind, took part of the harvest from them without recompense. In relation to the mass of peasants, these actions of the Dutch authorities provide a classic example of *compulsory market participation,* with powerful administrative pressure used to reorient production from serving local needs to producing for export. With small changes, this policy continued to be applied in Indonesia even in the nineteenth century, when authority had been transferred from the East India Company, nationalised in 1800, to the Dutch government. In 1829 a 'system of compulsory cropping' was introduced, under which 'Javanese peasants were compelled to grow for export the crops required by the Netherlands. Later, this production had to be processed in primitive enterprises belonging to the Dutch and delivered to government stores, to be sold by the Dutch treasury.'[13] The Dutch state 'became simultaneously both planter and merchant'.[14] But the commercial profits obtained by the state through compulsion were privatised through the system of private commercial enterprises that conducted trade in the finished products.

While expanding the existing production in their colonies, the Dutch rulers paid close attention to stopping the increased supply from lowering prices. Prior to the beginning of the industrial revolution, profits were maximised not through expanding output, but through monopolising the market.[15]

By the early seventeenth century the Dutch bourgeoisie dominated the world market, but this hegemony was commercial, not political. Meanwhile, the dominance of world trade by the Dutch not only failed to provide a stimulus to the economies of other European countries, but was also viewed as a sort of commercial parasitism. The high prices that were maintained artificially by the Dutch merchants held back development in the West. It is noteworthy that the commercial take-off in Holland coincided with the beginning of stagnation in the world economy, and the Dutch decline with a new period of world economic expansion.

Describing the flourishing of the Dutch republic, Giovanni Arrighi and several other authors of the 'world-system school' start from the premise that economic hegemony gives rise automatically to political and cultural dominance. But this is far from being the case. Holland was a serious military power, especially at sea, and politically influential. But it was not in a position to dictate terms to other powers, nor did it try to do so. France, Austria and even the declining Spanish Empire were incomparably stronger on the military and political level. In international politics, the Netherlands bourgeoisie made only extremely modest use of its financial strength.

The explanation for this state of affairs seems obvious at first glance: the Netherlands lacked the resources to carry on an assertive foreign policy. In terms of territory and population the republic was not on a level with the main European powers. It lacked mineral resources, and its harbours were shallow, meaning that building and providing bases for large fighting ships presented problems. But not even the British Empire at its height was able to employ its strength unilaterally, instead constructing a system of coalitions that for some 250 years allowed it to maintain a favourable relationship of forces in Europe. Throughout this time Britain never waged war alone on the continent, and never lost an armed conflict there (its sole defeat was in the American War of Independence, which involved almost no military operations in Europe). A significant proportion of state budget funds went on supporting allies – Russian, Prussian and Hanoverian – which with British money were able to maintain their own armies. As the British military historian Mark Urban notes, when the Duke of Marlborough in August of 1704 scored a sensational victory over the French at Blenheim, making the English military presence on the continent a reality, only 14 of his 66 infantry battalions were British.[16] To be fair, it should be pointed out that the British generals, who did not always trust their allies, nevertheless assigned their own soldiers to the most dangerous positions.

Giovanni Arrighi presents the policies of the seventeenth-century United Provinces as a perfect analogue of later British policy, painting an impressive picture of Dutch diplomatic hegemony. He maintains that it was the ruling groups of Amsterdam and The Hague that assembled the anti-Habsburg coalition in Europe, trained its armies and developed its strategy. In his words, the Netherlands even before the beginning of the Thirty Years War had 'established a strong intellectual and moral leadership over the dynastic states of northwestern Europe, and its diplomacy had developed proposals for a major reorganisation of the pan-European system of rule,' which 'found more and more supporters among European rulers until Spain was completely isolated'.[17] To back up his thesis, however, Arrighi does not adduce a single concrete example, unless we take into account Fernand Braudel's general remark that 'the threads of diplomacy were entwined and unravelled in the Hague'.[18] While citing the French historian, Arrighi nevertheless tactfully ignores the context in which that remark was made. Braudel in no way asserted that it was Holland that played the decisive role in the events of the Thirty Years War, merely noting that thanks to the behind-the-scenes activity of diplomats the Dutch role was more important than usually supposed, since 'we historians see in the forefront only Habsburgs or Bourbons'.[19]

The nineteenth-century French author Frédéric Ancillon also observed that Holland carried on vigorous diplomatic activity during the Thirty Years War, and that 'its political schemes encompassed all Europe'.[20] On closer examination, however, these schemes turn out to have been petty tactical intrigues whose main goal – pursued with the help of bribes – was to make use of second-ranking German princes to help ensure the security of Holland. Moreover, these intrigues, extremely short-sighted and inconsequential, met with defeat literally at every step. At the beginning of the Thirty Years War the Dutch wasted substantial funds supporting the Elector Palatine Friedrich V, who accepted the Czech crown after an uprising in Prague had expelled the representatives of the Habsburgs. The Palatinate was strategically important to Holland, since it threatened the 'Spanish Road', the system of communications that linked the Southern Netherlands with the Spanish possessions in Italy. Not only did this move fail to cut the 'Spanish Road', but Friedrich himself was driven out of his hereditary possessions, while the Palatinate lost its elector status, which passed to Bavaria. The defeat of Friedrich also had a demoralising effect on the protestant camp in Germany since the Dutch at the crucial moment refused to use their forces to support him.

The United Provinces, though concluding military alliances, never tried systematically to construct a system of coalitions. In wartime the country put its trust to a considerable degree on English and French diplomacy, trying to avoid giving anything in return so long as both these countries did not finish up among its adversaries. Similarly, the Dutch were reluctant to send their own contingents to support the military efforts of allies, a reluctance which often resulted in defeats. Political hegemony requires a certain responsibility, including a readiness by the leading power to support its allies, if necessary by force of arms. By contrast, the ruling groups in the United Provinces showed a stubborn refusal to take risks in support of German protestant princes, Swedes or Danes, supposing that all problems could be solved with the help of money.

The reason for this short-sightedness has to be sought in the very nature of the Dutch bourgeoisie. Engaging in intermediary trade, the Netherlands merchants had only one strategic interest, which was in keeping markets open. From time to time the United Provinces had to contend with foreign competition at sea and to compete with other powers in the colonies, but this rivalry did not presuppose long-term strategic conflict. Even in the cases of Spain and Portugal, the Dutch sought to trade at the very first opportunity.

Commerce in the Netherlands took the place of strategy, ideology, honour and even patriotism. This reached the point where provinces refused to finance the military efforts of the republic unless they saw direct commercial advantage for themselves, and where Dutch bankers at the height of the independence war earned money transporting silver to the city of Antwerp, occupied by the Spaniards.

The land forces of the republic were almost never used for strategic military operations in Europe. During the War of the Spanish Succession John Churchill, Duke of Marlborough, was forced to resort to blackmail to gain permission from the government of the United Provinces for the Anglo-Dutch army he headed to carry out a march into southern Germany. The English general was left with no option but to make a direct threat:

> As the argument continued with these sallow, stingy, narrow-minded men, Marlborough's patience and tact finally gave out. He told them plainly that they could agree to his terms – a march south to the Moselle by a *powerful* allied army – or he would take the English troops with him, leaving the Dutch behind alone. He brandished a warrant signed by Queen Anne, empowering him to do just that.[21]

It was only after a lengthy scandal that the union army received permission to move southward, where Marlborough won a historic victory at Blenheim.[22]

The Dutch oligarchy perceived the army not as a mechanism for carrying out strategic and national tasks, but as a sort of armed guard meant exclusively for defending the property and commercial interests of the merchants. For the latter, sending forces thousands of kilometres to Indonesia or Brazil to protect business interests or to carry out plunder was far more natural than to help their allies in European coalitions by shifting forces a few hundred kilometres to the south.

The use of Dutch technology and experts outside the country's borders began in a massive fashion long before the republic's independence was proclaimed, and an important role in this was played by the Habsburgs. After seizing extensive possessions in the Americas, the Spanish kings sent Dutch specialists there to carry out drainage works, sink mines and set up printshops. Not even the revolt of the United Provinces was allowed to change the situation; the Spanish Habsburgs continued making use of technologies and specialists from the Netherlands throughout the seventeenth century, though relying, naturally, on the southern part of the country that remained under their control. In Acapulco in 1615–16 the Dutch engineer Adrien Boot designed and built the fortress of San Diego, intended to repel possible Dutch raids. An important role in the spread of Dutch knowledge, technology and entrepreneurial culture was played by Calvinist emigrants from the Southern Netherlands who, after quitting their Spanish-occupied homeland, had preferred to make their way not to Holland but to other countries, from Denmark and Sweden to distant Russia.

Where the opportunity presented itself, protestant entrepreneurs from the Netherlands also went to work for the Habsburgs. One example was Hans de Witte, a Calvinist from Antwerp, who directed mines and smelting works for the imperial commander-in-chief Wallenstein in Bohemia. After Wallenstein was murdered, de Witte drowned himself in the pond of his own garden.[23] Most of de Witte's workmates were also protestants from the Netherlands. Later, during the war with Portugal, Dutch merchants unashamedly sold munitions to the Portuguese.

Patriotism and the concept of the national interest were unknown to the oligarchy of the United Provinces. Such ideas were developed by the politicians and ideologues of absolutist France, beginning with Cardinal Richelieu. The history of the Thirty Years War is striking precisely for the smallness of the role played in it by Holland. Within the context of the anti-Habsburg coalition its armed forces did not play a major role, and even the financial and diplomatic efforts of The Hague were of astonishingly little consequence (unless one counts the moment when the Dutch, breaking with the protestant ranks, provoked aggression by Sweden against the Danes, who had infringed on Dutch commercial interests).

The Dutch commercial hegemony in the first half of the seventeenth century rested on weak foundations. The development by Holland of its own production lagged behind the growth of trade, while the oligarchic elite doled out funds in extremely stingy fashion to anything that did not promise quick profits. The successful development of the English bourgeoisie objectively transformed it from an ally to a rival of Holland, with commercial and industrial competition starting to make itself felt even before political conflicts broke out.

The Dutch sought to undermine English trade in Africa, using gifts and compacts to persuade local rulers to close off access to their realms to ships of the English Royal African Company.[24] Their actions in Asia were no less harsh and aggressive. In 1623 the Dutch simply wiped out their English competitors at Amboina. The Amboina Massacre did not provoke prompt retaliatory action, since England still did not feel itself ready for a fight against the United Provinces. Moreover, the English monarchy was increasingly sunk in internal crisis, and the Thirty Years War that had begun in Europe was going badly for the protestants. The war required a consolidation of forces, and in the struggle against Spain the Dutch were still considered allies. The authorities in London reconciled themselves to the defeat, but forgot nothing. The Dutch bourgeoisie possessed more capital than the English. It had showed much greater energy and aggression in forcing its Portuguese predecessors out of Asia, in excluding the English and other Europeans from profitable markets, and in imposing its conditions of trade on local merchants and rulers. By the early eighteenth century, however, Holland had begun yielding its positions throughout the region to the British, who were capable of developing and implementing a long-term political strategy in the East that was closely tied to their actions in the West. The rulers of small Indian states themselves invited the English and allowed them to build fortified centres, hoping to undermine the Netherlands monopoly.

To Arrighi, however, it remains less than clear why the Dutch, after achieving complete success in all their initiatives, 'never governed the system that they had created. As soon as the Westphalia System was in place, the United Provinces began losing its recently acquired world-power status.'[25] But understanding the causes of the decline that had overtaken Holland by the end of the seventeenth century is perfectly simple if one recognises that the Netherlands had never exercised political hegemony. Just as the 'Westphalia System' was invented in hindsight by historians and political scientists, the strategic plan ascribed to the Dutch oligarchy had its origins in retrospective fantasising by theoreticians of the world-system school.

The weakness of Holland, as of Venice in earlier times, lay in the fact that its policies were too bourgeois, excessively subject to short and medium-term commercial interests. The Dutch oligarchy never developed the traits of political and commercial behaviour required for the successful exercise of hegemony. In England, by contrast, where the triumph of the bourgeoisie had been less complete, and where the ruling class represented a far more complex and at times contradictory coalition, a much more complex and many-sided foreign policy was able to evolve, one that also included taking account of the interests of numerous native partners and intermediaries.[26] During the seventeenth century the English in the East entered into struggles not only with the Portuguese, but later with the Dutch as well. In these struggles, however, they also relied on local allies. In 1622 Persian forces took part in a successful English expedition to seize the Portuguese port of Hormuz, while in the Amboina Massacre of 1623 the Dutch killed not only the English, but also Japanese who were collaborating with them.

The end of the Thirty Years War, coinciding with the installation of a republican system in England, became a turning-point in relations between the two maritime powers. The English parliamentary regime that had consolidated itself in the course of the civil war now had at its disposal a powerful army and a loyal, well-prepared fleet. The social energy set free by the revolutionary explosion redoubled the strength of the English, just as would occur with the French a century and a half later and in the early twentieth century, with the Russians. Oliver Cromwell, who headed the young English republic, was of a determined mind. For the United Provinces, hard times lay ahead.

Adopting the first Navigation Act in 1651, London threw down a challenge to the Dutch trading monopoly. From this time the export of English goods from the country was prohibited except in English vessels. Imports from any part of Asia, Africa or the Americas had to be carried on English ships, and from Europe, on English ships or on ships of the country from which the goods were being exported. The same rules applied in relation to English colonies. Dutch fishers lost the right to sell their catch in England. In the late eighteenth century the London *Political Journal* called the Navigation Act 'the guardian of the prosperity of Britain',[27] while the renowned liberal orator Edmund Burke, in a speech devoted to reconciling Britain with the American colonies, declared that it was this legislation that 'binds to you the commerce of the colonies', representing 'that sole bond which originally made, and must still preserve, the unity of the empire'.[28] From the point of view of the liberal doctrines of later times the Navigation Act, drastically limiting freedom of trade, was a harmful document that slowed the increase in the exchange of goods between countries. In practice, however, it not only led to a growth of British shipping, but also stimulated the development of shipping in other countries, from Denmark to Russia. English protectionism was a legitimate response to Dutch commercial monopolism and to the aggressive, short-sighted policies of the United Provinces.

Immediately after the Navigation Act of 1651 was adopted by parliament, the First Anglo-Dutch War broke out. This was a classic example of a trade war. The two countries had no territorial claims on one another. 'It was,' writes the American historian Paul Kennedy, 'a quarrel about who should rule the waves and reap the commercial benefits of that privilege; as a consequence, the naval and economic aspect was the dominant one.'[29]

The war revealed the weakness of the United Provinces. Although the Dutch fleet performed with great success in large sea battles, the coastal blockade mounted by the English proved effective in undermining the trade on which the prosperity of Holland was founded. The strategic advantage remained with the English, for whom the capture of enemy trading vessels became a profitable business.[30] For their part, the Dutch inflicted considerable damage on English trade in Asia and the Mediterranean. With support from their Danish allies, they succeeded in blocking English ships from access to the Baltic through the Øresund strait. Some historians maintain that English trade suffered even more than that of Holland.[31] Foreign trade, however, played a much smaller role in the English economy, and England's Atlantic ties continued to develop. Imports from Russia came via the northern route, through the White Sea.

The first Anglo-Dutch war ended for the republic in an acute economic crisis and a peace treaty under which the Dutch were forced not only to accept the Navigation Act of 1651 but also to compensate the losses suffered since 1611 by the East India Company. The Amboina Massacre was avenged.

The English Navigation Acts became an example to other countries. In 1662 France introduced a tax on foreign ships exporting French merchandise. For the Dutch, transporting cargoes between French ports became unprofitable, and French shipping developed accordingly. In Sweden a Commodity Act, drawn up on the English model, was adopted in 1724.

The maritime power of Holland was eventually overturned by an alliance between England and France. In 1672 the English and French joined in going to war on Holland. The United Provinces successfully resisted the superior forces of their enemies, and thanks to the genius of Admiral de Ruyter even inflicted serious defeats on them. But the country was incapable of waging war simultaneously with the English at sea and the French on land.

Nevertheless, the decisive factor in shifting hegemony from Holland to England was not the outcome of the wars at sea. The relationship of forces changed not so much through military actions as in the course of economic development. Exhausting the Dutch budget, the military operations undermined the country's might. In 1678 the state debt reached 38,000,000 guilders.[32]

In the interludes between wars Holland's economic position continued to decline. The Navigation Acts yielded their expected results,[33] and as English industrial output grew, the relationship of forces between the two leaders of the capitalist economy changed. In the 1650s the English merchant fleet had been no more than a quarter of the size of that of Holland, but by the 1690s the two were similar in tonnage and in the number of ships. Between 1702 and 1788 the tonnage of the British merchant fleet grew by 326 per cent,[34] and by the end of the eighteenth century the relationship of forces was two to one in favour of Britain. Under the impact of constant wars and internal disorders the financial position of the republic also deteriorated steadily. By 1713, even though Holland by this time was allied with Britain, which took on itself a disproportionate share of the expense and trouble of the war against France, the Dutch national debt had reached 128 million.[35]

By the end of the seventeenth century the general European economic crisis was being overcome, and this revival had clear links to the decline of Holland during the same period. The system of free trade which the merchants from the United Provinces had successfully exploited was giving way to the protectionist policies that were later to receive the name of mercantilism. The defence by governments of their internal markets led to a rapid growth of domestic production. The Dutch bourgeoisie lost on all fronts. As a centre of production, Holland was now meeting with competition from new factories and workshops established not only in France and England, but also in the German states, in Scandinavia and even in Russia.

As intermediaries in world trade the Dutch merchants lost their significance, since increasing quantities of goods were being produced from local raw materials for internal markets. The importance of domestic trade grew, and although world trade grew as well, the strongest positions within it went to countries with larger internal markets and more developed production. Within this overall scheme, England as a country with a substantially larger population held a huge advantage. But a no less important advantage under the conditions of mercantilism was the power of the state, defending the internal market, protecting the local bourgeoisie, and acting as an investor and customer. The less liberal and far more centralised English state, which in part retained the features of a feudal monarchy but which had turned these structures to serving the interests of capital, proved a far more effective tool for bourgeois development in this situation than the decentralised Netherlands republic.

The war of 1672–74, which Holland was forced to wage against England and France simultaneously, placed the republic on the verge of catastrophe. Military setbacks led to a social and political crisis that resulted in the fall of the Grand Pensionary Johan de Witt and the return to power of the House of Orange, banished from the levers of politics by the merchant oligarchy. The 21-year-old Prince Willem was proclaimed *stadhouder* of Holland and commander-in-chief of the armed forces of the republic, under the name of Willem III. In August 1672 the now-retired Johan de Witt, along with his brother Cornelis, was torn to pieces by a rebellious mob in The Hague. The first act of state by the new ruler from the House of Orange was to end the war with England. In February 1674 a separate peace was concluded between London and The Hague.

After the English had placed pressure on the Dutch with a series of military campaigns, a period of consolidation of capitals ensued. Overthrowing the Stuart King James II in 1688, the English parliament put an end to the prolonged struggle for power between bourgeois and aristocratic factions, and at the same time laid the basis for a new policy in relation to Holland. Chosen as the new king of England and Scotland was the same William III of Orange, whose right to the throne rested on the extremely tenuous basis of his marriage to Mary, daughter of the deposed James II.

This turn of events, which received the name of the 'Glorious Revolution', made it possible to formalise the Anglo-Dutch compromise – on the conditions of London. The 'Glorious Revolution' sealed one of the most successful deals in the history of world business; it 'had a character of an Anglo-Dutch business merger'.[36] The British bourgeoisie not only won access to the funds of the Dutch banks, but was also able to make use of their experience and knowledge. Similar institutions arose in short order in England. The opposition of the two maritime powers was replaced by an alliance directed against France. England, Scotland and Ireland received a Dutch king, and the British East India Company, Dutch shareholders. The number of foreign investors in the company grew steadily, as German merchants and people from other countries who had funds to spare ventured their capital.

British trade turnover grew rapidly, and by 1720 the British had substantially out-stripped the Dutch in the volume of their trade with Asia. But while the economy of the United Provinces stagnated, Dutch commercial capital fared relatively well, sharing in the profits of the British.

After suffering defeat in the wars of the seventeenth century Dutch capital, including in the first instance the VOC, depended on British arms for the defence of its interests. Until the Anglo-Dutch war that broke out in 1780, the British consistently and conscientiously provided this defence to their conquered foes, transformed now into junior partners. This allowed the Dutch to economise on military spending while retaining their commercial positions. Although the victory had clearly gone to the British, the terms of this compromise were by no means onerous for the Netherlands. The 'Glorious Revolution' was a classic example of a tactic that the British ruling class used later in Canada, India and South Africa: victory was consolidated through generous concessions to the vanquished. For the builders of the empire, the ability to compromise was to prove far more valuable than aggressiveness and a readiness to apply pressure.

The Franco–Swedish joint venture

While making commercial gains, the Dutch bourgeoisie willingly conceded the leading role in European politics to other powers. It was France, together with Sweden, that provided the decisive strength of the anti-Habsburg coalition, even though both countries had initially stood aside from the conflict. French policy, directed for a decade and a half by Cardinal Richelieu, provided a classic example of firmness, consistency and effectiveness. Advancing toward his goals in deliberate fashion, overcoming obstacles while refusing to force the pace, Richelieu laid the basis for a new diplomacy that was not subject to the search for momentary advantages, but to a long-term strategic plan.

Richelieu's problem was that a clash with Spain was in his view inevitable, but that France was not ready for war. In France during the religious wars the bureaucratic machine, whose foundations had been laid during the years of Valois rule, had not collapsed entirely but had split into parts, each of which functioned autonomously.[37] Richelieu had at his disposal already existing structures and institutions on the basis of which he could construct his new political order. But to make this unwieldy mechanism work precisely required enormous effort.

The modernisation of France that had begun under Henry IV and that continued under Richelieu served as a model for most of the countries of continental Europe. The key to changing society was to establish an efficient state apparatus. Despite later liberal myths, the development of a bureaucracy in no way restrained private initiative, but created favourable conditions for it; the more rational and predictable the actions of the government, the better the business climate. Max Weber showed with hindsight that the development of capitalism does not weaken bureaucracy but leads to its growth, to the spread of a bureaucratic type of rule. Long before the German sociologist, Cardinal Richelieu realised this in practice, creating an apparatus of power that was capable, through rational actions, of stimulating the country's economic growth.

Unhappy at the strengthening of the central administration, the aristocrats fomented conspiracies and revolts. The government was obliged constantly to use force, blowing up castles and creating a network of informers to warn it of internal threats. In such circumstances the cardinal could not allow himself a major war or a public break with Rome. But the objective logic of the struggle against Spain and Austria saw France counterposed to the policies of the Counter-Reformation being implemented by the pope together with the Habsburgs. Paradoxically, it was the Catholic Cardinal Richelieu who laid the basis on a European scale for government policies 'independent of the religious orientation of the state'.[38]

Even though the question of official state religion remained at the centre of the ideological struggle between the European powers until the beginning of the eighteenth century, the pragmatic French understanding of the state interest, the *raison d'état*, came to be generally accepted both by Catholics and by protestants. By the end of the seventeenth century these ideas had become so well implanted that they were followed unhesitatingly by all involved, including the pope. Richelieu sought to make up for the internal weakness of the state through an effective foreign policy. Beginning with the decade after 1610 French diplomacy showed a remarkable persistence in shaping an anti-Habsburg coalition in such a way that Paris, while retaining its political influence, could avoid as far as possible taking a direct part in war. During the years of Richelieu's administration the French concluded 74 international agreements; not even Russia remained outside the cardinal's attention. During the 1620s the main efforts of Paris were aimed at freeing the hands of Sweden, whose armies were to play a decisive role in the fighting. To wage war in Germany the Swedes needed to concentrate important forces, a situation that might have been exploited by neighbouring states with which the Swedes were in conflict. French diplomacy accordingly made titanic efforts to secure the rear of the Swedes. A diplomatic mission was sent to Moscow to try to reach agreement on the entry of the Russians into the anti-Habsburg coalition. Actions by Russia, it was intended, would tie down the forces of Catholic Poland, which might otherwise strike a blow against Swedish possessions. Although both Poland and Sweden were regarded with equal suspicion in Moscow following the Livonian war and the Time of Troubles, the choice was made – not without French influence – in favour of the Swedes. In 1632 Muscovy declared war on Poland. This conflict, known to history as the Smolensk war, did not end in decisive success for either side. The army of the boyar Mikhail Shein laid siege unsuccessfully to Smolensk, and his auxiliary detachments captured several small fortresses. In September 1633 the Polish King Władysław IV, approaching Smolensk with forces half the size of those of Shein, managed to surround the Russians and force them to capitulate. After Shein had surrendered in March 1634 his mercenaries crossed over to the Poles, and the boyar himself with 8,000 Russians returned to his homeland, where he was charged with treason and executed. After this another 'eternal peace' was concluded between the two sides, leaving the borders unchanged. The sole gain for Muscovy was that the Polish king officially renounced his claims to the Russian throne. Meanwhile, the main goal of French diplomacy had been achieved; the Swedes were spared the need to wage war on two fronts.

Richelieu, however, did not cease to pay attention to Poland. While the Russians were being incited to attack the Poles in order to support the Swedes, Poland and Sweden were being persuaded to conclude a truce. Despite their military successes, the Swedes under the influence of French diplomats were obliged to make serious territorial concessions. In 1629, with French mediation, the Altmark agreement was signed reconciling the Swedish King Gustavus Adolphus with his Polish kinsman Sigismund Vasa. At the same time a number of agreements were signed with German protestant princes, who received help from Paris in the war against the Habsburgs.

While Sweden was threatened in the south and east by the *Rzeczpospolita* and Muscovy, on its western boundary there remained unresolved disputes with Denmark. Here as well French diplomats intervened, seeking a truce between the rival Scandinavian powers.

French foreign policy was extremely pragmatic, but at the same time popular on the continent. As Frédéric Ancillon observes, Cardinal Richelieu while proceeding exclusively from interests of state acted to defend the rights and freedoms of his German neighbours:

> Political and religious freedom in the German empire was the best way of preventing its transformation into a new great power under the House of Austria, which opposed these principles. Here lay the whole secret of French policy: the princes of the empire had to resist Austria. Their power had to resist its power, and this goal was approved by all friends of humanity, since the existence of such independent states served to guarantee a general European harmony.[39]

To bring about a general European harmony in this fashion, powerful armed forces were required. The initial phase of the Thirty Years War showed that the German protestant princes could not defend themselves, even with the help of French and Dutch money. In January 1631 a treaty was signed with Sweden, and Gustavus Adolphus received from the French a financial subsidy of 400,000 reichstalers per year to conduct the war.[40] Summing up the results of his activity in his famous *Political Testament,* Cardinal Richelieu pronounced his famous words: 'Gold and silver are the tyrants of the world.'[41] Money from his deft hand also became one of the most important behind-the-scenes factors in international politics.

While France thanks to Cardinal Richelieu played a decisive diplomatic role in shaping the anti-Habsburg coalition, Sweden for 20 years represented its main military strength. The latter country provided a model, for imitation throughout the continent, of a military-state structure. If scholars at times describe Holland in the late sixteenth and seventeenth centuries as having the first modern economy,[42] Sweden on the same basis might be termed the first modern state. In his *History of the military art* Hans Delbrück states that the Swedes 'formed a military state of previously unseen strength'.[43] The population of Sweden was substantially smaller than that of various neighbouring countries, but the Swedish political system was quite different, and 'people, classes and king were combined into a single indivisible whole'.[44]

By the beginning of the seventeenth century Sweden was, in the words of an American historian, 'a nation in arms with a political culture directed toward war'.[45] The Swedish bureaucracy had been established with exceptional speed and virtually on an empty space. In the fourteenth century the country had amounted to a confederation of provinces, each of which had its own assembly, judges, laws and military organisation.[46] When King Gustavus Vasa came to power in the sixteenth century and founded a new dynasty, the realm he inherited, which included Finland as well as Sweden itself, had a total population of about one million. As acknowledged by Scandinavian historians, the kingdom represented 'an unknown and sparsely populated agrarian country at the edge of Europe'.[47] State centralisation was minimal. Unlike the case in the far stronger Denmark, here there was no regular army nor permanent navy. Wars with the Danes broke out frequently, and at first turned out badly for the Swedes. Prior to Gustavus Vasa there had been no clear line of succession to the Swedish throne, and a change of kings was almost always an occasion for strife. Trade was in the hands of the German Hansa. There was no normal capital; the king and his court led a nomadic existence, travelling from castle to castle, while in Stockholm, nominally the main city, the population did not exceed 10,000 people at the best of times. Of these, about a third worked directly or indirectly for the king.

Contrasting with the evident poverty of the kingdom was the wealth of the Catholic church. The Reformation in Sweden had one clear and obvious purpose: to strengthen the royal finances. Unlike the case in Germany, there was no popular movement for the Reformation in Sweden. King Gustav Vasa himself, according to historians, was not especially interested in questions of religion.[48] The urge to increase financial discipline and strengthen the state budget ran as a common thread through all his reforms. A crucial aim was to centralise the tax system. In earlier times the main tax, the *Grundsteuer,* had been paid by the peasant communities in natural form, while the government needed it in silver. But the countryside resisted such changes; even in the early seventeenth century, despite all the innovations 'both the new and old taxes continued to be paid in kind, while what the king needed was money'.[49]

The final drop that caused the cup of the king's patience to overflow was the crisis evoked by the need to pay Denmark for Alvsborg. This city was the sole Swedish port on the North Sea. In the course of one of the frequent wars with the neighbouring kingdom the city had been lost, and the Danes then demanded that Gustavus Vasa pay a huge ransom to receive it back. The treasury was empty. There was no way left to get the funds except through expropriating church property. In an assembly in 1527 a majority of representatives of the estates voted to adopt a resolution on reforming the church. The priests were made civil servants, the bishops were appointed by the king, and the budget of the church was incorporated into that of the government. Church taxes began to flow regularly into the treasury.

The Reformation did not lead to the creation of a 'new nobility' as occurred in England, but strengthened the position of the old, since landholdings that noble families had earlier deeded to the church were returned to them. Unpopulated lands were in essence nationalised; in 1542 Gustavus Vasa proclaimed them 'the property of God, the King and the Crown'.[50]

The restoring of church lands to the nobility not only strengthened support for the king among the ruling stratum, but also enriched him personally; lands that the Vasa family had earlier ceded to the church were returned to him. By the end of his life the king was among the richest people in the country, not only controlling more than 5,000 farms, but also owning important commercial enterprises.

Gustavus was a charismatic leader, an outstanding orator, the author of brilliant and convincing letters, and an energetic administrator. It was he who laid the basis for the renowned Swedish bureaucracy, which by the 1620s had taken on its mature form.

The administrative apparatus was established by experts who had been invited from Germany, and who set themselves to improving the work of the royal chancellery. They were also involved in putting the state finances in order. Foreigners had also to be invited in to organise the army and fleet. New fortresses were built, and garrisons were quartered in them to enforce control by the central authorities over the provinces. In conditions of internal peace and stability the population, consisting for the most part of free peasants, began growing rapidly.

To overcome a shortage of administrative officials, the authorities took up the question of education. In the mid-sixteenth century the university in Uppsala had been in deplorable condition, but a hundred years later Sweden was to be one of the European leaders in this field. New universities were established in all corners of the now-expanded state. To serve Livonia, a university was founded in 1632 in Derpt (Tartu); in Finland, another was established in Turku (Obo) in 1640; and for the internal regions of Sweden universities were founded in Greifswald in 1636 and Lund in 1668. Schools were opened in every town, and 20 grammar schools were established to prepare young people for university education. A military academy, the Krigskolleg, was organised to train officers.

The court in Stockholm spoke German; in the early seventeenth century King Gustavus II Adolphus was obliged to learn Swedish as a second language. Nevertheless, the Reformation and the work of the bureaucracy made their effects felt. National languages received a powerful stimulus to their development. Translation of the Bible into the Swedish and Finnish languages provided an impulse for the development of the literatures and education of both peoples. Books began to be published not only in Swedish, Finnish and German, but also in Estonian and Latvian. The first law in Europe on the preservation of the cultural heritage was even adopted, and something resembling a national museum was founded.

The Swedish-Finnish kingdom of the late sixteenth century could in some sense be considered the first example of a polyethnic national state. In all provinces the officials of the royal administration were primarily locally born people, and from the time of Gustavus Vasa operated according to common laws. Finns were able to participate in the Swedish parliament, and to hold official posts. One cannot, however, speak of full equality of rights for Swedes and Finns in the empire founded by the Vasa dynasty. In the main, government posts in Finland were held by local Swedes, while the Finns who sat in the royal parliament belonged mainly to the lower strata of society, and in consequence their political influence was not great.

The Vasa dynasty, which had come to power by election, sought to maintain the loyalty of the representatives of the estates, among whom were not only nobles, clergy and burghers, but also officers, state functionaries, peasants and even miners. In this respect the Swedish Riksdag, in its form still a thoroughly medieval estate assembly, was far more democratic than analogous institutions in most other countries of Europe.

The traditional Baltic trade with the German merchant cities did not by any means diminish during this period; on the contrary, it grew noticeably. Still more rapid, however, was the growth of trade connected directly to the new world economy. The overall volume of external trade increased, especially exports of honey and iron.

Meanwhile, Sweden's internal development was in sharp contrast to the principles of free trade professed by the first generations of leaders of the Dutch republic. It could be said that the rise of Sweden as a great European power and of its regional hegemony corresponded to a new stage in the development of the world economy, a stage in which opportunities for free trade had been exhausted and Europe was experiencing a drawn-out crisis. The Stockholm monarchs sensed acutely and succeeded in exploiting the opportunities which this crisis opened up before them even as it created difficulties for other, more powerful and developed states. However, the strict state regulation enforced by the Swedish kings in no way presented a challenge to Dutch hegemony or an alternative to it. On the contrary, these two tendencies organically complemented one another.

Just as the commercial hegemony of the Hansa cities in the Baltic rested on the military power of the German chivalric orders, and later on the Danish and Swedish kings, so Dutch commercial hegemony – which did not involve political dominance – would have been impossible without the support of strong military powers pursuing their own economic policies. In the West this role in the early seventeenth century was played by France, and in the East by Sweden.

Meanwhile Denmark and Sweden, integrated with Holland into a common commercial system and formally belonging to the general protestant camp, entered into a sharp struggle for control over the Baltic. This conflict had been exacerbated by Dutch intrigues. The merchants from the United Provinces were categorically opposed to the Øresund customs duties which the King of Denmark levied on them for entry to the Baltic.

The growing influence of Sweden brought with it a change in the relationship of forces in the region, as a result of which the Swedes were forced constantly to wage war. Trying to seize an opening for Russia onto the Baltic, Ivan the Terrible attacked the Livonian order, using as a pretext the failure by the Bishop of Derpt over many years to pay a tribute about which both sides had long since forgotten. The tsar's army entered Livonia and seized Narva. The war led to the collapse of the Livonian Order, already in crisis, after which Sweden and Poland intervened in the conflict. In 1582 the territories of the Order were divided between Sweden and Poland, while Muscovy gained nothing. In seizing Estland, the Swedes acquired a beach-head on the southern shores of the Baltic. Expanding this base, they subsequently established their power over a large part of the former Livonia apart from its southernmost region, the Dukedom of Courland. The former outposts of the Hansas in the eastern Baltic, Riga and Revel (Tallinn), were transformed into important centres of the new Swedish empire. But the Stockholm authorities, defending the interests of Swedish capital, did not exert themselves particularly to secure the development and prosperity of these German cities, redirecting trade to the benefit of Stockholm, Helsingfors and Vyborg.

Following the Livonian war Russia was weakened and could not be considered a serious adversary, but military conflict with Poland, with which Sweden now shared a common border, proved inevitable. In the early seventeenth century King Gustavus Adolphus inherited from his father a state at war with all its neighbours, Denmark, Poland and Russia. Despite all the efforts of earlier monarchs, state finances were again in deplorable condition. After the latest conflict Älvsborg was again in Danish hands, and the Swedes were again having to pay tribute, though diplomats from England and Holland were seeking to moderate the Danish demands.

This time, however, Sweden had on its throne a talented and determined king, with a no less efficient and decisive chancellor in Axel Oxenstierna, ranked justly with Cromwell and Richelieu as one of the outstanding politicians of the epoch. Between the king and his chancellor, a fortunate division of labour was worked out: the former concerned himself with military questions, and the latter with administration and diplomacy. Both achieved brilliant successes in their fields. The two understood and complemented each other wonderfully; Gustavus Adolphus was not only an outstanding military commander but also a firm administrator, who moreover was able to convince people and win them to his side by using his personal charm.

In the rapidly developing state apparatus the higher posts continued to be held by aristocrats, but certain routes for social mobility also became available to the less well-born, who had the opportunity for advancement on the basis of their service. Government documents show that earlier only 'members by birth of the Swedish nobility' could be appointed to key posts, but under Gustavus Adolphus a new formula was adopted: leading officials were now 'Swedes, primarily noblemen'.[51] As can be seen, higher state posts might in exceptional cases be entrusted to people from the non-noble classes. It was these lower orders of society which formed the main base of support for the monarchy in its struggle with the aristocratic opposition. The government, however, sought not revolution but compromise, trying to pacify and reconcile itself with the aristocracy while not losing the support of the masses.

Having drawn lessons from the social and political conflicts that had shaken the kingdom around the turn of the seventeenth century, Oxenstierna managed to ensure social peace and collaboration, winning the trust of the aristocrats. In other words, he pursued a Bonapartist policy of manoeuvring between social forces, seeking to consolidate society around a government acceptable to all. But in order to maintain stability under such conditions, funds were needed. 'Monarchy and aristocracy in Sweden,' a British historian states, 'were winding up their long-drawn-out feud on the only possible basis, a joint programme of war and expansion. From some points of view it was a national programme as well, or could be made to appear so.'[52]

The Treaty of Stolbovo, concluded with Russia in 1617 through English mediation, confirmed the Swedish hold over the territories on the eastern shores of the Baltic. In 1621 the campaign in Livonia led to the capture from the Poles of Riga, the largest port in the region. Profits from the Baltic trade replenished the Swedish treasury. With its German population of 30,000, Riga became the kingdom's largest city. Later, after the death of Gustavus Adolphus, the Danes were driven from the region of Skåne on the southern tip of the Scandinavian peninsula, and Sweden gained dependable access to the North Sea. These conquests became possible thanks to the radical military reform Gustavus Adolphus had undertaken.

Lacking the funds to maintain an expensive mercenary army, Sweden solved the problem by introducing universal military service. This has provided the basis for historians to single out the homeland of Gustavus Adophus as the first country in world history to establish a regular army.[53] Delbrück states that the Swedes 'were the first people to organise for themselves a national army'.[54] This assertion is not quite correct, since it ignores the English military reform of the fourteenth and fifteenth centuries, and also the experience of Holland, widely drawn upon by the Swedes themselves. But in relation to seventeenth-century Europe, the construction of Swedish military power was unquestionably innovative and revolutionary.

The armed forces created by Gustavus Adolphus rested on the class structure of the Swedish countryside, where the predominant layer was a free and economically independent peasantry with which both the nobility and the government were forced to reckon.[55] It was this peasantry as much as the urban bourgeoisie that became the base of support for the monarchy as it sought to strengthen its position in relation to the aristocracy.

In the words of an American scholar, the way the Swedes conducted hostilities 'resembled the total warfare of modern times'.[56] The kingdom of Gustavus Adoplphus was divided into six regions, each of which had to provide 18 infantry and six cavalry regiments. The obligation to furnish recruits was allotted on the basis of communities, with a particular number of households required to come up with a corresponding number of new soldiers. Adding to the military call-up was voluntary recruiting. This allowed the creation of a large and well-motivated army. A significant proportion of the units were formed in Finland, whose inhabitants at this time were loyal and patriotic subjects of Sweden. Under the Swedish system one out of every ten men fit for service was called up, while the remainder were numbered as reserves. But in Finland more were usually recruited, with the region providing nine infantry and three cavalry regiments.

Even during the era of border conflicts with the Novgorodians, the Swedish kings had held in high regard the ability of the Finnish hunters to wage partisan warfare. These forces were equally capable of using guerrilla tactics and of fighting on the battlefield, keeping formation precisely and displaying unshakeable discipline. The Finnish soldiers received the name of hakkapelis from their battle-cry 'Hakkaa päälle', which can be translated as 'Destroy, smash!'.

The morale of the Swedish-Finnish army was high. In transforming the church into a state institution Gustavus Vasa, perhaps without knowing it, took hold of a powerful ideological tool which his successors learned to use with notable success. As Delbrück stresses, 'Gustavus Adolphus built the morale of his forces not only through the leadership powers of his commanders, but also by developing religious feelings among his troops.'[57] The Swedish army introduced the institution of military chaplains, acting in essence as political commissars. Their task was less to tend to the soldiers' souls than to maintain morale and conduct ideological propaganda, explaining the king's policies and the goals and purpose of the war.

'Our infantry men have not been recruited with money,' Gustavus Adolphus stated,

> Nor have they been assembled in ignorance of the perils of war by the persuasive power of tavern keepers. They have been drafted into the service by careful selection from among rural population. They are in their prime, accustomed to doing work, to carrying burdens and to enduring cold, heat, hunger and lack of sleep, but not to the gratification of their appetites.[58]

The 70,000-strong army of Gustavus Adolphus in the early seventeenth century was larger in relation to the population of its country than the army fielded by Prussia against Napoleon in 1813.[59] The ability of the Swedish kings to mobilise human and material resources to achieve their military and political goals exceeded anything known elsewhere in the Europe of the time.

The lessons learnt from Maurits of Orange played no small role in the creation of the Swedish military machine. But Arrighi is mistaken in presenting the spread of military experience as a sort of 'technology transfer' organised consciously by the ruling class of the Netherlands. It is significant that the German protestant princes, direct neighbours and close allies of the bourgeois Netherlands, failed to assimilate these Dutch lessons. Sweden, whose army in the early seventeenth century came to be organised on a new model, was a quite different matter.

The power of the Swedish army rested not only on the organisational achievements of Gustavus Adolphus, but also on industrial development, to which the royal authorities assigned great importance. Thanks to improved casting, Swedish metallurgy began transforming itself into the basis for a real military-industrial complex. Here as in many other European countries private enterprise and state policy were closely linked. The Swedish military efforts were financed by the Amsterdam banker Louis de Geer.[60] The royal government paid for the credits and supplies by providing production concessions, often on newly conquered territories. These concessions in turn laid the basis for new Swedish industries. To operate their enterprises de Geer and his colleagues the de Besche brothers brought in large numbers of skilled workers both from Holland and from the Southern Netherlands. Of particular importance to Swedish industry were new methods of smelting metals. In the words of the American historian Franklin Scott, de Geer was not only a wealthy investor but also 'an organizing genius who lifted arms manufacture out of the handicraft stage to a factory operation and considerable export industry'.[61] In 1627, by which time most of his enterprises were concentrated in Sweden, he followed his capital and moved to the country.

The aggressive foreign policy of the Swedish kings acted on the whole to stimulate economic growth. The government controlled the 'commanding heights' of the economy. It owned a substantial part of the mining industry, and later began assuming other functions as well. Along with iron, deposits of copper that had been discovered in the 1570s were now worked for export, but these exports were used to pursue foreign policy goals.[62] Since iron and copper were used to produce weapons, they could rightly be described as strategic raw materials. After the end of the Thirty Years War the expanded military-industrial complex in turn began working for export. Between 1655 and 1662, for example, 11,000 cannon were produced, of which 9,000 were exported.[63]

For the first time in history a government not only supplied its army with weapons, but also engaged in the modernising and standardising of its armaments, conducting special research to this end. Purposeful work by experts, conducted on the direct orders of the royal authorities, led in 1629 to the appearance of a new weapon, a light 'regimental cannon' (*regementsstycke*). This four-pounder gun was drawn by one or two horses, a few soldiers could wheel it directly about the battlefield alongside the ranks of the infantry, and it fired case-shot instead of cannon-balls. The Russian historian S.A. Nefedov observes that the regimental cannon became the 'victory weapon' of the Swedish army in the Thirty Years War.[64]

Weapons were standardised, and made lighter. The calibre of the musket was reduced. The new, lighter musket was equipped with a wheel-lock firing mechanism (invented by Leonardo da Vinci). The musketeers could now fire their weapons without placing them on a stand. Paper cartridges and bandoliers were introduced. The infantry became more manoeuvrable and fired more rapidly. Well-trained and disciplined forces were now capable of carrying out swift marches, appearing where the enemy did not expect them. Awkward columns of two or three thousand soldiers were replaced by regiments of twelve or thirteen hundred. Since the musket now played a greater role than the pike, tactics changed as well. Deep columns were replaced by linear formations, making it possible to direct fire more effectively. Logistics were improved through the organising of stores and rear bases.

When the forces of Gustavus Adolphus landed in Germany the protestant forces had been smashed, and an attempt by the Danish king to defend his co-religionists had ended in a shameful defeat; meanwhile in Vienna, plans were being discussed for a post-war reordering of the political space that still bore the medieval name of the Holy Roman Empire. The pretext for the Swedish foray into Germany was provided by the Edict of Restitution (*Restitutionsedikt*) of 6 March 1629, under which the emperor effectively revised the conditions of the Peace of Augsburg.

The return of church property was to be accompanied by the implementing of active control measures by the imperial administration on the territories formally belonging to the protestant princes.

After his first victories over the imperial forces, Gustavus Adophus for practical purposes dominated the scene. But the Habsburg forces were by no means crushed. The decisive battle with the imperial forces of Wallenstein at Lützen ended in victory for the Swedes, but Gustavus Adolphus was killed while riding about the forward positions; the king was betrayed by his short-sightedness, as he approached too close to the enemy ranks while trying to reconnoitre the situation. The leader's death did not put a stop to the work of the military machine he had prepared, and which proved to be largely self-sufficient. But as the war dragged on, the resources of Sweden were exhausted. The army, which had taken pride in its discipline and martial spirit, had to be replenished with German mercenaries, and in Finland there were simply not enough men to replace those who had disappeared from the ranks of soldiers.

In 1634 the successes of the Swedes were replaced by a series of failures. After the catastrophic defeat at Nördlingen Chancellor Oxenstierna rushed to Paris to appeal for help. He was received by Cardinal Richelieu in April 1635. The chancellor seemed to the Cardinal to be 'somewhat Gothic and very Finnish',[65] but in sum, they readily found a common language. France was forced to openly enter the war.

The Swedes continued the struggle with energy and persistence, presenting all Europe with an example of northern determination. In the words of a French historian, after the death of Gustavus Adolphus the undertakings on which the heroic king had embarked 'were transformed into a general national cause'.[66] From that time onward, however, Stockholm depended totally on Paris, while the French were able to achieve their goals in full, but only at the price of active participation in military operations.

No diplomatic efforts could take the place of successes on the battlefield, where events unfolded in a way very different from what the Paris strategists had wanted. In August 1636 Spanish forces were approaching Paris, after seizing the fortress of Corbie that protected the capital. Contemporaries wrote of being able to see the bivouacs of the Spanish armies from the walls of Paris.[67] In various parts of the country revolts started breaking out as a result of the excessive tax burden. Court conspirators planned the murder of Richelieu. But the Habsburgs were no longer strong enough to build on their successes. The conspiracy, like all the others, was unmasked, and French forces took back Corbie. Three years later, after a long siege, the French captured the strategically important fortress of Breisach on the Upper Rhine and closed off the 'Spanish road' by way of which the Habsburg forces in the Southern Netherlands had been supplied. When Richelieu died in 1642, the French armies already felt themselves masters of western Germany, having taken Alsace and Lorraine. In 1644 the French seized the Rhine province. The forces of Marshal Touraine and the Prince de Condé, together with Swedish soldiers under General Wrangel, were nearing Vienna.

The Peace of Westphalia that ended the Thirty Years War made Paris the ruler of the destinies of Europe. In the words of Ancillon, the main goal of French and Swedish diplomacy was that 'the House of Austria should no longer be able to consider the princes of the empire its subjects, and the territory of the empire its provinces'.[68] The division of Germany into a multitude of small states was set down in international law. As a state entity Germany ceased completely to exist, to be reborn only in the second half of the nineteenth century. The socio–economic and demographic consequences were no less catastrophic. 'Not even the Second World War had such destructive consequences for Germany as the Thirty Years War. During the period from 1618 to 1648 the losses of population for the country as a whole were around 40 per cent, and in the cities around 33 per cent.'[69] The greatest losses were not inflicted by the battles, but by hunger, epidemics, and the plunder and violence carried out by mercenary forces.

While Germany, both protestant and Catholic, was the main victim of the war, the victor countries suffered considerable harm as well. The greatest losses were borne by Sweden. About half a million Swedish and Finnish soldiers were killed in battle or died of disease.[70] The losses to the male population were so great that in many of the country's provinces, especially in Finland, women took on male responsibilities. This was the case not only with peasant women, who had to plough the fields and cut firewood, but also with women aristocrats, who took on the management of estates. Nevertheless the number of Swedish subjects multiplied, as a result of territorial annexations under the Peace of Westphalia. When Gustavus Adolphus came to the throne the population of his kingdom had been about 1.3 million people, but at the end of the Thirty Years War about three million were under Swedish rule. The political success of Sweden made the country attractive to merchants and artisans and to industrial and military specialists, who moved there from diverse corners of Europe, opening offices or hiring themselves out for service. For Dutch entrepreneurs the dynamically developing Swedish monarchy opened new horizons, encouraging them to invest their capital in the northern kingdom and to settle there personally. Partly as a result of immigration, the population of Stockholm grew sixfold. Queen Christina, who succeeded Gustavus Adolphus, did not limit herself to inviting technical experts, but also brought in scientists and artists.

The main victor in the Thirty Years War was France. Its army moved freely about Western Europe, dictating its terms to the conquered. The fame of its generals, Touraine and Condé, knew no equals. Even the English dictator Oliver Cromwell, considered a great military commander, sent his 'ironsides' to serve under the command of Touraine. Spain, despite its huge overseas empire, lost its importance in Europe. Austria needed time to restore itself after the defeat. England remained an island state, preoccupied with internal conflicts. No court could compare for brilliance with that of the 'Sun King' Louis XIV. Overcoming the trials of the Fronde and stabilising the internal situation, the French monarchy seemed the most powerful political force on the continent, while the French bourgeoisie, whose strength had grown thanks to the policies of Jean-Baptiste Colbert, appeared just as impressive a force in economic terms.

Nevertheless the claims of France to hegemony in Europe, claims first made under Richelieu and then openly demonstrated by Louis XIV, met with resistance from a growing number of adversaries who were capable of mounting increasingly effective opposition to the military and political power of Paris. The traditional alliance with Sweden, maintained until the early eighteenth century, no longer compensated for the rise of new and increasingly broad coalitions, backed after 1688 by the joint interests of the ruling classes of Holland and England. A resurgent Austria and the new Kingdom of Prussia, formed through the unification of the Electorate of Brandenburg with the Prussian dukedom, put forward its own claims to influence in Europe.

In the first half of the seventeenth century the success of the Franco–Swedish alliance was ensured by the combination of French politics, founded on innovative centralisation and efficient bureaucracy, with the Swedish rational militarism on the basis of which the first national army of the modern era had been established. By the end of the century, however, the experience of both countries had begun to be consciously borrowed by other governments. The military methods that had brought success to the Swedes in the seventeenth century were no longer a secret, and the Swedish forms of military organisation were being imitated to perfection by other armies. Meanwhile, the political organisation of the French monarchy had become a model on whose basis the state machines of almost all European countries were being transformed.

In 1675 the Elector of Brandenburg Friedrich Wilhelm defeated a 15,000-strong Swedish army at Fehrbellin. The Prussians succeeded for practical purposes in forcing the Swedes out of Germany. An attempt by the Swedes to invade the Prussian territories of Friedrich Wilhelm ended in failure and in a rout that saw them seeking protection within the walls of Riga. France was then forced to involve itself to prevent the defeat of its ally. Under a peace treaty in 1679 Sweden regained almost all the territory it had lost.

Although Fehrbellin did not become a turning-point, it marked the rise of a new disposition of forces on the continent. Stockholm depended increasingly on Paris to maintain its empire, while French hegemony, so recently confirmed by the Peace of Westphalia and reinforced by the Treaty of the Pyrenees in 1659, was encountering growing resistance.

Mercantilism and the war economy

Just as the rise of regulated capitalism in the twentieth century was linked to a significant degree to the Second World War, mercantilism in the seventeenth century also grew out of the war economy of its time. The Thirty Years War and the civil war in England, along with a multitude of smaller internal and international conflicts, created new conditions with which governments that sought success were forced to contend.

The term 'mercantilism' made its appearance in hindsight in the works of Adam Smith and other theoreticians of liberalism, and was used by them to characterise a wide range of limitations imposed by the state on trade, limiting its freedoms and market relations in general. By contrast, the nineteenth-century Russian sociologist Nikolay Kareev characterised mercantilism as the 'commercial orientation' of the Western absolutist state.[71] The truth is that for some time the encouraging and development of trade had had nothing to do with free markets. Quite the reverse; free trade in the late sixteenth and early seventeenth centuries had brought on a drawn-out crisis throughout Europe, with the redistribution of resources from the entire continent to the benefit of a narrow group of Dutch merchant oligarchs. The new trading policy of the state differed from the old, first, in putting its stake on the regulation of markets and the limiting of commercial operations that could result in an outflow of resources from the country, and second, in directly tying support for trade to the development of industry and to the accumulation of capital within the country itself. Putting an end to the elemental process of global redistribution and accumulation of capital, and replacing it with a new type of accumulation that was concentrated within the structures of particular countries, mercantilism was a powerful factor in the development of national markets and the national state. The indissoluble duo of mercantilism and absolutism put the bureaucracy in order, adopted uniform rules in the area of education and imposed unified cultural standards on the court and government, enhanced the role of the capital in relation to the provinces, and forced all the territories under its power to orient themselves toward its attitudes, rules and style. In the process, it created not only national states, but nations themselves.

A market economy does not engage exclusively in the exchange of goods in accordance with the law of value, but this is its prime activity. In a market economy, furthermore, production is for the purpose of exchange; this is different from the function of the market in a traditional economy, which involves the exchange of surpluses of goods produced for personal use. In the absence of direct ties between producers and consumers in a market economy, the vacuum has been filled since ancient times by commercial intermediaries, who *in various ways* have subordinated both producers and consumers to themselves. It was this intermediary trade, whose masters were the Dutch, which in the early modern epoch became the quickest and most effective means of accumulating capital. This method of exploiting society, however, led to the degradation of production and restrained the growth of consumption; ultimately, it thus undermined the productive base of commercial capital itself. The transition from commercial to productive capital became a key question of development, but capital could not carry out this transition through its own forces, since doing so meant both rejecting an orientation toward the use of 'cheap' resources and also accepting a lower rate of profit.

The crisis of the seventeenth century, like analogous market failures in later epochs, posed the question sharply of the role of the state in the economy. The answer found by European governments lay in protectionism, the support of industry, and the creation of commercial monopolies under the patronage of the royal authority. Simultaneously with the change of state economic policy, a turning-point was reached in the very nature of bourgeois development. Through the agency of government intervention, large-scale capital was reoriented from trade to production, and organising industrial enterprises became profitable.

Just as the ideology of free trade propagated in the sixteenth century shows a clear similarity to the theories formulated by Adam Smith 200 years later, the mercantilism of Jean-Baptiste Colbert and his followers anticipated to a significant degree the ideas developed in the twentieth century by John Maynard Keynes. What was involved, of course, was a relatively simple view of the role of the state, a role that was reduced to two tasks. The government was required to ensure that the outflow of precious metals from the country never exceeded the inflow; in other words, the balance of trade had to be positive. From this followed the need to encourage national industry in such a way as to substitute for imports and expand exports. Where private capital could not or would not invest in production, especially large-scale production, the state itself became the investor, guaranteeing not only investment but also the sale of production, the implanting of new techniques and the training of workers, while carrying out strategic planning.

The class nature of mercantilist ideology was abundantly clear. 'The mercantilists,' Kareev wrote,

> in essence proclaimed the solidarity of interests of the state treasury and capitalist entrepreneurs in the fields of trade and industry. The theoreticians of this system were unconcerned with the interests of other classes of society, that is, of consumers, industrial workers, or landholders. Everything had to be sacrificed to commerce and industry.[72]

The absolute monarchy aided 'the rise of the commercial-industrial classes, and moreover of the topmost, capitalist, entrepreneurial layers among the groups engaged in industry and trade'.[73] For the traditional elites who were gradually losing their real socio-economic weight, the most important source of prosperity became state service, which allowed them to use their status as a sort of competitive advantage within the framework of the nascent capitalism. Occupying themselves with the tasks of providing political services to the growing trade and industry, the bureaucrats and military officers played a huge role in the success or failure of initiatives on which the accumulation of capital depended.

An important role in the development of industry was played by military orders, which were placed both with private enterprises and with state factories servicing the army and navy. The near-constant war or armed resistance that characterised the seventeenth and early eighteenth centuries created an ideal political setting for such economic activity. While the link between capital and the state in earlier times had mainly operated through the mechanism of credit, the time had now come for direct state encouragement of production.

It would be wrong to suppose that the military needs of the state were the sole motive for capital and the authorities to combine their efforts. Collaboration between the centralised monarchy and the bourgeoisie took place on a multitude of levels, starting with the formation of a postal service and ending with the regulation of commodity markets, with maintaining safety on the highways and with arranging luxurious court entertainments. The *rapprochement* between capital and the monarchy created a new structure of interests, and as these interests in turn collided, they gave rise to international conflicts, wars, and the opposition of states and coalitions.

In the transition by the European powers from the free market to mercantilism the keynote was set by France, which transformed itself rapidly into the political and economic leader of the continent. A policy of protection in relation to industry began in France as early as the time of Richelieu. The government not only placed military orders and built factories for the production of weapons, but also aided development in sectors that had nothing to do with the army or navy, for instance, in the textile industry. This was a case in which, to use the words of Marx, primary capital flowed directly into industry from the state purse.[74]

In the mid-seventeenth century, when the ideas of mercantilism were formulated and consistently embodied in the life of Jean-Baptiste Colbert, France underwent a sharp burst of economic growth, acquiring a weight in European markets that corresponded to its political influence. Analogous methods were employed in seventeenth-century England, regardless of who might at one or another moment might be in power – the Stuarts, parliament or Oliver Cromwell. British politics in the seventeenth and early eighteenth centuries was typified by a combination of free trade with forceful state intervention in 'strategic' areas. The English were the first to work out how to subordinate financial activity to the logic of mercantilism. In 1644 the Bank of England was founded; from then on the government could influence the state of finances not only by coining money and collecting taxes, but also by setting the bank interest rate. The French model was also adopted by the ruling groups in Prussia, Saxony, Austria and even Russia.

The military-political rise of Brandenburg and Prussia in the late seventeenth and throughout the eighteenth century was tied closely to mercantilist policies in the area of the economy. After the Thirty Years War Brandenburg presented a scene of total devastation. 'The country was ruined and depopulated; the traveller who passed along its roads beheld only smoking ruins and beggars.'[75] But vigorous efforts by the government led quickly to the restoring of the economy. The state lent its support to all the leading sectors – mining, saw-milling, and the production of linen textiles. It placed a form of control on the cutting of timber. There were state monopolies on particular types of production: silk and glass, and later porcelain and of course, weapons. Some enterprises and sectors were handed over by the government as concessions to private entrepreneurs. The production and sale of tobacco products was strictly regulated from the mid-eighteenth century.[76]

The policies begun by Friedrich Wilhelm in the seventeenth century were continued by his successors. The efforts of the monarchy were aimed at developing the textile industry and at draining marshes. In 1747 a system of foreign currency regulation was instituted; no-one was permitted to take from the country more than 300 thalers. In 1753, on the eve of the Seven Years War, the State Bank was established. In 1765 the Berlin Bank was founded, and in 1772 the Institute of

Maritime Trade. An indication of the government's concerns was the building of new factories. The power of the famous Prussian army was maintained not only through constant manoeuvres and care for the training of the officer corps, but also by the ability of the government to keep its finances in good condition.

In Saxony, production of porcelain was undertaken for the first time in Europe by Augustus the Strong. The factory in Meissen was organised in response to a decision by the king in 1710, after the secret of porcelain manufacture had been discovered by the alchemist Johann Friedrich Böttger. In Russia mercantilism first made its appearance with the New Trading Charter of 1667, which stressed that all prosperous states developed 'free and profitable trade', but that the governments 'watched over markets with great care'.[77] Commenting on this passage, Pokrovsky writes:

> The phrases concerning 'freedoms' and 'liberties' should not confuse us. What is concerned here is not 'freedom of trade' in the sense that the eighteenth century lent this term, but the abolition of all sorts of feudal constraints and extortions of a narrowly fiscal character that limited exchange for the direct small-scale benefit of the imperial and earlier, princely treasury.[78]

The state not only intervened in and organised the market process, but simultaneously 'freed' the market from feudal survivals, implanting bourgeois principles. The efforts of the first Romanovs were continued by Peter the Great, under whom the state itself established factories and stimulated industrial development, supporting private capital.

The Swedish kings were among the first to grasp the ideas of mercantilism, and implemented them with the exceptional energy, enthusiasm and effectiveness that were in general characteristic of most of the members of the Vasa dynasty. Their economic policies were in essence mercantilist even before this ideology took shape and spread about the continent. Sweden was not just another state that chose a mercantilist course, but a state which to a significant degree had itself been established on the basis of mercantilist policies. 'The whole seventeenth century,' an American historian writes, 'was characterized by increased emphasis on centralized planning and direction. Initiative for change came from Stockholm, often inspired by foreign example and assisted by foreign personnel and foreign capital.'[79]

Mercantilism, like Keynesianism in the twentieth century, ensured that state funds flowed into the modernising of infrastructure. France under Colbert again set an example to the rest of Europe when it began a massive programme of building and repairing roads. These efforts did not come to an end in later epochs despite changes of government and different political priorities. Almost everywhere in Europe the condition of roads was woeful, a fact largely responsible for the huge importance of water transport arteries, not only sea routes but also rivers and canals. France, which lay at a distance from the great European rivers, the Rhine and the Danube, and which lagged behind England and Holland in the development of sea-borne trade, needed an effective road network if its economy was to develop. From 1661 Colbert systematically addressed this question, and in 1669 special commissars, responsible for the state of bridges and roads, were appointed throughout the country. All land routes were divided into three categories – royal highways (chemins royaux), secondary highways (chemins vicinaux) and local roads (chemins de travers). For each category, standards were introduced spelling out the width and norms of maintenance. After the death of Colbert in 1683 the efforts of the government in this area gradually dwindled, partly because government attention was concentrated on foreign policy tasks. It is noteworthy that the importance of roads as a factor in military strategy was not yet fully realised. But the work that had been begun was renewed in the mid-eighteenth century, when a special academy was established in France to train road engineers. In 1668 it had been decided to assign 0.8 per cent of the state budget to the building and repair of roads, though in practice the sums spent were somewhat less. In the period from 1683 to 1700 the government spent an average of 771,100 livres per year for these purposes, between 1715 and 1736 spending each year averaged three million livres, and in 1786, on the eve of the revolution, the outlays came to 9,445,000 livres.[80] These efforts yielded an impressive result. To travel from Paris to Bordeaux in 1660 had taken 15 days, but in 1789 only five and a half days were needed.

Imitating France, the Spanish monarch Charles III in 1767 ordered the construction of 'royal highways' throughout his country. In Germany during the eighteenth century almost every state introduced measures analogous to those in France, beginning with Baden in 1733 and ending with Saxony in 1781 and Bavaria in 1790. In Britain the General Highway Acts were adopted in 1766 and 1773. The trip from Edinburgh to London, which in 1700 had taken 11 or 12 days, in 1800 required fewer than three. In the late eighteenth century, before the development of the steam locomotive, horse-drawn state railways made their appearance in Britain. A line stretching between Croydon and Wandsworth was used for the transport of goods, and another, from Swansea to Mumbles, for passenger transport. The existence of these railways encouraged engineers to consider using steam engines for transport purposes; the first experimental locomotives appeared in the late 1790s, and 1804 saw the successful testing of a locomotive capable of drawing ten tons of iron ore and 70 passengers at a speed of 8 km per hour. The development of transport went hand in hand with efforts to maintain order and safety. It was explained that governments needed not only to build roads, but also to guard them.

Curiously, the list of governments concerned with improving internal communications does not include Prussia; this again bears witness to the lack of understanding at that time of the military importance of a road network. Elsewhere in Europe rumours circulated that Frederick the Great considered bad roads good for the economy, since they ensured that 'foreign merchants had to travel for longer over bad roads, and hence left more money in the country'.[81] Whether this is true or not, Prussian roads in the eighteenth century were an object of complaints and mockery by most travellers, including Russians.

With the transition from the free market to a policy of encouraging industry, many regions of Europe saw their cities undergo rapid growth. This applied not only to such centres of textile production as Lyons, the northern Italian cities near the French border, and the quickly growing cities of England and the Scottish lowlands, but also to many cities of the Muscovite empire, such as Tula. It is true that the government in Russia, following on the initiative of Dutch entrepreneurs, decided to use serf labour in industry, and capitalism on the periphery did not develop in the same way as at the centre.

Mercantilism did not impede the development of trade, but directed its currents to points within the nascent empires. In 1669, some 14.4 per cent of English imports had come from the country's colonies; by 1773 this share had grown to 36.5 per cent.[82] By restricting imports and exports, state policies simultaneously aided the consolidation of internal markets and exchange between them. The result was impressive economic growth both in the mother country and in the colonies. The rapid development of the transatlantic economy can be traced in the figures for trade. In the late 1720s exports of British goods to North America were worth an average of £524,000 per year, while in the 1740s the figure was already around a million pounds. Correspondingly, exports to the West Indies rose from £473,000 to £732,000 per year. Even against this background, the increase in exports to India stands out; they grew from an annual figure of £112,000 to £522,000.[83]

After mercantilism had restored the European economy, creating the long-term preconditions for growth, a new expansion of financial capital began as well. Along with lending to states and private firms, this took the form of speculation of all conceivable varieties, possible now as a result of the mass of commodities and money accumulated in the preceding period. In the early eighteenth century the rapid growth of financial speculation led to a stock-market boom, followed by the inevitable crash.

The ending of the War of the Spanish Succession was accompanied by a quick rise in the prices of shares on the stock exchanges. This created favourable conditions for financial speculation, and for the inflating of stock-market 'bubbles' both in Britain and in France. In both countries the booms ended in collapses and scandals. In Britain this financial catastrophe went down in history as the 'South Sea Bubble', and in France it is associated with the 'John Law Affair'.

In Holland the price of shares in the VOC rose from 500 to 1,200 guilders, and in the WIC, from 40 to 400 guilders. The premises of the stock exchange in Amsterdam were 'too small to house all the speculators'.[84] The price of shares in the British East India Company rose at an equally dizzying pace. The shares were quoted at £100, and by 1717 at £200. For the next three years stock-market gamblers were seized by euphoria. In June 1720 shares in the East India Company sold at £420, but in the following summer the market collapsed, and the share price fell to £150.[85]

Both scandals had a political aspect. The South Sea Company had been founded with support from the Tory Party, which sought to make the firm a counterweight to the East India Company, dominated by Whigs. The rapid rise in the price of shares in the South Sea Company automatically buoyed the shares of the East India Company and other commercial firms, but at a certain point the Tories and the court circles associated with them were entitled to think they had achieved their goal; their fortunes had quickly expanded, and the company had attracted prominent and influential people from all Europe as shareholders. In France, the Scots economist John Law and the companies he founded achieved success when they won support from the regent Philippe d'Orléans. The Banque Générale Privée set up by Law in 1716 received the right from the authorities to issue paper money, and before long, without ceasing in essence to be a private joint-stock company, was granted the status of the Banque Royale. Law's activity, however, was not restricted to issuing paper money; he also acquired and reorganised the Mississippi Company, which was transformed into the joint-stock Compagnie de l'Occident. Later, it was merged with the Compagnie des Indes Orientales, with the Compagnie de Chine and with several other trading enterprises to form the Compagnie Perpetuelle des Indes. Its shares quickly rose in price. The growth of the stock-market pyramid was fed by the emitting of paper money. The initial success of this activity caused one of Law's most recent biographers to state that his hero 'behaved very much like a man of the twentieth century'.[86]

The collapse came in the summer of 1720. The South Sea Bubble burst. In France the devaluation of paper money was accompanied by a fall of stock prices and the discrediting of the government.

The financial adventures of the early eighteenth century rested on a genuine basis of economic growth. The new wave of expansion, however, was accompanied by radical changes in the European world-system. In the countries of the European centre, commercial capitalism gave way gradually to industrial capitalism. Holland remained the only country to consistently defend the principles of free trade throughout the seventeenth century, a fact which helped ensure the loss of its dominant position in the markets. Deprived of state support, Dutch industries fell gradually into decline, the textile industry in particular. The strengthening of the state, however, was a general tendency which not even Holland was to evade. Conflicts between regional elites and supporters of a stronger central authority ended in victory for the latter. The struggle between the *Stadhouder* of the Netherlands Maurits van Nassau, who sought to strengthen the central authority, and the Grand Pensionary of the Province of Holland Johan van Oldenbarnefelt, who defended the autonomy of the regions, ended with the triumph of Maurits. Oldenbarnefelt was charged with treason and executed on 13 May 1619. Later, the struggle between the House of Orange and its enemies among the merchant oligarchy repeatedly flared up afresh, and in 1651, after the death of Prince Willem II, the office of *stadhouder* was declared vacant. Members of the House of Orange, who earlier had acquired this post by inheritance, were banned from holding it. The triumph of the merchant oligarchy, however, did not lead to a rejection of centralist policies; only the emphases shifted. In place of the land army on which the House of Orange had relied, the navy was strengthened. External expansion was pursued more aggressively in the colonies, while plans for the incorporation into the republic of the Southern Netherlands, which remained beneath the power of the Habsburgs, were postponed.

As a Russian historian has noted, the position and interests of the commercial oligarchy changed dramatically in the course of the seventeenth century.

> After enriching itself fabulously during the first half of the seventeenth century, the trading bourgeoisie began to transfer its capital from the commercial-entrepreneurial and financial areas into land. It acquired rental properties, and took up lucrative posts in the government apparatus or in those of the states, municipalities and consistories. A sort of political oligarchy took shape, gradually transforming itself into a closed community which the commercial bourgeoisie could not penetrate as it wished.[87]

Although the United Provinces undoubtedly took a far more market-oriented approach than England, not to speak of France, there is no basis for regarding the Dutch state as weak, or as refusing to intervene in economic processes. The efficiency of the Dutch tax system was without precedent in the Europe of the time. The Grand Pensionary of Holland Johan de Witt complained repeatedly of the stinginess of his compatriots, who were not prepared to take money from their own pockets even 'for their own defence'.[88] But despite the fact that the population of the republic was only half that of England, budget revenues were greater, and from each taxpayer in Holland the state received three times as much money as in England or France.[89] This is explained in part by the higher level of incomes, but also by the political discipline that resulted from the powerful bond between citizens and the state. The Dutch bourgeois (including petty entrepreneurs) were ready to share with the state, recognising that they and the state were as one.

Controlling the traffic in goods between countries, the Dutch merchants received a sort of monopoly rent, appropriating a significant proportion of the profits. The shift from free trade to mercantilism also meant the beginning of the end for Dutch commercial hegemony. The English Navigation Acts, which provoked wars with Holland, were simply one manifestation of a general tendency. Following the example of London, the majority of states tried to restrict Dutch trade, seeking to have their exports conveyed on their own ships.

The successive political regimes in England were united in their desire to put an end to the Dutch trading monopoly, and in this enjoyed the complete support of France. The joint military, diplomatic and economic efforts of Europe's two strongest powers could not fail to yield a result. The decline of Holland, however, led not just to the emergence of England as the new commercial hegemon, but also to the strengthening of France as the country laying claim to political hegemony on a European scale. Anglo–French conflict became inevitable as a result of the victory of these two rising military-industrial powers over commercial Holland.

From dynasty to nation

The political result of mercantilism was the appearance of the national state, with all the consequences flowing from it, including the poetry of Pushkin and the music of Wagner. Britain, France and Holland, the countries that led the way in political and economic development, became the models for the rest of Europe, while against this background the Austria of the Habsburgs and the Prussia of the Hohenzollerns seemed exceptions, and the Russian Empire of the Romanovs an outright paradox. Meanwhile, the general tendencies inherent in advanced Western countries appeared visibly in the dynastic empires as well, despite the multi-ethnic and multi-linguistic nature of the populations of these states.

The first 'national' states in the modern sense were those empires, primarily trading empires, that developed as a result of overseas expansion in the period from the sixteenth to the eighteenth centuries. In the eighteenth and nineteenth centuries Britain and France were imperial powers no less than Austria or Russia.

Traditional historiography is inclined to draw a distinction between the formation of the national state in key European countries (Spain and Portugal, England and France) and their colonial expansion. The acquisition of empire is seen as something important, but fundamentally external with relation to the nation whose formation the authors try as far as possible to shift to earlier times. The truth is that before the beginning of the modern era we are at best dealing only with embryonic, potential nations, many of which did not realise their potential. 'The European national state,' political scientist Alla Glinchikova writes,

> would simply not have been able to take shape or to achieve its eventual economic and political form prior to or outside of the colonisation process. The European national states with their representative democracy, and the European type of market relations with their indispensable level of social uniformity, are equally the products of colonisation, and of colonisation of a quite specific type, in which the metropolis and the colonies were divided geographically and politically. It was also this that created the illusion and the possibility of abstracting the national state-metropolis as an independent, primary 'cell' of the modern epoch.[90]

In a European absolute monarchy where people were not citizens but subjects, the country and its population were identified with the crown, which for its part assumed responsibility for turning diverse territories and masses of people into a single enlightened state, corresponding to the ideas of progress and humanity of the time. The formation of nations, begun within the framework of absolutism, was continued by the bourgeois regimes.

The splitting of Germany into protestant and Catholic parts exacerbated its already divided nature. Nevertheless, state centralisation went ahead in Germany just as it did in Sweden or France. Saxony, Prussia, Bavaria and Austria were perfectly modern states for their time, with developed forms of bureaucratic and military organisation and with their own education systems and political traditions.

The problem did not lie with the limited extent of the territory, or with the rivalry of several states within a shared cultural space. Wherever a dynastic state remained, even if in apparently altered form, the solving of new tasks was rendered more difficult by the ambiguity of the political nature of the state. To this problem, the history of Austria–Hungary bears eloquent witness.

In the words of a Spanish historian, Habsburg rule both in Spain and in Austria was underlain by 'dynastic unity [*el sistema de unidad dinastica*], combined with broad regional autonomy'.[91] Despite the systematic efforts of the Habsburgs, trying to turn their patchwork empire into something like a modern nation, and despite the centralising reforms of Josef II and the decentralising compromises of Franz Josef, the national-state integration of Central Europe did not take place, to the misfortune of this region, which during the twentieth century experienced a series of bloody tragedies.

In the sixteenth century the Habsburgs had managed to secure the imperial crown for themselves by hereditary succession, reducing the rights of the elector princes to a pure formality, but in the process drastically weakening the ties of the electors to the empire. The possessions of the elector princes began turning into independent states. The Archduke of Austria, in reality the ruler of a vast empire, was nominally no such thing. But he was considered the emperor of Germany, over which in reality he had no power.

After successful wars with Ottoman Turkey allowed the Habsburgs to take possession of the entire territory of Hungary and to enter the Balkans, the geopolitical interests of Vienna began to shift in that direction, often coming into conflict with Habsburg policy in Germany.

In the battle of Mohács in 1526, the Turkish army routed the Hungarians, after which the Hungarian king recognised himself as a vassal of the Turkish sultan. In 1541 the Turks captured Buda and Pest, while the Hungarian territories that had become part of the Ottoman Empire were transformed into the Buda *paşahk*. Part of the Hungarian lands finished up under the control of the Austrian Habsburgs, and were turned into a base for a counter-offensive against the Turks. By a treaty of 1547 lands with a mixed Hungarian and Slavic population went to the Habsburgs. After the defeat inflicted on the Turks near Vienna in 1683 by the Polish King Jan Sobieski, the Austro-Hungarian reconquest began. In 1687 Austrian armies forced the Ottomans out of Hungary and Transylvania. In 1697 Prince Eugene of Savoy won a brilliant victory over the Turks at Zenta. The process of freeing the Hungarian lands continued until 1718, when Austrian forces occupied the most southerly regions of the country. Also in 1687 at a *sejm* in Pozsony, the present-day Bratislava, representatives of the estates recognised the hereditary right of the male line of the Habsburgs to the Hungarian throne. For Hungarian protestants, however, liberation turned into oppression and slaughter. The result of this policy was the revolt of Ferenc Rákóczi in 1703–11. Ultimately, the protestants were granted amnesty and religious freedom. Government posts in Hungary were required to be filled by Hungarians.

In the course of the War of the Spanish Succession the territory of Belgium, then the Spanish Netherlands, had gone to Austria. Meanwhile, the wars against the Turks moved the southern border of the empire to the Danube. Extensive domains throughout much of Europe, from the Southern Netherlands to northern Serbia, from Brussels to Belgrade, finished up beneath the power of Vienna. But these were heterogeneous territories, not integrated on any basis apart from a common ruling dynasty. This situation was well understood by the Vienna court, which made desperate attempts to consolidate the space under its political control. This task became central for successive emperors and their governments throughout the eighteenth century, though the methods used were different depending on who was in power in Vienna.

It was only in the mid-eighteenth century, when the male line of the Austrian Habsburg dynasty died out, that the 'patchwork empire' began turning into a genuine state, quite robust even if lacking in 'national' identity.

The first step along the road to imperial consolidation was the Pragmatic Sanction of 1713. Under this document the Emperor Charles VI, who had no sons, proclaimed the indivisibility of his dynastic possessions and determined that the succession to power in Austria could follow the female line. 'General acceptance of the Pragmatic Sanction,' the Belarusian historian Ya. Shimov states, 'became the main goal of Austrian politics under Charles VI.'[92]

In 1725 Spain recognised the Pragmatic Sanction in exchange for the House of Austria renouncing its claims to the Spanish throne, which as a result of the War of the Spanish Succession was held by the Bourbons. In 1726 the document was recognised by Russia, and in 1728 by Prussia. In 1731–32 they were joined by London and The Hague, and soon afterwards the Pragmatic charter won the support of the Reichstag of the Empire. Only in 1738 was recognition obtained from France. It appeared the goal had been attained, but two influential German states, Bavaria and Saxony, withheld their agreement. Since the Bavarian house had rights to the Austrian throne, its refusal to accept the new order of succession in Vienna had far-reaching consequences. Despite all the efforts of Austrian diplomacy after the death of Charles VI an international crisis broke out, growing into the War of the Austrian Succession of 1740–48.

Austria won this war, despite suffering territorial losses. A key role in deciding the outcome was played by Hungary. The right of the Austrian Princess Maria Theresa to the Hungarian throne was more than debatable, since the crown of István the Holy was heritable only by the male line. But when the Hungarian estates recognised Maria Theresa as their queen, they effectively confirmed the historic choice in favour of a common Austro-Hungarian empire.

Although Maria Theresa had been able to win and maintain her power only due to the loyalty of the Hungarians, her government followed a policy of administrative centralisation and of expanding the use of the German language. Laws and regulations began to be unified across the whole territory ruled by the Habsburgs. Special attention was paid to transforming the bureaucracy. A still more determined reform policy was pursued by Josef II.

By the early eighteenth century not only Britain, but all the major powers of Europe were no longer purely feudal monarchies. Instead, they represented the result of a class compromise between the traditional elites and the growing bourgeoisie, which was increasingly capable of dictating agendas especially in foreign policy, whose logic was closely connected to the overall conditions of development of the world-system.[93] The ideology of enlightened absolutism reflects quite adequately the demands and expectations which the rising class associated with the state authorities.

Many historians have considered the idea of enlightened absolutism the product of naivety, of utopian thinking, or of the political moderation of the French philosophers of the eighteenth century. But the French thinkers Voltaire, Diderot, D'Alembert and other authors of the famed *Encyclopedia* were in no way naïve, artless souls. Behind the utopia of enlightened absolutism can be discerned a perfectly realistic depiction of the norms and principles of state construction that suited most of the bourgeoisie at the time when these texts were written.

Enlightened absolutism was not just an ideology but also a real political practice, which in the conditions of eighteenth-century Europe was viewed as a thoroughly convincing alternative to the 'democratic' power of the oligarchies ruling in Holland and Britain. The problem did not lie in the fact that the monarchs and bureaucrats lacked enlightenment, but in their inability to cope with the tasks of capitalist development. In France, the most developed country on the continent, this contradiction manifested itself with great acuteness. But in Russia, Austria and Prussia, the commercial capital that was emerging was quite satisfied even in the late eighteenth century with a regime of enlightened absolutism, and made no claim to anything more.

The successes and failures of Josef II demonstrate better than any theories the possibilities and limitations of a policy of enlightened absolutism. In 1781 Josef II issued a decree on freedom of the press, and soon after, on religious toleration. The strict defence of Catholicism that was traditional for the Habsburgs was replaced by the principle of equal religious rights, extending not only to protestants and Orthodox, but even to Jews. Trying to support German culture, Josef mounted an attack on Italian opera in Vienna. The creation of a new German opera was entrusted to W.A. Mozart, who composed *The Abduction from the Seraglio* to a commission from the emperor.[94] In 1776 the Vienna Burgtheater was handed over to a German theatre troupe. In this respect Josef II differed sharply from Frederick the Great, who 'could not bear German literature'.[95]

Under Josef II monasteries met with persecution. The enlightened ruler considered monks 'the country's most harmful and useless subjects'.[96] By the time of his coronation the number of monasteries had fallen from 2,000 to 700. This, however, did not by any means signify a break with the Catholic church or cultural tradition. Josef's task was not to exterminate Austrian Catholicism, but to modernise it.

The government made efforts to remove numerous customs barriers dividing different parts of the empire. In 1775 internal customs barriers were abolished in Austria and Bohemia, though attempts to do this in Hungary were unsuccessful. British historian Tim Blanning notes that with the economic situation in Hungary and Transylvania effectively 'colonial', the local nobility strove to preserve 'what was deemed to be their fair share of direct taxation'.[97]

The Austrian Empire was not the only dynastic state whose existence was inseparable from the history of a ruling house. Just as the Austro-Hungarian empire was the expanded family appanage of the Habsburgs, Prussia was the familial estate of the Hohenzollerns, and Bavaria of the Wittelsbachs. Moreover, until the mid-nineteenth century the possessions of the Hohenzollerns, scattered about various parts of Germany and often with no territorial connection to one another, were even more deserving than Austria of being called a 'patchwork empire'. Later, when it expanded at the expense of Poland, Prussia could be called a multi-national country.

The rise of Prussia began in the sixteenth century when it merged with the Electorate of Brandenburg. In 1525 the Teutonic Order was transformed into the Dukedom of East Prussia, with the title of Duke assumed by the former Grand Master of the order, Albrecht Hohenzollern von Brandenburg-Ansbach, who had converted to Lutheranism. Poland, in the person of King Sigismund I, not only recognised the new state as its vassal, but also later guaranteed that the Brandenburg Hohenzollerns would inherit the territory when the male line of the Prussian Dukes became extinct, as occurred in 1618.

The Dukedom that arose during the Reformation on the lands of the former Teutonic Order was held in a personal unification with Brandenburg until merging with it to form a unified kingdom in 1656. In June of that year the forces of Brandenburg-Prussia, together with the Swedes, defeated a numerically superior Polish army in a three-day battle near Warsaw. The Prussians dispersed the Szlachecki militia, which in fleeing across the Vistula lost all its cannon when a bridge collapsed. A year later Poland recognised the complete independence of East Prussia. Soon after this, the Prussia of Friedrich Wilhelm entered into a new war, this time against its former ally Sweden, inflicting a sensational defeat on it at Fehrbellin. In Königsberg in 1701 Friedrich III was crowned King of Prussia, taking the title of Friedrich I. From then on the name of Prussia was applied to the whole Brandenburg-Prussian state.

Absolutism in Prussia rested on the firm support of the junkers – local landowners who built their prosperity on the well-organised and commercially oriented exploitation of the serf peasantry. The poet Adelbert von Chamisso formulated the relationship between government and landowners in the famous lines: 'Und der König absolut, wenn er unseren Willen tut.' – 'And the power of the king is absolute, provided he does our will.'[98]

By no means all historians, however, share the certainty of contemporaries about the omnipotence of the Prussian junkers. The British scholar Colin Mooers, for example, considers that 'the Junkers needed the absolutist state much more than the state needed them'.[99] In his view, the weakness in Prussia of the representation of the estates is to be explained not only by the fact that the bourgeoisie lacked sufficient influence in society, but also by the dependence of the junkers on the state. The royal power was the organisational form within whose framework landowner society was incorporated into the capitalist market – the same 'Prussian road to the development of capitalism' of which Lenin spoke.[100]

Unlike the situation in France, the bourgeoisie in Prussia lacked direct access to the royal finances, and as a result corruption was absent on any notable scale. The Berlin functionaries demonstrated 'bureaucratic efficiency far in advance of other absolutist states of the time'.[101]

Organisational harmony and logic were rare attributes of state administration in continental Europe in the eighteenth century. The absolutist regimes built their institutions in such a way that the appearance of new tasks and functions led not so much to the reorganisation or abolition of old state bodies, as to the appearance of new ones alongside them. The system grew steadily more complex, at times becoming completely chaotic. These traits could be observed in France, in Austria, and even in Russia, although the reorganisation carried out by Peter the Great in the early eighteenth century lent the political system of the St Petersburg empire a certain smoothness. In this respect the Prussian model of administration was not superior to that of France. If its efficiency was greater, this was not because the bureaucracy was better organised, but because it was better trained, and more disciplined and loyal.

The existence of a precisely functioning bureaucratic apparatus allowed the Prussian kings to establish a powerful army, whose strength was clearly out of proportion to the size and wealth of the state. Taking Sweden as their example, the Berlin monarchs achieved still more impressive results through the consistent militarisation of all aspects of state life. Visiting Berlin in 1770 the Italian poet Vittorio Alfieri complained that the city seemed to him 'a huge, loathsome barracks', and all of Prussia 'one vast guard-house'.[102] After a trip to Berlin one of the future leaders of the French Revolution, the Comte de Mirabeau, remarked ironically: 'War is Prussia's national industry'.[103] This joke was at least partly a compliment. The point was not only that the whole life of the Prussian kingdom was subordinated to the tasks of the army, but that among the Prussians war was subject to systematic rational organisation, becoming an 'industry'.

If vital national institutions include a massive army, composed of residents of the country who are loyal and ready to shed their blood for the government, then Prussia, which was not a nation in terms of the way nineteenth-century ideology understood this term, unquestionably outstripped most of its neighbours in forming a national state.

The oriental empire

At a time when the West was experiencing revolutionary cataclysms, in Eastern Europe a force was steadily and, it seemed, irresistibly arising and was entering into clear conflict with the nascent European world-system. That force was the Sublime Porte, the Ottoman Empire. The fall of Constantinople in 1453 proved a turning-point not only in political and economic respects, since it also induced the Portuguese and Spaniards to go in search of a western sea route to India.

The Turkish victory was a powerful blow to the Venetian military-commercial hegemony in the Eastern Mediterranean, especially since soon after Constantinople the turn came of Beirut and Alexandria, the main centres of Venetian entrepôt commerce. The fall of Byzantium marked the end of the medieval world, of its system of values, of its geopolitics and geo-economy, demonstrating to contemporaries the exhaustion of age-old traditions.

From the point of view of medieval legal thinking there could only be two emperors, the eastern and western, corresponding to the two parts of the ancient Roman Empire. The two empires had also corresponded to the two centres of the Christian church, Rome and Constantinople. After the fall of Byzantium the question of who was to inherit the Eastern title was an open one, but the Grand Prince of Muscovy acted quite logically in assuming the title of tsar (that is, Caesar), adopting the Byzantine two-headed eagle and proclaiming Moscow the 'Third Rome'. As ruler of the largest and at that time, the sole Orthodox power, he had every basis for doing so.

The integration of Russia into the nascent capitalist world-system had begun at the time of the Livonian war. From the sixteenth century Muscovy not only sought to develop trade with the West, but subordinated its entire foreign policy to this goal. The system of serfdom in Russia became established at the same time as, and in close association with, the development of the market economy and of international commercial ties. The products of Russian serf labour, like the cotton produced by black slaves in Virginia or sugar from the Caribbean plantations, stimulated and subsidised the development of free labour in the west, while simultaneously financing the consumption of the Russian ruling class. In essence, Russia was subjected to colonisation, not through the agency of a foreign power but through that of its own elite, which succeeded in establishing an impressive empire in Eastern Europe.

Ottoman Turkey for its part also laid claim to the heritage of Byzantium. Mehmed II the Conqueror, after setting up his capital in Istanbul, the former Constantinople, declared himself head of the Romans and head of the Muslims. 'He was at once Kaisar-i-Rum, Roman Emperor in succession to Augustus and Constantine, and Padishah, in the Persian idiom Vice-Regent of God.'[104]

The benevolent attention of the Sultan did not extend solely to the Orthodox Greeks. Everyone who was prepared to collaborate with the empire received support. The commercial privileges of the Genoese, whose rivalry with the Venetians had made them *de facto* partners of the Turks, were reaffirmed. Istanbul was rebuilt and populated with Greeks, Jews and Armenians, who had to be brought from other parts of the empire especially to replace the exiled residents.

Since the Sultans throughout the sixteenth and seventeenth centuries were in conflict with Spain and Austria, they opened their doors wide to everyone who had been persecuted in these countries. Calvinists fled to Hungary and Bosnia, which were under Turkish occupation. Spanish Jews, banished from their homeland in 1492, resettled themselves in Turkey. The sultans' tolerance had limits, but so long as followers of other faiths did not lay claim to political power, they were prepared to leave them to their own devices. Moreover, Islamic law laid down that most of the taxes that flowed to the treasury should be paid by non-believers. After the departure of the Turks, the Christian peoples who had lived under their power retained their own languages, culture, religions, and at times their social institutions as well, and were fully prepared for an independent political existence.[105]

The Ottoman state achieved remarkable successes in regions to the south-east, in short order establishing its sovereignty over the Arab lands of Asia and Africa. To the empire's new subjects the sultan in Istanbul was in the first instance a new Caliph, and this suited the Istanbul bureaucracy perfectly. In the West, the Turks achieved their greatest successes in the mid-sixteenth century. Under the Truce of Adrianople in 1547 the Habsburgs retained part of north-western Hungary, but Austria itself was forced to pay a tribute to the Sultan. Payments of this humiliating tribute ceased only after the war of 1592–1606. The sea-borne might of the Ottomans was broken by the combined strength of the Habsburgs and Venetians at Lepanto in 1571. But the defeats that the Turks began to suffer in the second half of the sixteenth century bore witness not so much to the decline of the empire as to the fact that after reaching its natural boundaries (coinciding largely with the eastern borders of the ancient Roman Empire), the Ottoman state lacked the strength for further expansion.

The military strength of the Ottomans rested on a solid economic basis, and the financial situation of the Turkish empire was significantly better than that of most Western empires of that epoch. Unlike the case in Russia, where the peasants were serfs dependent on the landowners, the Turkish peasantry was at once free and dependent on the state. In many ways the agrarian system that prevailed in Turkey recalled the early European feudalism, with the difference that the estates were not transformed into the private property of the landholders. The system under which state lands (*timar*) were distributed to outstanding participants in military campaigns and to government officials had been borrowed by the Ottomans from the Byzantines, and possibly from the Seljuks as well.

> The right to full property in land, an entitlement known as *rakbe,* belonged to the state, while the right to make use of land and to receive income from it belonged to the holder of the *timar.* The right to possession of the *timar* passed by inheritance from father to son, but the holder could not give the *timar* away, transfer it to an outside person, pledge it as security or bequeath it to anyone but his sons.[106]

Since the land belonged not just nominally but also in practice to the central authority, which regularly redistributed the peasant allotments, the economic and legal dependency of the peasants was obvious. But the personal status of the peasants had nothing in common with the position of serfs. No-one interfered in questions of production, and there was no compulsory labour.[107]

On the whole, this state of affairs was advantageous for the peasant population in the countries subjugated by the Turks. The social structure of rural regions underwent substantial changes. During the wars of conquest the old feudal aristocracy had been wiped out, brought to ruin or banished. Of its lands, a portion was distributed among the Turkish soldiers, who did not, however, receive hereditary rights to their new holdings. The result was that a powerful class of landowners did not become established as was the case in Russia or Hungary. But the favourable conditions enjoyed by peasant agriculture proved a crucial obstacle to the development of market and later, capitalist relations in the countryside. The compulsion to participate in the market that characterised European and colonial countries was virtually absent from the Ottoman territories until the nineteenth century, and this in turn increased the difficulties of accumulating capital and weakened the bourgeoisie.

The Ottoman empire fell victim to its own military–political success. The basis for the flourishing of the empire was the stability that the sultans invariably sought to maintain, despite recurrent palace revolutions. Unlike the Russia of the Romanovs, which actively sought to integrate itself into the developing European world-system, Ottoman Turkey pursued economic and political policies aimed at maintaining the traditional order. But the more this was successful, the weaker the empire became. The contradiction besetting the Ottoman empire was that unlike Japan, it could neither isolate itself from the influence and pressure of the world-system that was gathering strength in the West, nor assume a position within that system that suited at least an important part of the Ottoman elite, if not the population as a whole.

The Ottoman empire encountered many of the same dilemmas as the empire of the Romanovs. But it did not just seek to resolve these problems in different ways; over an extended period it failed to resolve them at all. This situation ensured that for two centuries the history of Turkey would be one of decline, occurring against a background of the contradictory and dramatic, but nevertheless obvious rise of Russia.

In the mid-seventeenth century the might of Turkey aroused respect and fear in the country's neighbours, and the armies of the sultans threatened Poland and Austria. By the end of the century the relationship of forces had changed radically and irreversibly. The turning-point was the siege of Vienna by the Turks in 1683. The Habsburgs were faring badly, and it was only the intervention by the Polish King Jan Sobieski that saved the situation. In a battle near Vienna on 12 September 1683 the Ottomans were crushed by the Holy League army which the Polish king had assembled.

This victory yielded almost nothing for Poland, which entered into a period of prolonged decline, ending in collapse. But for the Austrian Habsburgs the battle near Vienna marked the beginning of a triumphant move to the south-east, allowing them to regain their strength after the defeat in the Thirty Years War and to regain their position as a leading European power. The successes of Austria were achieved through the decline of Turkey.

From the first half of the seventeenth century Turkish technological backwardness steadily increased. The military defeats inflicted on the Turks by the Polish forces of Jan Sobieski, and later by the Austrian army of Eugene of Savoy, testified to the fact that the former glory of the Ottoman army had vanished into the past. In 1720 Sultan Ahmed III was forced to send a special mission to France with the aim of studying the latest European inventions. But despite the acute need for modernisation, recognised by a significant section of the elite, real changes occurred extremely slowly. It was not Islamic tradition or the rigidity of the dominant culture that blocked innovation, but primarily a fear of destroying the system of social and political relations that underlay the state.

Meanwhile, the integration of Turkey into the world economy was leading to the decay of the established system. The penetration of the empire by Western European exports increased steadily, as did the dependence of Ottoman society on these goods. From the West came not only weapons and new technologies, but also many items of everyday use. This process developed further in the nineteenth century. The growing dependence on the West also manifested itself in Turkish commercial policy, which became permeated by the principles of economic liberalism. The rights of foreign entrepreneurs were regulated by special 'capitulations', granting privileged status to representatives of Western nations with which corresponding agreements had been signed. The first such agreement was concluded with France in 1569, and others with England in 1580 and Holland in 1612. The economic liberalism to which the Sublime Porte adhered did nothing to aid the development of political liberalism, a situation which resulted in growing disillusionment among the educated intelligentsia of the capital, who dreamed not only of European goods, but also of European institutions.

The changes occurring in the West had an extremely negative impact on the life of the empire. The place of the Venetians, who traditionally had been enemies of the Sultan but who were also partners with Arab and Greek merchants, was taken by the Dutch, English and French. 'The Ottoman economy and monetary system collapsed in the 1600s,' English historians have recognised, 'mainly because of the aggressive mercantilistic economies of Western nations that replaced the Venetians in the Levant.'[108]

The internal market remained relatively narrow, while the Ottoman empire was unable to place on the world market any unique product which Europe could not obtain from other regions. 'World wide during the eighteenth and nineteenth centuries, international trade increased enormously but less so in the Ottoman lands,' notes the American scholar Donald Quataert. While foreign trade on the world scale increased by a factor of 64 times during the nineteenth century, in relation to the territories controlled by the Turks this index reached barely 16 times.[109] Although Turkey had played a major role in the European trade of the early seventeenth century, throughout the following two centuries its importance to the world economy steadily declined.

Incessant wars exhausted the treasury, and the need to maintain the navy turned into a ruinous burden for a state that was not conducting an active foreign trade. Most Turkish exports were conveyed on foreign vessels.

The army, earlier famed for its discipline, gradually decayed. The fearsome corps of the janissaries was drawn into internal political intrigues, and became a weapon for palace coups. Outside of their official duties, the janissaries engaged in artisanry and trade. A caste of professional warriors that had struck fear into all Europe was transformed into a class of petty shopkeepers.

Notes

1 C.R. Boxer (ed.), *Portuguese Conquest and commerce in Southern Asia*, London: Hutchinson, 1969, p. ix.
2 G.J. Ames, *The Globe Encompassed. The Age of European Discovery: 1500–1700.* Upper Saddle River, NJ: Pearson, 2008, p. 145.
3 *The Economist*, XIV (685): 1117, 11 October 1856.

4 See J.D. Tracy (ed.), *The Political Economy of Merchant Empires*, Cambridge: Cambridge University Press, 1991, p. 105.

5 H. Delbrück, *Istoriya voennogo iskusstva v ramkakh politicheskoy istorii* [History of the art of war in the context of political history], St Petersburg: Nauka, 2001, Vol. 4, pp. 107–8.

6 J. Israel, *The Dutch Republic. Its Rise, Greatness, and Fall*, Oxford: Oxford University Press, 1998, p. 267.

7 H. Delbrück, *Istoriya*, vol. 4, p. 112.

8 Israel, *Dutch Republic*, p. 267.

9 K. Yorgensen, M. Pavkovich, R. Rays, F. Shnayd and K. Skott, *Voyny i srazheniya Novogo Vremeni, 1500–1763* [English title: Fighting Techniques of the Early Modern World, AD 1500 – AD 1763], Moscow: EKSMO, 2006, p. 139.

10 Cited in Tracy, *Political Economy of Merchant Empires*, p. 4

11 Ibid.

12 See R. Blackburn. *The Making of New World Slavery. From Baroque to the Modern, 1492–1800,* London/New York: Verso, 1997, p. 195.

13 G.A. Shatokhina-Mordvintseva, *Istoriya Niderlandov* [History of the Netherlands], Moscow: Drofa, 2007, p. 299.

14 Ibid.

15 A. Calder, *Revolutionary Empire. The Rise of the English-Speaking Empires from the Fifteenth Century to the 1780s,* London: Pimlico, 1998, p. 171.

16 M. Urban, *Generals. Ten British Commanders Who Shaped the World,* London: Faber & Faber, 2005, p. 53.

17 G. Arrighi, *The Long Twentieth Century,* London/New York: Verso, 1999, p. 43.

18 F. Brodel', *Material'naya tsivilizatsiya, ekonomika i kapitalizm* [Material civilisation, the economy and capitalism], Vol. 3, Moscow: Ves' mir, 2007, p. 199.

19 Ibid.

20 F. Ancillon, *Tableau des révolutions du système politique de l' Europe* [List of the revolutions in the political system of Europe], Paris: Anselin et Pochard, 1823, Vol. 3, p. 201.

21 Urban, *Generals*, p. 45.

22 This battle, on 13 August 1704, also figures at times in the historical literature as the Second Battle of Höchstädt.

23 Israel, *Dutch Republic*, p. 272.

24 For complaints by English merchants about Dutch intrigues in Africa, see B. Davidson, *The African Slave Trade,* Boston/Toronto: Atlantic Monthly Press, 1980, p. 72.

25 Arrighi, *Long Twentieth Century*, p. 47.

26 For a comparison of English and Dutch policies in Asia, see Tracy, *Political Economy of Merchant Empires*, p. 87.

27 *The Political Magazine and Parliamentary, Naval, Military and Lottery Journal,* vol. 5, August 1783, p. 83.

28 E. Burke, *Selected Writings and Speeches,* ed. by P.J. Stanlis, Gloucester, MA: Peter Smith, 1968, p. 184.

29 P. Kennedy, *The Rise and Fall of British Naval Mastery,* London: Penguin, 2004, p. 50.

30 Calder, *Revolutionary Empire*, p. 164.

31 Israel, *Dutch Republic*, p. 721.

32 See T. Blanning, *The Pursuit of Glory. The Five Revolutions that Made Modern Europe: 1648–1815,* London: Penguin Books, 2008, p. 102.

33 J. De Vries and A. Van Der Woude, *The First Modern Economy: Success, Failure and Perseverance of the Dutch Economy, 1500–1815,* Cambridge: Cambridge University Press, 1997, p. 485.

34 See Tracy, *Political Economy of Merchant Empires*, p. 94.

35 See Blanning, *Pursuit of Glory*, p. 102.

36 N. Ferguson, *Empire: How Britain Made the Modern World,* London: Allen Lane, 2003, p. 24.

37 V.G. Kiernan, *State and Society in Europe, 1550–1650*, Oxford: Basil Blackwell, 1980, p. 93.
38 H. Schilling, *Höfe und Allianzen. Deutschland 1648–1763* [Courts and alliances. Germany 1648–1763], Berlin: Siedler Verlag, 1989, p. 52.
39 Ancillon, *Tableau des révolutions*, Vol. 3, pp. 244–5.
40 See K. Repgen, *Dreissigjähriger Krieg und Westfälischer Friede* [The Thirty Years War and the Peace of Westphalia], Paderborn/Münich/Vienna/Zürich: Schoenigh, 1998, p. 301.
41 Quoted in R. Bonney, *The European Dynastic States: 1494–1660*, Oxford: Oxford University Press, 1992, p. 418.
42 See De Vries and Van Der Woude, *First Modern Economy*.
43 Delbrück, *Istoriya*, Vol. 4, p. 119.
44 Ibid.
45 W. J. Stover, *Military Politics in Finland. Development of Governmental Control Over the Armed Forces*, Washington, DC: University Press of America, 1981, p. 32.
46 Ibid., p. 30.
47 H. Lindqvist, *A History of Sweden*, Stockholm: Nordstedts, 2006, p. 91.
48 Ibid., pp. 93, 94.
49 E. Jutikkala (with K. Pirinen), *Geschichte Finnlands* [History of Finland], Stuttgart: Alfred Kroener Verlag, 1976, p. 133.
50 Ibid., p. 83.
51 G. Barudio, *Gustav Adolf – der Grosse. Eine politische Biographie* [Gustavus Adolphus the Great. A political biography], Frankfurt am Main: S. Fischer, 1982, p. 112.
52 Kiernan, *State and Society*, p. 159.
53 See S.A. Nefedov, *Voyna i obshchestvo. Faktornyy analiz istoricheskogo protsessa. Istoriya Vostoka* [War and society. A factor analysis of the historical process. The History of the East], Moscow: Izdatel'skiy dom 'Territoriya budushchego', 2008.
54 Delbrück, *Istoriya*, vol. 4, p. 120.
55 C. Tilly, *Coercion, Capital and European States AD 990-1992*, Malden, MA: Blackwell Publishers, 1990, p. 57.
56 Stover, *Military Politics in Finland*, p. 33.
57 Delbrück, *Istoriya*, Vol. 4, p. 123.
58 Stover, *Military Politics in Finland*, p. 32.
59 See Delbrück, *Istoriya*, Vol. 4, p. 120. According to Delbrück the population of Sweden together with Estland and Finland was about a million people, which corresponded roughly to the combined population of Saxony and Brandenburg. These figures are somewhat underestimated. According to Swedish historians Gustavus Adolphus had about 1.3 million subjects.
60 Lindqvist, *History of Sweden*, p. 166.
61 See F.D. Scott, *Sweden. The Nation's History*, Minneapolis: University of Minnesota Press, 1977, p. 189.
62 Kiernan. *State and Society*, p. 159.
63 See Scott, *Sweden*, p. 190.
64 Nefedov, *Voyna i obshchestvo*, p. 26.
65 Lindqvist, *History of Sweden*, p. 205.
66 Ancillon, *Tableau des révolutions*, Vol. 3, p. 177.
67 A.D. Lyubinskaya, *Frantsiya pri Rishel'e. Frantsuzskiy absolyutizm v 1630–1642gg.* [France under Richelieu. French absolutism in the years from 1630 to 1642], Leningrad: Nauka, 1982, p. 82.
68 Ancillon, *Tableau des révolutions*, Vol. 3, p. 234.
69 Repgen, *Dreissigjähriger Krieg*, p. 313.
70 See Lindqvist, *History of Sweden*, p. 139.
71 N. Kareev, *Zapadnoevropeyskaya absolyutnaya monarkhiya XVI, XVII i XVIII vekov* [Western European absolute monarchy in the sixteenth, seventeenth and eighteenth centuries], Moscow: Gosudarstvennaya publichnaya istoricheskaya biblioteka Rossii, 2009, p. 256.

72 Ibid., p. 259.
73 Ibid., p. 260.
74 Marx and F. Engels, *Sochineniya*, Vol. 23, p. 767.
75 Ancillon, *Tableau des révolutions*, vol. 4, p. 46.
76 See D. Fraser, *Frederick the Great, King of Prussia*, London: Penguin, 2000.
77 Cited in M. Pokrovskiy, *Russkaya istoriya* [Russian history], St Petersburg: Poligon, vol. 2, p. 93.
78 Ibid., pp. 93–4.
79 Ibid., p. 188.
80 See Blanning, *Pursuit of Glory*, p. 7.
81 I. Sherr, *Germaniya Tsivilizatslya za 200 let*, Minsk: MFTsP, Vol. 2, p. 144.
82 See M. Radiker, *Between the Devil and the Deep Blue Sea. Merchant Seamen, Pirates and the Anglo-American Maritime World, 1700–1750*, Cambridge: Cambridge University Press, 1990, p. 303.
83 L. James, *The Rise and Fall of the British Empire*, London: Abacus, 2005, p. 66.
84 R. Roegholt, *Short History of Amsterdam*, Amersfoort: Bekking & Blitz Publishers, 2004, p. 79.
85 N. Robins, *The Corporation That Changed the World: How the East India Company Shaped the Modern Multinational*, London: Pluto Press, 2006, p. 25.
86 A. E. Murphy, *John Law*, Oxford: Oxford University Press, 1997, p. 1.
87 Shatokhina-Mordvintseva, *Istoriya Niderlandov*, p. 183.
88 Cited in A.T. Mekhen, *Vliyanie morskoy sily na istoriyu, 1660–1783* [The impact of sea power on history, 1660–1783], Vol. 1, Moscow/St Petersburg: AST/Terra Fantastica, 2002, p. 63.
89 Blanning, *Pursuit of Glory*, p. 102.
90 A. Glinchikova, *Raskol ili sryv 'russkoy Reformatsii'* [Schism or the failure of the 'Russian Reformation'], Moscow: Kul'turnaya revolyutsiya, 2008, pp. 43–4.
91 J. Vicens-Vives (ed.), *Historia de España y América* [History of Spain and America], Barcelona: Editorial Vicens-Vives, 1961, Vol. III, p. 198.
92 Ya. Shimov, *Avstro-Vengerskaya imperiya* [The Austro-Hungarian empire], Moscow: EKSMO/Algoritm, 2003, p. 125.
93 Alexis de Tocqueville was one of the first to discern, with hindsight, the evolution of the *ancien régime* in the direction of the new bourgeois order (see A. de Tocqueville, *De la démocratie en Amérique. Souvenirs. L'Ancien Régime et la Révolution* [Democracy in America. Recollections. The old regime and the revolution], Paris : Bouquins, Éditions Robert Laffont, 1986). But the necessity for changes, recognised by all including the traditional elites, did not by any means signify that the effective realisation of these changes was possible within the framework of the existing political system.
94 *Motsart. Istorii i anekdoty, raskazannye ego sovremennikami* [Mozart. Stories and anecdotes told by his contemporaries], Moscow: Klassika-XXI, 2007, p. 37.
95 I.V. fon Arkhengol'ts, *Istoriya Semiletney voyny* [History of the Seven Years War], Moscow: AST, 2001, p. 366.
96 I. Sherr, *Germaniya*, Vol. 2, p. 145.
97 Blanning, *Pursuit of Glory*, p. 31.
98 Quoted in F.A. Rotshteyn, *Iz istorii prussko-germanskoy imperii* [From the history of the Prussian-German empire], Moscow/Leningrad: Izdatel'stvo AN SSSR, 1948, p. 20.
99 C. Mooers. *The Making of Bourgeois Europe. Absolutism, Revolution, and the Rise of Capitalism in England, France and Germany*, London: Verso, 1991, p. 112.
100 See V.I. Lenin, *Agrarnaya programma sotsial-demokratii v pervoy russkoy revolyutsii 1905–1907 godov* [The agrarian program of the social democracy in the first Russian revolution of 1905–7]. *Polnoe sobranie sochineniy* [Complete works], 5th edition, Vol. 16.
101 Mooers. *Making of Bourgeois Europe*, p. 116.
102 Quoted in Rotshteyn, *Iz istorii prussko-germanskoy imperii*, pp. 19–20.
103 Ibid., p. 20.

104 J. Lord Kinross, *The Ottoman Centuries. The Rise and Fall of the Turkish Empire*, New York: Morrow Quill Paperbacks, 1977, p. 112.
105 See B. Lewis, *The Middle East. A Brief History of the Last 2000 Years*, New York: Touchstone, 1997, p. 127.
106 E. Iskanoglu (ed.), *Istoriya Osmanskogo gosudarstva, obshchestva i tsvilizatsii* [History of the Ottoman state, society and civilisation], Moscow: Vostochnaya literatura, 2006, Vol. 1, p. 187.
107 H. Inalcik and D. Quataert (eds), *An Economic and Social History of the Ottoman Empire*, Cambridge: Cambridge University Press, 1997, Vol. 1, p. 145.
108 Ibid., p. 22.
109 D. Quataert, *The Ottoman Empire, 1700–1922*, Cambridge: Cambridge University Press, 2003, p. 124.

5

THE RISE OF HEGEMONY

England in the early seventeenth century was an important country, but one experiencing difficult times, and which could hardly be considered a hegemon of the incipient capitalist world-system. The system overall had no hegemon, just as capitalism itself was not a formed and finished whole. This was despite the fact that the basic elements of the new social order were already present, not only in Holland but in many other countries as well.

A century later the capitalist system already appeared fully realised, and the elements of feudalism that remained in Western society were forced increasingly to assimilate themselves to this new order. Literally as people looked on, Britain was turning into an empire, not only dominating the world market, but also laying claim to a key role in world politics. The very concepts of the hegemon of the world-system and of its role and possibilities were founded with hindsight on the British experience.

Marx noted repeatedly that equality of commercial opportunities between two states of fundamentally unequal political strength was inconceivable. Meanwhile, the process of the centralisation and concentration of capital cannot fail to have political consequences. The rise of hegemony within the world-system is the natural and legitimate result of a general hierarchy of inequality and of the logic of accumulation of capital, which dictates the need for centralisation, including on the political level. This, however, does not occur immediately or of its own accord. Systemic hegemony arises and takes shape in the process of struggle, and bears the stamp of its origins.

Why Britain?

After the defeat in the Hundred Years War and the series of internecine conflicts that have entered history as the Wars of the Roses, the English state was weakened and had lost its earlier prestige. It could not claim a leading role in Europe, where a struggle was under way between two superpowers, France and Spain. Even the successes of the Royal Navy and the victory over Spain's Invincible Armada achieved by Sir Francis Drake and his comrades-in-arms in 1588 had not yet made England the ruler of the waves, and maritime power did not make up for weak land forces and a constant shortage of money.

Historians note that 'English arms failed to win any significant victories outside of the British Isles between Boulogne (1547) and the capture of Jamaica (1655).'[1] The growth of England's international influence which had begun during the reign of Elizabeth was replaced by a new decline in the early seventeenth century when the Stuart dynasty, which had succeeded the Tudors, was drawn into a lengthy conflict with the parliament. The place of the leading sea power, commercial and military, was taken with astonishing swiftness by the United Provinces, which in the time of Elizabeth had had trouble defending its right to existence as an independent state.

Nevertheless, England by the end of the seventeenth century had not only burst onto the European scene as a leading political, military and commercial power, but was also emerging victorious over all its rivals, who possessed far greater strength and resources. English commerce was outstripping that of the Dutch. English generals were prevailing over renowned French armies, and English productive industry, which not long before had been relatively backward, held one of the foremost places in Europe. Even in the areas of literature, art, science and philosophy, where traditionally the leading roles had been played by the French and Italians, the English now held one of the most prominent positions.

These gains would have been impossible had they not been based on the advantages of the English social and political institutions that had arisen from the crisis of the seventeenth century, a crisis which initially had weakened the country and left it for practical purposes outside the framework of European politics. What had happened for England to stand out so sharply and obviously against the general European background?

The political system based on parliamentary representation proved to be the ideal mechanism for the political development of the rising bourgeoisie. This system not only allowed the new ruling class to formulate and address in the best possible fashion the goals and tasks before it, but simultaneously helped to consolidate far broader layers of society around these goals. The point was not simply that bourgeois power had come into existence in England, but that this power was authoritative and stable.

In the mid-nineteenth century the British historian Thomas Macaulay, analysing the development of British parliamentary institutions, posed the question: why had representative organs, which existed in most countries of Europe, grown stronger in England by the end of the seventeenth century but fallen into decline elsewhere? 'One after another, the great national councils of the continental monarchies, councils once scarcely less proud and powerful than those which sat at Westminster, sank into utter insignificance.'[2]

During the seventeenth century the struggle between monarchic power and representative organs unfolded throughout all Europe, from England to Russia.

The central authority was forced not only to overcome the resistance of the bourgeoisie, demanding direct participation in the making of decisions, but also to wage a struggle against institutions, liberties and autonomous rights inherited from the Middle Ages. Almost everywhere, the government won. In France, the last sitting of the Estates-General before the Revolution had occurred in 1614, and in Castile the last time the Cortes had gathered before the Napoleonic wars was in 1664. In 1669 the last Landtag met in Bavaria. In Russia during the same years the 'silent' Tsar Aleksey Mikhailovich gradually but extremely effectively ended the importance of the Land Assemblies. In Brandenburg, Friedrich Wilhelm in 1688 managed to limit the representation of the estates, strengthening his centralised administration by effectively bribing the delegates. In Austria under the Habsburgs, the estate representation had lost its political significance and had been turned into an administrative instrument, used to restrain bureaucratic corruption.

Nevertheless, it is wrong to speak of the complete disappearance of the representative power in countries with absolutist regimes. In Sweden the Riksdag functioned, with even the peasantry represented along with the nobles, clergy and bourgeoisie (townsfolk). In France, even though the Estates-General had not gathered for many years, regional assemblies operated.

Consequently, the uniqueness of the English monarchy did not lie in the fact that it retained representative institutions, but in the fact that in the course of the seventeenth century these institutions gained the upper hand over the monarchy, creating a political system which in terms of the concepts prevailing in continental Europe was, as Macaulay recognised, 'anomalous'.[3]

From a historical point of view, this 'anomaly' is explained by two factors. Unlike the continental monarchs, the English kings were not forced constantly to wage land wars, and had no need to create the powerful military-political apparatus that was ultimately the basis for absolutism. Meanwhile, 'our Parliament, fully aware of the nature and magnitude of the danger, adopted, in good time, a system of tactics which, after a contest protracted through three generations, was at length successful.'[4]

Without question, the successes of parliament were linked to its political effectiveness. But this effectiveness in turn rested on the development of the bourgeoisie, which had managed to consolidate itself as a class and had set itself the thoroughly conscious goal of controlling the state. The bourgeoisie in France, after the defeat of the revolutionary movements of the Hundred Years War period, had spent the period from the fifteenth to the eighteenth centuries in a corrupt symbiosis with the state, exploiting the weaknesses of the feudal regime to serve its own interests. But the English bourgeoisie had set out to change the state, subordinating it fully to bourgeois tasks and principles. What was involved here was not just, of course, political traditions dating back to the Magna Carta, but also the fact that the social base of bourgeois development in England was broader, due to the active penetration of capitalist relations into the countryside. New social conditions gave the political leaders of the bourgeoisie the opportunity to develop, on this basis, a strategy that was at once realistic and quite radical.

Power and property

The main achievement of Western society from the point of view of liberal ideologues in later times was the defence of property. In this respect, Britain by the
mid-eighteenth century appeared to many thinkers and commentators to represent
a model of the liberal institutions without which both social and cultural progress
were impossible. The institution of private property, however, had taken shape
gradually in the course of the late Middle Ages, and England was far from leading the
way in this process. Even where private property existed in feudal society, it by no
means represented a general and universal economic principle. Relations of ownership
were regulated by numerous rules, decisions and customs which set out rights of
possession, use and inheritance. There was often no relation between these rights,
and at times they contradicted one another. The peasant allotment or the feudal
estate could often be inherited, but not alienated by those who held them. In
similar fashion, the lands belonging to the community were not in the strict sense its
property, since the very existence of the community assumed its connection with this
territory, and consequently the question of alienating the land, of renting it out or
of making commercial use of it, could simply not be posed. Rights in many cases
were not set down in any document, but were enforced through custom.

The appeals to antiquity that figured so prominently in the new culture of the
Renaissance were not least a reflection of the return to the principles of Roman
Law, which was destined to replace numerous 'truths', 'laws' and customs of the
feudal epoch. Roman legislation, with its precise and incontrovertible formulations,
codifying and regulating diverse aspects of life on the basis of general principles,
represented the ideal for the bourgeoisie. The real understanding of private property
and individual rights in antiquity, needless to say, differed from the later bourgeois
concept of property just as the ancient economy differed from the modern one.
Roman law was perceived by the epoch of the Renaissance as a juridical utopia, just
as antiquity as a whole was transformed from a real historical epoch into a moral and
ethical ideal, needed for carrying out the ideological tasks of the new era.

In England, an economic revolution had occurred in the mid-sixteenth century
with the enclosures, which involved the owners of large estates seizing common
lands, and also with the expropriation of monastery lands in the course of the
Reformation and the dividing up of these lands between the members of the 'new
nobility' (the peasants living there were driven off or placed in the position of hired
labourers). Both changes would have been impossible without state coercion. But
the mass expropriation of labouring people to which Marx pointed in the first volume
of *Capital*, the 'liberation' of working people from their hold over the means of production, required not only state coercion on an unprecedented scale, but also
deliberate work to determine the juridical and institutional shape the system would
assume. The formalising of bourgeois property rested on the replacement of old
laws with new, of customs with written law, and of informal mutual obligations
with commercial contracts. The establishing of private property rested on the
negating of earlier ownership rights, which were regarded as not having been rights

at all since they were not set down according to the new juridical practice, to which the lower orders of society did not at that time have access. The state guaranteed respect for the new property at the cost of ignoring and violating the old rights.

The spread of bourgeois relations did not always occur through the proletarianisation of the peasantry. As the experience of countries on the periphery of the capitalist world shows, the expropriation of direct producers often took other forms; the link between the peasants and the land might be preserved, but the peasants would be deprived of control over their production, which was taken from them by the estate-owners and the authorities. In both 'western' and 'eastern' variants, the role played by state compulsion was fundamental.

Resistance by the traditional majority to the introduction of bourgeois norms continued with greater or lesser intensity for several centuries. Even with reference to Western Europe, it would be wrong to suppose that the countryside was thoroughly bourgeois in the seventeenth or mid-eighteenth century. In Scotland, the process of enclosure could only be effectively carried through after the final union with England and the crushing of the Jacobite uprisings, when the highland clans sought the return to the throne of the heirs of James II, overthrown in 1688. In France traditional communal rights remained a factor restraining the development of capitalism in agriculture right up until the fall of the *ancien régime* in 1789. In other countries of Europe the transformation of landed property occurred even later, influenced to a significant degree by the French experience. It may thus be said that in respect of agrarian capitalism Britain until the end of the eighteenth century remained something of an exception. Even in Britain, however, parliament until the middle of the century had needed to pass acts doing away with the remnants of traditional relationships and obligations in the countryside. It is not hard to explain why the authorities in Britain waged a decisive and successful struggle against these 'relics of the Middle Ages', since as the historian Tim Blanning notes, 'Parliament represented the landed interests in the country,' and its acts were 'enforced by those same landowners, acting in their capacity as Justices of the Peace.'[5]

Throughout the sixteenth and early seventeenth centuries the royal authorities in England, referring to the prerogatives of the crown, kept open the possibility of intervening in property matters to regulate the mutual obligations of landowners and tenants. A revolution was needed to free the new nobility from this interference, and to consistently affirm the principle of private ownership of land. But the revolution, which became possible only thanks to the participation of the urban and rural masses, created a new threat to the landowners. This time the danger came from below, and in political terms, from the left. When the republic in England was replaced by the protectorate of Oliver Cromwell, the interests of the new landowners lay at the centre of attention of the authorities. The British historian Lawrence James notes that during those years 'the army had effectively replaced civilian government'.[6] The army, however, did not govern the country in its own interests; above all, it was a tough and effective tool of the new property-owning elite that had strengthened its position in the course of the revolution. The electoral qualification established during the years of Cromwell's dictatorship made parliament even less democratic than under the monarchy, and the policies of the regime toward the rural masses were even more harsh.

The military dictatorship was effective at suppressing the ferment of the masses who were dissatisfied with the social outcomes of the revolution, but it lacked legitimacy. The restoration of the Stuarts, carried out on the conditions of the victorious bourgeoisie, was no less necessary for consolidating the new economic and legal order than the revolution had been earlier.

Thomas Hobbes and John Locke summed up the outcomes of the revolution on a philosophical level, with the difference that the former stressed the role of state coercion, while the latter emphasised the need for legal norms and liberal institutions. Despite their apparent differences these two thinkers complemented one another wonderfully, showing the reader not only two sides of the newly emerged political system, but also two stages of its formation. The state coercion described by Hobbes in *Leviathan* could not fail to be in the forefront during the epoch of revolutions, when the institutions of the liberal order were still being established – with the help of the same coercion. Locke, living in a later period after the triumph of the Glorious Revolution and of the new social order, could allow himself a much more humane view of events, stressing the need for freedom, thanks to which a state of peace and goodwill would be achieved in society. Nevertheless, one should not be deceived where the class character of Locke's ideas is concerned. The concept of the citizen for Locke is inseparable from that of property. And although property from Locke's point of view is just as natural a right as the right to life, property paradoxically is not merely distributed unequally between individuals, but is not available at all to a significant proportion or even a majority of the population, who therefore cannot be members of civil society in the full sense.

In essence the benevolent philosophy of John Locke, lying at the basis of subsequent liberal thinking, is far more cruel and inhumane than the sober assertions of Thomas Hobbes, who merely formulated the fundamental indispensability for the state of compulsion and violence. It was Locke, however, who succeeded in expressing the key ideas of the new political order, combining the inequality of citizens in astonishing fashion with respect for the individual, and placing the constant readiness of the authorities to use compulsion and violence alongside respect for the rights of humanity.

As the British historian Colin Mooers observes, 'it was the historical novelty of the English state which allowed it both to directly intervene in the transformation of economic and legal relations on behalf of capital, and at the same time to maintain the façade of a seeming impartiality and neutrality.'[7] The property-owners, trusting in a government that represented precisely their interests, were much readier to part with their money, turning into conscientious taxpayers, while parliament, which controlled the ministers, granted the bureaucrats extremely broad powers not possessed in many cases by the functionaries of monarchic regimes. Powers which parliament had stubbornly refused to allow the governments of the Stuarts were willingly accorded to the new authorities. 'Strong government – and a large state – were thus to become as English as roast beef and warm beer,' Brendan Simms notes ironically.[8] After the revolutionary shocks of the seventeenth century, the English bourgeoisie had achieved its goal of cheap government. England spent far less on maintaining its bureaucrats and military officers than France, but time after time emerged victorious from wars. Treasury spending steadily increased, but unlike the dynastic states of the continent, which were constantly on the brink of ruin, the English authorities not only covered their own costs, but were able to provide subsidies to their allies. In any case, the government could easily borrow money from the bourgeoisie. Of £49 million spent during the war against France during the years from 1688 to 1697, the sum of £16 million was obtained through domestic borrowing.[9] The national debt of Britain rose steadily throughout the eighteenth century. By the end of the War of the League of Augsburg the debt stood at £16.7 million, by the end of the War of the Austrian Succession at £76.1 million, and in 1783, when the American War of Independence drew to a close, £242.9 million. At the end of the Napoleonic Wars it stood at £744.9 million.[10] Nevertheless, the government coped with its financial obligations, the British pound was stable, and production increased.

The parliament of the eighteenth and nineteenth centuries, elected on the basis of a property qualification, was the ideal representative organ for the bourgeoisie. This was bourgeois democracy in the most precise sense of the term, that is, a democracy that required both electors and politicians to be bourgeois, or more exactly property-owners, sharing the values and mode of existence of the ruling class. Meanwhile, this system provided certain advantages to the lower orders of society as well, such as the inviolability of the person and the chance to improve their status through joining the property-owning strata. Most importantly, the economic development that accompanied the political successes of British capitalism led initially to a gradual rise in the living standards of the masses. The wages of British workers were not only the highest in Europe, but were sufficient to create in the labouring masses a sense of well-being that continued until the industrial revolution of the nineteenth century.

In the sixteenth and seventeenth centuries England had experienced a demographic explosion. The population increased throughout Europe as a whole, but in England it grew at a substantially greater rate than in neighbouring countries. According to the calculations of historians, the population of France increased between 1500 and 1650 from 16.4 to 20 million people, in Austria and Bohemia from 3.4 to 4.1 million, and in Spain from 6.8 to 7.1 million. The Spanish population had grown to 8.1 million by 1600, but later began to shrink because of massive emigration to the American colonies. In England over the same period the number of inhabitants increased from 2.6 to 5.6 million, in other words more than doubling.[11] This growth is partly explained by the greater life expectancy on the island compared to the continent.

Nation and navy

In assessing the prospects for England, a seventeenth-century author declared: 'The sea is the only empire which can naturally belong to us.'[12] The emergence of

Britain at the forefront of world history as a sea power coincided with a period of impressive progress in navigation. The seafaring qualities of ships improved, their tonnage increased, and maritime routes were optimised. By the beginning of the eighteenth century English ships were taking a week less time to cross the Atlantic than in the mid-seventeenth century. Sails were improved, and the crews became smaller in number as they grew more professional.

The American admiral Alfred Thayer Mahan saw the main reason for the successes of the British navy as the fact that despite changes of government in Britain, the country's leaders concerned themselves constantly with naval matters. 'In its general direction,' Mahan remarked, 'this action has been consistent.'[13] The actual historical picture is somewhat more complex. It is by no means true that British governments invariably devoted sufficient attention to the fleet. For the British elites to fully appreciate the strategic importance of the navy and ensure its effective administration took a considerable time.

The appearance in the early sixteenth century of galleons, new seagoing ships with a displacement of as much as 1,500 tons, provided an impetus to the arms race when, following on Spain, other European states – notably France, Denmark, England and Scotland – began large-scale programmes aimed at establishing ocean-going fleets. Even such a second-ranked power as Scotland, trying to resist pressure from neighbouring England, was capable of efforts comparable to those mounted by leading European countries. Meanwhile, English shipbuilders quickly discovered the shortcomings of floating fortresses built on the Spanish model. To the heavy, high-sided ships of the Spaniards, the English counterposed lighter and more manoeuvrable vessels that were in essence floating artillery batteries. For that time, however, the cost of the shipbuilding programme was extraordinarily high. Between 1574 and 1605 the sum spent solely on creating the navy (involving ships, recruitment, the training and maintenance of the crews, and engaging merchant ships for auxiliary service, etc.), came to £1.7 million.[14]

In the early seventeenth century the army of the Stuarts was in an even more woeful state than the navy, and consequently, strengthening the fleet was perceived as the simplest solution under the conditions of the Thirty Years War. In 1634 Charles I, encountering a constant lack of funds for the building of ships, introduced a special 'ship money' tax. As a result he was able to create an impressive force of 19 royal warships and 26 armed merchant ships. It is true that this move, like other financial initiatives, did not arouse special enthusiasm among his subjects. Money for shipbuilding was given willingly only by the bourgeois of port cities, who felt a need for the defence of their commerce. As the historian Paul Kennedy notes, this fleet had 'poor personnel and badly-designed vessels'.[15]

During the revolution the importance of the navy increased. It was needed to defend the island from invasion by the monarchic powers of the continent. From this time the navy began to be viewed as a 'national' force, about which the whole country needed to be concerned. During the Restoration period, however, it ceased to receive the necessary financing, and fell into decline. During the war with Holland an enemy squadron managed to sail unopposed into the mouth of the Thames and set fire to warships at anchor there. If the conditions of the peace were finally advantageous for London, that was only because the objective relationship of forces too obviously favoured the English.

After the end of the Anglo–Dutch wars, when the need for active military operations at sea diminished, the state of the English navy declined still further. Squadrons ceased taking to the sea, and there were insufficient sailors. By the mid-1680s the situation had improved somewhat, but even the 'Glorious Revolution' and the war with France that followed did not immediately lend the fleet the importance it acquired in subsequent epochs.

Nevertheless, the readiness of parliament to assign funds for building new warships and the presence of a strong reserve of personnel made their effects felt. In France after the shattering defeat at La Hogue King Louis XIV was mainly worried not about the ships, but about the fate of Admiral de Tourville; in England, by contrast, the government could easily replace admirals. Making up the numbers of crewmen, however, presented greater problems. Although England had no shortage of experienced seamen, military service was much less advantageous for the sailors than signing on with merchant vessels. The authorities often had to press-gang sailors into military service by force. It was only toward the middle of the eighteenth century that the situation began to change as the pay rates for Royal Navy servicemen were raised, and became much better than for soldiers and officers in the army.

Amid the failures of the French regular fleet, Louis XIV and his naval ministry put their stake increasingly on privateers and pirates, who were entrusted with undermining English and Dutch trade. The government's calculation was not without a commercial component; the privateers were equipped by private individuals, and the state could avoid spending money to build ships; meanwhile, issuing patents for privateering brought in revenues.[16] But despite isolated successes the French privateers and fleet could not deal a decisive blow to English trade. During the War of the League of Augsburg more than 30,000 ships entered English and Dutch harbours, while the French managed to intercept only 1,000. In the most difficult years for the allies, 1691 and 1693, they lost 15 and 20 per cent respectively of their merchant ships, which of course dealt a serious blow to their economies. But a system of convoys was soon organised, the privateer bases were blockaded, and effective patrolling of the danger zones by ships of the Royal Navy transformed the situation. Meanwhile, the English in the course of their counter-attacks seized 1,296 French ships, many of which belonged to privateers.[17] Significant numbers of the ships that had been lost were won back.

The French challenge

Throughout the seventeenth century England and France were generally allies, first against the Habsburgs and then against Holland. In Flanders in 1657 and 1658 soldiers of Oliver Cromwell, the famous Ironsides, fought under the command of the French Marshal Touraine against the Spanish. Victory allowed the Lord Protector of England to annex Dunkirk to his possessions, intending that the port should become a gateway to the continent for the English. This acquisition did not alarm the French, and during the Restoration period, when the English monarch Charles II ran short of money and sold Dunkirk to his French ally, the transaction was not perceived as a blow to English strategic positions. Many people were of course dissatisfied, complaining that the king was squandering the fruits of the victories won under the Protectorate, but few would then have thought that Dunkirk would become a base for French raids against English shipping. In 1672 France and England again entered into an alliance against Holland.

The 'Glorious Revolution' sharply altered the situation, turning England and Holland from enemies into allies. The series of Anglo-French conflicts that followed not only determined the main features of European politics throughout the next century, but also exerted a huge influence on economic and social development.

Discussing British policy in the eighteenth century, the British historian Brendan Simms emphasises that it 'was driven by strategic, not economic considerations'.[18] In the readiness to pursue such goals, he sees a fundamental difference between the politics of the Liberal-Whigs, of William of Orange and the later Hanoverian regime, and the narrower understanding of the advantages of colonial expansion espoused by the Stuarts and later Conservative-Tories. Nevertheless, the goals and interests to which strategy was ultimately subordinate should not be forgotten. Ideological considerations such as the 'defence of protestantism' undoubtedly played a certain role, but they were never decisive. The interests of British capital as a whole (and not simply commercial advantages) remained constantly at the centre of attention of state figures, determining both the strategic reference-points of their policies, and also the limits to their freedom in choosing partners and allies.

The British elites understood perfectly that the main threat to their interests both on the European continent and in the colonies came from France. They spared neither efforts nor money to ensure their long-term strategic superiority over this adversary. The contest of English and French commercial capital that had emerged in the late seventeenth century differed substantially from the Anglo-Dutch conflict that had preceded it. England and Holland were powers similar to one another in many ways, and their ruling groups embraced largely similar strategic principles. In France, by contrast, the English bourgeois monarchy faced a power of a quite different type, which had developed its own strategy for exercising hegemony. This strategy was based on employing the political and military capabilities of French absolutism, along with the country's favourable geographic position and to some degree even its cultural influence. Transforming his court of Versailles into a model for imitation by all European monarchs, Louis XIV won not only the admiration of his neighbours, but also recognition by them of France as the leading country of the continent.

If English commercial hegemony rested on dominating the seas, and on controlling ocean routes and supplies to Europe of overseas commodities, the France of Louis XIV countered this by seeking to exercise political control over the European continent. The military-political strategy of the Sun King was connected in obvious ways with the protectionist ideas of Colbert. England needed to keep the continental markets open. Without access to European markets, colonial trade was worth little. London's continental strategy over more than two centuries could thus be reduced to a simple formula of balance. Political hegemony over the continent could not be allowed to fall into the hands of any single power, since in the conditions of mercantilism political control was inevitably followed by control over the market. By contrast, the French strategy for hegemony necessitated aggressive territorial expansion, the subjugation of neighbours and military-political domination, all of which allowed Britain to play the role of defender of 'European liberty'.

In this struggle London not only sought to weaken France, but also to maintain a durable political equilibrium on the continent, with no single country able to control the situation. As a result, and as historians note, London's foreign policy during this period cannot be reduced to rivalry with Paris, even though the British were obliged to go to war mainly against the French. 'British power-balancing occurred in a "mixed" states-system still fundamentally constituted by pre-capitalist, geopolitically accumulating states,' Benno Teschke writes.[19] As the sole capitalist state apart from the increasingly weak Holland, Britain enjoyed incontestable advantages, making use of the dynastic, confessional and territorial conflicts of the continental powers to pursue its goals, setting other powers against one another, and at times even instigating conflicts between them.

Nevertheless, it would be wrong to imagine the British elite as the sole genuinely conscious force operating in European politics, or the British bourgeoisie as the sole motive force of global capitalist development. In the dynastic states of the continent bourgeois relations were emerging vigorously, and forming their own influential interest groups able not only to direct development along capitalist lines, but also to mount a challenge to British hegemony and to the British scenario for the development of global capitalism. The differences between the British model of limited (though not yet constitutional) monarchy and continental absolutism were of course great, but they were not two fundamentally incompatible systems. In both cases the basis of power was not popular sovereignty, not democracy, but a compromise between elites. Only in Britain had a social contract been formalised and fixed clearly on a basis of bourgeois law, while what existed on the continent was an informal compact, subject to arbitrary revision and resting on feudal norms and traditions.

The French state played an even greater role in the development of capitalism than the British. With hindsight, liberal ideologues have seen the cause of the failures suffered by France in excessive intervention by the government. But the French experience can be considered a failure only by comparison with the British, and only insofar as the criterion for success was neither more nor less than world political and economic hegemony. Against the background of the other European powers (and especially of the Spanish empire with its vast resources), the development of France in the seventeenth and eighteenth centuries can justly be seen as a success story. In itself the ability to wage a struggle for global hegemony over a century and a half, despite a series of defeats, testifies to the power and effectiveness both of the French state and of the French bourgeoisie.

The French model of corrupt partnership between the state and capital was adopted spontaneously as a model by other European monarchies, including the Russian empire. In France this model was destroyed by the revolution along with the *ancien régime,* but in other countries it was to prove far more durable, having been reinforced by the habits and culture established on the basis it provided. By the mid-nineteenth century French political influence, which had spread not only to the ruling circles and to the elite groups of the bourgeoisie but to all educated layers, had enabled the spread throughout the continent of democratic ideas in a far more radical form than that in which they were formulated in Britain. Aristocratic imitation of the French court by the European elites created fertile soil for the ideas of the French enlightenment, while in Germany and Russia it aided the rise of the intelligentsia. But the ideas of bourgeois radicalism that captivated the minds of intellectuals found a much lesser reception among the bourgeoisie of Central and Eastern Europe, who in their development and social organisation recalled in many ways the commercial elites of *ancien régime* France. An informal agreement with the state permitted the accumulation of capital while reducing risk to a minimum and transferring the costs to the lower strata of society, who were least involved in the bourgeois economy. As the British historian George Taylor writes, 'the most spectacular operations of old regime capitalism were made possible by royal finance and political manipulation rather than industrial and maritime enterprise'.[20] Governments played a decisive role in organising trading companies and in the expediting of manufacturing production. But as modern-day researchers note, it would be wrong to suppose that 'private merchants always suffered'.[21] The bourgeois grew prosperous on state contracts, using the government-founded enterprises to serve their interests. The losses suffered by the crown turned continually into private profits.

In France under the *ancien régime* corruption was ineradicable, since it represented a form of compromise between the traditional elites and the bourgeoisie, a form of privatisation of government funds. It was for this reason that the Third Estate, or more precisely its topmost layer which had access to the financial and economic activity of the state, not only failed to mount a struggle against corrupt practice but up to a point had a direct interest in allowing it to continue. This corruption was partly institutionalised – as witnessed, for example, in the system through which taxes and other budget revenues were collected by tax farmers. Needless to say, treasury funds were not always embezzled. Colbert for a brief period succeeded in imposing a regime of strict economy and effective spending. His son Jean-Baptist, Marquis de Seignelay, managed as navy minister to build a strong fleet while spending comparatively modest sums; over 19 years of Colbert family administration, a total of 216 million livres was spent on the navy. In France in the early eighteenth century military spending consumed three-quarters of the state budget.[22] Special efforts were made to build up the navy. During the time of Colbert the government undertook an extensive programme of naval shipbuilding that included not only the launching of powerful warships, but also the construction of bases for the fleet. The French bureaucracy swiftly mastered the science which the Dutch and English had learnt over several generations. But the French government, for all the centralisation of power inherent in absolutism, was far less consistent in the creating of its fleet than the English had been. The reason needs to be sought in the class interests of the bourgeoisie, which were consistently and systematically represented in the Westminster parliament but not in the Versailles Palace of the Bourbons. Too much depended on individual people. After the death of de Seignelay in 1690 the situation changed immediately. Expenses began rising rapidly. In the last year when the marquis was active, the cost of maintaining the squadrons and port structures had come to 17 million livres, but in 1691 the sum of 24 million livres, and in 1692 a whole 29 million, was spent for the same purpose. The cost of a single serving of food to the sailors rose from 5 to 12 sous, though the sailors were not being fed any better. If the era of the Colberts is compared with the 19 years that followed, it is clear that spending more than doubled (to 495 million livres), while the fleet suffered one defeat after another.[23] In 1701 the death of the Count de Tourville robbed France of its sole admiral capable of winning victories over the English and Dutch.

The error of the Sun King

The War of the League of Augsburg was the first clash of English and French interests to be played out not only in Europe, but throughout the whole Atlantic. It ended in a tactical victory for the English; the goals which Louis XIV had set himself were not achieved, but both sides understood perfectly that the peace which ensued between them was no more than a brief interlude. The new pretext for war was provided by the dynastic crisis in Spain.

When Charles II, the last of the Spanish Habsburgs, died in November 1700, Louis XIV not only proclaimed Philippe of Anjou King of Spain, but several months later declared Philippe also his own heir as King of France. Louis' army occupied the Spanish Netherlands, placing its ports and commercial cities under French control. The first consequence of this Spanish-French union was the closing of Spanish possessions to English and Dutch commerce.

Perhaps unconsciously, Louis XIV sought to revive the global project of a world empire which the Habsburgs had failed to achieve. Now France, through whose efforts that project had been buried, sought the same status of global hegemon. But times had changed, and the Sun King's chances of success were small. As in the past, the French armed forces were the largest in Europe, and the country's navy, as the War of the League of Augsburg had shown, was well able to wage a struggle with England and Holland for dominance of the seas. But the outcome of wars is not decided solely by the big battalions. The political and social organisation of parliamentarist England was an advantage whose significance the other powers of Europe had not yet fully grasped.

While the War of the Spanish Succession was being waged in Western Europe, Russia, Denmark and Saxony began military actions against Sweden. This conflict, known to history as the Northern War, was a genuine gift to English policy, since it placed a fetter on the Swedish forces, robbing them of the possibility of supporting France, their traditional ally. In the West two coalitions confronted one another: France and Bavaria were fighting against England, Holland and Austria, while in Spain, whose throne was being disputed, a civil war was unfolding between supporters of the French Bourbons and the Austrian Habsburgs. In the east, the Swedes were fighting alone against an alliance of Russia, Denmark and Saxony, assembled with the support of Anglo-Dutch diplomacy. The relationship of forces, however, was by no means favourable to the allies, who suffered defeats every time the main Swedish forces appeared on the battlefield. In 1707 the Swedish King Charles XII, after routing the Saxons, hesitated as to whether to move eastward and strike a blow against Russia, whose forces were making use of his absence to seize one city after another in the Baltic region, or whether to go to the help of his French allies, whose position was becoming increasingly critical. The English government reacted to this danger by dispatching a diplomatic mission headed by the Duke of Marlborough, the commander of the British forces on the continent already famous as the victor at Blenheim. Through flattery, persuasion and perhaps threats the British general managed to convince the Swedish king to reject a campaign in the west, and the armies of Charles XII then moved into Russia. The upshot of this decision was the defeat of the Swedes at Poltava.

In the strategic sense the Battle of Poltava was no less effective in solving the problems of the British than in enabling the rise of Petrine Russia, since it removed once and for all the 'Swedish factor' that for 90 years had played a crucial role in French military strategy. But thanks to its successes the empire of Peter the Great clearly breached the bounds assigned to it in the British scheme of the 'balance of forces'. Russian troops soon appeared in Mecklenburg and Denmark, something which could not have failed to arouse alarm in the Elector of Hanover George I, soon to become King of Great Britain as well. Although the problems of Hanover were not a primary concern for the London cabinet, the British ministers would certainly have noted that the fears of the Elector coincided on the whole with the desire of England to maintain a balance. A naval squadron under Admiral Norris, sent originally to the Baltic to defend shipping against Swedish privateers, was now instructed to place pressure on those very Russians whom it had initially been supposed to help. Norris, however, did not make a great impression on the Russians. Peter's navy consisted mainly of galleys, and fought against the Swedes amid the islands of the northern Baltic, where Norris's heavy ships of the line could not venture. Until Peter's death, the relations with Britain of the St Petersburg empire he had founded remained strained and ambiguous, which did not prevent a rapid expansion of trade contacts and technical cooperation.

Meanwhile, events in the west were developing in their turn. In Flanders on 11 September 1709 a battle took place at Malplaquet that was to prove the bloodiest of the entire war. The French army was trying to lift the siege on the fortress of Mons, and the Duke of Marlborough and Eugene of Savoy forced them to retreat, but the losses of the victors were greater than those of the vanquished. In October 1709 the allies captured Mons and discussed invading France, but in London and The Hague the ruling circles gradually lost interest in the war.

The French were now so weakened that it was no longer the ambitions of Louis XIV that presented a threat to the continental equilibrium, but a possible strengthening of Austria. Initially, the Austrian Archduke Charles had laid claim only to the Spanish throne, but after the death of Josef I he had finished up ruler of Austria and head of the Holy Roman Empire. If Charles of Austria had managed to combine the domains of Austria and Spain under a single crown, a new world empire might have arisen. Moreover, possession of the former Spanish Netherlands, the present-day Belgium, made Austria an Atlantic power and a potential trade rival. Marlborough was recalled from the continent. After Britain in 1711 had departed from the war, the fortunes of the Austrians changed, and in 1712 they were defeated at Denain.

France was ruined and left impotent. The war was ended by two peace agreements, the Utrecht Treaty of 1713 and the Rastatt Treaty of 1714. In Utrecht, Britain and Prussia recognised the right of Philippe of Bourbon to the Spanish throne, and in Rastatt this right was affirmed by Austria as well. The question of unification, or of a union of France and Spain, was no longer posed. France in turn renounced its support for the British and French Jacobites who retained their loyalty to the deposed Stuarts, and recognised the right of the Electors of Hanover to succeed to the British throne on the death of the childless Queen Anne. Spain retained its overseas empire, but its European possessions were reapportioned. The territory of present-day Belgium became the Austrian Netherlands, and Vienna also obtained a part of the Spanish possessions in Italy. Britain obtained Gibraltar and Menorca, which for the British became key military and commercial stations in the Mediterranean. Another gain for the British bourgeoisie was the right to the *asiento* – a monopoly on the importing of black slaves to the Spanish possessions in the Americas, and also to a number of French possessions in the West Indies and North America.

European conflict

The defeat of France in the War of the Spanish Succession consolidated the hegemony of Britain in the world capitalist system, but this hegemony was neither solid nor universally recognised. After the failure of the expansionist plans of Louis XIV about two decades were needed for the French economy to recover, but along with the restoration by the mid-eighteenth century of industry and trade, the ambitions of Paris revived as well.

Providing the pretext for another great European conflict was an unsolved problem with the inheritance of the possessions of the Austrian House of Habsburg, whose male line had died out. The Pragmatic Sanction which ensured the transfer of power over the empire to Maria Theresa had been accepted by most of the states of Europe including France, but it was not recognised by Bavaria, and this created the conditions for renewed fighting.

Nevertheless, it was not Bavaria that unleashed the war, but Prussia. Friedrich II, the enlightened Prussian monarch who was praised while still alive as 'the Great', an intellectual and an admirer of Voltaire, simply attacked Austria in 1740 and occupied Silesia. The crisis that had broken out in Germany caused a chain reaction throughout Europe. The Anglo-French contradictions were superimposed on the age-old Franco-Austrian rivalry and on the new conflict within Germany between Berlin and Vienna. The British supported Austria; the French, Prussia and Bavaria; and although Prussia did not officially go to war with Britain, the British and French quickly finished up enmeshed in conflict.

This time the French armies were almost uniformly victorious. They captured city after city in the Austrian Netherlands, overcoming the resistance of the Anglo-Austrian forces. The military operations unfolding in India also turned out badly for the British. Nevertheless, British diplomacy proved more powerful than French arms. Spending extraordinary sums of money, London managed to settle the conflict between Prussia and Austria. Vienna reconciled itself reluctantly to the loss of part of Silesia, while Friedrich the Great, having achieved his aims, preferred not to tempt fate by entering into conflict with the might of Britain. In 1742 a peace treaty was signed between the two German powers, allowing the Austrians to concentrate all their forces on the struggle against France. It is true that in 1744 the war between Prussia and Austria resumed, again on the initiative of Friedrich, who, observing the failures of the Anglo-Austrian coalition, decided to exploit the situation in order to get his hands on the remaining portion of Silesia. The protestant population of the province, with no particular liking for the Catholic authority of the Habsburgs, was inclined to support the Prussian king. British diplomacy set to work again, winning from Vienna an agreement to renounce Silesia in return for recognition of Maria Theresa as the lawful heiress of the Habsburgs, and of her husband Francis I of Lorraine as German Emperor. After a series of defeats Maria Theresa was forced to agree to the loss of her Silesian territories.

Despite the diplomatic successes, it was well understood in London that wars are nevertheless won by force of arms. Responding to the successes of the French in India and the Netherlands, the British in 1745 captured the fortress of Louisbourg in America. The strategic importance of this strongpoint was so great that during the subsequent peace talks the French, in order to secure its return, were forced to surrender Madras, which they had occupied, and to withdraw their victorious forces from the Austrian Netherlands. Controlling Louisbourg and with mastery of the seas, the British were able to impose a total blockade on Canada and other French possessions in North America. The capture of Louisbourg was important, however, not only because it provided Britain with a trump card to be used in peace negotiations. After numerous failed attempts the British had finally learned how to carry out large-scale landing operations. The cooperation between army and navy worked out during the storming of Louisburg became a model for the future victories of the Seven Years War, the landings in Quebec and Havana.

The peace of Aix-la-Chapelle in 1748 essentially restored the pre-war situation, obliging the combatant sides to return what they had seized. For Britain, the main outcome of the war lay in the fact that it showed the key importance of the fleet for elevating struggle to a global level. A further achievement for Britain was the final crushing of the Jacobite movement in Scotland and the establishing of the

United Kingdom. The unification of the parliaments and armed forces of England and Scotland ensured the state centralisation of Great Britain, and made it possible to concentrate the resources of the two kingdoms on common goals.

During the War of the Spanish Succession, even though global interests of the parties were at stake, the military actions took place mainly in Europe, while the conflict in the Atlantic was fought out primarily at sea. The War of the Austrian Succession developed differently, demonstrating the growing globalisation of warfare. The military actions in Asia and the Americas took place not only at sea but also on land, with both sides striving to expand the zone of their control by drawing into the struggle local rulers in India and native American tribes in North America.

The greatest gains from the War of the Austrian Succession were made by Prussia, which consolidated its control over Silesia, seizing and holding the region in the course of two military campaigns. For the young Prussian monarch Friedrich II this was an extremely valuable acquisition, since it increased not only the territory of his kingdom but also its economic potential. The Silesian mines and industry played an important role in Prussia's subsequent development.

Prussia at the beginning of the eighteenth century had a model army, distinguished not only by its faultless discipline and training, but also by its effective, well-thought-out system of command. During battles, the 'living walls' of the Prussian infantry instilled fear in the enemy. As biographers of Friedrich have noted, his enlightenment enthusiasms and rationalist habits of thought combined organically with his militarism. Early in his military career the young king won fame as an outstanding commander. Most of his victories, however, would have been impossible had he not possessed an exceptional command staff. The Prussian officers and generals were capable not only of carrying out orders precisely, but also of showing initiative where this was indispensable. The equipment and logistics of the Prussian army were also a model to others.

The Prussian king must be given his due: he had no particular illusions concerning the feelings of his subjects, and grasped perfectly the class contradictions underlying the military-state system he had created. In his army, merciless punishments were employed so as to maintain the 'spirit of order' not only through moral influence but also through physical means. Nor is it surprising that the Russian army, despite the dislike felt by patriotic-minded nobles for 'Prussianism', adopted as its basis precisely this approach to order and discipline.

The Seven Years War

Both sides regarded the Peace of Aix-la-Chapelle as more of a truce, even though neither power saw any need to force events. In India, meanwhile, the clashes between French and British forces almost never ceased, and in the Americas a new crisis was ripening. Less than ten years had passed after the end of the War of the Austrian Succession when Europe was shaken by a new conflict, known to history as the Seven Years War.

This conflict was more deserving of the name of a world war even than the war of 1914–18. The theatres of the fighting were in Europe, the Americas, Africa and India. British and French forces fought one another in the Caribbean and in Senegal. Almost all the European powers, from England and France in the west to Russia and Austria in the east, were drawn into the conflict. The war proved not only to be the decisive round in the century-old confrontation between the British and French monarchies, but also a turning-point in the history of Central Europe. During these years Russia, which under Peter the Great had become a very important regional power, came to exert an influence on the overall course of European politics, seeking for the first time – though under duress, it is true, and without particular success – to act independently of Britain. Prussia reaffirmed its status as a great power, while Austria could no longer consider itself the leading force in Germany. The Seven Years War was accompanied by a 'diplomatic revolution' in which the old, tested alliances fell apart, and new ones were formed in their place. St Petersburg quarrelled for the first time with London, and Vienna came to an understanding with Paris. The British, who had viewed Austria as a counterweight to France, now supported Prussia as a counterweight to Austria.

The war represented a further stage in the globalisation of the military-political struggle between Britain and France not simply because of the scope of the military actions. In its origins this conflict differed sharply from the dynastic crises that had provoked the two previous European wars, since it had begun right outside the borders of Europe and had been caused by a direct and open clash of interests in the field of colonial policy.

The increasing rural population of the British colonies in North America, their growing economy and energetic commerce forced the colonial elites to recognise the need for an expansion of their 'living space'. Blocking their way to this external expansion was France, which laid claim not only to Canada, but also to the land along the Mississippi River all the way to New Orleans, around which the prosperous colony of Louisiana had grown up. The French possessions effectively closed off the possibility for the British colonies of moving into the interior of the continent, restricting them to a narrow space along the Atlantic coast.

In France, opening up the country's American territories was seen as a way of strengthening the existing social order. The French administration in Canada sought to create the conditions for the flourishing of a new aristocracy whose members had received large landholdings. The peasant settlers finished up in a subordinate position, as the French feudal system was reproduced on the new continent. In Québec, therefore, colonisation and feudalism were 'linked from the beginning'.[24] The French peasantry remained on the land, and the landowners in the 'old country' were fearful of losing their workers.

In the American colonies of Great Britain the population expanded more quickly. After the peasants in Britain had been driven from the land, a huge mass of 'excess' population had appeared, people who not only swelled the ranks of the proletariat, but who also provided the 'human material' for colonisation. Nor was there any shortage of soldiers or sailors. The population of England shrank somewhat between 1720 and 1750, largely as a result of mass emigration to North America, and in 1770 stood at around 7.5 million. Meanwhile, the population of the colonies by that time had increased to 2.3 million people, almost double the figure in the mid-eighteenth century.[25]

It is not surprising that the demographic relationship between Canada and the British colonies should have finished up unfavourable to the French. Meanwhile, the French authorities in colonial Canada were less successful than the New England farmers in wiping out the local native Americans, despite constant military conflict with them. The demographic pressure of the white settlers on the indigenous population was less, and the religious ideology of Catholicism, unlike Calvinism, demanded not the extermination of the natives but their conversion. Achieving more or less settled relations with the local tribes after a series of conflicts, the French managed to turn them into their allies against the British and the colonists. It is true that this alliance also had a reverse side. Since the tribes engaged in warfare with one another, collaboration with one of them led almost inevitably to conflict with others.

In London it was soon realised that the successes of the French in these circumstances depended not least on the support they received from the native Americans. The British representatives in America, imitating the French, began trying to attract native Americans to their side. The British press openly acknowledged that in conducting their war the Europeans in America were 'dividing Indians against each other, in a quarrel in which they had no interest'.[26]

Nevertheless, the policy pursued by the British toward the native Americans caused discontent among the colonists. In London it was understood that the native Americans could be drawn onto the British side only by guaranteeing them the right to the land. To the colonists the lands of the 'savages' were no more than unowned territories that had to be seized and divided up to allow the spread of plantations and farms. The contradictions between Britain and its colonies on the native American question were later to figure among the causes of the colonial independence struggle, but so long as the threat from Canada existed, the settlers were prepared to put up with collaboration between the British authorities and the natives.

The colonists demanded constantly that the mother country send new forces and make additional efforts to defend them from the French. Georgia, the new thirteenth colony that had arisen as a buffer zone between the British and Spanish possessions, needed to be defended against pressure from Spanish Florida. The settlers in the British colonies showed exceptional aggressiveness, provoking conflicts with the far less numerous French and their native American allies. As historians have noted, the colonial bourgeoisie understood perfectly how this would end, but was certain that support from mighty Britain would solve all the problems. 'Any new Anglo-American settlement in the Ohio Valley would come with a struggle and probably war. As American speculators and would be settlers will know, therefore, all this land and the great opportunities it afforded could not be obtained without the aid of the powerful British Empire.'[27] The settlers and bourgeoisie of the colonies not only waited for support from London, but quite consciously provoked clashes, understanding that only open conflict with France would force the empire to throw all its strength into supporting their initiatives.

As the American historian Robert Kagan notes, 'Mid eighteenth-century Anglo-Americans thus became the most enthusiastic of British imperialists.'[28] Brendan Simms emphasises that 'Imperialist vision, which later generations have sometimes seen as a corruption of the founding ideals, was thus part of the American project well before the independence.'[29]

The actions of American colonists who in 1754 attacked the French in the Ohio valley dragged Britain into the Seven Years War. A detachment of Virginia militia under the command of George Washington suddenly attacked and killed French soldiers accompanying a truce envoy who had been sent to the colonists with a proposal for resolving problems peacefully. Representatives of all the American colonies gathered in Albany in the spring of 1755 and demanded the immediate sending of regular troops. The parliament in London sought in every way possible to avoid a full-scale war, for which Britain was not ready. But the colonies insisted, and defeats suffered by the colonial militias showed that to rely on them in a struggle with the French and native Americans was impossible.

The ineffectiveness of the colonial militias resulted not only from their lack of discipline, training and military experience, but also from the fact that apart from the struggle with the French and native Americans the militiamen had another, very important matter on their minds: they could not leave their slaves unguarded.[30] The colonists, who had irresponsibly involved themselves in a fight with the French in 1754, stubbornly refused to set aside money for defending themselves, refused help to one another and demanded support from Britain. The constant failures of the colonial militias aroused growing dissatisfaction in London. The British diplomats were forced to act hastily, and this in part explains their crude errors which in the first years of the war left Britain and its Prussian ally on the verge of defeat.

Throughout the first half of the eighteenth century British diplomacy on the continent had displayed a good deal of competence. But this time, while trying to deal with tactical problems in several European courts at once, the diplomats simply failed to assess the strategic consequences of what they were doing. The government was concerned for the fate of Hanover, for whose defence Britain lacked the necessary strength. Attempting to solve the problem, the British diplomats urgently conducted talks in St Petersburg and Berlin simultaneously. In Russia they almost reached agreement on the sending of Russian troops to Hanover (effectively, by paying for them), while at the same time coming to an understanding with Prussia. Britain and Prussia quickly signed the Westminster Convention, which, however, provoked indignation in both Vienna and St Petersburg. Responding to Friedrich's *rapprochement* with Britain, the Austrian Empress Maria Theresa, for whom the return of Silesia had become a crucial foreign policy goal, decided to ally herself with the French Bourbons. The Franco-Austrian talks proceeded with astonishing smoothness. At the same time, agreement was reached on the future marriage of the newly-born Marie Antoinette to Louis, the heir to the French throne. Where St Petersburg was concerned, British gold proved far from all-powerful; the French and Austrian envoys also provided generous subsidies to their Russian partners.

Thus occurred the 'diplomatic revolution', known also as the 'overturning of alliances', which sharply altered the disposition of forces and put in question the results of London's efforts over many years to create a European 'equilibrium'. Britain and Prussia were forced in practice to wage war on their own, since they were virtually unable to provide one another with direct military aid. The sole consolation for London was the fact that after promising the Austrians that it would go to war on Prussia, the Russian government stipulated as a condition for its inclusion in the Austro-French alliance that it would not take part in the war on Britain.

The beginning of the war threatened to turn into a catastrophe for the British. Menorca was captured by the French, who then prepared to invade the British Islands, while the Prussian armies, which had been accustomed to defeating the Austrians, encountered a new and far more dangerous enemy in the Russians. Nevertheless, the sluggish but effective administrative machine of Hanoverian Britain moved into action, supplying the army and navy with all their needs. Ships were built, army regiments were fitted out, and the supply and financing of the fleet was organised. Special ranger units, trained in the tactics of partisan warfare, were prepared for fighting in the American backwoods. The red coats of the marksmen were replaced by a practical dark green uniform that provided camouflage protection in the forests.

On 20 November 1759 the French fleet, attempting to break out of Brest, encountered a squadron under Admiral Hawke and sought refuge in the bay of Quiberon. The British, who did not have pilots, took the risk of attacking the French in unknown waters during a storm, and were rewarded with a spectacular success. For the Royal Navy, historians consider Hawke's triumph was its 'most decisive victory until Trafalgar'.[31] The destruction of the French fleet altered the situation. In 1761 the *Gentleman's Magazine* reported with satisfaction that since the battle the French, who only a few years earlier had laid claim to dominance of the seas, had been 'without ships, without seamen, and without trade'.[32]

In the same year an Anglo-Hanoverian army commanded by Ferdinand of Brunswick defeated the French at Minden. The British and their German allies now controlled the situation on the Rhine. Meanwhile an expedition against Canada, undertaken by General James Wolfe, ended in a brilliant victory. British imperial ideologues were to term the capture of Québec 'one of the turning points in the world's history'.[33]

While the British were seizing Canada, the Prussians with some difficulty were repelling an offensive by the Russian and Austrian armies. Friedrich was not helped by his occupation of Saxony; he had seized the territory without declaring war, and was now using its human and material resources to serve his goals. The Saxon soldiers in the army of the Prussian king deserted in whole battalions. The numerical superiority and persistence of the Russian forces then resulted in disaster for Friedrich in a battle at Kunersdorf in August 1759. The victorious Russians could have proceeded calmly to Berlin, but instead the generals of the two allied empires wasted time arguing among themselves. With no unity between the Russians and Austrians, the Russian commander General Saltykov ultimately led his troops away, accusing the Austrians of breaching their obligations as allies. The Austrians levelled the same accusation at Saltykov. Friedrich described his unexpected salvation as 'the miracle of the House of Brandenburg'.

Berlin was captured by the Russians in the following year, but this was no longer of decisive strategic significance. Prussia had already restored its military might, and the resources of St Petersburg and Vienna were almost exhausted. After the death of the Tsaritsa Elizabeth in 1761 the Russian throne passed to Peter III, who made haste to conclude peace with Prussia – the 'second miracle of the House of Brandenburg'. Russian historians who complain at the sudden and unfounded concessions by Peter III that deprived St Petersburg of the fruits of victory over Prussia forget that for the Seven Years War, the Eastern European regions where the battles between Russia and Prussia took place were only a secondary theatre of action. The outcome of the struggle was decided elsewhere, and in no way to the advantage of France and its allies. In this situation the desire of the Russian emperor to conclude a separate peace and adhere to the winning side was a manifestation of elementary good sense. The Russian empire was on the verge of bankruptcy. While Prussia had regularly received British subsidies, France was incapable of providing Russia with analogous help. A victorious Russian army could not have been fed.

Friedrich, who even earlier had looked on the Russian empire with alarm, came to the conclusion that in future, conflict with it had to be avoided at all costs. When Catherine succeeded Peter III after a palace coup, the two monarchs continued an active collaboration, with their friendship ensuring catastrophe for their mutual neighbour – Poland, which they proceeded to divide between them, attracting the Austrians to the partition as well. The memory of Kunersdorf was an instruction to the successors of Friedrich the Great to follow a similar policy, and Berlin and St Petersburg did not go to war on one another again until 1914.

The position of France failed to improve after Spain entered the war on its side. Spanish colonial possessions were subjected to a series of well-planned and successful attacks. In August 1762 the British captured Havana, whose fortress and port had been considered impregnable, and in October they took Manila. When the Seven Years War ended, France had suffered defeat on all fronts, while Britain was at the summit of its power. The outcome of the war, as one historian remarks, was the 'transformation of the North Atlantic into an English inland sea'.[34] Even before the peace treaty was officially signed, it was clear that Britain had gained the upper hand in the struggle for global hegemony. The British historian Frank McLynn is not restrained in describing the impacts of this triumph; the year 1759, he states, 'effectively made Britain the global superpower of the eighteenth century; it was the first time a genuine British Empire could be discerned, and it laid the foundations for the dominance of the English language in the modern world.'[35]

Under the terms of the 1763 Treaty of Paris, France renounced all claims to Canada, Nova Scotia and the islands in the Gulf of St Lawrence. Britain also gained the Ohio valley and all the territory to the east of the Mississippi with the exception of New Orleans. Louisiana thus remained a colony of France, which, however, ceded it temporarily to Spain.[36] In Africa, Senegal passed to the British empire, but of the Spanish possessions only the small island of Grenada remained in British hands, with all other conquered cities and islands returned to Madrid. In India the warring sides returned to their original borders. But as later history was to show, it was in India that the British empire had won its most important victory in strategic terms.

Notes

1 L.H. Roper and B. Van Ruymbeke, *Constructing Early Modern Empires. Proprietary Ventures in the Atlantic World, 1500–1750*, Leiden/Boston: Brill, 2007, p. 5.
2 T. Macaulay, *History of England from the Accession of James the Second*, Leipzig: Bernhard Tauchnitz, 1849, Vol. 1, p. 42.
3 See Ibid., p. 25.
4 Ibid., p. 43.
5 T. Blanning, *The Pursuit of Glory. The Five Revolutions that Made Modern Europe: 1648–1815*, London: Penguin Books, 2008, p. 151.
6 L. James, *Warrior Race, A History of the British at war from Roman times to the present*, London: Abacus, 2002, p. 194.
7 C. Mooers, *The Making of Bourgeois Europe. Absolutism, Revolution, and the Rise of Capitalism in England, France and Germany*, London: Verso, 1991, p. 170.
8 B. Simms, *Three Victories and a Defeat. The Rise and Fall of the First British Empire, 1714–1783*, New York: Basic Books, 2007, p. 38.
9 See ibid., p. 39.
10 See James, *Warrior Race*, p. 272.
11 See R. Bonney, *The European Dynastic States: 1494–1660*, Oxford: Oxford University Press, 1992, p. 365.
12 Quoted in N. Ferguson, *Empire: How Britain Made the Modern World*, London: Allen Lane, 2003, p. 11.
13 A.T. Mahan, *The Influence of Sea Power upon History. 1660–1805*, London: Bison Books, 1980, p. 51.
14 See James, *Warrior Race*, p. 157.
15 P. Kennedy, *The Rise and Fall of British Naval Mastery*, London: Penguin, 2004, p. 44.
16 E. Sozaev and S. Makhov, *Bor'ba za gospodstvo na more. Augsburgskaya liga* [The struggle for dominance at sea. The Augsburg league], St Petersburg: Izdatel'svo SPBGU, 2008, p. 59.
17 See ibid., pp. 89–90.
18 Simms, *Three Victories*, p. 142.
19 B. Teschke, *The Myth of 1648. Class, Geopolitics, and the Making of Modern International Relations*. London: Verso, 2003, p. 11.
20 G. Taylor, 'Types of Capitalism in Eighteenth Century France', *English Historical Review*, July 1964, 79: 491.
21 J.D. Tracy, *The Political Economy of Merchant Empires*, Cambridge: Cambridge University Press, 1991, p. 95.
22 Ibid.., p. 95.
23 See Sozaev and Makhov, *Bor'ba za gospods*, p. 57.
24 E. McInnis, *Canada: A Political and Social History*, New York/Toronto/London: Holt, Rinehart & Winston, 1963, p. 63.
25 See Simms, *Three Victories*, p. 535.
26 *Gentleman's Magazine*, October 1760, XXX: 462.

27 R. Kagan, *Dangerous Nation. America and the World, 1600–1898,* London: Atlantic Books, 2006, p. 18.

28 Ibid.

29 Simms, *Three Victories,* p. 540.

30 Kagan, *Dangerous Nation,* p. 185.

31 A. Herman, *To Rule the Waves. How the British Navy Shaped the Modern World,* London: Hodder & Stoughton, 2004, p. 290.

32 *Gentleman's Magazine,* December 1761, XXXI: 596.

33 G.R. Parkin, *Round the Empire,* London/Paris/Melbourne: Cassell & Co. Ltd., 1892, p. 31.

34 Tracy, *Political Economy of Merchant Empires,* p. 252.

35 F. McLynn, *1759: The Year Britain Became Master of the World,* London: Pimlico, 2005, p. 388.

36 Under the terms of the agreement between France and Spain, the latter entered the war against Britain in exchange for the transfer to it of Menorca, at that point in French hands. The Treaty of Paris returned Menorca to the British, while France was forced to cede Louisiana to the Spaniards as compensation.

6

THE DISCOVERY OF 'THE WEST'

By the early eighteenth century the European economic and political presence in India had become significant, though it was far from dominant. Most of the subcontinent was under the control of the increasingly weak empire of the Great Moguls. As the power of this empire faded, the positions both of local rulers and of the European colonial companies grew stronger. The coastal cities and European trading stations provided export demand for local goods, stimulating the growth of production. While the activity of the British and Dutch East India companies helped enrich their respective countries and aided the accumulation of capital in Europe, this trade served just as much to encourage artisanry and bring about an increase in the wealth of India.

In Europe, meanwhile, admiration of the wealth, knowledge and refinement of the 'mysterious East' gave way gradually to a different inclination. Sensing their strength, the Western elites began demanding the right to reorder the lives of Asian peoples in line with European concepts and needs.

Enlightenment and 'despotism'

Among the main ideological innovations of the Enlightenment epoch was the discovery of the 'West' as a distinct civilisation, counterposed to the rest of the world. The ancient Greeks and Romans had categorised peoples as civilised or barbarian, with the mark of civilisation the existence of the civic institutions of the *polis*. The populations living to the West – the Celts, and later, the Germans – seemed to Greeks and Romans to embody the crudest barbarism. With such peoples, it was considered, Greek and Roman citizens had far less in common than with the enlightened Egyptians and Syrians, or with the people of Hellenised Bactria.

Medieval European society defined itself as Christian, and in this respect stood counterposed to the Islamic and pagan worlds. The division into West and East first began to acquire ideological significance with the schism of Christianity into Roman Catholicism and Byzantine Orthodoxy. But this schism had nothing in common with the new concept of the West that arose during the epoch of the Enlightenment. From this time on, it was to be the values of the Enlightenment that would be fundamental to the self-characterisation of 'European' or 'Western' civilisation: rationalism, the secularisation of the state, individualism, the rights of the individual, the existence of representative institutions, and so forth. Hence Western civilisation with its 'secularism', equal rights for women, and principle of a single, common set of rights for all rested not so much on the European history of the Middle Ages with its privileges and 'liberties' – a history with obvious analogues in the Moslem world (for example, in the Ottoman Empire) – as on radical bourgeois ideology, to which overcoming religious ideology and rejecting the earlier social and cultural hierarchy were of fundamental importance. The adherents of traditional values in the West felt no less hatred for the Enlightenment philosophers than did, in later times, the upholders of traditions in Asian and African countries. In other words, the new Western consciousness did not require a continuity with numerous existing norms and traditions typical of European societies, but on the contrary, a break with them. The extent of the break with these traditions also became the criterion according to which, later on, the level of 'modernisation' would be defined.

During the eighteenth century Europe freed itself from Christianity not only as an ideology, but also as a way of life. A peculiarity of Christian religious consciousness was that it reconciled itself to this situation, in line with the outcomes of revolutions. In the course of the reforms of Tsar Aleksey Mikhailovich and of his son Peter the Great the same process occurred in Orthodox Russia, though as Alla Glinchikova notes, the secularisation occurred not from below but from above.[1] This process culminated in the 'enlightened absolutism' of Catherine the Great. It is true that the functions of cultural control exercised by the church were taken over in this case not so much by civil society, as in the West, as by the state bureaucracy. From this time on religion ceased to be a public matter, becoming instead a question of private conviction and individual faith.

The identification, made with hindsight by liberal ideologues, of the values of the Enlightenment as the 'natural norm' of Western society strengthened the position of those who supported these values. The liberal conception of the 'natural norm', however, was innately contradictory. By proclaiming its political, social and cultural norms to be 'natural', liberal tradition lent them a general human significance. At the same time, the West presented itself as the bearer of these universal norms.

The idea of 'Western' civilisation, the historical product of the development of capitalist society, was presented as an extra-historical reality, a system of norms and principles that supposedly determined the superiority of the West over the rest of the world and that explained and justified this superiority. This duality inherent in the self-characterisation made by 'Western civilisation' reflected the contradictory nature of the capitalist world-system, which, while economically and politically an indivisible whole, at the same time could not exist without an internal hierarchical division into centre and periphery.

Later, the ideology of the Enlightenment and the eurocentrist vision of history would undergo harsh criticism. But in most cases, the critics themselves shared the same extra-historical and normative approach. Instead of showing that the idea of the West was just as historically restricted and transient as the concept of the Christian world, these critics were inclined to reject 'Western culture' as such, discounting the specific social conditions in which this culture took shape. Just as the ideologues of liberalism insisted on a sort of inherent superiority of 'Western civilisation', dating back to antiquity, so their critics, while rejecting the idea of superiority, did not think to consider that throughout most of human history the division into East and West has either meant nothing at all, or has had a meaning quite different from the one placed on it between the eighteenth and twentieth centuries. To paraphrase Rudyard Kipling, it might be said that rather than never meeting, East and West have repeatedly changed places, and united and divided while discovering one another afresh.

From the mid-eighteenth century, the idea became current in Britain and France that the countries of the East made up a world in which a harsh despotism prevailed, and in which any respect for human rights was lacking, along with even the rudiments of civic freedoms. The *Encyclopedia* of Diderot and D'Alembert refers peremptorily to the 'tyrannical, arbitrary and absolute government of a single man', stating that 'such is the government of Turkey, Mongolia, Japan, Persia and of almost all Asia'.[2] This type of rule debases 'the souls and hearts of Eastern rulers',[3] and is the most important cause of the misfortunes that beset their countries. Russia is assigned indirectly to the category of despotically run states, since according to the *Encyclopedia,* its 'government recalls that of Turkey'.[4]

The idea of 'Eastern despotism' was no less popular in Britain. Referring to French sources, an observer for the *Gentleman's Magazine* in 1762 drew a frightening picture of the oppression and humiliation which the peoples of Asia accepted as their due:

> In these countries there has been for a succession of many ages, no other law than the will of the sovereign, who has been regarded as a visible God, in whose presence the rest of mankind shrink into nothing, and before whom they ought to prostrate themselves in silence. In these unhappy countries, mankind implicitly kiss their chains; they adore their tyrant without any assurance either of property or life; and without any knowledge of human nature, or any exertion of human reason; they seem to have no virtue but fear, and what is still more astonishing, they push vassalage into heroism; they are almost insensible to life and death, and with a kind of religious imbecility, they bless the ferocious caprice which so frequently puts an end to their existence.[5]

Since the Enlightenment theory of the 'natural man' assumed that people originally were born free and felt themselves free, the horrors of Eastern despotism could not be explained on the basis of the primitiveness and savage condition of the Asian peoples, especially since visible facts testified to the opposite. 'We believe, upon the credit of history, that Europe was always brave and jealous of its liberty; and that Asia has been long absorbed in indolence and servitude; and, it is not strange, that this difference of character, so constant and uniform during a succession of many ages, should be imputed to the difference of climate, as a cause equally constant, uniform, and lasting.'[6] This suggestion was, however, disputed by other European authors, who recalled that the climate of southern Europe is not so different from, say, that of Turkey. This objection forced the observer for the *Gentleman's Magazine* to seek the main cause of the differences in culture and religion.

By no means everyone in this period agreed with the thesis of Asian despotism. The French traveller and orientalist Anquetil Duperron in his book *Législation Orientale,* published in 1778, wrote that the widespread ideas in Europe concerning Eastern despotism, and the absolute and unlimited power of Asian rulers over their subjects, did not correspond to reality. 'The accusations that we level against Eastern rulers are groundless, or they are based on instances of abuse which are recognised as such both by the rulers themselves and by their subjects.'[7]

Duperron wrote of the defence of property rights in the East, seeking to show that freedom of trade and enterprise was in no way constrained there. But his views were rejected and even ignored by most authors, who preferred simplified ideological schemes to concrete historical analysis. Even Karl Marx wrote of Asiatic despotism in the same words as his liberal opponents, emphasising that in those societies life and property were not secure, and that there was no stimulus to progress.[8]

Duperron observed openly that in depicting such Eastern countries as Persia, Turkey and India as 'barbarous', Western authors were trying to justify the policies practised there by Europeans, presenting Eastern peoples as capable only of 'serving as objects for our profit'.[9] The attempt might be made to justify the conquest of America on the basis of the savagery and backwardness of the local tribes, and all of Australia might be declared *terra nullius*, no-one's land, since the aborigines had neither a state nor, in terms of European concepts, a society. But India, which possessed an ancient civilisation and a flourishing economy, needed arguments of a different sort. The thesis of despotism supplied such arguments.

From the point of view of the Europeans, Indian rulers lived in an 'atmosphere of subtlety, treachery and fairy tale',[10] to which the British gentlemen counterposed their 'own best traditions of honesty'.[11] But the nobility of the true Englishman had its limits. Robert Clive in 1772 explained to members of the House of Commons: 'Indostan was always an absolute despotic government. The inhabitants, especially in Bengal, in inferior stations are servile, mean, submissive and humble. In superior stations they are luxurious, effeminate, tyrannical, treacherous, venal, cruel.'[12]

From Clive's point of view, this situation freed him totally from the need to follow the moral code of the British gentleman in a socio-cultural milieu where no-one observed these norms.

By no means everyone in Britain itself shared this approach. Edmund Burke declared resoundingly: 'Fraud, injustice, oppression, peculation, engendered in India, are crimes of the same blood, family and cast, with those that are born and bred in England.'[13] It is noteworthy, however, that the politician delivered his wrathful speeches on the crimes of the British administration in Bengal after Clive had completed his mission there. Still later, while unmasking the actions of the East India Company, Burke referred to the local context: 'All these circumstances are not, I confess, very favourable to the idea of our attempting to govern India at all. But there we are; there we are placed by the Sovereign Disposer: and we must do the best we can in our situation.'[14]

Meanwhile, Clive and other heroes of the colonial epoch, both British and Indian, not only behaved according to the rules of their milieu, but were themselves active in shaping this milieu. Analysing the social development of India, the British historian D.A. Washbrook reached an unexpected conclusion: the features of Asian society that Western authors characterised as age-old civilisational peculiarities had in fact been formed relatively late, and were the direct result of the peripheral integration of the East into the global capitalist economy.

> British rule restructured South Asian society and economy in ways meant to serve its own interests and which had the consequence of all but permanently precluding the transformation to modern industrialization. It was in this era that many of the social and economic features, understood by later generations to be the products of changeless tradition and taken by them to constitute the barriers of 'backwardness' to development, can be seen to have crystallized.[15]

As seen by Adam Smith, the dominance of the West was predetermined by the economic and technical relationship of forces. In its turn, Marxism points justly to the connection between the development of the productive forces and changes in society. Marx, like Smith, was convinced that a precondition for colonialism was the technical superiority of Europe. But technologically, financially and in organisational terms the Asian states in the sixteenth and even seventeenth centuries were undoubtedly stronger than those of Europe. By the late Middle Ages they had achieved a significantly greater level of development of the forces of production than Europe. Moreover, in the East we find many elements of the bourgeois economy, at times no less developed than in the West. As D.A. Washbrook notes, Southern Asia 'was responsible for a much larger share of world trade than any comparable zone and, between the sixteenth and eighteenth centuries, may have possessed upwards of one-quarter of the world's total manufacturing capacity'.[16] The economic might of China was also impressive.

Indian textiles filled the European market, and Indian spices were a highly prized product. According to recent calculations, by 1750 a quarter of global artisan and manufacturing production was taking place on the Indian subcontinent, while for Britain the figure was no more than 1.9 per cent. Dacca alone exported to Britain textiles worth 2.85 million rupees – an enormous sum for those times.[17] India might then have been considered the 'workshop of the world', and in any case merited the name, bestowed on it by contemporaries, of 'the richest country in the world'.[18]

Even in the mid-nineteenth century, when India was already under British control and when China had been forced to reconcile itself to political conditions dictated by London, the Asian countries as before exported more goods to Europe than they received from it. In 1856 the London *Economist* lamented: 'The drain of silver to the East has now continued so long and upon so large a scale, as to suggest that some permanent cause is in operation, which establishes a constant balance against the West, requiring to be satisfied.'[19]

The amounts of capital possessed by Indian entrepreneurs were extremely significant, and no less than those at the disposal of Europeans. 'From the fourteenth century,' Fernand Braudel notes, 'India had a lively money economy that was to move steadily along the road of a certain type of capitalism; however, this did not encompass the society as a whole.'[20] Even in Western Europe it was not until the early nineteenth century, or even later, that capitalism succeeded in 'encompassing the whole of society'. On the level of technological development, the gap between the West and the future 'Third World' appeared only in the mid-nineteenth century, as a result of the industrial revolution. In 1830 the relationship of production per head of population between the two groups of countries was approximately one to two, reaching one to seven by 1913.[21]

The dominant world position held by the West cannot be ascribed to the industrial revolution. European hegemony, and especially that of Britain, over the East had been established even before the industrial revolution transformed world trade. To the contrary, this hegemony was among the most important preconditions allowing the industrial revolution to succeed.[22]

Andre Gunder Frank is certain that the reason for everything was silver from the Americas. Thanks to this, the Europeans 'stole' first place from the East. But on its own, the flow of silver from the Americas to the old world would merely have strengthened the process of accumulation of capital in the countries of Asia, increasing its superiority over Europe. What happened was the reverse, and this was not simply because a positive trade balance is not in itself proof of economic dominance. India and China simply lacked the mechanism for the accumulation of capital that had taken shape in Europe. For this reason the silver that was received in exchange for spices, silks and later tea was not transformed into capital, but was spent on consumption or went to finance current operations.

In Europe, this mechanism of accumulation was underpinned not only by the activity of the bourgeoisie itself but also by its interaction with the state, and it was this latter factor that ultimately allowed the advantages of the bourgeois mode of production to be transformed into the source for a new global empire. It was not backwardness that became the cause of economic and political dependency, but on the contrary, the peripheral integration of the countries of Asia, Africa and Latin America that led to a growing lag behind the West.

Neither India nor China constructed a world-system around itself, consciously or even unconsciously. Spain, Holland and Britain, however, did precisely this. The process was not merely spontaneous or unconscious, but to an important degree deliberate as well. Thanks to conscious and prolonged efforts to organise a new system, the British empire was transformed into a mighty world power. In other words, the presence of imperial hegemony was an indispensable condition for the formation of capitalism as a global system, and not the reverse.

Asia: an entrepreneurial culture

Bourgeois development took place not just in Europe but in Asia as well, though at times in somewhat different forms. Asian merchants were well organised and fully able to defend their interests against local rulers, while the population was sufficiently mobile to make up an effective labour market, which in turn allowed production to develop in dynamic fashion. When British merchants established themselves in Calcutta, they found notable Armenian and Jewish communities there, actively carrying on entrepreneurial activity. Members of these communities immediately became the natural partners of the Europeans, who in turn were well acquainted with their way of life, culture and economic importance.[23] India during the seventeenth century was experiencing the same social processes that were under way in Western Europe. The same can be said of the Ottoman, Iranian and Chinese empires; scholars point to the fact that similar shifts were under way in each.

The main difference between East and West was that the East was richer, and not short of resources. Some historians even consider that the empire of the Great Moguls 'had too much money to need to trade off revenue for rights as European rulers had to do'.[24] The annual income of the ruler in 1600 was 20 times greater than that of the English monarch.[25] The Chinese government also functioned relatively well, and there seemed no necessity to change anything.[26]

The entrepreneurial culture that had arisen in the East was in no way inferior to that in the West. Lines of credit were well developed; the British borrowed money from Indian merchants, while the Dutch took out loans from the Japanese in Kyoto as the Portuguese had done before them. Muslim and Jewish money-lenders in Aleppo and Cairo were active in providing finance to Europeans.[27] To operate, European companies relied on local banking and trading networks. The obverse of this situation was the growth of the commercial debt owed by the British East India Company, which despite all the political successes of the British increased by a factor of almost six between 1786 and 1832.[28]

Despite sporadic and at times quite harsh interference by local rulers, trade in South Asia was relatively free. The state was drawn into the organisation of agriculture to a greater degree in places where it was required to maintain complex irrigation systems or to help the starving in case of famine.[29] Peasants provided the state (or local rulers who represented it) with a third to half of the harvest. Meanwhile, customs duties did not exceed 5 per cent of the value of goods, which to European ways of thinking was simply astonishing.[30] The trading corporations and guilds, which in Europe were tied closely to the state, in South Asia were based exclusively on the voluntary agreement of participants. The state was so little inclined to interfere in the lives of merchants that even the observance of sealed agreements was fundamentally a private matter, based above all on the concern of entrepreneurs for maintaining their reputations. If low taxes, free trade and the non-intervention of governments in the affairs of business are to be considered the main conditions for successful development, then the India of the Great Moguls would have become an advanced bourgeois society long before England and Holland.

The weakness of the Indian bourgeoisie (in striking contrast to its wealth and to the technological level it had attained) resulted not from state interference, but to the contrary, from its absence. While the government of the Great Moguls refrained from meddling in the affairs of merchants, and did not impose burdensome taxes or bureaucratic restrictions on them, it did not support them or provide them with help either. Still less did it undertake political initiatives in the interests of merchants. Here lay one of the main differences between the societies of East and West.

Analogous policies were followed by the Shahs of Persia. The governments of the Shahs showed no greater interest in local private entrepreneurs than the Great Moguls. The Ottoman Empire practised government control over the economy, but this was by no means as stringent as European travellers sometimes recounted. Merchants in Mameluke Egypt paid high taxes, but in other respects the state did not interfere in their business.[31]

In Asia, the commercial and political model represented in the history of the West by Venice and Genoa was to be found in such cities as Aden, Calicut, Malacca, Aceh and Bantam. Taxes and duties were low, and under favourable conditions such centres were transformed into something resembling offshore zones.

Studies of the economies of the Near East show that in Islamic culture, unlike Western Christianity, social status 'was much more positive'.[32] Usury, of course, was condemned by the Koran, but it was condemned by Christian doctrine as well. In any case, many of those who provided credit were not Muslims; most Eastern societies were not homogeneous in their ethnic and religious make-up. Along with Moslems they included Orthodox Christians, Armenians and Jews, not to speak of Hindus, who made up most of the population in the empire of the Great Moguls. Sharrafs or serrafs,[33] as bankers were called in India, almost always belonged to the Hindu community. In each village there was at least one such usurer or banker, who also dealt in insurance.

Western trade would have been impossible without the participation of local intermediaries, the banias.[34] Firms of banias often combined the capital of several blood relatives, but at times were partnerships based exclusively on business relationships. The banias did not make a show of their wealth, and scrupulously observed the requirements of religious ritual, their everyday conduct corresponding to the dictates of European Calvinist ethics.

Though weaker economically, the Europeans had a political advantage. Their state structures were aimed at supporting commercial expansion and strengthening the positions of 'their' capital. The European states were prepared at any moment to support the interests of entrepreneurs by force of arms and through administrative coercion, and because of this the Europeans held the initiative. Consequently, it was not Indian or Malay exporters who conquered the markets of Europe, but European entrepreneurs, together with their soldiers, sailors and administrators, who created a world market by establishing ties between continents and imposing their own rules.

In Asia, a significant proportion of trade was conducted through independent and semi-independent city-states, which at times were almost unconnected to the surrounding agricultural regions. These city-states provided ideal conditions for *entrepôt* activity and for deals between merchants, ensuring favourable conditions and security.

Regular and effective state intervention in the economy was something that arrived in most Asian countries together with European capitalism and the bourgeois system. This intervention by the state was not an obstacle to the development of capitalism; to the contrary, it was a crucially important factor allowing this development to occur. From the authorities, the commercial class required support and defence. The European merchants, behind whom stood the might of the state, were in a totally different situation compared with their Asian rivals, to whom the native authorities displayed a studied indifference.

The more bourgeois the temper and habits of the Europeans who arrived in Asia, the more inclined they were to establish monopolies on the new territory. For all their theoretical devotion to freedom of trade, the Dutch entrepreneur-colonists strove to establish monopoly control over the production and supply of the most valuable commodities, and maintained this control by force of arms. It was European monopolies that ensured the forcible economic integration of Asia into the new system of the world market.

With the coming of the Europeans, government intervention began affecting not only trade but also production, including not only traditional agriculture (which even earlier in the East, had often been unable to develop without irrigation organised by the authorities), but also production meant for the market and for export. Over several centuries, the compulsion placed by the Dutch administration on native communities to participate in the market was systematic, consistent, and merciless.[35] The Dutch authorities uprooted plantations and planted new ones, and decided which crops could or could not be grown.

Asia in the period from the fifteenth to the seventeenth century did not have civic institutions like those of the West, but the political life of the region was remote from the simplistic image of 'oriental despotism' to be found in European literature. The empire of the Great Moguls was in no way a state in which the will of the ruler decided everything. The authorities were forced to take account of traditions, caste privileges, communal rights, and local assemblies that often had judicial powers. Just as in Europe, the central government sought to consolidate its control over society, but it did this with far less persistence and success. Contrary to the later Western myth, the advantage enjoyed by the Europeans lay precisely in the fact that they possessed well-organised structures of authority, strict control and precise discipline, in contrast to the enfeeblement and chaos of the Eastern state.

In East Asia there were city-states ruled by Muslim merchant oligarchies. As in Italy in the late Middle Ages, the landowning aristocracy did not exercise power over the urban elite. Instead, people who had emerged from the bourgeoisie took power and used it to subordinate the aristocrats.[36]

The superiority of the Europeans lay in their possession of advanced means for organising violence – of state structures and policies aimed at defending the interests of capital, and on the 'tactical' level, in the existence of monopoly companies able to concentrate resources and which could develop themselves in close collaboration with the state. In other words, the strength of the West lay above all in its ability to construct a market economy by using non-market and even anti-market methods.

The European companies rested not on local but on global commercial networks, redistributing resources between diverse regions of the world while organising the division of labour and the mutual interdependence of consumption – in other words, in their ability to develop capitalism as a world system, and not simply as a particular set of productive and social relations on the local level. Military strength and commerce were closely linked, and the most consistent embodiment of this unity was the fleet.[37]

If there is something peculiar to the West that has ensured it a dominant position over two and a half centuries, its roots need to be sought not in Christian values, and not in the protestant ethic or in democratic traditions. The superiority of the West was ensured not by its culture but by a combination of the logic of development of capital with the interests of the state. The state was the instrument with whose help the bourgeois mode of production was transformed into the capitalist system. It was the ability of the Western bourgeoisie to become a conscious and politically organised class, putting state institutions at the service of its global project, that guaranteed its leading role in the incipient transformation of the world.

The offensive of the West: cannon as an argument?

The success of the Portuguese, Dutch and British was based on the absolute superiority of Western over local armaments.[38] Military superiority, however, must in the long term rest on superior state and social structures. Contrary to the thinking of liberal ideologues, the market does not exist in the form of an immutable, extra-historical system; it changes and evolves together with the evolution of society. The difference between the capitalist market and the traditional market lies in the fact that the decisive role in the former is played not by the competition of goods but by the competition of capitals. On this level, Western capital was incomparably more developed than that of the East.

Before the early eighteenth century the military superiority of the Europeans, already demonstrated clearly by the Portuguese admirals of the sixteenth century, did not bring the Western powers to political hegemony in Asia. Nevertheless, their superiority kept growing. In 1603 this unpleasant reality was discovered by the Chinese as well, when Spanish conquistadors drove them out of the Philippines. With the help of firearms, well-organised cavalry and advances in the field of for-tifications the Americas were seized by the Spanish and Portuguese, and Siberia by the Russians, without particular difficulty in the space of several decades. The empires of the Incas and Aztecs collapsed like houses of cards. The European methods of waging war shook the native Americans and Africans, since the armies of the whites sought not to capture slaves but to destroy their adversaries. The occupation of a region was often accompanied by a 'cleansing' that took the form of exterminating everyone who put up resistance. Or, of everyone who was there.

The sole Asian country that quickly and effectively assimilated European military experience was Japan. By the mid-sixteenth century, under the influence of the Portuguese, the musket had been put into mass production in Japan, and the infantry tactics developed by Oda Nobunaga recalled the reforms of Maurits of Nassau that had been worked out only 50 years earlier. The policy of centralisation that was pursued in Japan after unification of the country followed the same logic as in the West. The government disarmed the population, dissolved the private armies, and levelled splendid castles to their foundations.

This success in mastering Western military techniques anticipated the later successes in adopting Western capitalism. To the extent that Japan differed from China, it resembled Europe. Japan in the sixteenth century had large deposits of silver, second only to the vast resources of the Spanish Empire in the Americas. The production of Japanese silver was in the hands of the Shogun. But while the Spain of the Habsburgs used its silver for foreign expansion, ultimately becoming part of a new world economy dominated by other powers, Japan after its unification beneath the Shoguns closed itself off from the world market.

In China things worked out quite differently. The technical superiority of the Celestial Empire over the West was still a reality in the early eighteenth century, but in organisational and military respects the European states were incomparably more effective. The Chinese not only discovered gunpowder, but artillery appeared in China significantly earlier than in Europe. By the sixteenth century, however, Chinese firearms were decidedly primitive by comparison. European military organisation, born of the changing social nature of the state, created a demand for major improvements in firearms technology that had no parallel in China. In other words, the appearance of cannon and other new types of armaments in the East did not bring about a revolution in the art of warfare. By contrast, the reorganisation of the Western armies that began in the mid-fourteenth century spurred a rapid development of military technology.

Because of its sheer size China, despite its weak military organisation, remained beyond the grasp of the Europeans. In India the empire of the Great Moguls retained its dominant position until the mid-eighteenth century, but as early as the sixteenth century the superiority of European artillery was generally recognised in the East.[39] But even when Asian rulers obtained European artillery, they rarely managed to use it effectively, since they lacked the corresponding knowledge of tactics and military organisation. The Europeans in turn guarded this knowledge much more closely than they did the weapons and technologies themselves. The metal from which cannon were cast in India was, as a rule, of poor quality (a shortcoming that applied also to Turkish artillery of the seventeenth and eighteenth centuries). The Indian rulers hired military experts from Turkey and Europe, but rarely succeeded in improving the military capabilities of their forces to any serious degree. The organisation of the army was inseparable from the organisation of the state, and it was impossible to improve the one without changing the other.

The European powers came to Asia armed to the teeth, well organised and ruthless. It was precisely this that won them favour among local bourgeois layers who needed order, discipline and predictability if they were to follow the same capitalist road already pursued by the West. Meanwhile, each new wave in the European assault on Asia rested on a more powerful form of military-political organisation. The Dutch proved superior to the Portuguese, and the British surpassed the Dutch.

The British conquest of India might seem in hindsight to have been a consistent, systematically organised process. That was by no means the case. The Englishmen who in 1619 established their first trading outpost on the Coromandel Coast conducted themselves with extreme caution. In this, the Indian rulers might have thought, the English distinguished themselves favourably from the haughty and aggressive Portuguese. Nor were the English especially forward in undertaking missionary activity. The first protestant mission in India was established by the Danes.

The military-political expansion of the British East India Company was to a significant degree forced upon it. The last powerful emperor of the Great Moguls was Aurangzeb, who died in 1707. After the death of the emperor many rulers of the more distant Mogul territories seceded, founding independent princedoms and recognising the primacy of the empire only in nominal terms. The state finished up financially bankrupt, and local rulers felt themselves effectively independent. Beginning in 1739, Afghan and Persian forces invaded the Mogul domains with impunity, and a vacuum of power opened up. D.A. Washbrook notes that it was no accident that the decline and disintegration of the empire of the Great Moguls coincided with the arrival of the Europeans, and with the rapid development of trade and export production. The problem lay in the fact that commercial and economic development favoured the peripheral coastal regions of the empire, and not its central heartland. Attempts to strengthen control over these borderlands failed, and led to the appearance there of new regimes that used the same fiscal system as the Moguls, but with far greater success.[40] These regimes were not powerful enough to fill the increasing political vacuum, at the same time as the new politics gave rise to new contradictions and conflicts of interest. State structures 'were increasingly "farmed out" (or privatized?) to merchant and banking groups who utilized them as much, or more, for their own advantage than for that of their rulers'.[41] The commercial and bureaucratic elites, jointly taking over state power, launched an offensive against property and resources held in common, while carrying on a parallel privatisation (in practice, and at times formally as well) of state property. In this way a new elite came into existence, consisting of 'great households', groups known to history as vakil, dubashi, mirasidari and sometimes as 'new gentries' or 'commercial zamindars'.[42]

The disintegration of the empire did not in the short term bring a dramatic strengthening of the Europeans, and especially of the British, who initially were inclined to view the process as cause for concern. The local centres of power grew stronger, including the numerous princes and other rulers in whose hands lay financial, military and political control over the territories that nominally were still part of the empire of the Great Moguls. This, however, aroused the displeasure of the local bourgeoisie, who began to take issue with the rulers' arbitrary decision-making, extortions, and petty conflicts that obstructed the development of business.

Amid increasing political instability the British company, which even earlier had not restricted itself to peaceful trade, began a marked expansion of its armed strength. Adding to its need to defend itself in a context of political chaos was a natural desire to profit from the turmoil, enhancing its own position. 'Trade requires above all security and good faith,' a British imperial historian explained. 'When these vanished the traders became their own policemen. And to police India meant conquest.'[43]

A second factor driving the militarisation of British commercial strategy in India was rivalry with the French: 'The presence of these evil passions, however, led to the adoption of another policy, and to the initiation of a carrier of territorial conquest and spoliation, which till now, had never been so much as dreamed of.'[44]

It was the French who first conceived the idea of using the military-political crisis in India to serve their interests. Joseph François, Marquis de Dupleix, who in 1742 was named governor-general of the French Compagnie des Indes, quickly realised that in the conditions of political instability Europeans with the help of small contingents of well-trained professional soldiers could exert a disproportionate influence. Intervening in internecine conflicts on the side of particular claimants, the French weighted the balance to their advantage. These interventions brought about a marked increase in the French sphere of influence, from which British entrepreneurs were forced out. Dupleix also thought to take over the collection, on the territory under his influence, of taxes meant for the Great Moguls. In this way, the most important function of the imperial power passed to the French. The company set up its operations so as to ensure that its activity was self-financing, and that it could maintain its European forces using money obtained in India.[45]

For French capital, which was inferior to the British in resources and experience, it was quite natural to transfer the rivalry to the military-political plane, especially since the French monarchy possessed a good deal of diplomatic experience and armed strength. But in challenging their British competitors, the French politicians and entrepreneurs in India did not realise how quickly and effectively the East India Company would succeed in adopting the same model.

The War of the Austrian Succession, which had broken out in Europe, provided a pretext for military conflict between the British and French in India. The French Admiral Labourdonnais captured Madras, which belonged to the East India Company. In 1746 Dupleix's forces seized the British outpost of Fort St George. Then in a battle on the Adyar River the French, with only 300 of their own troops and 700 native soldiers, used musket volleys to scatter a force of 10,000 Indian troops fighting on the side of the British. The use of Indian soldiers in European armies was nothing new, but it was the French who thought to train and arm them according to the Western model, and then to place them under the command of European officers.

Realising the extent of the threat, the British company began constructing its own armed forces on the model of the French. 'Dupleix might be said to have provided the impulse for an uncontrolled development of events,' the French historian Marc Ferro writes, since after he was summoned back to his homeland the failures began that would later give rise to the myth of the 'loss of India', said to have been 'taken from us by the British.' In fact, it was the policies of Dupleix that provoked the British to act in response, and that forced them to embark on a conquest that initially had not entered into their plans.[46]

Under the peace treaty signed in 1749 at Aix-la-Chapelle, Madras was returned to the British, but while Europe experienced an interlude of peace, the struggle in India never ceased. The local Indian rulers, discovering the effectiveness of European forces, themselves called on the British and French to intervene in endless conflicts unfolding both within the princedoms and between them. As a result, the conflict between the two European powers assumed the typical form of struggle between two claimants to one or another princedom.

The financial resources of the British were substantially greater than those of the French. The volume of Britain's trade with India was four times that of France, and the funds not only of a great number of British merchants but also of many Indian ones were in the accounts of the East India Company. These funds were directed toward resolving military questions. In 1758 two battalions of sepoys were in the company's service; in 1759 this figure was five, and in 1765 no less than ten, with a total of 9,000 soldiers.[47] Compared to the size of the native armies such contingents might have seemed insignificant. The overall number of troops under the command of the Great Moguls reached a million men, though such a mass of people could not be assembled in one place or even for a single campaign.[48] Meanwhile, even in the eighteenth century the well-organised, disciplined and trained units of professional soldiers established by the Company held the upper hand over militias whose numbers were many times greater.

The Company was also successful in its choice of competent personnel. At first this was an administrative and commercial question; as trade developed, the need grew for the Company to exclude from its work open adventurers who might threaten its policies through irresponsible actions. It was soon discovered, however, that astute administrators could also turn out to be first-class soldiers. From among the employees of the British East India Company came the conqueror of Bengal Robert Clive, along with many other well-known colonial figures.

Clive and his closest comrades were former clerks of the company who had 'learned the art of war on the march and on the battlefield'.[49] But it was these non-professional soldiers and the hastily assembled troops they led who dealt a crushing defeat to the French generals and Indian feudal armies.

As a politician, soldier and administrator Clive was the direct opposite of the aristocrat Dupleix. He measured his ambitions precisely against the forces at his disposal, and as a result, gradually came to achieve successes beyond his wildest imaginings. He took risks readily, but these risks were always carefully calculated. With insignificant resources, Clive outplayed his opponents tactically.

With the beginning of the Seven Years War the French government sent substantial reinforcements to India, hoping to achieve a breakthrough in the situation.

But in 1759 the French, despite huge efforts, were unable to capture Madras a second time. The 8,000-strong army of Count de Lally, supported by powerful artillery forces, could not break the resistance of the 4,000 defenders of the city, a significant number of whom were Indians. After 1759 the French generals, their attention diverted by the war in America and Europe, were unable to send new reinforcements to deal with Clive.

The counter-offensive begun by the British eventually laid to rest the plans of the French to establish their own empire in India. Each new campaign increased Clive's superiority. In 1761 Pondicherry, the capital of French India, surrendered to his soldiers. Although the Peace of Paris returned these possessions to the defeated side, the relationship of forces had changed irrevocably. Britain remained the sole European power wielding political influence in India.

The 'Bengal revolution'

With hindsight, the expression 'the Bengal revolution' that was used in the eighteenth century to describe the coup staged in 1757 by Robert Clive and his local allies has come to be viewed as a terminological curiosity, born out of the imprecision of the political language of that period. On closer examination, however, it turns out that these events actually represented a unique form of social overturn, a bourgeois revolution of a colonial type. Analysing the structures of power that became established in the course of these events and the social base of the new regime, the Englishman Washbrook concluded that the state constructed by the British East India Company bore clear marks of its indigenous, Indian provenance.[50] The fact that the British administration in India was foreign was not in itself a serious problem either for the population or for a significant section of the elites in India. This country had undergone repeated conquests, and had got on superbly with the new rulers, who in turn had fallen beneath the spell of the local culture (the British in this respect were no exception).

The Great Moguls who had preceded the British were themselves conquerors, a foreign dynasty and, moreover, infidels whose actively proselytised Islam was no less in conflict with Hinduism than the Protestantism of the British gentlemen. Nick Robins in his history of the East India Company shows convincingly that the conquest of Bengal by the British in the eighteenth century not only rested on the support of the local commercial bourgeoisie, but was also actively financed by it.[51] The class of native entrepreneurs, the banias, developed successfully beneath the protection of the British authorities in Calcutta, accumulating extraordinary riches. It was the banias who managed the day-to-day affairs of the Company, acting for the British as commercial intermediaries and creditors.

The formal pretext for the conflict which ended in the Battle of Plassey was a raid by the Bengali Nawab[52] Siraj against Calcutta. Those who suffered in the course of this raid included not only the company, which controlled the city, but also the local population, especially the Hindu and Armenian merchants. After restoring British control over the city, Clive directed his efforts toward deposing Siraj and replacing him with a loyal company ruler. Selected for this role was Mir Jafar, a relative of the ruler. The conspiracy was supported by many people in the court of the nawab himself, as well as merchants who had suffered from his actions. The British press wrote with enthusiasm of the inhabitants of Bengal who 'hugged themselves in the expectation that the English would defeat the nabob, and deliver them from his tyranny and oppression'.[53]

The weakening of the Great Moguls led to a worsening of the tyranny of the local rulers, whether Muslim nawabs or princes who were part of the Maratha Confederacy. The former oppressed their subjects with an unbearable burden of taxation, while the latter simply resorted to plunder. Neither group was capable of ensuring an effective legal system, respect for property rights or guaranteed access to markets. In all these respects the power of the East India Company seemed the most attractive option amid the political collapse that accompanied the decline of the empire.

A striking example is provided by Nabakrishna Deb, who not only acted as a go-between for the conspirators at the court of the Nawab of Bengal in their dealings with the British, but who also provided food supplies to Calcutta when it was besieged by the forces of the nawab in 1756. After the victory at Plassey, Nabakrishna rewarded himself by taking part in the pillage of the harem in Murshidabad; from it, the victors took gold, silver and jewels worth 80 million rupees. Receiving the title of maharajah and a salary of 2,000 rupees from the East India Company, Nabakrishna after Plassey returned to his home city of Sovabazar on a lavishly decorated elephant, scattering silver coins about the streets.

Even many years after Plassey, Nabakrishna's financial position remained far better than that of the victors in the battle. In 1780, when the Governor of India Warren Hastings ran into financial difficulties, he found his only solution was to appeal to the same Nabakrishna for a loan of 300,000 rupees.[54]

The battle that took place at Plassey on 23 July 1757, and that decided the outcome of the struggle in Bengal, was strictly speaking not a battle but a brief artillery duel in the course of which the light batteries of the British prevailed over the heavy weapons of the Bengali ruler. The huge imbalance of forces (800 British soldiers, 2,200 sepoys and eight cannon confronted 68,000 Bengalis and 50 cannon) had no effect on the course of the encounter. Panic began to seize the Bengali ranks, and a section of the Bengali forces fled the battlefield, in order soon after to join the forces of the East India Company. Clive reported with satisfaction to the directors of the company that the British forces had lost only 17 men, 'those chiefly blacks'.[55] Ultimately, the victory had been won not by force of arms but by politics; an important section of the Bengali elite had put their stake on the British.

The significance of the victory at Plassey would not have been so great if the rout of Siraj's forces had not been followed by a political revolution in Bengal organised and supported by a substantial part of the local elite. Originally, the company had planned to rule Bengal through puppet nawabs, but it soon became clear that this scheme would not work. It was discovered that Mir Jafar had been flirting with the Dutch. The nawab was replaced, but the new ruler, his son-in-law Mir

Qasim, proved an even less successful choice and soon entered into open conflict with the British. After the Bengali forces had again been defeated, Mir Jafar was restored in 1765 to the Bengali throne, where he remained until his death two years later. In May 1765 Clive returned to India after a five-year absence, just in time to receive the news of the death of Mir Jafar.[56] The situation was dismal. The company's managers in Calcutta were confused and demoralised. A mutiny had broken out among the sepoys, though this was quickly suppressed, and Mir Qasim with the support of the Great Mogul had returned to Bengal at the head of a large military force. In a battle at Buxar in 1764, however, the company's army, consisting mainly of sepoys, had scored another victory over the significantly larger army of Mir Qasim.

Most of the subcontinent was now under the control of the victors, but Clive and the company's council in Calcutta were not ready to take on the role of rulers of India. After making peace with the Great Mogul they forced him to sign a decree (*firman*) handing over to the British the right to collect taxes in Bengal and the neighbouring territories, the *diwani*. In exchange, the Company bound itself to pay 2.6 million rupees annually into the treasury of the emperor.[57] Ultimately, the Great Mogul was turned into a pensioner of the Company, living on a budget which it assigned to him.

Initially, the Company received the right to collect taxes in the provinces of Orissa and Bihar as well as in Bengal. The revenues in the years from 1762 to 1764 came to £2 million, and in the period from 1766 to 1769 reached £7.5 million.[58] These resources were quickly put to use strengthening the Company's military might. New fortresses were built, the size of the armed forces was increased, and successful campaigns were waged in the provinces of Deccan and Mysore. By 1782 the number of troops under British command in India had reached 115,000 men, 90 per cent of them sepoys. The Company now exercised political, military and financial control over an extensive, densely populated and wealthy territory substantially greater than Bengal itself. The administration of the nawab as well was now maintained at the expense of the Company. The initial outcome of this system was managerial chaos and generalised corruption, in which both the British and their Indian partners participated alike. Attempts by Clive to impose order were only partially successful, and it was only in 1773 that his successor Warren Hastings managed to establish a more or less effective administration that was, naturally, completely in the hands of the British.

The political and legal institutions on which the British administration in Bengal rested enjoyed the support of the local bourgeoisie; in the words of one historian, these institutions proved able to 'attract the support and flatter the ambitions of the newly dominant classes'.[59] Thanks to the new authorities the informal privatisation of rights and property to the advantage of the new commercial elite, a process already under way in Indian society, was formalised in legal terms. The Company provided the bourgeoisie with defence against the encroachments of rulers and sultans, and also against the poorer classes who sought the return of the communal property they had lost.

The Indian bourgeoisie played a decisive role in the formation of the colonial state, and it was this that explains the surprising ease with which the Company, its administrators and its generals achieved brilliant successes with comparatively small forces. Concealed behind the façade of the British colonial presence were powerful commercial interests of entirely local origin. As Washbrook states, 'the achievement of state power in most parts of South Asia was accomplished through, and on the back of, these groups', while 'colonialism was the logical outcome of South Asia's own history of capitalist development'.[60]

Each successful conquering expedition by the East India Company ended in a reconciliation with the conquered, and with their inclusion in the inchoate political system. As in Scotland, where after the crushing of the Jacobite revolt of 1745 first the elites and then broader layers of society turned into supporters of the new perspectives of empire that were opening up for them, in India as well former enemies were turned one after another by the Company into supporters. The Marathas were recruited in large numbers to the Company's forces, attracted by the pay and by the prospect of advancement through service. The same also occurred with the Sikhs, who began enlisting in the army after the 1850s.[61] Not only the army but the civil service as well actively incorporated members of the indigenous population, without whom the conquerors in India could not have advanced a single step.

The trade balance between Britain and India came to favour the latter. Each year the British traders left silver in India to cover the trade deficit. In Bengal huge fortunes were accumulated, Calcutta prospered, and production and employment increased. The banias could quite logically have considered that although they were prevented (in the conditions of caste society) from having their own political and military structures, they were making use of the British administration to attain their own ends. A century later, Marx wrote that British dominion had led to the greatest and indeed, the only social revolution ever experienced in Asia.[62] In essence, the Indian bourgeoisie with the help of the British army freed itself from the old political and state system that had hindered its prospects.

Why, then, did the relationships in this case change radically by the early nineteenth century? Why was India, followed later by China as well, transformed into part of the periphery of the world capitalist system, while the commercial relations between Europe and Asia changed dramatically to the disadvantage of the latter? The decisive role was undoubtedly played by the industrial revolution in Britain. While the Indian bourgeoisie with the help of the soldiers in red coats and the gentlemen in powdered wigs were installing mercantile capitalism in South Asia, in Britain industrial capitalism was coming into being.

In the development of industrialisation the logic of global accumulation, characteristic of the capitalist world-system, played a decisive role. The commercial and financial relations between India and Britain in the eighteenth century did not yet provide a basis for talking of India – despite the military and political presence of foreigners – as a 'periphery'. But European capitalism had developed as the centre of a world-system, mobilising and redistributing the resources of many regions of the planet, while Indian commercial capitalism remained a profoundly local phenomenon, participating in the global economy only to the extent to which it became part of the British commercial system whose embodiment was the East India Company. Success led to a dramatic change in the relationships within the camp of the victors. The Indian merchants and bankers who had financed Clive received their investments back with interest, but to employ a chess term, 'lost quality'. Winning access to the tax base of Bengal, the Company made itself independent of the Indian bankers, and in banishing the competition of other European companies, the British also acquired the ability to dictate terms to their Indian partners. The Indian bourgeoisie, which had put its stake on the British colonial regime as a tool for realising its own ambitions, underestimated the power and resources of the state – especially, of a state that was directly included in the management of global processes, a state-hegemon. The result was a social transformation, but not the one on which the people who invested money in Robert Clive and his administration were counting. The economic and political reconstruction of Bengali and later of Indian society sub-ordinated its capitalist development to the needs of external, European accumulation. The key role in organising the economy, Washbrook concludes, was 'taken out of the hands of indigenous capitalists and passed, via the monopoly powers of the state, to British ones'.[63]

Twenty years after the start of British expansion Indian traders and artisans, who initially had welcomed the imposing of British rule, had discovered that the new rulers, though different from the old, were not much better. The British, along with their closest partners among the Hindus and Armenians, imposed their commercial conditions stringently, and did not shrink from resorting to coercion and the use of squads of sepoys to intimidate recalcitrant suppliers. Bribe-taking became standard practice, along with extortion.[64]

Even a conservative British historian was forced to admit that employees of the company 'in general combined incompetence and corruption to a remarkable degree'.[65] By the 1780s news of the cruelties and lawlessness practised by the British administration in India had reached London, and could no longer be ignored. Even King George III wrote of 'shocking enormities in India that disgrace human nature'.[66] Public opinion demanded punishment of the guilty, and the head of the British administration, Warren Hastings, became the scapegoat on whom the rage of newspaper commentators and parliamentary orators was unleashed.

After Hastings, the British administration in India was headed by Lord Cornwallis, who succeeded in putting an end to the most blatant excesses that had accompanied the operations of the East India Company in previous years. The new, formally organised bureaucratic state closed off the opportunities the local bourgeois had enjoyed for enriching themselves through informal privatisation. Property rights were strengthened and consecrated as the newly emerged Indian bourgeoisie had wanted, but the formalising of these rights was accompanied by the ending of the systematic appropriation by the bourgeoisie of treasury property. Many financial magnates were transformed into petty usurers and speculators.[67]

The combination of commercial monopoly with a political monopoly on power was the strategic tool with whose help the economy of Bengal, and then of India as a whole, was transformed. The fruits of the victory were distributed unevenly, with the main advantages accruing to the British. But the Indian bourgeoisie did not rise in revolt. The rules that had been set in place as a result of the British victory were far worse for the Indian financiers and merchants than they had anticipated. But even these conditions were advantageous for them.

One of the first consequences of imposing the market regime on Bengal was the catastrophic famine of 1770. Crop failure and hunger had happened before in India, but they became more frequent after the coming to power of the British. The problem was not simply that the foreigners did not understand the details of the local agriculture and of the local irrigation systems, but also that the British had brought capitalism with them. As Marx noted, in India agriculture that was not capable of developing in accordance with the British principle of free competition went into decline.[68] Warren Hastings stated two years later that in the course of this disaster no fewer than 10 million people died, a third of the population of the region. If Hastings' assessment was anywhere near correct, the Bengali famine was a monstrous shock that dwarfed both the 1931 famine in Ukraine and the policy of genocide carried out by Pol Pot in Cambodia. Other writers have spoken of 3 million dead, and the Indian scholar Rajat Datta considers that the British sources exaggerated the scale of the catastrophe, and that 'only' 1.2 million Bengalis died. Even if Datta's calculations are closer to the truth than the estimates of contemporaries who, shaken by what they had seen, most likely cited unverified and clearly excessive figures, we are still confronted with one of the most appalling calamities ever to have been caused by policies of economic liberalisation and deregulation.[69]

The administration of the Moguls had responded to the regularly recurring crop failures by lowering taxes, regulating prices, and establishing state food reserves. With the taking of power in Bengal by the East India Company, all this came to an end. The main financial instruments had passed from the government to the hands of corporate managers who answered to their shareholders in London, not to the local population. Since the crop failure and famine could have lowered share prices on the stock exchange, the company reacted to the events by raising dividend payments to its shareholders, and to cover these expenses, it not only left tax levels unchanged, but even raised them. At the same time, entrepreneurs linked to the Company began buying up foodstuffs so as to resell them at speculative prices – perfectly rational behaviour from a market point of view.

Today even the most single-minded adherents of market economics are prepared to admit that the state should intervene in times of natural disaster. Unfortunately, for the state to intervene in such circumstances it needs to have economic levers, the tools of intervention and regulation, under its control during 'normal' times as well.

The birth of 'traditional society'

As the world-system took shape, a more developed capitalism, a society with more advanced bourgeois relations, as a rule came to prevail over less developed forms.

But for the most part, this success was not achieved on the commodity markets, but on battlefields or in the course of diplomatic discussions.

The problem facing the Asian entrepreneurial class did not lie in any lack of initiative, but in the fact that in Asia, unlike the case in Europe by the end of the seventeenth century, nothing even resembling a national state had been established. The sole exception was Japan, which by the middle of the century had overcome its internecine internal wars. This fact contributed substantially to the country's later transformation into the sole Asian imperialist power.

Victory over the French in India secured for Britain the position of the leading world power. The effect that we observe in India was totally different. Even if we reject the nationalist interpretations that reduce colonial history to oppression, plunder and insults, it is easily seen that the integration into the world market to which the local bourgeoisie aspired yielded an unexpected result that in many ways altered the direction of social development.

The Indian bourgeoisie reconciled itself to the role assigned to it within the colonial state, since this system, while forcing local capital into a secondary role, nevertheless allowed it to develop. Local companies grew, their owners enriched themselves, and their property rights were reliably defended. Through delegating political power, risks and responsibilities to a foreign state, Indian capital gained the opportunity to secure for itself certain economic niches that suited it perfectly. 'After a few early misunderstandings, South Asia's capitalist social classes became the most loyal supporters of the British Raj and sustained it throughout the middle and later decades of the nineteenth century.'[70] During the sepoy revolt the bourgeoisie gave decisive support to the British, while the mutinous soldiers received backing from feudal clans that had fallen into decline.

The flourishing of the bourgeois segment of Indian society, however, was in flagrant contrast to the 'traditionalisation' and socio-cultural decline of society as a whole. It might be said that within the colonial model the bourgeoisie guaranteed its own prosperity at the expense of sacrificing not only the interests of the masses, but also the prospect of national development. The Indian population in the early nineteenth century underwent a 'peasantisation', in which town-dwellers returned to the land as they were driven out of production and semi-nomadic tribes were settled forcibly as agriculturalists.[71] Corresponding to this economic process was a socio-cultural de-modernisation or growth of traditionalism at the lower level. In other words, Indian society was far more backward in relation to Europe at the end of the nineteenth century than it had been when the century began. By reinforcing ancient customs, Anglo-Indian legislation turned them into unchanging and constantly self-reproducing practice, strengthening the conservatism of society. 'Peasantisation' and 'traditionalisation' were advantageous not only for British capital, but also for capital in general. Within this system local capital received its share, and the problems that colonial practices caused it were not particularly great compared to the advantages it derived.[72]

The tax policy of the East India Company conduced to the steady decline of the countryside.[73] The inevitable consequences of such a policy included peasant revolts, which occurred during the period before 1857 with the regularity of a natural phenomenon. The company's activity, aimed at maximising the extraction of surplus product for commercial use in the cities and for sale in Western markets, blocked capitalist development in the villages. In other words, exactly the same occurred in India as happened in most countries of peripheral capitalism from Russia to South America; the acceleration of capitalist development 'from above', stimulated by the world market, blocked tendencies to bourgeois development 'from below'.

After the revolt of the sepoys the Anglo-Indian government enacted reforms that somewhat alleviated the situation of the peasants. In the process of land redistribution, notables and other influential people, and also temples, received title to significant allotments. As a result, a British historian notes, a new class of landowners was 'thereby created by State patronage'.[74] The new system, resting on a European type of administration, required the establishing of a large bureaucratic apparatus at the local level, accompanied in turn by the development of Indian education and by the appearance of new middle layers tied to the colonial government and the bourgeoisie. Ultimately, it was not the foreign official, nor the soldier in his pith helmet, but precisely this local bureaucrat, standing in counterposition to the village community, who became the main support for and practical embodiment of the British Raj.

The colonial state expedited the accumulation of capital through the expropriation of the lower orders of society, and the redistribution of property and incomes. The state itself, in line with liberal principles, did not lay claim to the managing of business or property. All the advantages flowing from the process of destruction and creation that accompanied the reordering of society went to the private sector, including, and even primarily, at the local level. Capital increased its profits not through technical innovations and the modernisation of production, but through the exploitation of cheap labour. From the point of view of accumulation this second route is simpler, cheaper and more easily followed.

A degraded society could not, of course, exercise strong demand for the goods and services produced by Indian capital. But as early as the 1820s new foreign markets had begun opening up, in China, Ceylon and Europe.[75] The decline of the internal market resulted in a cheapening of the commodities placed on foreign markets and, accordingly, in a competitive advantage for the Indian bourgeoisie. This situation not only bound the local bourgeoisie to the empire and to the world market that for the moment was inseparable from the empire, but also turned Indian capital into a force directly interested in the strengthening and growth of British world power. The less the contribution of local capital to the formation and development of the internal market, and the more society became traditionalist, the less actively the modernisation of India then went ahead; the stronger the vested interest of the Indian bourgeoisie in the empire and its markets, the more 'globalist' the bourgeoisie became in its ideology. The Asian state that had come into being on the basis of colonialism was not simply capitalist, but proved to be ultra-capitalist. The might of the Company united in a single structure both 'sultanism' and capitalism; the private corporation became transformed into a sultan, and the state into the property of the firm.[76]

It is not surprising that the brilliant economic successes of India in the early nineteenth century were devalued by the reconstruction of the capitalist world-system that followed. The local bourgeoisie retained its capital, but lost its strategic position. The altered relationship of forces gave rise to new relations, contradictions and conflicts, which, as they accumulated and grew more acute, led ultimately to the mutiny of the sepoys. After crushing the mutiny, the British administration was obliged once again to form a partnership between the representatives of the metropolis and the local elite. But these relations were now constructed on a completely different basis from those in the time of Robert Clive.

Notes

1 See A. Glinchikova, *Raskol ili sryv 'russkoy Reformatsii'* [The schism or the failure of the 'Russian Reformation'], Moscow: Kul'turnaya revolyutsiya, 2008.
2 *Encyclopédie ou dictionnaire raisonné des sciences, des arts et des métiers*, Paris, 1754, Vol. 4, p. 886.
3 Ibid., p. 887.
4 *Encyclopédie ou dictionnaire raisonné des sciences, des arts et des métiers*, Neufchastel: Samuel Faulche & Co, 1765, Vol. 14, p. 443.
5 *Gentleman's Magazine*, XXXII: 299, July 1762.
6 Ibid., p. 300.
7 A.-H. Anquetil Duperron, *Legislation orientale*, Amsterdam, chez Marc-Michel Rey, 1778, p. vi.
8 Marx and Engels, *Sochineniya*, Vol. 14, p. 292.
9 Anquetil Duperron, *Legislation orientale*, p. v.
10 C.F. Lavell and C. E. Payne, *Imperial England*, New York: The MacMillan Co., 1920, p. 99.
11 Ibid., p. 11.
12 L. James, *Raj. The Making and Unmaking of British India*, London: Abacus, 2003, p. 49.
13 Quoted in C.C. O'Brien, *The Great Melody. A Thematic Biography and Commented Anthology of Edmund Burke*, Chicago/London: University of Chicago Press, 1992, p. 343.
14 Ibid., p. 325.
15 D.A. Washbrook, 'Progress and Problems: South Asian economic and social history *c.* 1720–1860', *Modern Asian Studies*, 22 (1) (1988), p. 79.
16 Ibid., p. 60.
17 See N. Robins, *The Corporation That Changed the World: How the East India Company Shaped the Modern Multinational*, London: Pluto Press, 2006, pp. 67, 148.
18 Ibid., p. 67.
19 *The Economist*, XIV (685): 1117, 11 October 1856.
20 F. Brodel', *Material'naya tsivilizatsiya, ekonomika i kapitalizm, XV-XVIII vv.* [Material civilisation, economy and capitalism, XV-XVIII centuries], Vol. 2, p. 94.
21 See E.J. Hobsbawm, *The Age of Empire, 1875–1914*, London: Weidenfeld and Nicolson, 1987, p. 15.
22 Washbrook, 'Progress and Problems', p. 61.
23 See *The Gentleman's Magazine*, XXVII: 307, July 1757.
24 J.D. Tracy, *The Political Economy of Merchant Empires,* Cambridge: Cambridge University Press, 1991, p. 57.
25 See ibid., p. 52.
26 Ibid., p. 68.
27 Brodel', *Material'naya tsivilizatsiya*, Vol. 2, pp. 94–5.
28 See Washbrook, 'Progress and Problems', p. 74.
29 Tracy, *Political Economy of Merchant Empires*, p. 52.
30 See ibid., p. 97.
31 Tracy, *Political Economy of Merchant Empires*, p. 66.

32 Ibid., p. 61.
33 In European literature the spellings shroffs, sharrafs and serrafs are encountered.
34 Some sources give this word in a different form, as banyans.
35 Tracy, *Political Economy of Merchant Empires*, p. 3
36 Ibid., p. 18.
37 Tracy, *Rise of Merchant Empires*, p. 10.
38 See Tracy, *Political Economy of Merchant Empires*, pp. 142, 195; H. Kamen, *Spain's Road to Empire. The Making of a World Power*, London: Penguin Books, 2002, p. 11.
39 C.R. Boxer (ed.), *Portuguese Conquest and Commerce in Southern Asia*, London: Variorum Reprints, 1985, p. 160.
40 Washbrook, 'Progress and Problems', p. 69.
41 Ibid.
42 Ibid.
43 Lavell and Payne, *Imperial England*, p. 101.
44 W.C. Pearce, *History of India*, London and Glasgow: William Collins, Sons & Co., 1876, p. 64.
45 F. McLynn, *1759: The Year Britain Became Master of the World*, London: Pimlico, 2005, p. 169.
46 M. Ferro, *Histoire des colonisations. Dès conquêtes aux independences, XIII–XX siècle*, Paris: Seuil, 1994, p. 91.
47 See Tracy, *Political Economy of Merchant Empires*, p. 183.
48 See ibid., p. 183.
49 James, *Raj*, p. 21.
50 Washbrook, 'Progress and Problems', p. 68.
51 See Robins, *Corporation that Changed the World*,
52 In some sources the title of the ruler of Bengal is given as 'nabob'. For the sake of uniformity this will be rendered here as nawab, irrespective of the form used in the source.
53 *The Scots Magazine*, June 1757, p. 315.
54 See Robins, *Corporation that Changed the World*, pp. 58–9.
55 James, *Raj*, p. 35.
56 R. Harvey, *Clive: The Life and Death of a British Emperor*, London: Hodder and Stoughton, 1998.
57 P. Griffiths, *Empire into Commonwealth*, London: Ernest Benn Ltd, 1969, p. 95.
58 See Tracy, *Political Economy of Merchant Empires*, p. 184.
59 Washbrook, 'Progress and Problems', p. 75.
60 Ibid., p. 76.
61 James, *Raj*, p. 73.
62 Marx and Engels, *Sochineniya*, Vol. 9, p. 135.
63 Washbrook, 'Progress and Problems', pp. 79–80.
64 James, *Raj*, p. 29.
65 Griffiths, *Empire into Commonwealth*, p. 97.
66 Quoted in ibid., p. 357
67 Washbrook, 'Progress and Problems', p. 80.
68 Marx and Engels, *Sochineniya*, Vol. 9, p. 133.
69 For an account of the famine of 1770 see Robins, *Corporation that Changed the World*, pp. 92–3.
70 Washbrook, 'Progress and Problems', p. 84.
71 Ibid., p. 81.
72 Ibid., pp. 85–6.
73 James, *Raj*, p. 193.
74 A. Wells, 'Imperial Hegemony and Colonial Labor' in *Rethinking Marxism*, April 2007, 19 (2): 188.
75 Washbrook, 'Progress and Problems', p. 86.
76 Ibid., pp. 87–90.

7

AN EPOCH OF WARS AND REVOLUTIONS

The late eighteenth century was a time of global revolutionary turmoil which affected not just North America and France, but all of Europe as well. By the beginning of this epoch of revolutions the capitalist world-system already existed in its main outlines. The bourgeois revolutions rested on already-formed capitalist relations not just on the local but also on the global level. Orthodox Marxists in the late nineteenth century were led by their understanding of this fact to conclude that the revolutions concerned were in essence political overturns, and that their basis lay in a conflict between bourgeois societies that had already been established, and feudal states that no longer corresponded to the new social forms. Paradoxically, this theory was not profoundly different from the liberal view of revolution as a revolt by civil society, which had taken shape 'in natural fashion', against a state that held back its development. In fact, both the state and the society were torn apart by internal contradictions. It was precisely for this reason that the conflicts themselves took on so dramatic and bloody a character. In the course of the revolutions, societies that *still were not completely bourgeois* became transformed, while at the same time entering into conflict with state formations that were *no longer completely feudal*.

The American revolt

In the eighteenth century commodity exchange between the colonies and the metropolises grew at impressive rates, testifying to the fact that the political limitations which the European powers placed on this process had by no means paralysed it. Contrary to the ideas of liberal economists, politically enforced monopolism did not raise the prices of goods and reduce production, but had a directly opposite effect. The industries of the European metropolises, gaining access to raw materials and labour power at extremely favourable prices, and with guaranteed sales on extensive colonial markets, were able to dispose of their products much more cheaply on other markets as well.

The contradictions between Britain's American colonies – which were highly developed economically – and the 'mother country' arose not because London restrained the development of its overseas possessions, but because colonial capital, enjoying broad opportunities for growth and unlimited access to the broad market of the new global empire, quickly outgrew the limits prescribed for it, and began developing its own system of goals and interests.

In the seventeenth century the colonies of New England had been conceived of as suppliers of raw materials, providing Great Britain with timber, pitch, hemp and other commodities that earlier had been imported from Russia. The real economic structure of the northern colonies, however, came closer to replicating the economy of the metropolis than to complementing it. The British government in turn showed less and less interest in New England, directing more attention to the tropical colonies. Politically as well, the American colonies were to an important degree self-sufficient. Their self-government was in considerable measure a result of the English revolution, during which the local protestant bourgeoisie, taking advantage of the discord in the metropolis, effectively took power into its own hands.

From the late seventeenth century, the North American colonies and the mother country grew increasingly remote from one another in economic terms.[1] From the point of view of British bourgeois interests it was the planter economies of the south that developed more successfully, furnishing European markets with rice, sugar, cotton and tobacco grown using the labour of black slaves. In this respect the southern colonies resembled the Caribbean islands that had come under British control. The slaveholding colonies of Jamaica, Barbados and Virginia were the first self-governing territories to found their own electoral institutions in the late seventeenth century – though only, naturally, for white settlers. In time, the bodies set up there acquired counterparts in other colonial possessions, and the legal precedents established were used to settle contentious issues elsewhere.

By the mid-eighteenth century Boston, Philadelphia and New York were numbered among the leading commercial centres of the empire. Contemporaries described the Philadelphia market as 'the best of its bigness in the known world, and undoubtedly the largest in America'.[2]

The struggle for control over markets, as in the case of most capitalist conflicts, heightened the tensions between the metropolis and the American colonies. Seeking to demonstrate the importance of the colonies for Britain, Edmund Burke referred to the huge market for British goods that was opening up beyond the ocean. The American bourgeoisie, however, had other plans. Exports from the metropolis not only met with growing competition from colonial producers, but also with more direct resistance; it was no accident that as the conflict with the metropolis developed, boycotts of British goods became a favourite form of opposition to the 'tyranny' of London. Until the end of the Seven Years War the New England colonies, despite their economic self-sufficiency, still required British support, since they were in constant need of defence against the native Americans, the Dutch and

Spanish, and later against the French. The British flag was also necessary to the shipowners of Boston and New York, giving protection during voyages in neutral waters; the threat alone of revenge from the Royal Navy was usually enough to guarantee safety. But relations of this type with the colonies were relatively burdensome to the metropolis, which, as its American territories developed, spent increasing sums on them while receiving less and less in return.

At the height of the Seven Years War the colonists saw no problem with the presence on their territory of British troops and officials. In 1763 Benjamin Franklin extolled the 'glorious peace' signed in Paris, a peace that would allow Britain to take possession of all of North America and to create a 'universal empire of that extended coast'.[3] A certain William Smith, one of the ideologues of colonial expansion, wrote: 'Would to God we have a little more government here.'[4] A turning-point was the establishing in 1763 of the Proclamation Line. This decision guaranteed the right of the native Americans – as subjects of the crown – to the lands to the west of the old border, while the colonists were prohibited from driving the indigenous population out. The privatisation of lands to the west, begun while the war was still under way, came to a halt, and a number of the decisions were annulled. At first, the colonists did not take the Proclamation seriously, regarding it as a demagogic document meant to placate the 'redskins'. Ordinary settlers wanting to move westward, together with innumerable speculators and smugglers who were developing their business on native American lands, ignored the Proclamation openly. But once it was discovered that the king's government was serious about fulfilling its obligations to the native Americans, discontent within the colonies began to grow. As early as 1763 a revolt broke out among the native Americans, whom representatives of the royal administration managed to pacify by declaring support for their demands. In 1768 the British superintendent of Indian [sic] affairs Sir William Johnson signed a new agreement with the Iroquois at Fort Stanwix, but his policy of seeking reconciliation with the indigenous people of America aroused indignation in the colonies, and failed to receive the necessary support from London. Johnson was forced to resign.

All attempts by the British authorities to extract at least some financial gain from their North American colonies met with furious resistance from the settlers. The situation was exacerbated by the Stamp Act of 1765. Through this tax the government in London sought to force the American colonies and the East India Company to pay some part of the costs of the war. It should be noted that by the standards of the eighteenth century British taxes were not excessively burdensome.[5] Moreover, the demand made by parliament was in essence perfectly just. It was events in America and India that had drawn the country into war, and the army had been sent to the colonies at the request of colonial representatives. Meanwhile, the American colonies and the East India Company had made enormous gains from the victory. In 1766 the British government demanded that the company pay the sum of £400,000 per year.[6] The company, while expressing some reluctance, agreed to pay. The colonists, by contrast, categorically refused.

In economic terms the southern colonies, which supplied tobacco and cotton to the world market, were tied more closely to Europe. But they too were encountering problems with the London government. The local elites were unhappy with the taxes, and indignant at the abolitionist mood that was becoming increasingly widespread in Britain. The propaganda in favour of abolishing slavery was fraught with the collapse of the entire economic system of the American south. Meanwhile, the growth of the economy of the north was turning it into an important partner for the southern colonies.

Despite their differing economic systems and distinct interests, the colonies of north and south were increasingly united in the claims they placed on the metropolis. In 1767 the British government introduced new customs duties in the colonies, arousing a storm of outrage among the settlers, who in response organised a boycott of British goods. Three years later, British soldiers in Boston opened fire on a rebellious but unarmed crowd, after which an escalation of the conflict became inevitable.

The colonists sought to show that the parliament in Westminster had no right to levy taxes on them, since no colonial delegates represented them there. Meanwhile, subordination of the American colonies to the London parliament had been anticipated in the Navigation Acts of the seventeenth century, that is, in the legislative decisions without which successful expansion in America would scarcely have been possible. In the event, London was forced to renounce its stamp duty, though it passed the Declaration Act, affirming its right to impose taxes on the colonies. Each concession by London, however, merely spurred new demands and claims from the colonists.

In the eighteenth century New England had become an important market for tropical products supplied by the East India Company. But this profitable trade also drew the attention of the London government as it sought to cope with financial difficulties after the end of the Seven Years War. By 1772 the East India Company was on the verge of bankruptcy, and in May 1773 the government of Lord North was forced to implement the famous Tea Act, imposing additional duties on the colonists. These duties were met with another revolt and with the Boston Tea Party, during which tea was thrown overboard from the ships in which it had been imported. The commercial dispute grew into a political revolution.

In the early twenty-first century, when hostility to American imperialism has come to a head not only in countries of the 'periphery' but also in the public opinion of most Western countries, the question has naturally arisen of whether the significance of the American revolution has been exaggerated. While the revolution was earlier seen as democratic in character, and as a national liberation movement, there are now people inclined to view it as a separatist revolt whose subtext was the self-interest of the colonial elites.

The conservative-minded Niall Ferguson remarks that the American War of Independence 'was indeed a civil war which divided social classes and even families'.[7] There was not even the semblance of national unity in the colonies, and at first even Benjamin Franklin wavered. Loyalists and supporters of the Tory party, who maintained their allegiance to the crown, made up a substantial part of the colonial population and took part in military actions, using partisan tactics against the forces of George Washington. When the radical delegates to the Continental Congress in July 1776 voted for the Declaration of Independence, by no means all residents of the colonies responded with enthusiasm. John Adams acknowledged that independence was supported by approximately a third of the population.[8]

An even harsher 'revisionist' view of the American revolution is expressed by Samir Amin:

> In their revolt against the English monarchy, the American colonists did not want to transform their economic and social relations; they just no longer wanted to share the profits with the ruling class of the mother country. They wanted power for themselves, not in order to create a different society from the colonial regime, but to carry on in the same way, only with more determination and more profit. Above all, their objective was to pursue westward expansion, which implied, among other things, the genocide of the Indians. Maintaining the institution of slavery was not questioned. Almost all of the important leaders of the American Revolution were slaveholding property owners whose prejudices in this regard were resolute.[9]

The protestant sects that migrated to New England were, in Amin's view, supremely authoritarian, cruel and aggressive, as shown by the fact that they had been forced to leave the Old World, whose society had been unwilling to tolerate or encourage their aggressiveness. The loyalist emigrants, who fled in large numbers from the independent United States to Canada, laid the basis there for a much more humane society, within whose context workers came to possess a far greater degree of class consciousness.

The efforts by a section of the British public to free the slaves in the colonies poured oil on the flames of civil conflict. The decision to abolish slavery was taken by the British authorities in America at the height of the revolt, and was clearly aimed at winning the support of the black population of the south. Thousands of black Americans joined the British army, taking part in constructing fortifications and in transporting supplies for the forces; at times, they also fought in the ranks. At the end of the war those of them who had remained in New York and had not been evacuated along with the departing units were sold back into slavery.

Unfortunately, the declaration emancipating the slaves brought turmoil to the ranks of the loyalists, among whom there were also slave-owners, while also consolidating the white population of the south around anti-British positions. When a few radical-minded supporters of independence tried to counter the British initiative and for their own part condemned slavery, they did not win broad support. In Britain itself, Edmund Burke sharply derided the idea of freeing the slaves, ridiculing its advocates and panegyrists. He recalled that Britain was itself involved in the slave trade, and argued that the slaves would not accept liberation, since in the main they were 'much attached to their masters'.[10]

Other politicians and commentators expressed themselves much more harshly. 'To arm negro slaves against their masters,' the Duke of Richmond argued indignantly, 'to arm savages, who we know will put their prisoners to death in the most cruel tortures, and literally eat them, is not in my opinion, a fair war against fellow subjects.'[11]

John Wilkes, a Middlesex member of parliament known for his radical-democratic views, wrote that there was nothing more appalling than Indians [sic] who had risen up against whites receiving weapons and assistance from British generals: 'Human nature shrinks from such a scene.'[12] Indians, he stressed, were almost as repellent and cruel as Jews.

The abolitionism of the British government was inconsistent at best. This is illustrated particularly by the situation that arose after the conclusion of peace, when it was decided to resettle freed American slaves in the African colony of Sierra Leone. 'The "Land of Freedom", as Sierra Leone was to be called, also happened to be the province of slavery,' the prominent historian Simon Schama points out. 'The Royal Navy, which was to escort and possibly protect the infant colony of the free, was at the same time assigned to protect the busy British slave-trading depot on Bance Island, a little way up-river from the estuary.'[13]

It might be said that in the years from 1775 to 1781 the elites of the North American colony-states used 'their' lower social classes against the British just as the elites in the southern states 90 years later were able to rely on the mass of the white population in the struggle against the north.

Through one device and another, the New England bourgeoisie managed to create a broad social bloc that on one side included the planters of the south, and on the other the radical-minded small property-owners and farmers of the north. In other words, they achieved their goals through successfully imposing a political hegemony that could, however, be maintained only at the price of making serious concessions to the petty-bourgeois lower orders of society. For precisely this reason, a revolt that began as an egoistic action by the colonial elites and the middle layers connected to them ended as a revolution, and gave rise to the most demo-cratic state that had ever existed. Needless to say, even before the struggle for independence reached its conclusion the main concern of the American elites became restraining the democratic pressure from the masses. On the whole, the founding fathers coped successfully with this challenge. As soon as the question of relations with Britain had been more or less dealt with, the original Articles of Confederation were replaced with a far less democratic, but more demagogic Constitution.

The majority of scholars who analyse the military aspects of the American War of Independence agree that the British acted with striking indecisiveness and ineptitude, in sharp contrast with their conduct during both the Seven Years War and the Napoleonic wars. This is scarcely to be explained on the basis of a lack of good commanders or of unfamiliarity with the semi-partisan tactics used by the colonists. Such methods had been practised during earlier campaigns, and the reg-ular army had learnt how to combat them effectively. Moreover, the large numbers of native American and American loyalists who fought on the British side were thoroughly familiar with the local conditions, and employed the same tactics.

The loyalists complained constantly that they did not receive enough support from the British generals.[14] Lawrence James observes that the main problem facing British commanders in America was 'confusion over objectives'.[15]

The real reason for the ineffectiveness of British actions lay not in the military but in the political and economic area. The people making the decisions in London understood perfectly that military victory would not guarantee a strengthening of the authority of the crown over the remote American territories unless that victory were followed by a political compromise. This was the characteristic strategy of the British empire, with whose help it overcame the resistance of the Scottish clans in the eighteenth century, and which it was later to employ in India following the revolt of the sepoys and in South Africa after its victory over the Boers. The main question was the price of the compromise.

Edmund Burke, who actively (and not without an element of self-interest) defended the interests of the colonies in Britain, constantly reminded his audiences of the need for concessions: 'Peace implies reconciliation; and where there has been a material dispute, reconciliation does in a manner always imply concession on the one part or on the other.'[16] The main question was not whether compromise was necessary in principle, but 'what our concession ought to be'.[17]

The situation in the American colonies, and especially in New England, was such that any effective compromise would be less economically advantageous for Britain than recognising the claim of the former colonies to independence. The prominent thinker and commentator Josiah Tucker wrote during the War of Independence that the American colonies were 'a Millstone hanging about the Neck of this Country'.[18] Adam Smith held a similar view.

At the same time, the fact of the secession of the colonies not only dealt a blow to the prestige of the empire, but also created a dangerous precedent that could be used (and that was used) in quite different situations. The inconsistency of British policy with regard to the 13 rebel colonies was exacerbated by a split in the ranks of the British elites themselves. The response of conservatives to the political principles of the colonists was one of revulsion, and for this reason they were inclined to take a positive attitude to the departure of the colonies from the empire. By contrast, liberals found these principles rather impressive, and as a result sought to keep the rebels within the framework of the empire through negotiations and concessions.

These objective contradictions predetermined the inconsistency of British policy. Following as a consequence was the lack of any clear strategy or decisiveness in the conduct of military operations.

War and peace in America and Europe

Supporting the revolt of the colonies, France entered the war in 1778, to be joined a year later by Spain and then by Holland as well. The French action was dictated not only by a desire to take revenge for the defeat in the Seven Years War, but also by a fear that the aggressive-minded American colonies would reach agreement with London, and as the price of compromise, would demand a new expansion – this time at the expense of the possessions that after the previous war had been left to the French in Louisiana.[19] 'They will hurl themselves on us with such force as if there had never been a civil war,' Louis XVI wrote to his cousin Charles III of Spain. It was this fear that compelled him in short order to recognise the independence of the United States, and to support its military efforts 'in order to prevent its reunification with the metropolis'.[20]

In London, it had not been anticipated that the colonists would resort to armed struggle. An even greater surprise to British politicians was the fact that the colonial leaders would readily find allies in Europe. For the British bourgeois monarchy in earlier times, the internal enemies who had allied themselves with foreign enemies had been traditionalists – Catholics and Jacobites, the supporters of the deposed Stuart dynasty. These were hostile to the liberal-bourgeois regime, and it was entirely logical that they should attract absolutist Europe to their side. But London was not ready for American liberals to adopt the same position, while appealing to the principles of the British constitution. In their pragmatism, though, the founding fathers of the United States were worthy pupils of the British Whigs, who despite their liberalism were also prepared to collaborate with any continental regimes, even the most authoritarian, if they found this to their advantage. In the new situation London was forced to confront the hostile attitude of former partners and allies, who were dissatisfied with the position in which the new conditions of British hegemony had placed them. Russia and Prussia proclaimed an 'armed neutrality', declaring that they would not permit the Royal Navy to search their ships under the pretext of searching for military contraband. London was obliged to reconcile itself to this 'revolt of the allies', with the British government instructing the navy that 'Russian ships should be left unmolested'.[21] During the whole period of military operations, the only seizure of Russian ships that occurred was not carried out by the British but by the Spanish, who were allied with the Americans.

Finding itself in conflict simultaneously with the French, Spanish and Dutch in several theatres of war, the British navy for a time lost its control of the Atlantic. In 1781 the 80,000-strong British army of Lord Cornwallis was blockaded in Yorktown, and lacking the expected support from the sea, was forced to surrender. This defeat was a direct result of the loss of naval supremacy, though it is true that the British navy was to reach Yorktown – five days too late.[22]

The Mediterranean had been abandoned, leading to a sharp decline of British trade, since ships sailing under the British flag became easy prey for French corsairs. In the West Indies a number of islands were seized by the French, and a threat hung over Jamaica, the most important economic and political centre of the British empire in the region. The Franco-Spanish coalition made preparations to invade the British Isles (the Channel Islands had already come under attack), and the main strength of the Royal Navy had thus to be concentrated near the coasts of Britain itself. The response to these dangers, however, was an unprecedented mobilisation of British naval power, with the number and fighting potential of the Royal Navy's ships growing continuously. The garrison at Gibraltar stood firm against a French and Spanish siege, ensuring that the British fleet would be able to return to the Mediterranean. In

October 1782 the besieging forces were compelled to withdraw. The British navy, which in 1778 had possessed 66 ships of the line, in 1780 had 95. Its personnel strength grew from 16,000 at the beginning of the war to 60,000 at its height, and to 100,000 when the peace was signed. In April 1782 Admiral George Rodney dealt the French fleet a decisive defeat at the Battle of the Saintes, restoring British naval supremacy.

Fearing problems in Ireland, the British government substantially softened its anti-Catholic legislation, thus gaining numerous recruits for its navy and especially for its army, which also expanded. In 1774 the British land forces had comprised 72 battalions; in 1778 this number stood at 118.[23] The military efforts were accompanied by an impressive psychological and cultural mobilisation, with patriotic and civic enthusiasm taking hold of society.

The outcomes of the war at sea do not by any means suggest that Britain was the losing side. In 1783 the London *Political Journal* published a list of the losses that includes 80 ships captured by the enemy, of which 25 were later seized back. Only 22 British ships were sunk. The list of enemy ships (American, French, Spanish and Dutch) that were captured or sunk covers two full pages in the same issue of the journal. Of French ships alone, 129 were captured and 11 sunk.[24]

Despite the victories at Saratoga and the capitulation of Yorktown, George Washington's armies were significantly weaker than those of the British. War-weariness, however, took its toll of both sides. Mutinies occurred in the American forces, and the British commanders complained of an epidemic of drunkenness among the king's officers.[25] In practice, military actions in America ceased from October 1781, when Yorktown surrendered. Both sides remained in position, with neither the strength nor the desire to launch attacks on one another. When the war ended, the British still had strong garrisons in many strategically important cities and strongholds, enjoyed the support of the native American tribes to the west, controlled New York, and were fully capable of continuing military operations. What they lacked was not military strength but political will.

Britain was financially exhausted. At the beginning of the 1780s, some 56 per cent of the annual budget was being spent on servicing the national debt, which exceeded £240 million.[26] But the country's continental enemies were no less exhausted, and during the Napoleonic Wars British finances sustained a national debt almost two-and-a-half times as great. In March 1782 the cabinet of Lord North resigned, and the new government set as its main goal achieving peace with the Americans and with their allies in Europe. The British diplomats who negotiated the peace treaty with the United States made exceptionally generous concessions, while the Americans did everything possible to keep their dependency on France, their erstwhile ally, to a minimum. The concessions were so major, and so obviously not dictated by military necessity, that critics in the homeland reproached the chief British negotiator, the Earl of Shelburne, for destroying the British empire. On territorial questions the concessions were so far-reaching that they aroused the 'outraged protests of Canadian merchants'.[27]

Those who suffered most from the Anglo-American peace agreement were the North American Indians. In 1783, even before the treaty had been signed in Paris, a London journal reported that the Indians [sic] had received news of the impending reconciliation of Britain with the United States, France and Spain 'with noble indignation'. Appealing to the British governor, delegates of the indigenous inhabitants of America recalled their loyalty and the threat that hung over them: 'You engaged us with fair promises to take part in your dispute, and you now desert us in our misfortunes – you turn your backs like sheep upon the enemy, advise us to sue for peace, from the men you have taught us to despise.'[28] But for the sake of good relations with their former enemies, the London authorities decided to sacrifice the interests of their faithful supporters.

The loyalists among the settlers were given the opportunity to move northward, to the Canadian lands that remained under British control. Contrary to the expectations of many supporters of American independence, Canada remained a peaceful rear for the British throughout the entire war. The relatively small number of French settlers needed the support of the state to defend themselves against the native Americans, and did not have the political strength to do this on their own. Meanwhile, the goods they produced were only of value if their sale in European markets was guaranteed. Consequently, the French settlers were doomed to be loyal British subjects, just as they had earlier been faithful subjects of the French monarchy. The British authorities in turn sought to manage relations with the native Americans through mutual concessions and guarantees – not from humane motives, but because this was cheaper and easier. The French settlers had found that the British merchants offered them new openings for sales, and Quebec was now part of the British trading system.[29] A massive migration of loyalists from the now-independent colonies of New England strengthened the ties between Canada and Britain. Even Woodrow Wilson in his highly patriotic *History of the American People* was forced to acknowledge that immediately after the gaining of independence, the victors began repressing their political opponents, and that the flight from the new state took on mass dimensions: 'Thousands upon thousands crowded to New York to seek the shelter of the British arms.'[30] British figures indicate that more than 40,000 loyalists moved to the provinces of Ontario, Nova Scotia and New Brunswick.[31]

Immediately after the signing of the Paris peace, Britain and the USA began negotiating a commercial treaty that was meant to embody a 'family compact between two nations'.[32] While having seized independence from Britain politically, the American bourgeoisie began to insist on retaining, at least in part, the privileges and positions it had earlier possessed in Britain and in other countries when the Americans were still subjects of the crown. The British ruling class for its part was perfectly ready to meet its former enemies half-way, while reminding them that in declaring independence they had deprived themselves of all their rights: 'If they are placed in the footing of the most favored nation, they must surely applaud our liberality and friendship, without expecting that for their emolument, we should sacrifice the navigation and the naval power of Great Britain.'[33]

Following the resignation of the Earl of Shelburne, the British government of William Pitt pursued the same course of reconciliation. Before 1781 was out the American Intercourse Bill was passed, exempting the still-not-recognised United

States from the Navigation Acts and dramatically expediting American trade with the West Indies. On the eve of their independence the 13 colonies, together with the West Indies, had consumed some 37 per cent of British exports; in 1797–98 this figure amounted to 57 per cent.[34] Since the main concern of the British bourgeoisie was not to retain sovereignty, but to keep its positions on the markets of the former colonies, London was prepared in matters of legislation to make almost any concession in order to achieve this latter goal.

The 'second British Empire', whose beginning was marked by the independence of the United States, was by no means short of territory. As well as the limitless expanses that were available for westward colonisation in Canada, the possessions of the British crown had been augmented through the annexation of Australia. The vast territory of this continent, along with New Zealand, was viewed in London as a replacement for the lost American colonies. Meanwhile, the conquest of Bengal had opened up new prospects in the East. To a considerable degree, however, the new empire needed to be constructed afresh, according to different principles, and on the basis of lessons that had still to be drawn from the events of the American revolution. Canada, Australia and other self-governing colonies, and later India as well, would be guaranteed sovereignty in matters of taxation, so as to exclude any repetition of conflicts such as the 1765 dispute over stamp duty. Simultaneously, measures would be taken to strengthen the political ties between the colonies and the metropolis. In expanding its empire around the planet, the British ruling class was concerned to ensure that none of the 'white colonies' (later to become dominions) would become excessively strong and self-sufficient in economic terms. At the same time, their close association and mutual interdependence were encouraged; the empire was no longer bound together solely on vertical lines, but also on horizontal ones.

In America itself, the end of the war heralded a new outburst of social conflicts and political changes. For the lower orders of American society independence was valuable not in itself, but above all because it promised to allow the oligarchic nature of British politics to be overcome; the masses could now increase their social weight and force the elites to reckon with them. By the end of the War of Independence, however, the most important concern of the American elites was no longer the struggle with the former metropolis, but the question of how to keep their own popular masses under control. The American generals were obliged to devote far greater attention to suppressing mutinies within the ranks of their own armed forces than to the expiring war.

Against a background of economic crisis, business in America strove to make up for its losses, shifting the burden onto farmers and other petty-bourgeois layers – that is, onto the very 'people' whose support had allowed the war to be won. With the ending of the military conflict the material situation of the masses not only failed to improve, but deteriorated. Farmers had been ruined by debts and taxes. The workers, artisans and peasants of New England found to their surprise that the new democratic order installed by 'their' bourgeoisie could turn out to be worse than foreign oppression. In 1786 and 1787 Massachusetts experienced a rebellion headed by the War of Independence veteran Daniel Shays.[35] The founding fathers responded to this initiative from below with their own outburst of class hatred.[36] It was in connection with these events that James Madison pronounced his famous dictum: 'Liberty may be endangered by the abuses of liberty as well as the abuses of power.'[37]

The elites met Shays's rebellion not only with repression, but also with changes to the American state system. The Articles of Confederation were replaced with a new Constitution of the United States which strengthened the authority of the central government. Political control returned to the hands of the privileged social layers. In the process, the American bourgeoisie successfully carried out its own Thermidorean coup even prior to the beginning of the French Revolution, to which we are indebted for that term.

The successes of the revolutionary armies of France, followed by the victorious expansion of Napoleon's empire, frightened the leaders of the USA and forced them to draw closer to Britain. Hamilton's pro-British policy, however, was counter-balanced by French compliancy. In ceding Louisiana to the United States, the French emperor acted with a great deal of foresight; he not only received acutely needed money from the Americans, but also rid himself of an overseas territory which his fleet, after the catastrophe at Trafalgar, could not effectively defend, and with which neither contacts nor trade were continuously maintained. The USA for its part gained the opportunity for further expansion to the south-west, of interest chiefly to moderate leaders of the slave-holding south. After the purchase of Louisiana, the foreign policy orientation in Washington changed decisively. Under conditions in which war with republican and then Napoleonic France required a growing concentration of effort, less and less attention was paid in London to events in the New World, where the seeds of a new conflict were quickening. Continuing resistance from the native Americans was among the factors which prompted the United States to invade Canada. In 1812, when the empire of Napoleon had seemingly attained its greatest might, and when French armies were moving toward decisive clashes with Wellington in Spain and Field Marshal Kutuzov in Russia, American forces invaded Canada, trying to tear this defenceless colony from the British grasp. The British forces did not exceed 4,000 troops, so the outcome seemed preordained. But the Canadian militias swiftly cooled the ardour of the attackers. French volunteer units defeated the Americans at Chateauguay and Lacolle.

The war which had begun in 1812 with an American invasion of Canada ended in a draw when the Treaty of Ghent was signed in 1814, entering into force in 1815. As after the preceding war, London again showed itself to be extremely accommodating, refraining from trying to exploit its obvious military and political superiority after the defeat of Napoleon. Once more the British empire sacrificed the interests of its indigenous allies, handing over to the vicissitudes of fate the native Americans who had fought against the American forces. London was completely satisfied with the fact that for Canada, the threat of invasion from the south had been done away with. The main outcome of the war was the establishing of a new system of relations between the British empire and its future geopolitical heir, the American republic. After the conflict of 1812 the two English-speaking powers no longer entered into open conflict. Throughout much of the nineteenth century relations between the USA and Britain were by no means uniformly friendly, but, despite everything, American capitalism developed in the shade of its British counterpart, accepting the rules set in place by the British bourgeoisie.

British trade with America not only continued after the United States became independent in 1783, but began expanding rapidly. Particular growth was registered by exports of raw materials from the southern slaveholding states. The industrial revolution that was unfolding in Britain led to dramatic increases in demand for the cheap raw materials produced by Russian serfs and Afro-American slaves. From Russia came foodstuffs and cheap metals, and from America cotton. During the 1780s shipments of raw cotton from the United States averaged 15.5 million pounds weight, but by 1800 this figure had almost doubled to 28.6 million pounds. By 1840, 80 per cent of Lancashire's supplies of raw cotton came from America.[38] During the Napoleonic Wars, when as ill luck would have it Britain's agriculture suffered from crop failures, American grain helped until 1812 to feed Wellington's army. The shipments continued, though with reduced volume, even after the two countries went to war.

Relations with the United States came to occupy a special place in Britain's imperial policies. For a century and a half London was prepared to make concessions in order to shape this partnership. Initially, the reward for this policy took the form of a lack of any serious imperial challenge from America; later, it appeared as collaboration between the 'old' and 'new' empires in handling the transfer of hegemony. Throughout the nineteenth century Great Britain remained the largest trading partner of the USA, accounting in the 1890s for more than half of American exports and for a quarter of imports.[39]

A far more acute problem for British hegemony was the revolution in France, and thereafter, the unprecedented expansion of the empire of Napoleon.

From democracy to empire

During the seventeenth and eighteenth centuries the British and French models of the development of capitalism – at least on the political level – seemed directly contradictory. In Britain the bourgeoisie entrusted its affairs to the state, while in France the government subcontracted its business to the bourgeoisie. In neither case did the nascent bourgeois class lose, since it received commissions and profits, but in each case the question of control arose.

In England under the Stuarts the monarchy tried to free itself from the control of the bourgeoisie, while in France the bourgeoisie sought to rid itself of control by the monarchy. The result was that the revolutionary processes unfolding in the two countries were directly opposite to one another. The defeat of the Fronde, occurring in the seventeenth century at a time of successes for the London parliament, deepened the contrast between the English and French models.

The English revolution was to a significant degree conservative (and its conservative features were reproduced on an even greater scale, almost to the point of caricature, in the American revolution). Meanwhile, the French revolution from its inception unfolded as a radical, innovative movement.

Throughout almost the entire eighteenth century it was possible to observe the initiatives of the Versailles court ending in failure one after another. The reason why France could not become an enlightened monarchy was not that the bourgeoisie was weak, but to the contrary, because this class was too strong and presented excessively high demands, to which the government and the traditional aristocracy could not agree. As is seen repeatedly in history, the authorities sought to resolve the internal contradictions through external expansion – the wars with Britain were meant to increase France's share of the world market and in the process, to satisfy bourgeois appetites without sacrificing the position of the aristocracy. These wars, however, ended in defeats.

For the French monarchy, each new clash with Britain proved more calamitous. The War of the Austrian Succession had an indeterminate outcome (the only undisputed victor was the Prussia of Frederick the Great, which won control of Silesia), the Seven Years War ended in a French defeat, and the American War of Independence, though formally resulting in victory for the Bourbons, turned for France into a definitive catastrophe.

The fact that the war for the independence of the United States ended successfully for the latter was to an important degree due to French intervention. But the Paris peace agreement of 1783 yielded little for France. The return of Senegal could in no way be considered sufficient recompense in a conflict fought at the cost of huge expenditures and losses. From the bourgeois point of view this was an obvious failure of the state. In economic terms the outcomes of the war were catastrophic. Trade suffered once again. The fleet suffered colossal losses. Not without an element of *Schadenfreude,* a British journal stated in 1783: 'The French who gave the Americans credit are all bankrupts.'[40] The monstrous budget deficit to which the war gave rise in France became one of the reasons that in 1789 forced Louis XVI to convoke the Estates-General, marking the beginning of the revolution.[41]

Before the bourgeoisie could benefit from the changes, it was obliged to confront a new danger that quickly came to overshadow all the problems it had needed to cope with under the *ancien régime*. As if by magic, the return to the scene of medieval class representation in the form of the Estates-General set free the spirits of the past. The masses, who earlier had been suppressed and who at best had followed enthusiastically behind their bourgeois leaders, suddenly acquired their own voice. This was a voice of class hatred. The images of revolutionary Paris in the late eighteenth century call to mind the urban uprisings of Marcel and Caboche. But this time, the outcome of the struggle was to be the very opposite. The royal power collapsed in bloody convulsions.

The old order was too strong, and the leading bourgeois circles too closely tied to it and corrupted by it, for the necessary changes in the political system to occur without the participation of the masses. But in the event, the democracy that replaced the *ancien régime* proved 'excessively' radical and obviously anti-bourgeois. Max Weber was later to note that political freedom derived not so much from the nature of capitalism, which had no special need of it, but from the conditions in which capital took shape and came to power.[42] Nothing confirms this thesis as clearly as the history of the French Revolution.

A series of revolutions, coups and civil wars were needed for democratic republicanism to become consolidated in bourgeois Europe. The question of how to combine political freedom and universal suffrage with the class hegemony of capital continued to pose an insoluble dilemma for European society until the era of imperialism, when the external expansion of the West made it possible to turn colonial conquests and the economic subjection of the countries of the periphery into a mechanism for the redistribution of wealth within the 'centre'. But this solution, thanks to which the loyalty of the subject classes was ensured with a minimum of concessions on the part of the elite, was arrived at only toward the end of the nineteenth century, and even it could not guarantee European society against acute social conflicts. In the first half of the century neither the extent of European dominance over the outside world, nor the economic mechanisms available to European capital, nor the internal political order in the Western countries themselves provided any such possibility. France in the time of Bonaparte was a country cut off from overseas markets by British competition and blockade, and its field of expansion became Europe itself.

The mechanism used for consolidating society was to be patriotism. This time, however, the patriotism concerned was revolutionary in nature, bound up inextricably with the idea of change and liberation. It was in this form that patriotism seized the minds of the French population, and it was from this combination that a distinct 'model' arose, to be employed by numerous later national movements, including some that possessed none of its democratic content.

The French Revolution marked the beginning of mass 'popular' armies, based on universal military conscription. The cohesiveness of the French battalions; the vertical mobility that provided the forces with a virtually unlimited reserve of cadres for the officer corps; the closeness that arose on this basis between officers and soldiers, each of whom, as Napoleon put it, carried a marshal's baton in his knapsack; and finally, unprecedented mobilisational efficiency, all made the French army practically invincible for two decades, from the Battle of Valmy in 1792 to the confrontation at Borodino in 1812. Only the appearance in Europe of new patriotic movements, transforming the nature of war after 1812, put an end to this succession of French victories.

During the first years of the nineteenth century the French expansion seemed irresistible, and its armies effectively unconquerable. But in its path stood two obstacles that were too important even for the power of the newborn empire or the military genius of Napoleon to overcome. These obstacles were Britain and Russia.

The irreconcilable hostility displayed by the British ruling class toward revolutionary France contrasted strikingly with the desire for compromise with the rebellious colonies during the American war. In the case of France, of course, hostility toward a traditional rival and competition between commercial interests both played a role. But there was also something that extended outside the framework of these familiar motives. The French Revolution represented the first popular revolution since the

Middle Ages in the course of which the bourgeoisie lost its control over the political process. During the Dutch and English revolutions this control had been maintained, albeit with great difficulty; the dictatorship of the 'Lord Protector' Oliver Cromwell was aimed at least as much against aristocratic reaction as against the revolutionary masses. In the United States the founding fathers managed to keep the movement under their control, crushing the protests of the lower social orders after the end of the war. It was only in France that the masses broke through to the forefront of political history, spontaneously repeating the scenarios of the medieval popular revolts. This dynamic of the revolution, in essence anti-bourgeois, made the British elite an irreconcilable adversary of the French republic. Although bourgeois political control was restored in the course of the Thermidorean overturn, and then strengthened by the regime of the empire, the inertia of the conflict between Paris and London had already taken on enormous force.

The struggle between Britain and France in the early nineteenth century became reminiscent of the fabled contest of the elephant and the whale. British hegemony at sea was counterbalanced by the invincibility of the French armies on land. Until 1812 none of the coalitions supported by British money on the continent was able to prevail over Napoleon Bonaparte and his marshals. The culmination of this struggle was the Battle of Trafalgar, which showed that the armed forces of Napoleon's empire would not be able to break out of their captivity on the continent. Not only would Bonaparte be unable to strike a blow across the channel at Britain, but the French bourgeoisie would not be able to burst through and seize an economic expanse of global scale for its operations. After this, Bonaparte had no other road open to him apart from trying to expand his dominance over the continent, until the point in 1812 when his military machine overextended itself, coming up against popular warfare in Russia and Spain.

Having established his control over most of the continent, Bonaparte tried to exclude British goods from European markets, redirecting supplies of raw materials from Eastern and Central Europe to France. This 'continental blockade' was no less the essence of the Napoleonic wars than the well-known battles and famous victories of the French marshals. But on this field, the emperor was not to achieve success.

The unplanned result of this system was an increase in production and the beginning of industrialisation in most of the countries of continental Europe, including Russia, but for French industrialists the new situation was largely bad news. The French industrial interests were unable to conquer the new markets from which the British had been forced out. French products were more expensive than those of local competitors, and had to be transported over long distances on bad roads, since the sea lanes were closed. Even where industrial growth occurred, it was soon affected by the narrowness of the market. Crises of overproduction became universal. Under Napoleon's rule economic crises occurred twice, in 1806 and 1811, each time demonstrating the weakness of the 'continental system' the emperor had set up.

Britain also underwent economic crises, but the government's military orders provided an important support to industry. Meanwhile Russia and other countries of Eastern Europe, cut off by the 'continental blockade' from the British market, experienced great difficulties in selling their raw materials. The currency rapidly became devalued; in Russia a paper bill of exchange with a face value of one ruble now fetched only 26 kopecks in silver. The landowners who until this time had been the main purchasers of French manufactures were ruined both by the wars and by the blockade.

The economic logic of the crises impelled the ruling elites of Russia and Eastern Europe to try to break the blockade, while France sought continually to expand the unified continental market and to turn it into a counterweight to the global market. Developments were similar at the western end of the empire, in Spain and Portugal, for which French hegemony also signified an effective loss of contact with their own overseas colonies (and ultimately, was to mean the loss of large sections of their empires).

For Napoleon, exercising control over the continental expanse of Europe was a strategy that was forced on him, and that made inevitable a deadly conflict with Russia, as the largest continental power. In other circumstances the emperor would have preferred to coexist peacefully with the Russian state, and might well have succeeded in doing so. Instead of this he finished up in Moscow, locked with his army in the burning city, from which he had then to retreat to Paris.

In planning his Russian campaign, the emperor proceeded on the basis of his earlier experience of fighting the Russian army, which despite being a formidable opponent for the French had continually suffered strategic defeats. All the Russian generals of the period had shown an inability to plan a campaign on the strategic level. Even Suvorov's famous march into Switzerland almost ended in catastrophe.[43]

So long as he held the strategic initiative, Bonaparte was certain of his ability to dictate the conditions of war and peace to all his adversaries. But with the 'continental system' expiring, the state of affairs had begun to change. For France, the demands of military necessity resulted in economic crisis, while attempts to solve all problems through the use of force led to catastrophe. Grasping the dynamic of the situation acutely, Napoleon's conquerors, Prince Kutuzov and the Duke of Wellington, stuck to defensive tactics and exhausted their enemy through a struggle that for the French emperor was arduous and pointless.

Revolutionary and imperial France had not only defeated feudal armies, but had also infected Europe with its ideas, and this also worked catastrophically against the political system which Bonaparte established. Among the key ideas of the new order was patriotism. By spreading national self-consciousness throughout the continent, the French conquerors placed in the hands of the conquered a powerful ideological weapon of struggle against the empire itself. This became fully apparent during the campaigns of the years from 1812 to 1815, when the French generals found to their astonishment that they were now confronted not by feudal but by national armies, founded in the image and likeness of their own and not only using similar tactics, but also possessing a similar consciousness. Even before Bonaparte's tactical schemes were shattered against the unbreachable defence of Wellington's infantry at Waterloo, his strategy had been defeated.

The Congress of Vienna, convened by the victorious powers after the fall of Napoleon, drew up a balance-sheet of the period of wars and revolutions, fixing in place in the most conservative political form the changes that had occurred. Europe and the world, however, were now radically different compared to the years before the French Revolution, and even the monarchs and bureaucrats who gathered in Vienna were compelled to recognise this. What late twentieth-century commentators in their illiteracy termed the Westphalia system in fact came into being only at the Congress of Vienna. Europe was transformed into a community of independent, sovereign and formally equal states. In imitation of France, all these states sought, in greater or lesser degree, to become nations.[44]

By no means all, however, succeeded in forging a new identity for their power. Throughout the following decades the European dynastic monarchies attempted with greater or lesser success to fulfil this task, and in the century that followed the failures they encountered along this path turned into the collapse of empires that had seemed thoroughly stable and 'natural' from a geopolitical or geographical point of view. The first to start disintegrating under the impact of the growing national movements was Ottoman Turkey, after which the crisis would infect the Austro-Hungarian and by the early twentieth century, the Russian empire. The Hohenzollerns, declaring themselves Germans, managed to cope better with the problem than the Habsburgs, though the ethnic make-up of their subjects too was far from homogeneous. Germany, Italy, Spain and other Western countries in one measure or another sought to become like France, but at the same time to place a conservative stamp on the nationalism borrowed from that country. In France, which provided the rest of Europe with a model of the national state, a conservative interpretation of nationalism was also triumphant.

French nationalism became oriented increasingly toward the past. The recollection of past conflicts and victories proved to be a useful tool for consolidating the people in the present.

Notes

1 G.L. Beer, *The Old Colonial System, 1660–1754*, Gloucester, MA: P. Smith, 1958, Part 1, Vol. II, p. 232.
2 Quoted in M. Radiker, *Between the Devil and the Deep Blue Sea. Merchant Seamen, Pirates and the Anglo-American Maritime World, 1700–1750*, Cambridge: Cambridge University Press, 1990, p. 70.
3 Quoted in B. Simms, *Three Victories and a Defeat. The Rise and Fall of the First British Empire, 1714–1783*, New York: Basic Books, 2007, p. 502.
4 Quoted in ibid., p. 540.
5 L. James, *Warrior Race, A History of the British at war from Roman times to the present*, London: Abacus, 2002, 2002, p. 272.
6 See L. James, *Raj. The Making and Unmaking of British India*, London: Abacus, 2003, p. 50.
7 N. Ferguson, *Empire: How Britain Made the Modern World*, London: Allen Lane, 2003, p. 95.
8 L. James, *The Rise and Fall of the British Empire*, London: Abacus, 2005, p. 115.
9 S. Amin, *The Liberal Virus. Permanent War and the Americanization of the World*, New York: Monthly Review Press, 2004, p. 59.

10 E. Burke, *Selected Writings and Speeches,* ed. P.J. Stanlis, Gloucester, MA: Peter Smith, 1968, p. 167.
11 Quoted in Simms, *Three Victories,* p. 594.
12 Ibid., p. 595.
13 S. Schama, *Rough Crossings. Britain, the Slaves and the American Revolution,* London: BBC Books, 2006, p. 221.
14 Ferguson, *Empire,* p. 96.
15 James, *Rise and Fall,* p. 114.
16 Burke, *Selected Writings and Speeches,* p. 153. It should be noted that Burke had a material interest here; he was receiving a salary as the representative in Britain of the New York assembly.
17 Ibid.
18 Quoted in B. Semmel, *The Rise of Free Trade Imperialism: Classical Political Economy, the Empire of Free Trade and Imperialism 1750–1850,* Cambridge: Cambridge University Press, 2004, p. 20.
19 The status of Louisiana remained ambiguous; it had been transferred to Spain, but could be returned to France, as later occurred. In addition, Paris was concerned for the safety of islands belonging to it in the West Indies. For London, in fact, one of the possible means of achieving a compromise with the colonists would have been to try to satisfy their appetites at the expense of a third party – France. Consequently, the alarm felt by French political figures was not unfounded.
20 Quoted in *Frantsuzskiy ezhegodnik 2008* [French Yearbook 2008], p. 119.
21 *The Cambridge History of British Foreign Policy,* Vol. 1, p. 135.
22 It is noteworthy that the surrender at Yorktown had no effect on the career of Lord Cornwallis, though in formal terms its consequence was the loss of the North American colonies. Several years later we find Cornwallis in the post of Governor of Bengal, a clear promotion, especially considering that this post was not just prestigious and responsible, but also extremely lucrative. His fate may be compared with that of Admiral John Byng, whose failure led to the loss of Menorca. Byng was court-martialled and shot. The defeat of Cornwallis, even if it was not welcomed by the entire British elite, at least suited those important elements who were seeking a pretext for ending the war and finding reconciliation with the former colonies.
23 See Simms, *Three Victories,* pp. 618, 666.
24 *The Political Magazine and Parliamentary, Naval, Military and Lottery Journal,* vol. 5, August 1783, pp. 89–95.
25 See James, *Rise and Fall,* p. 118.
26 See James, *Warrior Race,* p. 272.
27 E. McInnis, *Canada: a Political and Social History,* New York/Toronto/London: Holt, Rinehart & Winston, 1963, p. 160.
28 *The Political Magazine and Parliamentary, Naval, Military and Lottery Journal,* vol. 5, July 1783, p. 13.
29 McInnis, *Canada,* p. 132.
30 W. Wilson, *A History of the American People,* New York/London: Harper & Brothers, Vol. 3, p. 26.
31 G.R. Parkin, *Round the Empire,* London/Paris/Melbourne: Cassell & Co. Ltd., 1892, p. 32.
32 Ibid., p. 150.
33 *The Political Magazine and Parliamentary, Naval, Military and Lottery Journal,* vol. 5, August 1783, p. 83.
34 See Semmel, *Rise of Free Trade,* p. 30.
35 For a detailed account of Shays's rebellion, see J. Fresia, *Toward an American Revolution. Exposing the Constitution and other Illusions,* Boston, MA: South End Press, 1988.
36 See H. Zinn, *A People's History Of The United States,* New York: Harper, 1995, pp. 93–4
37 E. Foner, *Give Me Liberty! An American History,* New York: W.W Norton & Company, 2006, p. 219.

38 James, *Rise and Fall*, p. 119.
39 *Chambers's Encyclopaedia. A Dictionary of Universal Knowledge*, London & Edinburgh, 1895, Vol. 10, p. 381.
40 *The Political Magazine and Parliamentary, Naval, Military and Lottery Journal*, vol. 5, July 1783, p. 84.
41 See *Frantsuzskiy ezhegodnik 2008* [French annual 2008], p. 116.
42 'Today's "freedom"', Weber wrote, 'arose out of a unique confluence of circumstances and conditions, which will never be repeated.' M. Veber, *K sostoyaniyu burzhuaznoy demokratii v Rossii* [On the state of bourgeois democracy in Russia], Paris: Sintaksis, 1988, no. 22, p. 94.
43 A Khramchikhin, *Kak Rossiya osvobodila Evropu* [How Russia liberated Europe], *Russkaya zhizn'*, 2007, no. 17, p. 74.
44 B. Anderson, *Imagined Communities: reflections on the origins and spread of nationalism*, London: Verso, 1991, p. 85.

8

THE BOURGEOIS EMPIRE

For the capitalist world-system, the defeat of Napoleon marked the end of a struggle for hegemony that had been waged continuously from the late seventeenth to the early nineteenth century. Britain had won. At the height of the Crimean War in 1856 the London *Economist* stated:

> In a word. We desire nothing in the way of personal aggrandisement that is not already ours. If a grateful world, awakened to tardy appreciation of our merits, were to propose to 'pleasure' us by some welcome present, it would be scarcely possible to discover any one possession which, for our own sake, we would like to have.[1]

In Britain, the long reign of Queen Victoria was accompanied by a sense of stability, but it was also a time of dynamic technical progress and of a general confidence in the inevitability of cultural and social progress as well. Wars, revolutions and other conflicts broke out here and there, but they no longer took on the dimensions of global shocks. Liberal opinion in the countries of continental Europe saw in these disturbances merely signs of the imperfection of the political or social order in particular countries that had not attained the advanced level evident in Britain and to some degree, in France. Against the background of the previous and subsequent periods the Victorian epoch appears as a time of prosperity and calm. The European empires collaborated with one another and gradually became global. All of them stressed their readiness to abide by the norms of international law, humanity and civilised behaviour.

The demand of the ruling classes for state intervention quickly diminished. The existing system of institutions made it possible to reproduce the bourgeois order more or less automatically, though the need remained to resort regularly to violence when the lower orders of society tried to escape from the structures to which they had been consigned, whether in the course of the Chartist movement in Britain or during the revolutionary events of 1848 and 1871 in France. State violence, however, was now exclusively conservative and sporadic. Its goal was not to transform society but to defend it against any encroachment of revolution. Liberal social thinking assigned the government the role of a 'night watchman'; from the point of view of the bourgeoisie and its interests, the state power had already carried out its tasks of constructive transformation.

Needless to say, this limitation on the role of the state applied only in relation to the countries of the Western 'centre', and to the most developed of them. On the periphery, by contrast, the use of state violence and the compelling of people to participate in the market remained everyday realities.

The imperialism of free trade

In Britain in the mid-nineteenth century the traditional imperial policy of favouring monopolies and state protectionism came to be replaced by a liberal course that corresponded to the market doctrines of Adam Smith. These changes reflected a new stage in the development of capitalism and the altered situation of Britain within the world-system, with its hegemony no longer disputed seriously by anyone. But this did not in any way signify that external expansion had been abandoned. Not only did the British empire keep growing in this epoch, but the United States as well shifted its boundaries decisively to the west, occupying the territories of native American tribes and seizing the border provinces of Mexico, which had just gained its independence. Bernard Semmel describes this period as one of 'free trade imperialism'.[2]

The liberalism of this most liberal of all world empires was never, of course, absolute. Compared to France and other European powers, Immanuel Wallerstein notes, the British state is considered to have 'regulated less and taxed less' during the 'epoch of free trade', but state orders provided a constant stimulus to industry.[3] Often, it was not the invisible hand of the market that instigated production, but the British state itself, whose cautious but effective intervention 'remained invisible'.[4] Questions of the development of agriculture, navigation and many other sectors were constantly under consideration by parliament, but state intervention was aimed at removing restrictions on the market.[5]

The psychological and ideological basis for the policy of free trade lay in the sense of Britain's obvious superiority in the world. At the dawn of the industrial revolution Britain had made active use of protectionism, for example, to defend local textile manufacturing from Indian competition. The task was made easier by the fact that both sides of the market, exports and imports, were controlled by one and the same state. The beginning of industrialisation in Britain was accompanied by a simultaneous rise in the import duties on textiles in Britain itself, and the opening of the market in India.[6]

The industrial revolution swiftly altered the world economy and the global division of labour. By 1793 the productivity of a Lancashire textile worker was

400 times as great as that of an Indian weaver. It is not surprising that after free trade was introduced in India in 1813, the first consequence was the collapse of local production. Prior to this, India's balance of trade with Britain and the rest of Europe had been positive, but over the following 20 years Indian imports of textiles from Britain rose by a factor of 50, while textile exports to Britain declined by three-quarters.[7] For the Indian weavers, the results were catastrophic. Dacca, which in the eighteenth century had been a flourishing centre of textile production, became a virtual ghost town; over the same 20 years its population shrank from 150,000 people to a mere 20,000.

The industrial revolution enhanced and strengthened Britain's commercial and military superiority over the other Western powers. During the period from 1760 to 1830 the United Kingdom accounted for two-thirds of the growth in world industrial output. In the mid-eighteenth century Britain had been responsible for less than 2 per cent of world manufacturing production, but in the first half of the nineteenth century its share increased to 10 per cent, and by the 1860s, to 20 per cent. Some 53 per cent of world iron-smelting took place in Britain. A country that was home to a mere 2 per cent of the global population accounted for approximately half of humanity's industrial capacity.[8]

Protective tariffs vanished into the past, along with the Navigation Acts; meanwhile, restrictions on the exporting of industrial machinery were repealed. The protectionist system, however, was dismantled gradually and very cautiously; meanwhile, the differing views of supporters of protection and partisans of free trade remained an important dividing line between the parties in parliament. The Liberal-Whigs called for all restraints on trade to be abolished, while the Conservative-Tories insisted on the defence of local producers, and above all, of agricultural interests

It was by no means accidental that the ending of Anglo-French hostility coincided with the first wave of the industrial revolution. The military collapse of Napoleon's empire did not by any means see France excluded from European or world politics. As a military and even commercial power, the country soon regained a notable position on the continent. But unlike the case in previous decades, this did not lead to conflict with Britain. From this time, the former rivals acted constantly as partners – at Navarino, where the navies of both powers joined with the Russians to smash the Turks; in Crimea, during the war against Russia; in Egypt, for the purpose of building the Suez Canal; in China, during the periodic interventions; in the dividing-up of Africa; and finally, on the battlefields of two world wars.

Underlying the changes in geopolitics were economic causes. British and world capitalism were once again undergoing reconstruction. The new situation brought with it the opportunity for a compromise that was agreeable both to British and to French capital. Britain's industrial pre-eminence not only made it more tolerant of French commercial and financial expansion, but also gave it an interest in furthering this growth. A sort of division of labour arose. From the 1840s French capitalism developed in symbiosis with its British counterpart, occupying primarily the niches that the British bourgeoisie had left unoccupied. As the industrial revolution proceeded and British capital shifted from trade to production, France by contrast witnessed an increase in its maritime trade, followed by a development of ship-building and of a number of other sectors. French financial capital also expanded, collaborating actively with British industry. But unlike the case in the previous century, the growth of French trade and credit did not cause alarm on the other side of the Channel; to the contrary, it was seen as altogether positive. The French merchant fleet was transformed into a major carrier of British goods.

The principles of free trade dominated British politics until the Great Depression of 1929–32, in no way impeding the aggressive expansion of the empire. In outward terms this process appeared natural and spontaneous; the empire grew 'less like a structure than an organism, less like a city than a forest'.[9] But just as forests (and still more, cities) for all their elemental growth are subject to certain natural laws and logic, so the growth of the empire allowed the fulfilling of essential tasks that confronted not just British capital, but also capitalism as a whole.

The role of hegemon in the world-system involved a certain responsibility, irrespective of whether this was recognised by the ruling class of the dominant power. The British elite of the nineteenth century was conscious of this responsibility. During this epoch, maintaining equilibrium in the system became a crucial political goal, toward which the forces of the state were directed no less than toward the defence of Britain's own 'direct' interests. The burden of hegemony was not always easily borne; the empire found itself drawn constantly into local and regional conflicts which seemingly did not affect it directly.

The efforts by the empire to maintain global peace and order yielded benefits. As noted by the Russian political scientist Vladimir Malakhov, British hegemony meant that 'a relative peace prevailed throughout the entire century'. Subsequently, 'the weakening of British hegemony in the early twentieth century brought with it a destabilising of the international system'.[10] Within this scheme two world wars, the Russian revolution, the collapse of the European continental empires, fascism and totalitarianism can been seen as the results of a crisis of hegemony in the capitalist world-system.

The British empire in the Victorian era saw itself not just as a military or economic power, but also as a global moral force. This claim, moreover, was recognised by a significant part if not by most of the world community, unlike the analogous pre-tensions by the leaders of the USA in the early twenty-first century. The struggle against the slave trade was undoubtedly an important moral ace in the hands of the empire. By this time the economic importance of slavery was much less than it had been in previous centuries. Political reforms in Britain, and the expansion of the franchise after the parliamentary reform of 1832, had made the British elite more sensitive to public pressure, while public opinion was more oriented toward democratic values. Abolitionist propaganda gained increasing currency in Britain, forcing the ruling groups to reckon with the popular mood, while the industrial revolution made free labour more productive.

Often, the empire found itself obliged to counteract the ambitions of regional powers, even when the latter were not directly opposing it. This is how the Anglo-Russian conflict of the mid-nineteenth century needs to be understood. In themselves, the imperial ambitions of St Petersburg were in no way a threat to Britain, either economically or in the geopolitical sense. Moreover, the British in entering into conflict with their former ally placed at risk their strategic positions in Asia, positions which the Russian empire in earlier times had reliably protected. But the desire of the St Petersburg authorities to control the entire Black Sea, and their unconcealed goal of dismembering Ottoman Turkey, provoked instability that was fraught with unpredictable changes for the whole global relationship of forces. The attempts by Tsar Nicholas I to do away with the 'sick man of Europe', as Turkey was then known, led to the first large-scale European war since the defeat of Napoleon. Britain and France, supported by Piedmont, fought on the side of the Ottoman empire, which was perceived by public opinion in the West as the victim of aggression. Defeating Russia in the Crimean War, the Western powers stimulated an accelerated transformation of Russian society. The following years in Russia saw the beginning of the 'epoch of great reforms'.

By contrast, the regroupment that took place within the political expanses of Germany and Italy aroused no such pained reaction in the British elites, since it did not at first imply a destabilisation or unpredictable changes to the situation outside the borders of those countries. But in the wider scheme, the reforms in Russia and the processes of unification in Germany and Italy were part of a broad global process of reconstruction affecting not only Europe and America, but Asia as well.

The empire in Asia

The exploits of Robert Clive did not bring about the conquest of India by the British, but led to the establishing of British economic and political hegemony over the subcontinent. Meanwhile, neither the East India Company itself nor the government in London perceived the resulting situation as temporary or transient. No plan of conquest had been prepared in advance, and neither was there any certainty as to whether British territorial acquisitions should be expanded.

The new stage of British expansion in the early nineteenth century, as in the mid-eighteenth century, was motivated by changed circumstances and by a fear of losing earlier gains. The arrival of Napoleon in Egypt had aroused panic among British politicians and the directors of the East India Company, who feared that if the French were to consolidate their power over the land of the Pharaohs they would make a further leap into India. Napoleon was unable to hold Egypt as a base for colonial expansion, but by the time this became clear, the situation in India had changed irreversibly. Armies under the command of Arthur Wellesley, the future Duke of Wellington, carried out a series of successful campaigns against the Maratha princes and significantly expanded the boundaries of British possessions. After this the conquest went ahead practically without let-up, until the whole territory of the subcontinent was united beneath the Company's rule.

The final conquest of India not only enhanced the economic opportunities for British capital in Asia, but also brought about a dramatic increase in the might of the empire. As a British historian notes, the 'military resources of India, once under

European control, were to prove decisive for the further rise of the West'.[11] The Indian armies became a crucially important prop of the empire. As early as 1762 a small contingent of sepoys had taken part in a British expedition against Spanish-held Manila, and in the course of the nineteenth century Indians saw service across the whole expanse of the empire, in Burma, Africa and East Asia. As bureaucrats and businessmen, technical experts and soldiers, members of the new Indian elite not only served the empire, but to a significant degree determined its appearance, practice, institutions, ideology and agenda.

By the early twentieth century India had a status recalling that of the dominions rather than of the other colonies, though unlike Canada or New Zealand, it did not have a democratic government. As a British writer of the time noted, 'this empire, it must not be forgotten, although a dependence, has passed beyond the colonial stage, and in many details, is governed like an independent state'.[12] India represented a sort of imperial centre, furnishing everything without which the empire would have been inconceivable – people, commodities and ideas.[13]

The expansion of Anglo-Indian capital had a dramatic impact on the fate of China, when it was discovered that opium, grown in India, was virtually the sole import for which there was a demand in the Celestial Empire. In 1793 a British dip-lomatic mission brought to China examples of the finest achievements of European knowledge and civilisation, but the imperial government appraised them as 'strange and costly objects', unworthy of any interest.[14] Europe, however, needed Chinese goods, which it was prepared to consume in growing quantities. Once tea-drinking had become part of the way of life in Britain and North America, the East India Company made trade in this product one of its most important pursuits. Since the East India Company was unable to sell anything in China, European and American consumers were forced to make up for its expenses, and this became one of the causes of discontent in the North American colonies.

Opium was cultivated and used in India as a medicine. Early in the eighteenth century it had been imported to China, but opium-smoking was soon forbidden by imperial decrees. Despite the imposition of another strict ban in 1799 this trade developed rapidly. In 1820 imports amounted to 5,000 cases per year, and by 1840 had reached 40,000 cases.[15] 'By 1830, the opium trade was probably the largest commerce of its time in any single commodity, anywhere in the world', a British source states.[16]

In 1835 a further attempt by the Chinese authorities to stop the illegal trade led to a military clash with the British. Opening the Chinese market to the products of British industry became especially important in the context of an economic depression that broke out in 1836. In London, there were no illusions as to how insubstantial the British position was from a moral point of view, but the economic gains to be made from incorporating China into the world-system were too great. In 1840 an escalation of the conflict, which had periodically taken on violent forms, led to full-scale war.

By the beginning of the nineteenth century the Chinese army had become extremely backward in terms of its armaments, but the bureaucratic system of the

Celestial Empire made it possible to mobilise and maintain large numbers of disciplined troops, and for a time this provided a counterweight to the technical superiority of the West. But the creation by the British of the Indian army sharply altered the relationship of forces in East Asia. The forces commanded by British generals now possessed both technical superiority and sufficient numerical strength to prevail over any other army in Asia.

The First Opium War ended in victory for the British, who in 1842 imposed their peace terms on the Chinese empire. Hong Kong passed under British control, to become for many years a strategic base for the Royal Navy and a strongpoint for further offensives against China. After the defeat of 1842 the Chinese empire fell increasingly into decline. In the 1850s the country was shaken by the Taiping rebellion, and a drawn-out civil war began. The European powers made use of any pretext to intervene in internal Chinese affairs. The Europeans were soon joined by Japan, transformed by the success of modernisation in the 1860s into a major military power.

The Second Opium War of 1856–60 saw China fighting not only the British but also the French. Entering Beijing, the European armies subjected it to systematic plunder.[17] Joining in the attack on China was Russia, which in 1860 took advantage of the weakness of the neighbouring empire to impose an unjust border treaty on it. British entrepreneurs gradually penetrated the Chinese internal market; after the opening of the interior provinces of the empire to foreign business interests, British vessels gained the ability to serve internal trade routes. By 1898 Britain accounted for 82 per cent of China's foreign trade.[18]

Reconstruction

The great Russian economist Nikolay Kondratyev characterised the period from the mid-1840s through the 1870s as marked by a 'rising wave' in the development of the world economy.[19] In the second half of the 1850s, however, the world market experienced a profound crisis, followed by a wave of social and political shocks which led to a major restructuring of capitalism.

By the end of the 1850s Britain, with the only industrial economy on the planet, had become the 'workshop of the world'. From being a rival, France had been transformed into a partner, while the rest of the world, including even the dynamically developing United States, lagged far behind Britain. But over the following decade changes occurred in Europe and America that radically altered the relationship of economic forces. While remaining the leading power, Britain lost its industrial monopoly. Paradoxically, this took place with the active collaboration of British capital itself, which needed new markets in which to sell its products. Until mid-century Britain had mainly exported the products of its manufacturing industry, but the leading place was now taken by exports of technology and equipment. If this had not happened, British machine-building would simply have choked on its own products.

Statistical data bear witness to a sharp change in the structure of British exports during the second half of the nineteenth century. In the decades between 1850 and

1870 exports rose across all categories, but by the end of the 1880s exports of the most important types of finished products had declined noticeably. The losses were made up in part by the fact that exports of machinery and industrial equipment continued to grow. Hence, for example, the United Kingdom in 1854 exported textile goods to the value of £31.7 million, and in 1870 to the value of £71.4 million, or more than twice as much. But in 1887 British textile exports were worth only £71 million. The picture is still more striking in the case of other types of goods. British exports of iron had a value of £11.7 million in 1854, and of £111 million in 1870, but of only £107.1 million in 1887. Correspondingly, exports of linen goods amounted to £5.1 million, £10.4 million and £8.7 million, and of woollen goods, to £10.7 million, £26.6 million and £24.6 million. By contrast, exports of equipment continued to grow, more than doubling each decade from £2.2 million in 1854 to £5.3 million in 1870 and £12.8 million in 1887.[20]

Just as Britain unexpectedly and voluntarily ceded a substantial part of its seaborne commerce to France, in this new stage it readily renounced its industrial monopoly, while retaining its technical and economic leadership. In the rest of Europe and in North America, by contrast, the transition from mercantile-agrarian to industrial capitalism followed a complex path. The world-system underwent a painful period of restructuring, accompanied by dramatic political, economic and social changes.

During this period most European countries implemented major reforms, at times almost revolutionary in their scope. Changing the map of the world and the relationship of forces within it were the ending of serfdom in Russia; the Civil War and the abolition of slavery in the United States; the Meiji Revolution in Japan; the transforming of Canada into the first British dominion; the dissolution of the East India Company and the establishing of the Indian empire under the control of London; the *risorgimento*, with the formation of a unified Italian state beneath the leadership of Piedmont; and finally, the Austro-Prussian and Franco-Prussian wars, which culminated in the rise of the German Empire.

From the point of view of the development of world capitalism, the United States in the first half of the nineteenth century represented an anomaly, combining two types of development within a single state. In relation to the world-system, the north was part of the centre, while the south developed in line with the logic of the periphery. This, however, did not in any way prevent the elites of the slaveholding south from feeling completely comfortable, and even from displaying aggressive imperial ambitions. Though slavery was officially outlawed in the northern states, the economic and political interests of the southerners substantially affected not only general American priorities, but also the views and positions of politicians who were themselves from the north. The historian Robert Kagan emphasises that throughout most of the nineteenth century 'slavery shaped American foreign policy'.[21]

The number of slaves in the southern states continued to grow, though not of course as fast as the numbers of the 'white' population, which were increasing as a result of immigration. In the United States in 1790 there had been some 3,172,000 whites, about 58,000 free 'coloured' citizens and 697,000 slaves. By 1820 the population had more than doubled, comprising 7,862,000 whites, 233,000 free 'coloureds', and 1,538,000 slaves. By 1860 there were 26,922,000 whites living in the country, along with 488,000 free 'coloureds' and 3,938,760 slaves.[22] The slaveholding south and industrial north had distinct interests, but were both in equal degree oriented toward expansion. Satisfying the demands of the north, the government of the United States sent its cavalry to crush the native American population to the West of the Mississippi. Serving the interests of southerners, the government went to war on Mexico, and prejudiced its relations with Britain, which opposed slavery.

This symbiosis between two bourgeois societies which were oriented toward expansion, but which were organised in different fashion, was able to continue so long as the armed forces they shared protected the interests of both sides. But in the mid-nineteenth century these armed forces, after stripping Mexico of Texas and California and breaking the resistance of the native Americans, emerged onto the Pacific Ocean. Continental expansion had reached its natural limits. From that moment the contradictions between north and south quickly worsened, culminating in civil war.

The ruling classes of the south sought to turn the United States into a peripheral empire like serfholding Russia. But the bourgeois development of the north was in clear contradiction with this perspective. The point was not that the south was backward, but that its resources were being used directly for the development of the world economy, and in the first instance of British industry, instead of serving the industrialisation of the north.

When war broke out between north and south, British public opinion was deeply divided.[23] Officially, slavery was condemned, but the southern states supplied Britain with 75 per cent of the raw cotton used there, providing work for a fifth of the population of the island.[24] The blockade imposed by the northerners on the coastline of the southern states quickly made its effects felt on British industry. But the southerners had miscalculated in believing that their raw material was irreplaceable. The British government applied itself energetically to increasing cotton production in its colonies.[25]

The leaders of the south had made an error which a century later was to be repeated more than once by ambitious leaders of rising powers on the periphery. Overestimating the strategic importance of their raw materials, they failed to realise that the countries of the 'centre' always have much greater room for economic and political manoeuvre than appears at first glance. Re-unifying the United States under their power after the Civil War, the ruling groups of the north not only undertook a wide-ranging reconstruction in the south that radically changed society there, but also provided the impulse for a new stage of industrialisation that rested on a policy of protectionism and import substitution. The resources of the south, both of labour power and of raw materials, were directed to serving the industrial needs of the north. The south was to remain a relatively backward part of the country for further decades, but on the whole Reconstruction fulfilled its aims. In 1895 a contemporary noted: 'The South is rapidly becoming a prosperous manufacturing community.'[26] Nikolay Kondratyev observed that after the completion of Reconstruction the USA began to be drawn 'especially strongly' into the orbit of the world economy.[27] The consolidation of the US internal market acted as a guarantee of the success of these efforts, since the size of a 'protected' market has a direct relationship to the chances of such a policy being viable.

While the conflict between north and south was unfolding in America, in Europe the question was being posed of the unification of Italy and Germany. For centuries, political atomisation in both countries had been accepted as inevitable by the majority of the population, not to speak of the elites. This was despite growing criticism from the democratic and nationalist intelligentsia, influenced by the ideas of the French Revolution. But from the late 1850s the situation changed sharply. Industrialisation in America and continental Europe was proceeding against a back-drop of growing protectionism. This was aimed primarily against British imports, the restriction of which was a vital condition if local production was to begin developing and eventually to take the place of foreign goods. But this in turn created a situation in which the only countries that had a chance of success were those that could guarantee their industries a sufficiently large 'national' market. In Europe in the second half of the nineteenth century the expansion of industry and the spread of romantic nationalism went hand in hand. Nationalist ideology, however, also began rapidly to penetrate and infect more backward regions of the continent, where it did not rest on the necessary economic, social and cultural conditions. This nationalism quickly took on a reactionary nature, providing a platform for the consolidation of embittered petty-bourgeois elements and incompetent members of the provincial intelligentsia.

The ruling groups in Prussia and Piedmont quickly recognised the new opportunities and historic tasks with which they were confronted. In Prussia Chancellor Bismarck, though remaining an ideological conservative, borrowed readily from the ideas of socialists and laid the basis for the first modern pension system in Europe, while reforming the education system and initiating a 'cultural struggle' (*Kulturkampf*) against clericalism. In Italy, Count Cavour went even further, making use of the revolutionary militia commanded by Giuseppe Garibaldi to seize Naples.

After the capture of Naples, Cavour's government managed without great difficulty to shift Garibaldi into secondary roles. The Piedmontese armies went into action, seizing the neighbouring provinces. In February 1861 a parliament representing most of the country's regions proclaimed the Piedmontese monarch Victor Emmanuel King of Italy. The leading role of Turin was determined in advance by its level of industrial development; Piedmont's foreign trade in 1859 made up a third of that of Italy as a whole, while the region's railway network, the first to be constructed on Italian territory, had reached a total length of 800 kilometres.[28] As well as accomplishing national tasks, the *risorgimento,* the process of unifying the country, created the conditions for the further development of industry in Turin.

Full unification of Italy was delayed almost for a decade, since the leaders of the new kingdom were obliged to manoeuvre between far stronger powers, Austria and France. With the help of the French Emperor Napoleon III, the Italians first managed to force the Austrians out of the north-eastern provinces and to annex Venice. Then, taking advantage of the defeat of the French in the war against

Prussia and the collapse of the Second Empire, Italian forces in 1870 captured Rome, making it the capital of their kingdom. The unification of the country was complete, but major tasks still lay ahead. As one of the politicians of the epoch of the *risorgimento* remarked, 'We have created Italy; now we have to create Italians.'[29]

Germany, up to a point, was confronted by the same problem. It is usually considered that the Thirty Years War, by reinforcing the divisions within the country, delayed the creation of a single German nation by a good 200 years. No less important, however, was the fact that the numerous states that remained on the territory of the Holy Roman Empire were for the most part too small for a nation in the proper sense to come together on their basis. Ultimately, it was this high degree of dismemberment that acted as the precondition for the development of a unified culture, a shared economy and eventually, a common German society. The bourgeoisie found its opportunities constricted within a framework of free cities and princedoms, and sought so far as it could to develop its enterprises on the whole territory of the empire. Prominent intellectuals and ambitious bureaucrats moved from one kingdom or princedom to another seeking recognition for their services. If the conflicts of the sixteenth and seventeenth centuries had ended with the dividing of the empire into a number of more or less powerful kingdoms which swallowed the free cities and petty princedoms, then instead of a single German nation a number of related nations might eventually have arisen (evidence of this might be seen in the gradual differentiation of Austria and the independent development of Luxembourg).

The German nation was 'open', and to an important degree was constructed in the mid-nineteenth century. The starting-point was provided by the Napoleonic wars, which awakened national consciousness, and the culmination was the revolution of 1848, which saw the formulation of an all-German democratic project. But it was the industrialisation of the mid-nineteenth century that acted as the turning-point, after which the formation of the German nation changed from being a cultural-ideological to a practical project.

Just as the formation of the British Empire coincided with the rise of capitalism, the German imperial project became possible in an epoch of further reconstruction of the capitalist system, when Europe and North America were undergoing a wave of industrialisation. These circumstances placed their stamp both on the formation of the cultural traditions of society and on the organisational shape which the life of the state assumed. In the mid-nineteenth century Germans still thought of themselves as visionary and impractical, inclined more to poetry than to commerce or industry, which were regarded as the preserve of the pragmatic British.

As often happens in a country where the lack of a strong, unified state limits the career opportunities of young people from the 'middle class', Germany exported specialists, energetic and enterprising people who preferred to seek happiness and success in Eastern Europe. Here, encountering populations that were even more patriarchal and traditional than at home, the Germans acted as bearers of European progress and entrepreneurship. In the West, meanwhile, they experienced an inferiority complex and a constant sense of humiliation, as they encountered the advanced economic existence of the British and French.

The revolution of 1848, which in Germany ended in defeat, merely deepened the sense of national backwardness. Accordingly, the wars in which Prussia defeated Denmark, Austria and finally France were perceived by German society as a long-awaited revenge. The bourgeois modernisation culminated in a 'passive revolution' (or 'revolution from above'), carried out in the process of unification by Chancellor Bismarck and the Prussian bureaucrats. This political triumph was reinforced by no less impressive economic successes. For the German nation, the industrial revolution was an experience just as unifying, and just as fundamental for shaping society, as the socio-political revolutions had been for Britain and France.

In Germany, political unification and industrial revolution not only coincided in the temporal sense, but represented a single, internally indivisible process whose various elements nourished and supported one another. The mass migration of the population from the countryside to the cities, factory discipline, and the new means of communication and transport gathered and blended together people who had come from different traditional regions, undermined 'local patriotism', and discouraged the use of regional dialects at the level of everyday life, finally replacing them with the dominance of the literary language. These advances, however, were achieved under the leadership of the authoritarian Prussian bureaucracy, and to a significant degree thanks to its actions.

Meanwhile the successes of Italy, which had established a more liberal system, were far less impressive. When unification was completed in 1870, the new kingdom was one of the most backward countries of the West. The financial position of the state was dismal. As calculated by British economists, the Italian national debt, which in 1861 had been about £125 million, increased by 1895 to £492,314,300, an espe- cially heavy burden 'in proportion to the productivity of the country'.[30] Although 60 per cent of the country's population supported themselves by working on the land, agriculture was extremely backward in technological terms.[31] In central and southern Italy, semi-feudal forms of landholding persisted. The government, though far more liberal than that of Germany in its economic and social policies, could do nothing to end the gap between north and south. The backwardness of the south has remained a crucial problem burdening the development of Italy throughout all the country's subsequent history.

The last major shock to be experienced during the epoch of reconstruction in the 1860s was the Meiji Revolution in Japan. The meaning of this strange 'revolution-restoration', which was accompanied by a reimposing of the authority of the imperial house, was not fully grasped by European observers, even though in its scale and consequences it proved to be among the most radical transformations of the period. A brief civil war in 1868 ended in the overthrow of the feudal regime of the Shogunate, which had kept the Tokugawa family in power for two and a half centuries. Under the pretext of giving the emperor back his nominal property, land nationalisation was carried out and feudal domains were abolished. The new centralised state carried out an administrative reform. In place of the former princedoms, prefectures were established, with their borders quite different from the old feudal landholdings. Different social classes were given equal rights.

The centralised state set about organising an army and navy on the European model. A rapid, often forcible modernisation occurred of daily life, government and education, with peasant children compelled to go to school: 'The spending by the government of Japan on education was equal to the defence budget.'[32]

Where possible, feudal traditions were placed at the service of modernisation. Through strengthening the government apparatus, Japan in the space of 20 years was transformed into a state that was highly individual, but entirely able to bear comparison with the countries of the West. The effects of this were quickly felt by the neighbouring Asian countries on which Japanese imperialism hurled itself as soon as the opportunity arose.

Passive revolution in India and Canada

While the processes of unification in Italy and Germany are widely cited as classic examples of 'revolution from above' or 'passive revolution',[33] the developments during the same period on the expanses of the British empire have mostly attracted less attention. Nevertheless, similar changes were taking place there.

The most radical changes occurred in India during the 1860s. Not only were the forms of political organisation on the subcontinent refashioned, but to an important degree, the social and cultural forms as well.

The impulse for change was provided by the Indian Mutiny. This uprising, provoked when British officers insulted the religious feelings of Indian soldiers, took place against the background of a worldwide economic crisis. The mutiny in the army attracted support from a section of the traditional aristocracy, and was accompanied by mass peasant revolts against the *zamindar* landowners, who doubled as local representatives of the East India Company. The revolts were aimed not only at the British authorities, but also against the established social system, which was profoundly at odds with the aims and ideology of the rebels. The targets of popular anger included the local bourgeoisie, whose property was subjected to plunder. As Lawrence James observes, 'it was far from clear whether or not the mutineers would forge a permanent alliance with the rural insurgents. What was beyond question was that attacks on property, pillaging and assaults on bankers and businessmen convinced men of substance that they had a common cause with the British.'[34] Paradoxically, the 'mutiny' of 1857 helped consolidate the alliance between the colonial authorities and the Indian bourgeoisie. The British agent in Delhi Mohan Lal reported that irrespective of their religious beliefs, business people awaited the return of the colonial forces, who would bring back 'British laws and courts'.[35]

The ensuing civil war was marked by numerous atrocities, with the victims including any Europeans, even women and children, who fell into the hands of the sepoys. These barbarities were used by the colonial propaganda to justify repression. Meanwhile, significant sectors of Indian society were no less outraged and terrified than the British, or even more; the British at least were able simply to abandon the country that had torn itself free from their control.

The British administration was able to prevail in the struggle only because massive numbers of Indians fought on its side. Indian troops in the Company's army carried on fighting against their compatriots, while well-off people sacrificed their funds to maintain the colonial forces, supplying them with provisions and ammunition. Numerous agents, by no means all of them hired, informed the generals of the movements of the enemy, suggested the best roads to follow, and led detachments along secret paths. A particular role in defending the positions of the empire was played by Sikhs.

> The noble devotion with which these lately conquered people followed our standard is unique in the history of the world. It was the highest possible exhibition of political honesty, and forms, with the subsequent rejoicing which upon the suppression of the revolt, prevailed among all peace-loving society, the highest tribute to the benignity of our rule, or at least to the power and wisdom of our race.[36]

Drawing up a balance-sheet of the war, an imperial historian stated triumphantly: 'The mutiny proved that India was not, and probably never will be, a country which can be united to oppose our rule.'[37]

However the ideologues and propagandists might have reassured themselves, the uprising furnished proof of the viciousness of the established system of rule and of the presence in India of massive discontent. If the power of the empire was to be consolidated, radical changes were essential, and these duly followed. The political reform that began after the suppression of the mutiny radically altered the structure and to a degree even the nature of British rule. The East India Company was nationalised, and in 1876 Queen Victoria, after some hesitation, assumed the title of Empress of India. Administrative practices underwent sharp change, and the state, which earlier had entrusted its functions to the zamindars and other local intermediaries, now took on a direct presence at all levels of collective life.

Despite the imposition of order within the government, the new administration did not have a uniform character throughout the territory of India. Direct British rule was introduced only on the territories that earlier had been controlled by the Company. The princes and local rulers retained their possessions, but were obliged to submit to regular British inspections.

Britain's Indian empire was supposed to be seen not only as a new form of organisation of the colonial regime, but also as a continuation and restoration of the state system of the Great Moghuls. The royal proclamation that announced the founding of the new state emphasised that it would be based on the 'ancient rights, usages and customs of India'.[38] The British administration was indeed guided in its activity by Indian traditions, in the form in which these had been established or were retained in the mid-nineteenth century. The only problem was that these traditions and norms had themselves changed radically under European influence.

The reorganisation of the administrative system was accompanied by a sweeping programme of public works, aimed in the first instance at developing infrastructure – at building railways and highways, canals and government buildings. With the development of transport came the first steps toward industrialisation, and the birth of a local working class. Under the East India Company railway construction had been subject to commercial interests, had depended on private investors, and hence had developed weakly. British soldiers, to whom the roads were of strategic rather than commercial interest, had complained openly that the Company was making 'little progress in the physical development of India'.[39] Now the responsibility for 'material development' was assumed directly by the administration.

In parallel with the efforts of the administration to modernise infrastructure, there appeared what Lawrence James has described as an 'educational revolution'.[40] The period directly following the revolt of the sepoys saw the founding of five universities, which opened affiliates in various parts of the country. By 1900 the University of Calcutta was the largest in the world in terms of the number of its students. Higher education was provided in English, with the young people also required to have a knowledge of Latin and Greek. With the growth of an educated middle class the press developed rapidly as well, not only in English but also in local languages.

The efforts by the government to increase the number of Indians in all the organs of the state apparatus were so successful that they aroused disquiet among the 'white' population. The latter even established the Anglo–Indian and European Defence Association, holding noisy meetings that were reported sympathetically in the London *Times* and *Daily Telegraph*.[41]

Such protests inevitably inspired mobilisations in response by the educated layers of Indian society. In Calcutta in December 1885 the first general assembly of the Indian National Congress (INC) took place. The organisation united numerous small groups and associations that were active already in various parts of the country. It seems not to have entered anyone's head that such a coalition might challenge the very foundations of British rule. Only as a remote strategic prospect did the participants in the Congress see India gaining self-governing status in the manner of Canada or of the 'white colonies' of Australia, at this time still to undergo federation.

At gatherings of the Indian National Congress, Queen Victoria was referred to as 'Mother', and one of the ideologues of the movement, Achyut Sitaram Sathe, eloquently explained his love for Britain: 'The educated Indian is loyal by instinct and contented through interest. The English flag is his physical shelter, the English philosopher has become his spiritual consolation.'[42]

The pacification of the country that was achieved by the Victorian administration after the East India Company was shut down proved so successful that the colonial regime managed to win support in broad layers of society. Portraits of Queen Victoria – a sort of remote white goddess – adorned the walls of peasant homes. But by no means everyone was so content with the course of events in British India. The efforts at modernising the country did nothing to improve the condition of the rural poor. During the same years when the government of Lord Canning was reporting proudly on the latest successes, India experienced an appalling famine, which according to the calculations of the British themselves took as many as half a million human lives.

While India by the end of the nineteenth century had become a model for Britain's other 'native colonies', Canada during the same period became a model for the white settler colonies that were being transformed into dominions. The War of 1812 had been Canada's first 'national' triumph. The population of Canada at the time did not exceed 300,000, compared with 8 million in the United States; nevertheless, it was the Canadians who emerged victorious.

Despite the consolidation of society resulting from the war with the USA, the British authorities in Canada were far from being able always to rely on unanimous support from the population. French-Canadian patriots under the leadership of Louis-Joseph Papineau demanded increased autonomy, and in 1834 the parliament of Lower Canada sent a list of 92 resolutions to London, demanding additional rights for the provinces of British North America. London replied with ten resolutions in which it rejected the main demands of the Canadians, after which the Rebellion of the Patriots began in 1837, with significant numbers of Anglo-Canadians joining in. The Republic of Canada that was proclaimed by the rebels was quickly smashed by the regular army. Papineau fled to France, and many of his supporters were hanged, but in 1848 he was able to return to the country and again to engage in political activity. As usual, military successes and repressions were followed by concessions and consolidation. In 1867 the Dominion of Canada was proclaimed, as a semi-independent state within the British empire. Its status later became a model for other countries gaining self-government.

It should be noted that the right to self-government was tied openly to the racial and cultural make-up of the inhabitants of the territory concerned. Imperial ideologues constantly stressed the fundamental difference between the 'white colonies' and other possessions of the empire. Canada provided a model for Australia and New Zealand. Since the populations there were by this time 'chiefly of British or European descent', a commentator stated, 'this same plan of leaving the people to govern themselves is followed. Where the people of a colony are chiefly of other races, this cannot be done ... '.[43]

Needless to say, the reason for these differences was not to be sought in the racism of British administrators, but in the natives themselves and their culture: 'In India people are governed. They had been accustomed to this for ages before we got possession of the country. How much longer the same kind of rule will be necessary it is impossible to say. In Eastern countries things come very slowly.'[44]

Notes

1 *The Economist*, XIV (645): 8, 5 January 1856.
2 B. Semmel, *The Rise of Free Trade Imperialism: Classical Political Economy, the Empire of Free Trade and Imperialism 1750–1850*. Cambridge: Cambridge University Press, 2004, p. 4.
3 I. Wallerstein, *Modern World-System III. The Second Era of Great Expansion of the Capitalist World-Economy, 1730–1840s*, San Diego, CA: Academic Press, Inc., 1989, p. 19.
4 Ibid., p. 21.
5 Ibid., p. 19.
6 Cited in N. Robins, *The Corporation That Changed the World: How the East India Company Shaped the Modern Multinational*, London: Pluto Press, 2006, p. 148.

7 See ibid., p. 148.
8 See P. Kennedy, *The Rise and Fall of Great Powers. Economic Change and Military Conflict from 1500 to 2000,* London/Sydney/Wellington: Unwin Hyman, 1988, p. 151.
9 C.F. Lavell and C. E. Payne, *Imperial England,* New York: The MacMillan Co., 1920, p. 84.
10 V.S. Malakhov, *Gosudarstvo v usloviyakh globalizatsii* [The state under the conditions of globalisation], Moscow: KDU, 2007, p. 133.
11 J.D. Tracy (ed.), *The Political Economy of Merchant Empires,* Cambridge: Cambridge University Press, 1991, p. 184.
12 H.C. Morris, *History of Colonization,* London/New York: MacMillan, 1908, p. 255.
13 G. Blue, M. Bunton and R. Croizier (eds), *Colonialism and the Modern World. Selected Studies,* Armonk/London: M.E. Sharpe, 2002, p. 26.
14 J. Beeching, *The Chinese Opium Wars,* London: Hutchinson, 1975, p, 17.
15 See A.A. Del'nov, *Kitaj. Bol'shoj istoricheskij spravochnik,* Moscow: JeKSMO, Algoritm, 2008, p. 559.
16 Beeching, *Chinese Opium Wars,* p, 39.
17 Del'nov, *Kitaj,* p. 585.
18 See *The Nation,* 66 (1708): 217. 24 March 1898.
19 See N. Kondratyev, *Problemy ekonomicheskoy dinamiki* [Questions of the economic dynamic], Moscow: Ekonomika, 1989, p. 181.
20 *Chambers's Encyclopaedia. A Dictionary of Universal Knowledge,* London and Edinburgh, 1895, Vol. 5, p. 377.
21 R. Kagan, *Dangerous Nation. America and the World, 1600–1898,* London: Atlantic Books, 2006, p. 185.
22 *Chambers's Encyclopaedia,* Vol. 10, p. 380.
23 A. Wood, *Nineteenth-Century Britain, 1815–1914,* London: Longmans, 1960, p. 240.
24 Ibid., p. 243.
25 Ibid., p. 244.
26 *Chambers's Encyclopaedia,* Vol. 10, p. 389.
27 Kondratyev, *Problemy,* p. 211.
28 K. Bris, *Istoriya Italii* [History of Italy], St Petersburg: Evraziya, 2008, p. 407.
29 Ibid., p. 421.
30 *Chambers's Encyclopaedia,* Vol. 6, p. 246.
31 Bris, *Istoriya Italii,* p. 428.
32 E. Deynorov, *Istoriya Yaponii* [History of Japan], Moscow: AST, 2008, p. 569.
33 It may be recalled that it was on the basis of the *risorgimento* that Antonio Gramsci also formulated his concept of 'passive revolution'.
34 L. James. *Raj. The Making and Unmaking of British India,* London: Abacus, 2003, pp. 72–3.
35 Ibid., p. 73.
36 W.C. Pearce, *History of India,* London and Glasgow: William Collins, Sons & Co., 1876, p. 209.
37 G.R. Parkin, *Round the Empire,* London/Paris/Melbourne: Cassell & Co. Ltd., 1892, p. 210.
38 Cited in Pearce, *History of India,* p. 211.
39 Cited in James, *Raj,* p. 185.
40 Ibid., p. 344.
41 See ibid., p. 351.
42 Quoted in ibid., p. 352.
43 Ibid., p. 34.
44 Ibid., p. 229.

9

IMPERIALISM

The global reconstruction of the 1860s changed the economic and political map of the world, but did not undermine the dominant position of the British empire. Its might remained uncontested, resting not only on military power but also on a number of economic advantages. In an epoch of protectionism the size of the 'defended' market came to have an extremely important bearing on further development, and on this level the empire of Queen Victoria with its huge resources and population of many millions had no equal. It was not simply the largest state formation on the planet, but also the largest integrated market, access to which was extremely important for industrialists of all other countries.

Nevertheless, the changes occurring in the world had negative aspects where Britain was concerned. Felt most acutely of all by the country's industries were the consequences of the spread of protectionism. The glory of the former 'workshop of the world' was on the wane. The role of global hegemon, bringing with it not just numerous advantages but also a significant burden of cares and responsibilities, came at an increasing price. While the United States, Russia and the unified Germany were making a gradual transition to protectionism, in Britain the policy of free trade remained in place throughout the second half of the nineteenth century and even into the twentieth. This policy was far from optimal from the point of view of the British entrepreneurial class, and in the dominions and colonies it aroused open discontent. But this was the cost the empire had to pay for its role as leader of the capitalist world.

Large-scale railway construction created demand for the output of metal producers, coal mines and machine-building works, but simultaneously led to a relative decline in sea-borne trade, and reduced the importance of naval power. The transport of goods within Europe now occurred mainly by land.

Toward the end of the nineteenth century the 'social question' began to take centre stage. The industrial revolution, while enriching British entrepreneurs, had devastating consequences for the country's working class. The replacing of people by machines was accompanied by a massive growth of unemployment and by a lowering of wages. By the mid-nineteenth century the situation had begun to improve, but not by enough to smooth out the blatant social contradictions.

So long as Britain remained the 'workhop of the world', the sale of its products in foreign markets was guaranteed. The low purchasing power of workers within the country itself did not pose a problem for industry, but on the contrary, stimulated the dynamic development of business by keeping wage costs low. But as Britain lost its industrial monopoly, the situation changed. The new industrial powers could not repeat the British experience, since they lacked a monopoly position in world trade. The development of global competition turned the 'worker question' into a genuine headache for capitalists. The organised proletariat, even if it did not lay claim to power, at least demanded political freedoms and economic rights. Meanwhile, the bourgeoisie itself could no longer develop unless it made concessions to the labour movement. The problem, however, lay in the difficulty of increasing the incomes of hired workers without sacrificing capitalist profits. Even people who categorically denounced the socialist ideas that were coming into fashion acknowledged that something had to be done about the 'social question'. But higher wages meant lower returns for the capitalists, and reduced competitiveness for industry on foreign markets. Resolving this contradiction proved impossible within the context of the Western economy during the nineteenth century.

The late Victorian depression

In retrospect, the difficulties encountered by the world economy in the 1870s and 1880s came to be described as the 'late Victorian depression'. Beginning in Britain, this downturn spread gradually throughout the entire world.

The building of factories, the construction of railways and the development of trade at times continued at almost the same rate as earlier, but prices fell. The scale of the depression is illustrated by the dynamic of British exports. In 1854 commodity exports from the British Isles had been worth £97.2 million, and in 1870 £199.6 million; in other words, exports doubled during the period of global reconstruction despite all the protectionist barriers. But in 1887 they came to £221.4 million, an insignificant rise for so lengthy a period.[1] Between 1873 and 1896 the level of prices in Britain fell by 40 per cent, while to the horror of entrepreneurs, 'wages could not be and were not proportionally reduced'.[2]

Industrialisation brought about an acceleration of capitalist development, a growth in the power of the bourgeoisie and an increase in the efficiency of production, but at the same time led to a decline in the rate of profit in all the leading Western economies and on the global scale. Liberal authors have been inclined to blame this on workers, who by demanding wage increases, forced capital to reduce its share in the overall income. Marx, by contrast, showed that the rate of profit declines not because labour becomes less productive, but because its productivity increases.[3] Also making an impact may be such factors as the saturation of markets and strengthened competition, in circumstances where the buying power of workers is limited. But the main cause driving profit rates lower is the change in the organic composition of capital, in other words, the need to spend ever-greater sums on the technical equipping of production. As more expensive and complex technology is installed, the relationship of constant capital (invested in equipment) and variable capital (invested in the exploitation of labour) changes to the advantage of the former, while the profit is derived from the latter. In turn, this tendency to a reduced rate of profit means that capitalism experiences the need from time to time for new markets and economic sectors, for new commodities and for the drawing into the labour market of new masses of workers who can be exploited using simpler and 'cheaper' methods.[4] At first, these new markets are all highly profitable, as demand outstrips supply. But after a time the potential of every such 'wave of innovation' is exhausted, and for the next wave to arise an external impulse is required, not only in the form of scientific and technical discoveries, but also in the form of social changes that make these discoveries the objects of felt needs. Successive technological revolutions, accompanied by radical changes in consumption and lifestyles, make it possible to radically alter the state of the market, and through reviving it, to raise the rate of profit. Meanwhile, the completion of technological revolutions is just as inevitably accompanied by crises and by falling profitability. Here, commercial capital comes to the aid of industrial capital, creating new markets and opening up different areas of life, previously uncommercialised, to commercial exploitation.

Periodically repeated crises of profitability within the framework of industrial capitalism give rise just as regularly to the resurgence of commercial and financial capital, 'returning' to world history in ever-new forms, along with ideological justifications for free trade, open markets, and the shameless exploitation of people and resources.

This occurred too in the course of the 'late Victorian depression'.[5]

The scramble for colonies

Commercial capital is unable to conquer markets without the participation of the state, without coercion and violence. The new wave of colonialism that began in the 1870s brought an expansion of the Western world at the expense of 'barbarian' territories earlier though undeserving of attention, and of pressure on Asian states that had retained their independence. The colonial expansion, dictated by economic necessity, was maintained as a result of the demographic preponderance of the West. Europe in the nineteenth century experienced a demographic explosion. At the end of the eighteenth century Asians had made up two-thirds of the population of the planet, but by 1900, as Eric Hobsbawm indicates, their share had diminished to approximately 55 per cent. During this time the number of Europeans doubled.[6]

The main thrust of colonial expansion was into Africa, viewed by Europeans as empty territory that outside powers were entitled to divide among themselves. Until the mid-nineteenth century the seizure of colonies in Africa had been linked to the need for anchorages, naval bases and storage sites. Some historians are inclined to think that during this period the Royal Navy 'was not so much an adjunct to empire, as empire – or at least much of it – was an adjunct to the navy'.[7] By the end of the century, however, the situation had changed radically. By this time not just Britain and France, but all countries with at least some military and maritime potential were taking part in the 'scramble for conquests'. Germany, Belgium and Italy were creating their own overseas empires. Portugal's African possessions were extended into the interior of the continent, while Holland sought to consolidate and expand its control over Indonesia, Russia occupied Central Asia, and Japan attempted to establish bridgeheads for itself in China and Korea.

In 1800 European powers had laid claim to approximately 55 per cent of the planet's territory, but exercised real control over no more than 35 per cent. In 1878 they held 67 per cent of the world's land area, and this time the control was genuine. By 1914 some 85 per cent of the globe had been incorporated into the European empires.[8] During the period from 1876 to 1914 the population of the colonies increased from 314 to 570 million people, that is, by 81 per cent.[9]

The new wave of colonial expansion left almost no chance for the states of the periphery to maintain an independent existence. From this point their independence was ensured only by the goodwill of the great powers, in cases where the latter preferred to retain them as buffer zones between the possessions of the major empires. In Asia by the beginning of the twentieth century only four independent states remained – Persia, Afghanistan, Thailand and China, not counting Japan, which was itself an imperialist power, or Nepal, an unacknowledged protectorate of British India. In Africa the only country to remain independent was Ethiopia, with which the poorly trained Italian army had proven unable to cope. At times (for example, in Morocco, Malaya, Oman and to some degree in Nigeria) the European powers had been forced to compromise, maintaining native governments in the form of protectorates. The Anglo-Egyptian administration in the Sudan provided a unique example in which an occupied Arab nation acted as a formally equal participant in a colonial conquest.

Where no state-political tradition existed, or where it was weak, this tradition was established by colonialism. The decisive role, it follows, was not played by the technical backwardness of the colonised peoples, but by their level of political orga-nisation. Serious problems for the Europeans in the colonies began arising only later, once the efforts in Africa of European bureaucrats and soldiers had resulted in the installation of a state system at least to some degree resembling that of the West.

The European empires united the planet in a single political, economic and even social whole to such an extent that the globalisation of the late twentieth century can be considered only a repetition of the imperialist experience of the final decades of the previous century. Even in the first years of the present century a historian could observe that 'this colonial world was far more globally integrated than the postcolonial world between 1950 and 1990, possibly even our world today'.[10]

During the twentieth century the widespread growth of anti-imperialist senti-ments, taking hold not only of leftists but also of a substantial section of the liberal intelligentsia, brought a dramatic re-evaluation of the colonial experience. Taking the place of imperial propaganda and the myth of the 'white man's burden' was a simplified concept of colonialism as no more than conquest and compulsion. A petty-bourgeois political correctness triumphed, with condemnation and bans taking the place of attempts to penetrate to the essence of the phenomenon. There was no demand for critical analysis of colonialism, since relations between rulers and ruled, Europeans and non-Europeans, 'whites' and 'coloureds' were reduced to the relations between master and slave, violator and victim, to the simple counterposing of two worlds.[11]

Such a discourse ignores the complex socio-political hierarchy of the colonial world, the key element of which was the 'native' elites. It was only later, when the illusions associated with decolonisation had vanished into the past and the newly independent states had shown their ability to serve the interests of international capital far more ruthlessly, cynically and zealously than the earlier colonial administrations, that a more critical view of the problem began gaining a foothold among historians and sociologists.

The colonial world that had taken shape by the end of the Victorian epoch was a complex and contradictory formation: 'Imperial control has always depended on a measure of co-operation or collaboration between colonial rulers and influential local interest groups. Establishing such collaborative relations has always required considerable political skills on both sides.'[12]

The creation of a state of the European type, penetrating everyday life and directly present at grass-roots level, required large numbers of administrative workers, police and military personnel, not to speak of jurists, notaries, translators, postal workers, technical experts and managers. The systematic training of local functionaries was a major concern and headache for all colonial administrations, and the effectiveness of rule over the territories depended on the quality of these officials. For their part, the 'native' officials could always resort (and often did resort) to bureaucratic sabotage when they encountered completely unacceptable or incompetent initiatives from the Europeans.

'Imperial policies,' writes the historian Kevin Reilly,

> had to be implemented by thousands of colonial nationals: collaborators, agents, officials and soldiers, and colonial ambitions could often be frustrated by untold 'natives' and middling people, including lawyers trained in European law schools who were adept to turning it against the Europeans. Nor was there always a single imperial policy. Rather, there were disagreements: between the foreign office and the colonial governor, or between the policy makers and those in charge of implementation or enforcement … The same is true of what [is] to be called, perhaps too simplistically, the other side. For some of the colonized, a particular policy was repressive, for others progressive. The colonized of one colony (for example the Sikhs of India) might be imperial enforcers in another … [13]

Ultimately, the tasks of colonialism were economic. Hence the denial of national sovereignty, liberalism, the encouragement of industrial development, the construction of transport infrastructure, measures to spread enlightenment and political repression were all linked in one way or another with meeting the main challenge: integrating the new territories of the global periphery into the capitalist world-system.

Hardest of all was creating a labour market. 'Nowhere in Africa, in the initial period of colonialism, did the natives voluntarily hire themselves out to work. The idea of leaving his village and land, the property of his tribal group, to go and earn money, of which the native did not know the value, in places a considerable distance from his home, seemed to the African of those times neither proper nor just.'[14] To accustom the population to the labour market, the colonial state was forced to resort to various forms of compulsion, ranging from harsh methods in the German colonies and the Belgian Congo to milder ones in the British possessions, where taxes were levied on the natives in order to induce them to earn money. Nevertheless, it was only toward the end of the colonial period that it was possible to speak of such methods as having been successful, at least in a number of African countries. Meanwhile, European capital still needed an economic space which, as explained earlier, grew far more slowly than the physical space occupied by the colonies.

The Victorian epoch ended with proud talk of peace and progress, into which notes of doubt increasingly inserted themselves. The entire globe was divided between the leading European powers, joined now by the United States. There was no more free space for expansion anywhere on the planet, and as before, capital found itself cramped. In the forefront now were the contradictions between the western empires themselves.

The theory of imperialism

By the end of the nineteenth century the world empires had achieved unprece- dented military and economic power, while leading capitalist firms had transformed themselves into global corporations, subjecting the lives of hundreds of thousands and even millions of people to their will. As before, these firms were linked to one or another country, whose government zealously protected their interests, but these interests had now become global, encompassing different continents and the most diverse countries. Overseas investments were no less important than conquests, and the credit of European banks became available in the most remote and 'barbarian' corners of the planet.

The economy of the free market was disappearing into the past even where gov- ernments adhered to liberal principles. It was not protectionism that was banishing competition; this was being accomplished by the concentration and monopolisation of capitals. The logic of accumulation was taking precedence over the logic of the market. Companies vied not for consumers, but for market share and raw materials.

All these phenomena had been known since the very dawn of capitalism. If there had not been large masses of capital and rivalry between them, then the wars and other socio-political shocks that defined the character of Europe in the early twentieth century would not have occurred. In precisely the same fashion, monopoly companies had been known long before this epoch, as had international credit and corporations. But the concentration of production made possible and inevitable monopolies of a new type, combining production and trade, the extraction of raw materials in centrally organised fashion, and resource transport and processing. The competition of capitals became incomparably more important than the competition of goods. In the first half of the nineteenth century a number of large companies had raised themselves above the mass of middle and small firms like the tip of an iceberg, but now the concentration of capital had reached such a degree that small and medium business was totally subordinate to large, and survived in the niches which the monopolies themselves had earlier assigned to it.

In practice, the combining of concentration of production with formal observance of the requirements of free trade increased the ability of corporations to control the market. The figure of the individual capitalist, the owner conducting the affairs of the family firm, was increasingly superseded. Management was transformed into a complex, bureaucratised process. The bureaucracies of the state and of the corporations developed in close symbiosis, exchanging personnel and servicing one another's needs.

The British economist John A. Hobson was the first to describe the new quality which the capitalist system had taken on, defining the new era as that of imperialism. This term was seized upon and filled with new content by Marxist writers including Rudolf Hilferding and Nikolay Bukharin, and then by V.I. Lenin, who published his famous book *Imperialism, The Highest Stage of Capitalism*. Lenin's brief monograph proved to be a classic text, of significance even for historians and economists alien to the Marxist tradition. Although Lenin did not 'discover' imperialism, and was not the first to describe its key traits and identifying characteristics, it was he who summarised and systematically generalised the work performed earlier by other authors, turning the theoretical discoveries, observations and commentaries of others into a consistent analytical system.

The new imperialism, according to Lenin, represents a specific form of organisation of capitalism that arose in the late nineteenth century, differing sharply from the previous economic, social and political model. As the defining features of imperialism, Lenin notes the following:

> 1) The concentration of production and capital has reached such a high level of development that it has created monopolies which play the decisive role in economic life; 2) the merging of bank capital with industrial capital and the creation, on the basis of this 'finance capital', of a financial oligarchy; 3) the export of capital, as distinguished from the export of goods, takes on especially great significance; 4) the formation of international monopoly associations of capitalists, which divide the world between them; and 5) the territorial division of the world between the largest capitalist powers has been completed.[15]

Financial and industrial capital become increasingly entwined, with banks no longer merely providing credit for production, but also directly controlling it. Private firms are transformed into many-faceted business empires, tied closely to the government.

On the one hand, 'the free market departs increasingly into the realm of the past'.[16] But on the other hand, Lenin constantly associates imperialism with more intense and ruthless competition: 'The higher the degree of development of capitalism, the more strongly the shortage of raw materials is felt. Competition becomes more acute, the worldwide hunt for sources of raw materials more intense, and the struggle to acquire colonies more desperate.'[17] The explanation for this apparent contradiction lies in the fact that rivalry between petty producers, striving to attract the consumer, has been replaced by a struggle to divide up markets and resources, a struggle that would be impossible without the participation of the state and that does not exclude the use of protectionist measures. In other words, the age of great-power competition has dawned. From this, Lenin draws his conclusion concerning the close ties between the monopolisation of capital and colonial expansion.

In the history of capital, the free market in fact represents an episode or a particular stage. It has appeared repeatedly in the course of historical development, and its emergence, naturally, is far from accidental. The great-power competition of the early twentieth century was a new phenomenon not in relation to the entire history of capitalism, but in relation to the preceding epoch, to the time when Victorian Britain flourished as the world centre and effective monopolist in the area of industrial production. Britain at this time had no need to use protectionist measures itself, and sought however it could to resist their introduction by other countries.

Nevertheless, Lenin was correct in judging that imperialism represented something new. Society had changed because production had changed, and because a new level of accumulation of capital had been achieved: 'The concentration of production; monopolies growing up as a result; the merger or intertwining of banks with industry – here we find the history of the rise of finance capital and the substance behind this concept.'[18]

The novelty of imperialism also lay in the fact that for the first time foreign expansion was viewed in ruling circles not only as a means for accelerating the accumulation of capital and raising the rate of profit, but also as a means of solving the 'social question'. The British entrepreneur and colonialist Cecil Rhodes formulated this connection in supremely simple terms when he argued in 1895 that Britain needed to 'acquire new lands to settle the surplus population, to provide new markets for the goods produced by them in the factories and mines'. This was not merely 'a solution for the social problem', but the only way to avoid 'a bloody civil war'. In other words, he maintained, 'if you want to avoid civil war, you must become imperialists.'[19]

The empire in the epoch of imperialism: Britain

The ending of the British industrial monopoly did not by any means mark the end of British world hegemony. Just as the commercial superiority of the Dutch in the seventeenth century did not lead to the United Provinces achieving global political dominance, so the loss of industrial supremacy did not mean the sun had set on the British empire. The political role of the empire was still to endure throughout an entire epoch.

Initially, the industrialisation of continental Europe that began in the 1860s aided the continuation of economic growth in Victorian Britain. This period saw the empire flourishing to its fullest extent. As the largest importer of raw materials, Britain shaped world markets with its demand. The British empire in 1870 possessed a merchant navy with a tonnage 12 per cent greater than that of the commercial fleets of all other European countries combined. Its industrial installations smelted 53 per cent of all the iron and steel produced in the world, and furnished almost half of all the textile goods. The growth in the economy of the unified Germany was seen at first as a positive factor, since the expanded market meant increased sales for British products. Britain acted as the global creditor, including with relation to the quickly growing economy of the United States. Even on the eve of the First World War Britain accounted for 44 per cent of world capital investments.[20] The country's cultural influence, far less important in Europe during the first half of the nineteenth century than that of France or even Germany, steadily increased. In London in the Victorian era, it was proudly declared that English was 'becoming the language of the world'.[21]

Paul Kennedy in his book *The Rise and Fall of Great Powers: Economic Change and Military Conflict from 1500 to 2000* notes that the British empire in the mid-nineteenth century acted in a geopolitical vacuum – it had no serious rivals on the global level between 1816 and the 1880s. The USA experienced the Civil War and its aftermath. French military might was significant only on land, and the evolution of French capitalism had transformed the country from a rival of Britain to a junior partner. The result of this geopolitical disposition of forces was the 'splendid isolation' of Britain. 'Hence the pleasant situation occurred in which Britain's naval superiority rose while her expenditure on the fleet fell or was at least kept steady.'[22] The British bourgeoisie could allow itself a unique combination of overwhelming military might and relatively low military expenses. Defence spending made up only 2–3 per cent of gross domestic product: 'The size of the British economy in the world was not reflected in the country's fighting power.'[23]

In the period between 1860 and 1890 the only power whose development aroused any concern in London was the Russian empire. In Russia, liberal economic policies were again replaced by protectionism. Meanwhile, the war of 1877–78 in the Balkans showed that St Petersburg had recovered from its defeat in the Crimean War and was seeking as before to improve its position in the Black Sea basin. Its victory over the Turks, achieved this time on its own, had not been without difficulty. But by the end of the war the Ottoman empire was on the verge of destruction, and Russian forces were on the outskirts of Istanbul. Further intervention by British and French diplomacy, backed by a demonstration of naval strength, was needed to save the Turkish capital. But even from this crisis, Britain managed to extract the maximum advantage. In exchange for British guarantees of security, Turkey surrendered Cyprus, which became a base for the Royal Navy in the Eastern Mediterranean. The conditions of the Treaty of San Stefano, dictated to the Turks by the Russian military, were revised. In Russia, memories of the Crimean War remained fresh.

No longer the sole country in its class, Britain remained the first among equals, and was recognised as such by all other participants in world processes. But as the industrial strength and colonial positions of Germany grew more potent, concern began to be felt in London.

By the time when the 'scramble for colonies' began, Victorian Britain already had ample territories, and its traditional policy was oriented less at territorial control than at retaining and developing its commercial pre-eminence. But active colonial expansion on the part of other powers, above all the quickly developing Germany, forced the British to make additional efforts to expand their own empire. Hence the conquest of Kenya and other territories in East Africa resulted not so much from London's own plans as from the need to restrict the Germans, who had gained a base in Tanganyika.[24]

Although the situation in the world was changing, the British ruling class remained unshakeably convinced that the country's dominance of the seas guaranteed its strategic superiority over any possible adversary. In January 1904, however, Halford Mackinder delivered a lecture to the Royal Geographical Society in which he warned of the end of the 'epoch of Columbus' and the beginning of a new era.[25] From then on, industry and railways would be more important for the might of the state than powerful navies: 'The successful powers will be those who have the greatest industrial base.'[26]

The new strategic importance of railways was only fully revealed during the First World War. Earlier, the supremacy of the British fleet had guaranteed that even with comparatively small forces, the imperial generals could always be the first to appear, at the necessary time and place, and that they would invariably hold the initiative. Now, it was easier to move reinforcements by land than by sea. But even before the military implications of massive rail construction had come to be understood, its economic results were making their effects felt, dramatically accelerating the industrialisation of America and Germany.

American imperialism

In February 1898 the administration of William McKinley made use of the explosion of the American battleship *Maine* in Havana harbour as a pretext for intervening in the affairs of the Spanish colonies, where for some years a war for independence had been raging. The explosion of the American warship remained unexplained, marking the beginning of a tradition of strange incidents setting off American military actions abroad (from the sinking of the *Lusitania* in 1915 and the Tonkin Gulf incident of 1964 to the attack by terrorists on the World Trade Center in New York in 2001).

The US government declared itself the defender of Cuba, insisting that it disclaimed 'any disposition or intention to exercise sovereignty, jurisdiction or control over the said island except for the pacification thereof'.[27] This promise was formally observed – in the case of Cuba, but not of the Philippines or Puerto Rico, also occupied by the Americans in the course of the war. On the basis of such declarations, future US President Woodrow Wilson in his *History of the American People* even concluded in retrospect that where Cuba was concerned, 'intervention had come, not for the material aggrandizement of the United States, but for the assertion of the right of the government to succor those who seemed hopelessly oppressed, to recover the peace and order of its coasts, to free its trade ... '.[28]

In reality, the USA was of course an aggressive imperial power from the moment of its birth, and it was the need of the American elites for independent expansion that predetermined not only their resolve to part ways with Britain, but also the ability of the ruling groups of north and south to unite and to work out a common project of independence. Robert Kagan observes reasonably enough that the shift of US policy in the direction of imperialism in 1898 did not by any means involve a break with national traditions, as maintained by opponents (and even a few supporters) of the course being pursued. To the contrary, 'it grew out of old and potent American ambitions', already manifested by the founding fathers.[29] For American public opinion, however, the war with Spain was a moment of truth, when masses of citizens who had sincerely believed in republican values suddenly recognised the imperialist character of their own state.

Defending the need for colonial expansion, the American ruling groups simultaneously stressed that their actions were to an important degree forced on them, and that American colonialism would be quite different from that of the Spanish, British and French. The annexation of the Hawaiian islands, for example, was justified on the basis that 'if we did not take Hawaii England would'.[30] Assessing the prospects for the future American colonial empire, the liberal-progressive newspaper *The Nation* stated: 'British rule in India in the first instance was the despotism of a private trading company irresponsible to the last degree. We have nothing in our system of government which corresponds to it. We have no way of ruling a dependency except by the ballot.'[31] Such colonialism could only be of benefit to those subjected to it, just as the victory of north over south in the Civil War and the subsequent policy of Reconstruction was an undivided blessing to the conquered.

> We must undertake in Cuba what we undertook in the South thirty three years ago. It will be nothing short of reconstruction, but it will be more difficult than reconstruction in the Southern States was, because it must be imposed upon a people who do not speak our language, who do not think our ideas, and who will be sure to hate us if we try to coerce them.[32]

Declaring war on Spain, the USA easily overran Cuba and Puerto Rico. In the Philippines, however, it encountered active resistance from the very insurgents it had arrived in order to defend. A colonial administration was installed in the Philippines and Puerto Rico. Guam, a southern island in the archipelago of the Marianas, which had been subject to the Governor-General of the Philippines, was transferred to the United States under the Treaty of Paris, and in February 1899 Spain sold the remaining Mariana Islands to the German empire.

According to various assessments, the colonial war begun by American forces in the Philippines cost the local population from 200,000 to a million lives. As the Russian historian V.V. Sumsky notes, 'the counterinsurgency methods which the Americans used in Vietnam during the second half of the twentieth century were first tried out, and with frightful savagery, in their Asian colony.'[33] The success of American colonial policy, however, was guaranteed not only by the punitive operations, but in the first instance by the collaboration of the local bourgeoisie, which readily supported the new bosses. In 1900 the US authorities set about organising a system of representation which allowed for participation by the local elites in colonial rule.[34]

Woodrow Wilson was quite open in explaining the policy shift the USA had carried out:

> It had turned from developing its own resources to make conquest of the markets of the world. The great East was the market all the world coveted now, the market for which statesmen as well as merchants must plan and play their game of competition, the market to which diplomacy, and if needed be power, must make an open way. The United States could not easily have dispensed with that foothold in the East which the possession of the Philippines so unexpectedly afforded them.[35]

For the sake of this, the Americans had even had to sacrifice certain ideals, and abandon principles, that had been 'professed by every generation of their statesmen from the first'.[36]

As American colonial expansion developed, the tone of the press changed, and illusions were dispelled concerning the particular democratism of the American empire. On the pages of *The Nation,* idealism was replaced by pragmatism:

> If we are going to annex and rule over countries the population of which differs from us in race, religion, language, in history and every variety of antecedent, and who will probably hate us and treat our rule as a 'yoke', we shall have to get administrators ready, as well as guns and ships. We shall have to do what the other conquering and colonizing nations do, what England does, what Russia and Germany do.[37]

Of course, the question of how to reconcile republican values with imperial ambitions could not be totally ignored by the liberal wing of public opinion. The answer provided by commentators in those years was cynically straightforward: there would be no such reconciliation. If the British parliamentary system and the French republic could ignore this contradiction, crushing the resistance of the local populations in Madagascar and the Sudan, why could American democracy not act in exactly similar fashion in the Philippines and Puerto Rico? 'It is indeed, a diffi-cult feat for democracy to swallow its fine words about the rights of man and go brutally ahead on the supposition that Malagasy and Sudanese and Philippine

Islanders have no rights which a conquering republic is bound to respect, but democracy is no more obliged to be consistent, when it does not want to, than any other form of government ... '[38]

By no means all citizens of the American republic, of course, shared so pragmatic a view of the matter. On 19 November 1898 the Anti-Imperialist League was founded in Boston, followed by the rise of analogous bodies in all states. A year later these groups had a total of around a million members. In October 1899 the American Anti-Imperialist League was established on a national basis. The leading role within the league was played by the liberal intelligentsia and by members of the petty-bourgeois 'populist' opposition. The league spoke out against the Treaty of Paris, under which the Philippines and Puerto Rico had come under US control, and after the ratification of the treaty in February 1899 called for an end to American intervention in the Philippines, demanding that the archipelago be granted independence.

Among the ideologues of the league was the famous writer Mark Twain, who stated his determined opposition to 'having the eagle put its talons on any other land'.[39]

By 1901, however, the activity of the league had gone into decline. Unable to compel changes to the government's course, the movement was obliged to reconcile itself to the consequences of US actions. During the First World War the Anti-Imperialist League did not speak out against US participation in the conflict, though some of its members expressed disagreement with the administration's policy. In 1921 the league was dissolved. While its legacy had a certain influence on the ideology of the American left, the league left almost no trace on American mass consciousness, for which the contradiction between the democratic functioning of domestic politics and anti-democratic practices in foreign policy was not a topic of serious consideration until the Vietnam War period of the late 1960s.

The conquered Philippines, meanwhile, became a base for American expansion in East Asia.

In 1884 the Chinese government suffered defeat at the hands of France, and in 1895, of Japan. These military setbacks created the conditions for a social explosion. The floods of 1898 were followed by the popular uprising of the Boxers, which soon turned against the foreign presence in the country. In 1900 the Boxers killed the German envoy to Beijing, along with large numbers of other Europeans and Chinese Christians. This provided the pretext for a further intervention, in which French, Austrian, Italian and Russian forces all participated alongside the Germans and British.

The American public had been well primed to support participation in the carving-up of China.

The acquisition by the USA of its own colonies in the course of the Spanish–American War forced American bourgeois opinion to re-evaluate the actions of other colonial powers. British colonial practice was now presented in a positive light, while the need for collaboration between the two powers was no longer justified on pragmatic grounds, but on the highest considerations of principle. While the Americans concerned themselves with developing democracy in the former Spanish colonies, the mission of the British empire lay in spreading enlightenment in Asia. Hence any weakening of Britain's position in the East 'would mean rolling back the tide of civilization for at least a century'.[40]

It was not only the British who were styled as agents of civilisation. In 1900 the American newspaper *The Nation* noted with envy and admiration that in conquering Manchuria, Russia had 'acquired one of the richest provinces of the world'.[41] Like other acts of colonialist predation, the Russian expansion would be exclusively to the benefit of the subjugated people, and under the power of the Romanovs Chinese barbarism would yield to civilised Russian ways: 'Russia will surely introduce into this region a higher civilization, and in the wake of her rule will spring up better established order and prosperity is sure to attend it.'[42]

These hopes, however, were not to be borne out. The dividing-up of booty in northern China turned into a war between Russia and Japan. Crushing the Russian forces on land, the Japanese concluded the war of 1904–5 with a naval victory in the Straits of Tsushima and the capture of the fortress of Port Arthur. For Russia, the outcome of the war marked the beginning of an epoch of revolutionary convulsions, and for Japan, signified its emergence as a new imperialist power.

For America, the Japanese success meant the appearance of a new and unanticipated rival, with which a bloody conflict lay ahead.

Notes

1 *Chambers's Encyclopaedia*, Vol. 5, p. 377.
2 E. J. Hobsbawm, *The Age of Empire, 1875–1914*, London: Weidenfeld and Nicolson, 1987, pp. 37–8.
3 K. Marx and F. Engel's, *Sochineniya* [Works], Vol. 25, part 1, p. 263.
4 A. Shubin, *Velikaya depressiya i budushchee Rossii* [The Great Depression and the future of Russia], Moscow: Yauza, 2009, p. 9.
5 Hobsbawm, *Age of Empire*, p. 66.
6 Ibid., p. 14.
7 B. Moore and H. Van Nierop, *Colonial Empires Compared: Britain and the Netherlands, 1750–1850*, Aldershot: Ashgate, 2003, p. 4.
8 See H. Magdoff, *Imperialism: From the Colonial Age to the Present*, New York: Monthly Review Press, 1978. pp.19, 35.
9 See V.I. Lenin, *Polnoe sobranie sochineniy* [Complete works] (5th edition), Vol. 27, p. 434.
10 G. Blue, M. Bunton and R. Croizier (eds), *Colonialism and the Modern World. Selected Studies*, Armonk/London: M.E. Sharpe, 2002, p. ix.
11 Typical here are the works of Frantz Fanon. See F. Fanon, *Peau Noire, Masques Blancs*, Paris: Editions du Seuil, 1952.
12 A.N. Porter and A.J. Stockwell (eds), *British Imperial Policy and Decolonization, 1938–64*, London: Macmillan Press, 1987, Vol. 1, p. 5.
13 Blue et al., *Colonialism*, pp. vii–viii.
14 *Istoriya, sotsiologiya, kul'tura narodov Afriki* [History, sociology and culture of the peoples of Africa], Moscow: Nauka, 1974, p. 265.
15 Lenin, *Polnoe sobranie sochineniy* (5th edition), Vol. 27, pp. 386–7.
16 Ibid., p. 381.
17 Ibid., p. 380.
18 Lenin, *Polnoe sobranie sochineniy*, Vol. 27, p. 344.

19 Quoted in R. Palme Dutt, *The Crisis of Britain and the British Empire*, London: Lawrence & Wishart Ltd., 1957, p. 79.

20 See V.S. Malakhov, *Gosudarstvo v usloviyakh globalizatsii* [The state under the conditions of globalisation], Moscow: KDU, 2007, pp. 76–7.

21 *The Federation of the British Empire*, London: Gibbs, Shallard & Co, 1886, p. 7.

22 P. Kennedy, *The Rise and Fall of British Naval Mastery*, London: Penguin, 2004, p. 178.

23 P. Kennedy, *The Rise and Fall of Great Powers. Economic Change and Military Conflict from 1500 to 2000*, London/Sydney/Wellington: Unwin Hyman, 1988, p. 153.

24 *Istoriya, sotsiologiya, kul'tura narodov Afriki. Stat'i pol'skikh uchenykh* [History, sociology and culture of the peoples of Africa. Articles by Polish scholars], Moscow: Nauka, 1974, p. 255. It might be said that the logic of the European powers in East Africa in the late nineteenth century remained identical to that of the Portuguese conquerors in the time of the Estado da India.

25 *Geographical Journal*, April 1904, XXIII (4).

26 Ibid., p. 441.

27 Quoted in W. Wilson, *A History of the American People*, New York/London: Harper & Brothers, Vol. 5, p. 274.

28 Ibid., p. 274.

29 R. Kagan, *Dangerous Nation. America and the World, 1600–1898*, London: Atlantic Books, 2006, p. 416.

30 *The Nation*, 66 (1708): 216, 24 March 1898.

31 *The Nation*, 66 (1707): 199, 17 March 1898.

32 Ibid.

33 V.V. Sumsky, *Fiesta Filipina*. M.: «*Vostochnaja literatura*», 2003, book 1, p. 329.

34 For a more detailed treatment see ibid., pp. 323, 329 etc.

35 Wilson. *History of the American People*, Vol. 5, p. 276.

36 Ibid., p. 294.

37 *The Nation*, 66 (1716): 377, 19 May 1898.

38 Ibid., p. 375.

39 *New York Herald*, 15 October 1900.

40 *The Nation*, 66 (1716): 375, 19 May 1898.

41 *The Nation*, 71 (1837): 207, 13 September 1900.

42 Ibid.

10

THE CRISIS OF HEGEMONY

Politicians and economists in the mid-nineteenth century, just as in the first years of the twenty-first century, were convinced that the internationalisation of capital and the development of trade ties would bring about peace and prosperity. 'Liberal bourgeoisie of that age,' Palme Dutt wrote ironically in 1936, 'even while they pursued the policy which corresponded to the interests of their domination and maximum exploitation of the world, believed that the realisation of the goal of universal free trade and international capitalist relations at which they aimed would shatter national frontiers and lead to world peace, harmony and unity ... '[1]

In reality the politics of global integration, pursued through the joint efforts of major world powers, did not lead to the disappearance of the contradictions concerned. To the contrary, these contradictions took on an unprecedented scale, intensity and complexity.

Evaluating the prospects for imperialism, Lenin referred correctly to the unevenness in the development of the leading Western countries: 'There cannot be uniform development of separate enterprises, trusts, industrial sectors or countries under capitalism.'[2] The accelerated development of Germany and America, catching up with and outstripping the old European powers, brought about an inevitable redistribution of influence, roles and resources.

Fortunately for Britain, the claimants to the leading world role had to deal not only with the old hegemon but also with one another, and also with such rising regional powers as Russia and Japan. The ruling classes of the USA and Germany worked out two counterposed strategies with relation to Britain, and it was the collision of these strategies that to a significant degree determined the course of the conflict between the imperialist powers in the twentieth century.

The German strategy was tough and aggressive. It looked toward confrontation, the seizure of colonies and the undermining of influence. Even if the main object of the aggression was not Britain but Germany's continental neighbours, Russia and France, the British ruling class was in no doubt that its global hegemony was under threat. The empire was thus prepared to defend French, Belgian and Russian interests with unexpected resolve and unselfishness.

By contrast, American strategy in the context of the German challenge consisted of supporting Britain. Throughout the twentieth century the USA showed a consistent readiness to act as Britain's partner and defender, displaying no less loyalty and disinterestedness with regard to London than the latter did in relation to Paris. But the gradually ageing empire, besieged by its enemies, was turning into a hostage of its ally.

The German challenge

'When one compares Germany's most important economic indices,' the Soviet historian V.I. Dashichev wrote, 'the specific weight of its colonial possessions, its exports of capital and its foreign trade with its place in world industrial production, it will become clear why German imperialism was marked by a particular aggressiveness.'[3] This 'injustice' in the distribution of the global influence of European countries and peoples aroused the indignation not only of Germany's ruling class, but also of a significant section of its society. The right of the Germans to expand their 'living space' became understood and approved even among social democrats. If the solving of the 'social question' was linked to the expansion of empires and the seizure of colonies, did German workers not have the same right to material prosperity as their colleagues in Britain and France?

On the eve of the First World War the German General Friedrich von Bernhardi published a book on the looming conflict. German industry, he argued, could not develop without new markets, but

> we have not the assured markets which England possesses in her colonies. Our own colonies are unable to take much of our own products, and the great foreign economic spheres try to close their doors to outsiders, especially Germans, in order to encourage their own industries, and to make themselves independent of other countries.[4]

The only way out of such a situation was through an expansion of empire. That was a goal Germans had to 'fight for, and win, against a superior force of hostile interests and Powers'.[5] The future of Germany could be summed up as 'world power or downfall'.[6]

The first attempt by German imperialism to test the strength of the British empire occurred during the Anglo-Boer War. The clash between Britain and two small Boer republics in southern Africa was perceived by European opinion as a heroic struggle by a handful of white settlers against the Leviathan of the empire. The reality was somewhat different. In 1896 German forces had been sent to Africa, prepared if need be to support the Boers in the Transvaal and the Orange Free State, while German cruisers steamed to the shores of Mozambique, gaining permission from the local Portuguese authorities for German military units to cross through their territory. The Boers prepared assiduously for war, while Germany equipped their armies with the most up-to-date weapons, including modern machine-guns and large-calibre artillery that was considerably superior to that of the British. It was this technical superiority of the Boers that explains the severe defeats that were suffered by the British forces, and that were accompanied by appalling, unprecedented casualties.

The Anglo-Boer War, like the Russo-Japanese war that followed, not only marked the beginning of a new era of struggle for an imperialist redivision of the world, but was also a prototype for a whole series of twentieth-century 'peripheral' wars in which great powers engaged in indirect conflict. Local wars figured as elements in a global stand-off.

The war in South Africa was met with a wave of enthusiasm by the populations of Britain and its dominions.[7] For the British empire this conflict represented the high point of consolidation and of a sense of internal unity. The ranks of the army fighting against the Boers were filled out by numerous volunteers from Canada, Australia, New Zealand and even India. None other than Mohandas Gandhi, the future leader of the Indian struggle for independence, helped form the Indian Ambulance Corps, in which he personally served and won a military award. After the death of Queen Victoria he headed an Indian mourning procession in Durban, and in the name of Indian subjects of the crown in Africa, sent a telegram to London expressing condolences with the royal family on the death of 'the greatest and most loved Sovereign on earth'.[8]

Under the command of General Roberts the British forces learnt to avoid head-on confrontations with an adversary whose firepower exceeded their own, and to prefer flanking manoeuvres aimed at encircling the enemy. All the major towns of the Transvaal and the Orange Free State were captured. The struggle continued for some time as the Boers, after suffering defeats on the battlefield, resorted to the tactics of guerilla warfare. But the British generals countered the partisan warfare of the Boers with their own innovation, which was also to play an important role in the twentieth century – concentration camps, in which, as British historians have admitted, no fewer than 20,000 women and children died.[9]

Nevertheless, the decisive role in ending the war was not played by repression against the civilian population, but by the ability of the British authorities to use the indigenous African population against the Boer colonists. The British did not trust the Africans, and tried to stop them gaining access to firearms, but ultimately it was the native population who decided the outcome of the struggle.

As usually happened in the history of the British empire, the suppression of armed resistance was followed in 1902 by a compromise. The Treaty of Vereeniging proved to be extremely advantageous for the defeated side. The place of the British colonies and Boer republics was taken by a new dominion, the Union of South Africa, in which the Boer elites gained decisive political influence. In 1914 South African forces, commanded by battle-hardened Boer generals, fought for the British empire against the Germans in Africa.

The next international crisis arose once again in Africa, but this time in the north of the continent. In 1830 the French had seized Algiers, and in the period of the 'scramble for colonies', had established control over Tunis. Next in line was Morocco. In 1904 Italy, Britain and Spain agreed to recognise the 'special rights' of France in Morocco, with the Sultanate destined to become a French protectorate. Germany, however, did not take part in the negotiations. In 1905 the German Kaiser Wilhelm II arrived unexpectedly in Tangier. The German monarch delivered an inflammatory speech promising support to the Sultan in the struggle against France. The General Staff in Berlin had already prepared the famous Schlieffen Plan, according to which German forces would rout the French in the space of a few weeks, before the Russian army in the east could mobilise. The French were forced to make concessions. An international congress, convened in January 1906 in the Spanish city of Algeciras, managed to avoid war. But in 1911 a new crisis broke out in Morocco. A German gunboat arrived in the Atlantic port of Agadir, and the government in Berlin announced its intention to establish a naval base there. Once again the French managed to avoid war by making concessions. Cameroon was transferred to Germany.

The war that twice had almost broken out in Africa began as a result of the murder in Sarajevo of the Austrian Archduke Franz Ferdinand. But even if the shot fired in Sarajevo had not rung out on the fateful day of 28 June 1914, Europe would still have gone to war. The ease with which a local diplomatic crisis grew into a world war resulted from the fact that all the leading powers were ready for war and all, in essence, wanted it. The economic crisis that had begun in 1914 threatened to figure as one of the most severe in world history (as the Great Depression was later to become). A war seemed the best way out.

The outcomes of the World War

The First World War almost turned into a triumph for Germany. The Schlieffen Plan came close to being successful. The plan of the British, to conduct the struggle with the help of a naval blockade and operations in the colonies, while leaving the land war to France and Russia, proved completely unrealistic. The Russian armies managed to begin military operations on the Eastern Front unexpectedly quickly, holding up the German offensive against Paris, but were made to pay for this by suffering a heavy defeat in August 1914.

The British were obliged to use their forces to save their ally, sending massive reinforcements to the continent. Thanks to the efforts of Moroccan and British forces, the German attack was halted in September; the Miracle of the Marne took place.

Throughout the war the British proved unable to turn their naval power into a decisive strategic factor. The Battle of Heligoland Bight in August 1914 and the Battle of the Dogger Bank in January 1915 ended to the advantage of the British, but the Battle of Jutland in 1916 was a clear German success.[10] The strategic consequences of this victory for the Germans, however, were the same as if their fleet had been completely shattered and sunk. The German military leaders proceeded on the basis of definite rational assessments, calculating the acceptable level of losses, while the British admirals, like the Russian generals, believed in the need to attack at any price. Hence the British navy, despite its failure, continued seeking to engage the enemy, while the German navy, despite its success, hid itself away.

Trusting to their industrial might, the German ruling groups underestimated the other factors in the struggle, relying above all on their organisational and technical superiority. Conducting a drawn-out war on two fronts proved beyond the powers of Germany, and the entry of the United States into the struggle in 1917 made the German position hopeless. The highly organised industrial society proved able to bear the extremely heavy burden of the four-year conflict, but Germany's less economically developed allies – Turkey, Austro-Hungary and Bulgaria – were a hindrance to it rather than an asset.

By the end of the war conquerors and conquered were equally exhausted. In Russia revolution was raging, with the Bolsheviks under Lenin having come to power – alarming news for all the ruling classes of Europe. Austria-Hungary was disintegrating into its component parts, the Ottoman empire was in its death throes, and the survival of Turkey as an independent state was in question. Within Germany itself, the Russian example inspired the left wing of the labour movement to determined action. But in France as well the army was demoralised, while Britain had only with difficulty survived the experience of the first general mobilisation in its history.

Against this backdrop, the United States and its President Woodrow Wilson appeared as the sole force capable of restoring peace to the old continent. Wilson's peace plan, the famous 'fourteen points', foresaw not only an end to war, but also a democratisation of international life and the self-determination of nations.

Wilson's radical-democratic declarations were aimed not only at demonstrating that a return to the old conservative order was impossible, but also at preventing the growth and spread of revolution in Europe, seizing the initiative from the Russian Bolsheviks. While the Bolsheviks called first and foremost for social liberation and for realising the class interests of workers, seeing national self-determination as one element of a more general transformation of the political world-system, Wilson's concept of self-determination, aimed clearly against the old empires, ignored the link between national and social oppression, making its appeal above all to national movements. The map of Europe became filled with new states. Poland was reborn, while Finland appeared in the north. Czechoslovakia won its independence, and Yugoslavia took shape in the Balkans.

The neo-romantic concept of the nation that had spread throughout Europe against the background of the Italian *risorgimento* and the unification of Germany perceived the people as a sort of integral, collective organism, with its own distinct history representing not the development of social contradictions, but a single process through which the national spirit manifested itself. The national territory became an essential attribute of the people, which if it lacked its own geographical space did not have an authentic existence. Just as obligatory as a condition of 'authenticity' was for a people to have its own state. When compared to actual history, this conception stood reality on its head. While in historical terms it was the development of the state that formed nations, the romantic view perceived the nation as something existing a priori (though sometimes not revealing its potential), while the need for a people to establish their own state flowed from the age-old existence of the nation.

Arising out of this philosophy was the slogan 'the right of nations to self-determination', understood as the right of a particular people to establish 'its own' state on 'its' territory. This ideology took hold of the masses of the Slavic intelligentsia in Austria-Hungary, forced the educated layers of society in Finland to make the switch from their native Swedish to the difficult Finnish language, and provided the impulse for national revival among the peoples of the Baltic, dividing the supporters of the rebirth of the *Rzeczpospolita* into Polish and Lithuanian patriots. The same ideology was ultimately to give rise both to Ukrainian nationalism and to Zionism among the Jewish population of Poland and Ukraine.

By the early twentieth century the idea of the 'self-determination of nations' held such sway in left circles that Rosa Luxemburg and the Austro-Marxists, who took a different view, were seen as dissidents among the ranks of the social democrats. Meanwhile, it could not be said that such attitudes had any basis in the theories or views of Karl Marx. Supporters of the 'self-determination of nations' invariably cited Marx's writings on the Irish question, where the author of *Capital*, referring to the British, stressed that no people that oppresses another people can itself be free. Marx, however, was addressing the question of oppression, not of some set of metaphysical, inborn 'national rights'. The problem at issue here might be solved through founding a national state, or by overcoming inequality through transforming a shared state. With regard to Poland, Marx and Engels were ardent supporters of independence, but when the discussion turned to Central Europe, they wrote of the reactionary role played by the 'non-historical peoples' whose national strivings had figured among the decisive factors in the defeat of the revolution of 1848–49 in Hungary. Marx, it follows, was neither a supporter of the 'territorial integrity' of states, nor an adherent of 'self-determination'. For Marx, everything depended on the specific conditions of social struggle and on the relationship of class forces.

Lenin, who in his pre-revolutionary works had defended the right of all peoples to 'self-determination up to and including secession' as a matter of principle, stressed repeatedly that secession and the formation of a national state was a right, not an obligation. This was the case even with regard to the everyday practice of colonial empires: 'When we advance the slogan of freedom of self-determination, *that is*, freedom of secession, we demand of the oppressors in **all** our agitation: try to retain your hold through culture and through providing benefits, *not* through coercion.'[11] While giving verbal recognition to the 'right of nations to self-determination', Lenin as a practical politician was, paradoxically, much closer to the logic of Marx and Engels than to the rhetoric of his contemporaries. Ultimately, the Soviet Union represented an attempt to solve the national question not on the basis of the romantic ideology of self-determination, but on that of a policy of equal rights and 'positive discrimination'. This policy was pursued within the framework of a state that remained a single whole, but that was transforming itself and that had altered its class nature in the course of a revolution.

While the Russian revolution offered national minorities the chance to join with Russians in founding a new state in which they would have equal rights, the liberalism of Wilson aimed at achieving the gradual disintegration of the old empires, which were to be replaced by a world of small and weak 'national states', a world in which the arbiter (and later, hegemon) would be the great and free America.

From the outcomes of the Balkan wars of 1912–13, it was possible to foresee that the practical result would be the appearance of numerous unviable and mostly authoritarian states, together with ethnic cleansing, inter-ethnic carnage, and the cultural degradation of entire regions. The new borders determined for Central Europe by the Versailles Treaty yielded the same result, but on a larger scale. Subsequently, each new wave of 'self-determinations' would inevitably have the same consequences, but this experience went unreflected on the level of political theory. The undisputed rule of the dogmas of national self-determination, both among liberals and leftists, proved one of the most effective tools of the new ideological hegemony on the global level.

The disintegration of Austria-Hungary led to the appearance in its place of 'mini-empires', multi-national states. Among these were Czechoslovakia, Yugoslavia, and even Poland, which within its borders of 1920 included German, Ukrainian, Belarusian and Lithuanian territories. The problem lay not in the fact that these societies were multinational in their ethnic make-up, but in the fact that despite their ethnic and cultural heterogeneity, they sought to organise their political structures as if they were homogeneous national states.

The new national states were constructed on the model of older ones, above all France and Germany, but having arisen in a later epoch, they encountered numerous problems for whose solving they had neither the finances nor the capability. Though they were equipped with aggressive nationalist ideologies, their sovereignty was fundamentally weak, since with few exceptions they lacked the ability to create an independent military-industrial complex. By the end of the First World War, the military-technical revolution that had begun decades earlier in the area of naval armaments had totally changed the nature of armies. Armed forces had been mechanised, and war itself had become inseparable from the development of industry. Military conflicts had been transformed into contests of industrial and transport systems. By no means all countries were in a position to produce tanks and aircraft. Advanced military equipment could be purchased (and this was to make arms exports one of the main sectors of the world market), but in the course of an actual war they had to be repaired, replaced and provided with ammunition. A country that lacked its own productive capacity could not do this independently under the conditions of a prolonged military conflict. The result was the rapid and inevitable transformation of countries with weakened sovereignty into satellites of one or another of the leading powers. After orienting itself initially to the victors of the First World War, Eastern Europe after the Great Depression – with the exceptions of Poland and Czechoslovakia – moved gradually into the orbit of German politics, thus determining the nature of later conflicts in the region. After the Second World War and the decolonisation of the countries of Africa and Asia, the same trends re-emerged with new force, with dependence in the area of military technology exacerbated by dependence on foreign economic aid and technical assistance. The newly independent states were forced in most cases to join one of the two camps of the 'Cold War', orienting either to the USA or the Soviet Union. After the collapse of the latter, the independent states created out of the fragments of the Soviet bloc were forced into similar alignments.

The democratic international order proposed by Woodrow Wilson was supposed to rest on the equal representation of countries in the League of Nations. But here the American president met with a humiliating defeat: the United States, subject to growing isolationism, did not join the League. Nor did Wilson's efforts to limit the imperialist ambitions of the conquerors enjoy particular success. France won the right to huge reparations payments from Germany, along with agreement that it could station its forces on the territory of the conquered country. The free Arab state propagandised by Lawrence of Arabia as he helped raise a revolt against the Ottomans was not established. The territories seized from the Germans and Turks were transferred to Britain, France, Belgium and Japan – though not, it is true, as colonies but on the basis of League of Nations mandates that foresaw the later granting of independence. In practice, however, the methods of rule in the mandated territories and the policies pursued there were no different from those in normal colonies. The United States expanded its overseas empire, receiving a number of islands in the Pacific Ocean under a League of Nations mandate. Various British dominions also became colonial powers, with the Union of South Africa receiving a mandate over the former German South-West Africa (the present-day Namibia), while Australia received New Guinea and New Zealand, Samoa.

The Soviet challenge to capitalism

For all the popular and attractive declarations voiced by Wilson, the achievements of his foreign policy proved extremely modest. But one of his efforts was eminently successful: the revolutionary wave that had arisen in much of Europe and that had begun to be felt in Asia was suppressed.

Revolutions erupted in Hungary and Germany, but the Hungarian Soviet Republic was smashed, and in Germany the moderate social democrats kept the process under control. The left-wing leaders Karl Liebknecht and Rosa Luxemburg were killed in January 1919, and the workers' uprising in Berlin was defeated. The same fate awaited the Bavarian Soviet Republic.

While the nationalist movements largely achieved their goals within the framework of the Versailles system, the forces of the left met with failure. But even after the revolutionary wave of 1918–19 had ebbed, the threat of mass workers' protests remained very real for the ruling classes, and required a corresponding strategy. The revolutionary process continued in China, and in Germany and France powerful communist parties arose. Left-wing currents in Italy remained extremely radical and influential, with their positions destroyed only by the fascist coup carried out under Benito Mussolini in 1922.

To an important degree, attempts to find an answer to the challenge of the Russian revolution of 1917 defined the content of liberal and social democratic politics in Europe and America throughout the entire period between the two world wars. The situation was relieved in part by the dying out of the revolutionary impulse in Soviet Russia itself, where the proletarian revolution traversed all known phases from the dictatorship of a radical party to a creeping Thermidorean coup and ultimately, the installing of a Bonapartist regime headed by J.V. Stalin. The Soviet Union, which replaced the Russian empire, shifted gradually from a foreign policy course aimed at supporting world revolution to a *Realpolitik* based on manoeuvring between imperialist powers.

Even in the form of a Bonapartist regime, the Soviet state represented a problem and a challenge for global capital to the degree to which it showed the possibility of a victorious anti-bourgeois alternative. Soviet practice exerted a growing influence on public opinion in Western countries.[12]

Responses to the Soviet challenge included the democratisation of state institutions in many countries; the granting of universal suffrage, including for women; and also efforts at reform in the fields of social welfare, health care and education. But these measures had an inconsistent and unsystematic character, and in countries where crisis and class conflict had been felt more sharply, an opposite variant appeared in parallel with the attempts at democratic reform: a tightening of the screws, dictatorship, and in extreme cases, fascism.

Politics ceased to be a monopoly exercised by the 'educated classes'. The reforms from above were aimed, as usual, at avoiding revolution from below. But the question came to be posed of the scale, specific paths and limits of the changes. The reforming of capitalism proceeded through trial and error, and the period of the 1920s and 1930s can be thought of as a time when unsuccessful attempts and serious errors predominated. It was only considerably later, after the end of the Second World War, that it was possible to speak of a transformation of capitalism arising from the 'welfare state'. For such a transformation to occur required enormous efforts, an acute struggle, and most importantly, not just changes to particular aspects of the social policy of various countries, but structural changes encompassing the capitalist world-system as a whole. Among the elements of this global process was also a change of hegemon.

An empire under threat: Britain between the two wars

After the Great Depression Britain retained its leading position in world trade, followed by the United States, whose production to a degree remained confined to the internal market. Since the economic damage suffered by Britain in the course of the First World War was far less than that borne by France and Germany, British industry once again for a short time held the dominant position in Europe.

It was after the First World War that the British empire reached its maximum extent. Its territory expanded considerably compared to the 'golden age' of Queen Victoria. In 1931 the empire occupied an area of 34.65 million square kilometres, with 485.5 million people. This was a quarter of the Earth's inhabited land surface, and home to every fourth dweller on the planet. The empire accounted for 20 per cent of the world harvest of wheat, 23 per cent of rice, and 27 per cent of cotton. It provided pasture for 36 per cent of the world's cattle and 38 per cent of its sheep, while producing 40 per cent of its wool, 55 per cent of its rubber and 100 per cent of its jute. A third of the world's tea crop was harvested on the possessions of the empire, and about a third of the sugar cane. Under its control were as much as a quarter of the world's known reserves of oil and 28 per cent of global coal production.[13]

Also worthy of note was the strategic importance of the new acquisitions. When it took possession of German-held Tanganyika, the British empire gained control of a huge and continuous swathe of Africa extending from Capetown to Cairo. The empire also derived great strategic advantages from its gains in the Near East. The mandate obtained over Palestine strengthened the British position in the Eastern Mediterranean, adding the port of Haifa to the commercial and naval centres on Cyprus and in Egypt, while possession of Iraq and the protectorate over Kuwait ensured British control over an important part of world oil production.

Writing with hindsight about this period, historians have spoken of an 'over-extended empire', or even of 'imperial overstretch'. In the same connection many authors expound a thesis that characterises the empire as a chance conglomerate of countries and territories.[14] Closer examination, however, raises doubts about such arguments.

The process of formation of any empire includes 'chance' acquisitions, resulting from unplanned tactical successes. But on the whole, all important empires, beginning with that of Rome and including even the Austro-Hungarian empire, have arisen and functioned on the basis of their own internal logic. The territories acquired have augmented and strengthened one another, and their resources have been exploited so as to consolidate the system. When changed socio-political and socio-economic conditions have undermined this internal logic, the end of the empire itself has been approaching.

The crisis of the British empire may have taken on the appearance or been perceived by politicians as 'imperial overstretch', but this was merely an illusion, a banal and superficial explanation. If the problem had really lain in the excessive extent of British possessions, it could readily have been solved through abandoning various territories and consolidating strategically important positions, just as Marcus Aurelius succeeded for a whole century in halting the decline of the Roman empire. After the First World War London without particular hesitation renounced its control over Ireland, in nominal terms granting it the status of a dominion, but in fact conceding its independence.

Moreover, if we consider how the imperial system coped with the numerous problems and challenges confronting it after the First World War, we might con-clude that its existing structure was remarkably durable. Britain was once again the sole global power. France, despite its vast colonial empire, which had also been expanded at the cost of former German possessions, was so exhausted by the war that it could not play an independent role. In Victorian times French imperialism had also played the part of Britain's junior partner; now, it was confirmed definitively in this role. Germany, defeated in the war, had lost its colonies. Russia, after experiencing revolution, laid claim to the leading role in the world movement of the socialist proletariat, but not in any way in the global capitalist system. The United States, though dramatically strengthened both politically and economically, still lacked both the military and political infrastructure that would allow it to act as a global empire.

Paradoxically for the sole global empire, Britain lacked the strength to exercise undivided hegemony on the regional level as well. In every part of the world it faced a regional power whose strength was comparable to its own or that exceeded it. On the continent was the reviving Germany; in the Mediterranean, Italy was gaining strength; and in the Pacific, Japan had consolidated its influence. On the Atlantic Ocean, the USA had strengthened its positions, and in Latin America, British imperialism conceded the dominant role entirely to the Americans.

The main problem was not a lack of resources for defending the empire, but the fact that it was becoming increasingly difficult for Britain to cope with the additional tasks that flowed from its role as world hegemon. Maintaining the empire now depended exclusively on diplomacy, on the art of constructing coalitions. This art was well known to the British elite, but in earlier times none of Britain's allies had possessed the resources that might potentially have allowed it to take the place of Britain in the global capitalist system. Now things were different.

The greatest problems had arisen in India. Since the late nineteenth century local political parties had been able to influence events in the country through elected municipal authorities and through the legislative assemblies of the provinces, despite lacking any real ability to control the executive power. By the beginning of the First World War the Indian National Congress was maintaining completely loyal, even friendly relations with the colonial administration, whose higher ranks attended its deliberations. In 1914 the Congress adopted a resolution calling for 'a speedy victory for the Empire'.[15] The resolution was supported by Gandhi, who by this time had returned from Africa.

From 1916 the key question of Indian politics became the demand for self-determination – Home Rule (by analogy with Ireland, where this demand had already been raised in the nineteenth century). This by no means excluded a loyal attitude to Britain. Gandhi explained that his task, to 'gain a status of full equivolity for my countrymen', in no way contradicted the development of the empire.[16] The radicalisation of the anticolonial movement was a result of the crisis of the First World War, with the influence of the Russian revolution playing a far from minor role. The Indian bourgeoisie used the mass movement to strengthen its position in relation to the British authorities, but also experienced a certain unease at what was occurring.

In the form it had assumed under Queen Victoria, the Indian colonial regime, the Raj, disappeared long before the official proclamation of independence. As Lawrence James notes, after 1919 the old order was replaced by a strange, multi-layered system 'shaped by Westminster politicians, run by Indians and supervised by a dwindling band of British officials'.[17] In 1917 the British government issued a Declaration of Policy, known also as the Montagu Declaration in honour of the British Secretary for Indian Affairs Edwin S. Montagu, in which it promised India self-government, but named no specific date and provided no list of specific reforms, stating merely that 'substantial steps in those directions should be taken as soon as possible'.[18] From 1919 some administrative functions in the provinces were transferred to Indian ministers chosen by the legislative assemblies. India took part in the discussions at Versailles, signed the peace treaty, and was represented in the League of Nations. Dominion status, analogous to that of Australia and Canada, was promised but again, no date was specified. During the subsequent years no new steps followed.

The transitional system that was established following the reforms of 1919 did not satisfy the demands of anyone in full, but gave rise to a 'catastrophic equilibrium' in which none of the major forces, either in Britain or in India, was able to alter the situation sharply in its favour and in the process, to impel the government to enact a new series of reforms. To conservative ideologues of empire any retention of British power in India had not only economic, but also political and symbolic significance. Meanwhile, the Indian bourgeoisie and middle classes insisted on a constantly growing list of concessions. The system of government was clearly lagging behind the demands of a changing society, and the colonial bureaucracy confronted growing problems. Against the background of a dismal political situation a radicalisation of the masses was under way, and was gradually coming to affect bourgeois public opinion as well. After the Amritsar Massacre of 13 April 1919, when troops opened fire on an unarmed crowd, killing or wounding several thousand people, the Indian opposition became radicalised, and the demand for political reform was replaced by calls for independence. The British parliament was forced to begin an investigation into the actions of Brigadier-General Reginald E. Dyer, who had ordered his forces to open fire on the demonstrators. The parliamentarians concluded that the general had been guilty of unjustified and excessive use of force, and recommended to Minister of War Winston Churchill that Dyer be removed from his post.

As British historians have stated, these events helped transform the leaders of the Indian National Congress 'from loyal subjects of the King-Emperor into implacable nationalists'.[19] There is no doubt, however, that this evolution in the views of the local politicians had causes extending far beyond their emotional reactions. The Indian bourgeoisie had grown in strength, and was demanding a higher place in the hierarchy of the empire. Denied what it sought, it began to question the imperial project as such.

In the late nineteenth century the wave of nationalism that had arisen in Western Europe engulfed Eastern Europe as well, and by the 1920s had rolled on to the colonial countries of Asia. As Benedict Anderson observes, this nationalism was inspired to an important degree by imperial propaganda itself, and was nurtured by the education system that had been established on the Western model: 'For the paradox of imperial official nationalism was that it inevitably brought what were increasingly thought of and written about as European "national histories" into the consciousnesses of the colonized – not merely via occasional obtuse festivities, but also through reading-rooms and classrooms.'[20] In this way 'national' historical myths, constructed in Europe after the event, became a tool shaping a new self-consciousness among the intelligentsia and elites of the conquered peoples of the periphery.

In India, Gandhi was able to develop his own specific version of nationalism that appealed to traditional values. Despite having a reputation as an idealist, Gandhi was a successful practical politician who understood the advantages of the tactic of non-violent resistance. This approach allowed him and his supporters to conduct a struggle against the British authorities while remaining within the bounds of legality. More than likely, an attempt at an armed uprising would have led not only to acts of repression by the colonial regime, but also, and as the history of the sepoys showed convincingly, to a civil war within Indian society itself.

Gandhi, with his critique of industrialisation and Western society, was precisely the figure whom the increasingly powerful Indian bourgeoisie needed if they were to draw the traditional masses onto their side. He promised the people an independence different from the one of which other leaders of the Indian National Congress dreamed. He condemned earlier concepts of independence as 'English rule without Englishmen'.[21] But Gandhi's propaganda, which promised to transform society in the process of decolonisation, did not take the form of a distinct political alternative. The appeal to the traditions and ideals of the masses became a factor in the political struggle, and influenced its methods, but did not in any way affect its goals.

On Gandhi's initiative a boycott campaign was begun, aimed against British institutions and goods in India. This campaign included a rejection of honorary titles and offices, along with boycotts of official receptions; of British schools and colleges; of courts and elections; and finally, of foreign goods. The campaign that began in August 1920 continued until February 1922, when Gandhi himself called a halt to it because the protests had begun taking on a violent character. Effectively, the revolt by the Indian national movement against the colonial yoke turned at its height into an uprising against the international market.

The Great Depression

With the departure by Russia from the capitalist world-system, the relationship of forces within the system changed fundamentally. Britain's field of manoeuvre was sharply restricted, and favourable conditions were created for the rise of America. Following the war, new markets appeared for American products. Between 1914 and 1924 the gold reserves of the United States grew from $1,924 million to $4,499 million, a sum calculated by economists to amount to about half of the world's total gold holdings.[22] Between 1913 and 1929 the US share of world industrial production more than doubled, reaching 43 per cent, while the country's national wealth increased by 40 per cent.[23] It is true that by the mid-1920s, as output in the European countries started to revive, American exporters began encountering difficulties in selling their goods. But no-one then understood the real significance of what was occurring.

As in the case of all previous crises, the narrowness of the internal markets of the leading Western countries made depression inevitable. After the period of recovery had ended, the world-system again found itself in much the same circumstances as before the First World War, when the conflicts between the leading Western powers unfolded against a background of shrinking demand for industrial products.

The crisis, it follows, was just as much social as economic. The problem did not lie in the fact that the reviving European economies were creating competition for the Americans, but in the fact that the opportunities for economic growth within the existing social model were fundamentally limited. The result was that industrial growth, while causing markets to become saturated, not only failed to feed on itself but prepared the way for a crisis of overproduction.

As early as 1924 a decline was experienced, and the Federal Reserve System moved to overcome it by increasing the mass of money in circulation. But just as occurred later, in the early years of the following century, a substantial proportion of the funds did not finish up in the real sector but went into financial speculation, resulting in the appearance of successive 'stock-market bubbles'.

The disturbances in India, along with the German inability to pay reparations, exacerbated the financial problems of Britain. Bankers in the City of London found themselves acutely short of money. Seeking liquid funds, the British financiers began a massive sell-off of their American assets. The upshot came in October 1929 when the New York Stock Exchange was smitten by 'black Thursday'. Share prices collapsed, causing genuine panic. Over the next few weeks the shares quoted on Wall Street lost more than a third of their value, some $32 billion. But the end had not yet come; the decline in share prices continued almost without let-up. Over the following three and a half years the fall in production was to have catastrophic consequences throughout most of the world.

The economies of Germany and France suffered no less catastrophically than that of the United States. Somewhat better off was Great Britain, where the fall in industrial output amounted to about 10 per cent, while in Germany production declined by almost half. The crisis also dealt very substantial blows to the British empire. While the share of the colonies and dominions in Britain's exports kept growing, especially during the depression years (increasing from 34.5 per cent in 1913 to 43.5 per cent in 1930 and 46.8 per cent in 1931), the portion of British imports derived from the imperial territories did not increase, and during the years of the crisis even declined (amounting to 27.7 per cent in 1913, it came to 29.2 per cent in 1930 and 27.3 per cent in 1931).[24] The share represented by Great Britain in the imports and exports of its dominions fell noticeably. Contemporaries observed that a 'weakening of internal economic ties' was occurring within the empire.[25]

The Colonial Development Act of 1929 yielded nothing or almost nothing. The colonial elites were increasingly uninterested in maintaining the existing order, finding the conditions of imperial trade less and less favourable to them. After the crisis struck, serious anticolonial protests erupted in Africa, and nationalist moods in

India grew stronger. It was no accident that a new wave of anti-British protests arose in India at the height of the Great Depression in 1930–31.

The Westminster Statute of 1931, which markedly expanded the rights of the dominions, was supposed to unite the empire by helping to strengthen economic ties within it. This was especially important at a time when a further wave of protectionism was sweeping the capitalist world, including Britain itself. But both the dominions and the colonies, as they sought to cope with the crisis, continued to seek new markets outside the empire, above all in America.

As always occurs during crises, faith in free trade was quickly replaced by calls for protectionism. In 1926 a group of bankers from Britain and other countries had signed a 'Plea for the Removal of Restrictions upon European Trade', in which it was argued that 'economic freedom is the best hope of restoring the commerce and credit of the world'.[26] Four years later the same British bankers issued the following appeal: 'Great Britain must retain her open market for all Empire imports, while being prepared to impose duties on all imports from all other countries.'[27]

The British ruling class gradually came to reject the policy of free trade, attempting, as historians note, to lock itself away in its own commercial and financial orbit.[28] This was perfectly logical as a means of stabilising the empire. But it also signified the end of Britain as the global hegemon of the capitalist system.

Notes

1 R. Palme Dutt, *World Politics. 1918–1936*, London: Victor Gollancz Ltd., 1936, p. 85.
2 V.I. Lenin, *Polnoe sobranie sochineniy* [Complete works] (5th edition), Vol. 27, p. 417.
3 V.I. Dashichev, *Bankrotstvo strategii germanskogo fashizma. Istoricheskie ocherki, dokumenty i materialy* [The bankruptcy of the strategy of German fascism. Historical sketches, documents and materials], Moscow: Nauka, 1973, Vol. 1, p. 31.
4 F. von Bernhardi, *Germany and the Next War*, London: Edward Arnold, 1914, p. 82.
5 Ibid., p. 84.
6 Ibid., p. 85.
7 See T.C. Caldwell (ed.), *The Anglo-Boer War. Why Was It Fought? Who Was Responsible?* Boston: D.C. Heath & Co, 1965, p. x.
8 P. Brendon, *The Decline and Fall of the British Empire. 1781–1997*, London: Jonathan Cape, 2007, p. 229.
9 See Caldwell, *Anglo-Boer War*, p. viii.
10 See Kh. Vil'son, *Linkory v boyu. 1914–1918 gg.* [Battleships in action. 1914–18], Moscow: Izografus. EKSMO, 2002.
11 Lenin, *Polnoe sobranie sochineniy*, Vol. 27, p. 436.
12 A typical example of these sentiments is to be found in the book by Sidney and Beatrice Webb, *Soviet Communism: A New Civilization?* (London: Longmans Green & Co., 1947). While information on the Stalinist repressions and labour camps and on the horrors of collectivisation was unavailable in Western Europe, or was not regarded as trustworthy, news of the successes of industrial development in the USSR, of the system of free health care and education, of the rapid progress of popular education and of other achievements of Soviet society circulated widely.
13 *Malaya sovetskaya entsiklopediya* [Small Soviet encyclopedia], Moscow: OGIZ, 1932, Vol. 2, pp. 98, 100.
14 See P. Kennedy. *The Rise and Fall of Great Powers*; G. Arrighi. *The Long Twentieth Century*, London/New York: Verso, 1999; etc.

15 Cited in R. Palme Dutt, *India To-Day*, London: Victor Gollancz Ltd., 1940, p. 299.
16 Cited in ibid., p. 300.
17 L. James, *Raj. The Making and Unmaking of British India*, London: Abacus, 2003, p. 640.
18 Cited in Palme Dutt, *India To-Day*, p. 431.
19 N. Collett, *The Butcher of Amritsar. General Reginald Dyer*, London: Hambledon Continuum, 2007, p. ix.
20 B. Anderson, *Imagined Communities: reflections on the origins and spread of nationalism*, London: Verso, 1991.
21 Quoted in T. Ahmet, 'Gandhi: the man behind the myth', *International Socialism*, Summer 2009, 123: 126.
22 Palme Dutt, *World Politics*, p. 67.
23 See V. Galin, *Politekonomiya voyny. Tupik liberalizma* [The political economy of war. The dead-end of liberalism], Moscow: Algoritm, 2007, p. 333.
24 *Malaya sovetskaya entsiklopediya*, Vol. 2, p. 102.
25 Ibid.
26 Cited in Palme Dutt, *World Politics*, p. 97.
27 Ibid., p. 98.
28 D. Reynolds, *Britannia Overruled. British Policy and World Power in the 20th Century*, London/New York: Longman, 1991, p. 207.

11

THE CHANGE OF HEGEMONY

From the time of the first popular revolts in medieval Europe, every revolutionary uprising of the masses has threatened to grow into an anti-bourgeois revolution, but each time the bourgeois leaders of political life have managed to cope with the danger. The Paris Commune of 1871 showed that workers' organisations could for a certain time, if only briefly, take power under socialist slogans. Meanwhile the Russian revolution, though unable to bring socialism to realisation in the form in which the revolutionaries proclaimed it, provided the whole world with an example of the political success of a radical anticapitalist party.

By the end of the 1930s, however, the socialist alternative in Europe had met with defeat. The failure of the Spanish revolution and the defeat of the Communist Party of Germany bore witness to the fact that despite the hopes of many on the left, the social crisis that arose out of the Great Depression had not ended in a new revolution but in the triumph of reaction.

The sharper the social conflicts within each individual country, the stronger was the temptation to solve them through foreign expansion. On the ideological level this demand for expansion was best expressed by fascist or Nazi ideology. A wave of aggressive nationalism seized hold of the country that had lost the First World War. German public opinion had felt the defeat keenly. Meanwhile in Italy, which formally had been in the camp of the victors, it was recalled that the army had managed to lose all its battles.

Imperialism and fascism

Recovering from the political and economic crisis associated with the military defeat, bourgeois circles in Germany sought a means of regaining their earlier position in the world. The rise to power of Hitler and his national socialists allowed several problems to be solved simultaneously. It was possible now to put an end to the Communist threat, to guarantee the loyalty of the masses, to placate the working class with social reforms, and to prepare for a new war.

By the mid-1920s the relationship of forces between the countries that laid claim to the role of global hegemon in place of the weakened British empire had changed. The loss by Germany of its colonies was seen in Berlin as a major strategic problem, seriously reducing the prospects for industry. The First World War and the Treaty of Versailles had put an end to the German economic presence outside the borders of Europe. In 1913 foreign investments by German capital had amounted to 35 billion marks. In terms of this index Germany was effectively tied with France (36 billion) for second place in the world after Britain (75 billion), and outstripped the United States (13 billion). By the mid-1930s, however, the picture had changed dramatically. The USA had now taken the lead, with 102 billion marks. Britain (71 billion) was in second place, while Germany was at the end of the list, with its foreign investments amounting to no more than 10 billion marks. Compared to their pre-war level the foreign investments of the United States had increased by some eight times, outpacing those of Britain, while German foreign investments had declined over the same period by more than 70 per cent.[1]

If Germany was prepared to reconcile itself to the loss of its overseas colonies, this was only on the condition that these losses were made up by opportunities for expansion in Eastern Europe. Nazi leaders spoke of this openly and clearly. Addressing Wehrmacht generals soon after taking power, Hitler explained his political perspectives to them as follows: 'The British are more afraid of economic threats than of military power. Our eighty-million-strong people have solved their ideological problems. Now they have to solve their economic problems ... This cannot be done without invading foreign states and seizing the property of others.'[2]

The new continental empire did not have to be built through taking back the former colonial possessions. Eastern Europe was closer and, it seemed, easier prey. The Anglo-French elites, however, could not allow an uncontrolled expansion of Nazi Germany to the east. Such an expansion might seem to remove a direct threat to British and French colonial possessions, but at the same time it would radically alter the general global relationship of forces. The transformation of Eastern European markets into the exclusive domain of German capital would be bad news for British and French industry. For the same reason, the idea of unifying Austria and Germany aroused extreme aversion in London and Paris.

The British ruling circles vacillated between understanding the danger posed by fascism and giving way to their fear of communism. Within the British elite, alarm at the Nazi threat issuing from Germany was not by any means always paramount. Hostility to Germany was dictated less by a dislike for Nazi ideology and for the policies of Adolf Hitler than by geopolitical and economic rivalry. Meanwhile, communism was understood not only and not so much as the ideology that held sway in the USSR as the real mass movement that had developed in Western Europe. The British elite could have closed their eyes to the excesses of German Nazism had it not been for the hegemonic claims of Berlin. Similarly, they could have reconciled themselves to coexisting with Moscow had it not been for the

Soviet link with the Communist International. Understanding this, Stalin at the height of the Second World War ordered the Comintern dissolved.

Adding to the indecisiveness of the British government was the fact that it did not feel it had reliable support from the empire. When the Czechoslovak crisis broke out in 1938, the dominions gave the Westminster cabinet to understand that they were not prepared to go to war with the Germans in order to save a small state in Central Europe.[3] It is possible that British Prime Minister Neville Chamberlain was using the discontent of the dominions as a sort of political alibi when he set off to sign the shameful Munich Pact with Hitler. Little more than a year later, when war nevertheless broke out over Poland, all the dominions apart from Ireland entered the struggle against fascism. But the opposition of the dominions in 1938 was genuine, and deepened the sense of confusion in London.

While the ideological and geopolitical vectors in Britain were in contradiction, throwing the ruling class into disarray and creating numerous problems for them in the decision-making process, in Berlin these two vectors largely coincided. Conflict between Germany and the USSR was inevitable because the logic of ideological opposition coincided with the logic of geopolitical expansion, though here too events did not pass off without hesitations and contradictions. The Moscow-backed Communist movement of the early 1930s presented a threat to the capitalist order in Germany and Central Europe, helping to persuade important numbers of the corporate bourgeoisie to choose in favour of fascism – at that time the only effective political alternative to social transformation. The radicalism of fascism (and especially of German national socialism) made it possible to block revolutionary impulses in societies that had experienced the humiliations of the Versailles Treaty, the horrors of the Great Depression and sharp outbursts of class struggle. But the threat of the communist alternative had been removed from the agenda in Germany by the mid-1930s, and the defeat of Republican Spain in the Civil War of 1936 to 1939 and the disintegration of the Popular Front government in France showed that the revolutionary tide had begun to ebb. At this point it became possible for the Nazi leaders in Germany to reach agreement with the Stalin leadership in the USSR, which for pragmatic reasons was in turn becoming inclined to seek a pact with Hitler. The conflict between Nazism and communism, however, was superimposed on the geopolitical conflict between German imperialism and the Atlantic world-empire – with Britain and later with the United States, which was gradually coming to act in its place. The logic of the struggle for hegemony within the world-system again brought Germany, as a continental power, back to its starting-point of conflict with Russia, only this time it was not socio-ideological but geostrategic considerations that were crucial. As in the case of Napoleon, victory over an Atlantic empire in such a conflict would only have been possible for a continental power if it had managed to consolidate its control over the entire European continent. This would have necessitated a clash with Russia. The ideological opposition between Nazism and communism would now have served a new purpose – providing a basis for mobilising the military and political strength of Europe, under the power of Berlin, for another 'crusade'.

The Germans, however, had learnt the lessons of the First World War, and this time began the war in the west after securing their rear in the east. Once the pact with Stalin had allowed Hitler to solve this problem, the Second World War became a reality. After Poland came the turns of Denmark, Norway and France.

The defeat of France in 1940 doomed the British empire not so much to isolation as to the inevitable loss of its global role. Victory over Germany on a one-to-one basis was theoretically possible for the British even in this period, but only if they concentrated all their resources in Western Europe. This meant the inevitable twilight of the empire.

Once again, the maritime strategy failed; it proved impossible simultaneously to wage total war against Germany in Europe and to defend British imperial interests throughout the world. By the beginning of the Second World War the renowned Royal Navy, whose main forces had earlier been concentrated in the North Sea and the Mediterranean, was forced to carry out diverse tasks on all the world's oceans at the same time. As a Russian military historian notes, the British navy during the Second World War waged perhaps its best-ever campaign, since 'it was forced to conduct a type of war that had not been foreseen for it even in its golden age of undivided domination of the seas. The Royal Navy was forced to fight simultaneously on three oceans: the Atlantic, the Arctic and the Indian.' To this might be added the navy's Mediterranean and Pacific operations, in which war was waged 'with no less scope and intensity'.[4]

The British empire fought heroically, and Winston Churchill was unquestionably right in terming the Second World War its finest hour. But the sun had already set on the empire, and new powers, the United States and the Soviet Union, had come to the forefront of history.

Global 'castling' – the rise of America

Hitler's invasion of the Soviet Union sharply altered the nature and scale of the war, creating a new geopolitical situation. The failure of the 'Blitzkrieg' in 1941 in practice robbed Germany of the chance of global victory, but this was still far from obvious to participants in the events concerned. Meanwhile, the future relationship of forces between the victors depended on the further course of the war.

In 1942, in the context of the successes achieved by Hitler's Japanese ally, the final attempt was made in Berlin to seize the global strategic initiative through a simultaneous attack in the Near East and in the Caucasus. The military historian Aleksey Isaev characterises the German campaign of 1942 as a 'campaign for oil'.[5] The German offensive, unleashed simultaneously in the Caucasus and Africa, was the last 'global project' of German imperialism.

By the late spring of 1942 the German army had reached the Volga and the Caucasus, and was at the approaches to Alexandria. The Nazi command was counting on seizing the oil riches of the Caucasus, on cutting the supply route between the Soviet Union and the outside world via Iran, and on drawing Turkey into the war. This was aimed not just at putting the Soviet Union on the brink of catastrophe, but also at creating favourable conditions for waging a further struggle against Great Britain.[6] But the German military machine had exceeded its capacities. With the rout at Stalingrad, Germany had lost the war irrevocably. Now, the main question of the war for the allies lay in determining who would reap the fruits of victory.

The behind-the-scenes rivalry of the USSR and the Western powers within the framework of the anti-Nazi coalition is well known. But alongside this contest another, far less noticeable, was unfolding – between London and Washington. To the British leaders it was already quite clear during the war that the main role in the system of world capitalism was shifting to the USA. The specific conditions of this political 'castling', however, were still not completely obvious. The role of Britain as the second great power of the West needed to be determined afresh, and the relationship of forces between the allies changed both in the latter years of the war and after it ended.

On the diplomatic level the crossroads was reached at the Tehran conference in 1943, when the American President Roosevelt actively supported Stalin in a controversy with Churchill. As is well known, Churchill urged the opening of a second front in the Balkans, which would have been perfectly feasible by the late summer or autumn of that year. Stalin insisted on a landing in Normandy, also in 1943, though all the participants in the talks understood perfectly well that this could only occur later.

From a purely military point of view the Balkans scenario had a whole range of advantages, the chief of which was that in technical terms it would be easier to implement, and a second front could thus be opened earlier. The events that had followed the landing by the allies in Sicily confirmed Churchill's suggestion that pressure on the Germans from the south could substantially ease the position of the Soviet forces. At the height of the Battle of Kursk, on 13 July (the day after the unsuccessful Soviet counter-attack at Prokhorovka), Hitler in a conference with the General Staff declared to his generals that the operation on the Kursk salient should be halted as a result of the Anglo-American offensive in Italy.[7] Field Marshal Manstein was to complain with hindsight that this decision by Hitler had 'robbed' him of an inevitable victory at Kursk.[8]

Soviet historians add correctly that even without the developments in Sicily the Germans would have lost the battle on the Kursk salient. But the events in Sicily showed that in the Mediterranean theatre of operations highly significant strategic results could be achieved quickly and with comparatively small forces. The allies had the chance to land their forces at virtually any point on the long coastline of the Balkans and Southern Italy, creating a prospective threat to Rumania, and in the case of rapid success, to the German forces on the southern flank of the Eastern Front, to Budapest and Vienna. In northern France, by contrast, it was necessary to attack a comparatively narrow area whose defence had been painstakingly prepared, and where the positions were supported by excellent rear communications.

It is usually considered that in rejecting Churchill's Balkans plan, Stalin acted on the basis of geopolitical logic, seeking to extend Soviet influence eventually to the Balkans and Eastern Europe. But he was not in the least directed by strategic considerations. Although the 'Balkans plan' would have done more to relieve the position of the Soviet forces in 1943 and 1944 than opening a second front in France, it would have done far less to bring forward the total defeat of Germany and the end of the war than a landing in Normandy. The latter move would have threatened the industrial and population centres of the Third Reich. In other words, while Churchill's plan was primarily tactical, Stalin's demands were dictated by considerations of strategy.

While Stalin had sufficient reasons for rejecting Churchill's Balkan plan, it was far less obvious why Roosevelt should have supported Stalin in Tehran. From the point of view of the general logic of rivalry between East and West, Roosevelt's positions should have coincided with those of the British Prime Minister. But the leadership of the United States in that period was primarily concerned not with holding back communism, but with seizing global hegemony from Britain.

The British historian Peter Clarke notes that long before the Tehran conference, a 'long-lasting strategic dispute' had emerged between the allies. The plans of the British Prime Minister were systematically rejected by US leaders. 'It was not just that Stalin was unavailingly pressing his Western allies for a Second Front; Churchill and Roosevelt were themselves at odds on the issue for nearly two years.'[9]

In 1942 the armed forces of the British empire were still substantially more powerful than those of the United States, but American military might was growing by the day, in a context where the dependence of the British on economic aid and weapons supplies from across the ocean was increasing. In these conditions American politicians constantly insisted that joint operations be conducted under the command of their generals, even though the latter were much inferior to their British counterparts in both experience and competence.

Through solidarising with Moscow, the American leaders systematically weakened the influence of London. The landing in Normandy definitively altered the military-political relationship of forces in the West. In the Balkans, the British with their navy, military experience and political ties might have played the decisive role, but the expensive and technically extremely complex operation in Normandy could be carried out only beneath the undisputed leadership of the USA.

The military and technical superiority of the USA was reinforced following the development and use of atomic weapons.

Japanese diplomatic codes had already been broken by the British and Americans in the middle of the war, and the Western allies were well informed about the state of affairs in Tokyo. There was no particular doubt that the will to resist of the Japanese leaders had been undermined. In 1946 American officers acknowledged that Japan would in any case have had to capitulate before the end of 1945, and that this would have happened 'even if the atomic bombs had not been dropped, even if Russia had not entered the war, and even if no invasion had been planned or contemplated'.[10] The atom bombing of Hiroshima and Nagasaki served no military purpose, but was an act of terror aimed not so much at the Japanese as at America's allies. The Russians were supposed to take fright, and the Western allies to understand the scale of the technical gap between them and the Americans. In the latter case the calculation did not prove justified; not only the Soviet Union, but also Great Britain and France, and later China, could equip themselves with nuclear weapons. But the growth of their American and Soviet nuclear arsenals during the 1960s and 1970s led to a situation in which only the USA and USSR possessed a strategic nuclear potential.

The post-war reorganisation of capitalism consolidated the new relationship of forces. A system of institutions was constructed with the goal of ensuring American hegemony. The Bretton Woods agreement established the leading role of the US dollar. This status of the American currency not only served to confirm the might of the US economy. The British pound, despite the political and financial might of the empire, had never played such a role. The global role of the dollar made the monetary policy and Federal Reserve System of the US instruments of global hegemony. The power of the dollar finally destroyed the economic unity of the British empire. The disintegration of the unified economic space, that had begun during the time of the Great Depression, was now confirmed by official agreements.

The new world order rested on a new social practice that was established during the years of the Second World War and that was continued through post-war reforms. A system of regulated capitalism took shape, with its basis in the ideas of John Maynard Keynes. State intervention and a policy of ensuring employment, measures which allowed an increase in the living standards of the working class and of the socially deprived as a whole, became a new orthodoxy that forced classical liberalism onto the sidelines. Against the background of the economic ruin that prevailed in Europe, American economic leadership was indisputable. In 1945 the United States accounted for 60 per cent of world industrial production.[11] In 1947 came the adoption of the European Recovery Program, which received the name 'Marshall Plan' in honour of US Secretary of State George Marshall who had proclaimed it. This programme envisaged extensive investments of US government funds in the Western European countries that had suffered from the war. The plan was not, however, entirely disinterested; it created orders and new markets for American industry.

The rise in wages now to be observed throughout the West brought a dramatic expansion of the market and created new opportunities for economic growth even after the problems of post-war recovery had been solved. America, as the greatest industrial power and the largest consumer market, simultaneously became both the centre of attraction and the economic locomotive for other countries.

As the Finnish economist Heikki Patomäki emphasises, this eventual agreement 'represented a partial victory of productivism over financial capital'.[12] The new system limited speculative opportunities for financial capital, encouraging investments in production.

In parallel with Western Europe, Japan was undergoing restoration as well. Its post-war economic rebirth, like the subsequent rise of South Korea, was linked directly to the dominance of Keynesian principles, both on an international and a national level. The United States not only refrained from forcing its partners to renounce defending their domestic markets, but on the contrary, viewed such policies as sensible and logical, and as according with the general perspective of defending the 'free world'.

The 'Cold War'

After the Second World War the League of Nations was replaced by the United Nations Organisation, in which a privileged position was granted to the 'leading world powers' that had won the war – the United States, Britain, the Soviet Union, China and France, the latter restored to the status of a 'great power'. The decision to admit France to this status was aimed at reducing the specific weight of Britain in the process of political reorganisation of the West.

Until the 1980s China did not play a substantial role in the United Nations, especially since its place in the Security Council continued to be held by the bourgeois government that had been overthrown by the 1949 revolution and that controlled only the island of Taiwan. As the influence of Britain and its ability to conduct an independent foreign policy declined, the UN was transformed into an arena of struggle between the United States and the Soviet Union, with the remaining countries of the West compelled to submit to American leadership.

The confrontation between the two superpowers, the USSR and the USA, began immediately after the victory over Germany, and of course resulted from the general logic of global rivalry. But it contained a further important element: it was exceptionally advantageous to Washington, since it transformed the USA into the guarantor of the security of the West. In the face of the 'Soviet threat', the capitalist countries of Europe and Asia were obliged to rally around America.

The political structure of the imperial hegemony of the United States, unlike that of earlier colonial empires, was built on a system of military bases, of military-political blocs, and later of economic blocs as well. In 1941 the USA gained access to British naval bases in the Atlantic in exchange for hundreds of obsolete destroyers. The same year, the Americans occupied the Danish military bases in Greenland and Iceland.

Following the victory over Germany the foreign military presence of the USA did not diminish, but increased. Australia, Denmark, France and Britain demanded that military bases occupied during the war be returned to them. Joining these countries were Panama and Iceland. In 1949 some bases were shut down, but the logic of the incipient Cold War required a new expansion of the American presence abroad. For waging the struggle against the Soviet Union a network of military-political alliances was created, encompassing the main zones of potential conflict: the North Atlantic (NATO), the Near East (CENTO) and the Far East (SEATO). In the longer term only NATO retained its military and political significance, but the mechanisms for the penetration of American power into the Near East and East Asia that were created within the frameworks of CENTO and SEATO continued to operate after these blocs had passed into history.

In the United States in 1947 the National Security Act established something like a parallel government, handling strategic matters including military-political relations with other countries. In this fashion, effective military-political control was combined with a lack of direct administrative-territorial control, and with an absence of direct responsibility for what was occurring.

The scale and importance of this system extended far beyond the bounds of military necessity, in the view of many scholars constituting the basis for a sort of informal empire, an infrastructure of foreign domination 'created with the apparent agreement of officials acting in the name of the current sovereign local state'.[13] In many cases, it is quite legitimate to point to the 'voluntary' nature of the military collaboration. In South Korea, for example, a decision by the Americans in 2003–4 to consider a partial withdrawal of their forces in line with the general change of the strategic situation aroused such acute displeasure within the local elites that one local expert felt obliged to publish a press article calling on them to deal with the issues 'in a sagacious manner', to reconcile themselves to a 'harsh reality', and to 'come to recognize that the primary responsibility for the defense of its country lies with the Korean people themselves'.[14]

The military-political and economic hegemony of the USA aided in the formation of local elites that were incorporated into the new imperial system no less organically than the earlier colonial elites had been, and that perceived dominance by a foreign power as a crucial condition for maintaining the existing social order and the very existence of the local state. In the same fashion, the Eastern European republics that became independent of the USSR following the disintegration of the Soviet bloc immediately sacrificed many elements of their long-awaited sovereignty to the benefit of the European Union and of the North Atlantic alliance.

The rapid growth in the number of American military bases began during the Korean War and continued during the war in Vietnam. By 1967 America's foreign military presence had reached the same level seen during the Second World War.[15] On the ideological level this new reality was justified by a doctrine according to which the system of bases was 'a legitimate and necessary instrument of U.S. power, morally justified and a rightful symbol of the US role in the world'.[16]

The geography of the American presence reflected not only the strategic priorities of the new global power, but also the scale of its influence. Many bases were closed under pressure from local governments and at the demand of public opinion. The defeat in Vietnam forced the USA to abandon its military installations in Indochina. But despite this the global network of military bases continued to grow, and the ending of the Cold War, like the victory in the Second World War, was the occasion not for a curtailing but for an expansion of America's overseas military presence. In 2008, when the presidency of the younger George Bush drew to a close, the US military presence around the globe reached its culmination:

> Officially, over 190,000 troops and 115,000 civilian employees are massed in 909 military facilities in 46 countries and territories. There, the U.S. military owns or rents 795,000 acres of land, and 26,000 buildings and structures valued at $146 billion. These official numbers are entirely misleading as to the scale of US military basing, however, excluding as they do the massive

building and troop presence in Iraq and Afghanistan over the last many years, as well as secret or unacknowledged facilities in Israel, Kuwait, the Philippines and many other places.[17]

Defending its own ideological priorities and geopolitical interests, the Soviet Union was objectively doomed to respond to the strengthening of the US global role. Revolutions in countries of the capitalist periphery, in China, Vietnam and Cuba, opened new fronts in the Cold War, whose course in the early period was not by any means always favourable to the West.

'Hot' wars were not always avoided, but now the conflicts that erupted on the periphery of the system did not expand into global armed conflagrations. The Korean War continued from June 1950 to July 1953, and several times military conflicts broke out in the Near East between Israel, enjoying the support of the USA, and Arab countries receiving aid from the USSR. In October 1962 the two superpowers almost went to war as a result of the Caribbean Crisis, when the Soviet Union tried to install missiles in Cuba. Moscow was eventually forced to abandon this attempt, while the Americans removed their missiles from Turkey.

The Vietnam War, which had begun as a struggle by Communist insurgents against the French colonialists, grew into a drawn-out military conflict involving the participation of the USA. The American defeat in Vietnam in 1975 dealt a heavy blow to US world prestige, as did the Islamic revolution which the USA was unable to prevent from coming to victory in Iran. By the end of the 1970s, however, US foreign policy had learned lessons from its failures and was taking on a new aggressive energy. The American revenge for the defeat in Vietnam came in the form of the war in Afghanistan, where the Soviet Union in turn had become involved. From the early 1980s the Cold War began increasingly to turn in favour of the Americans, since the Soviet leadership was faced with a growing shortage of resources and had begun to fall behind in science and technology.

Faced with American hegemony over global capitalism, the Soviet Union sought to establish its own parallel world-system. The main challenge the USSR presented to the West, however, was not in the area of the arms race. Throughout the early post-war years, the social programmes implemented in societies of the Soviet type continued to arouse envy in many capitalist countries, showing how a society freed from the dictates of profit and the market could solve its problems. For its part, the United States unleashed its own propaganda counter-offensive, pointing to the lack of civil liberties in the USSR and the states associated with it, while also stressing the social progress achieved by the West.

The new social contract established within the framework of regulated capitalism opened the way for social democracy to take power painlessly in a number of European countries. The victories achieved by the labour movement were impressive, but the results were to prove relatively modest. Within the framework of the mixed economy, the elements of socialism played the role of propping up the edifice of capitalism, damaged by wars and crises. A side effect of the reforms was the stabilisation of Western democracy. The compromise between democracy and imperialism that had not been attained either in the nineteenth or in the first half of the twentieth century was achieved on the basis of consumer society. The redistribution of resources between centre and periphery continued, perhaps even on a larger scale than in the era of classical imperialism in the early twentieth century, but a significant proportion of this wealth went to improving the position of workers in the countries of the 'centre'. State social programmes, in accordance with the ideas of Keynes, made it possible to mobilise funds in order to solve the key tasks with which the market had failed to cope.

The tolerance shown by American foreign policy toward the moderate left in the countries of the 'centre' (though by no means in the 'periphery') bore fruit in the form of a consolidation of Western society, whose citizens on the whole were satisfied with the conditions of the post-war compromise and with the weakening of Soviet influence. By contrast, the Soviet system encountered growing difficulties as centralised bureaucratic planning, which had showed its advantages during the years of industrialisation and war, was forced to immerse itself in the problems of developing an increasingly complex and demanding consumer society. There was not enough money to provide 'butter and guns' simultaneously. The success of the USSR in the arms race contributed to its defeat in the area of social rivalry.

Nevertheless, all the gains achieved by the West during the first thirty years of US hegemony were made possible only by its continuing control over the periphery. This control, which provided the system with indispensable resources, figured as a major strategic question throughout the entire period of the Cold War.

Decolonisation

The logic of the political mythology in the newly independent states required that decolonisation be presented in hindsight as the outcome of national liberation struggle. The paradox, however, lay in the fact that by the early 1960s, when the process of decolonisation reached its peak, anticolonial uprisings had in most cases been crushed where they had occurred at all. The defeat of the first wave of anticolonial revolts became an important precondition for decolonisation taking on the form it assumed in practice.

It is noteworthy that during the Second World War, when the French state in practice ceased to exist, the colonial administration did not encounter serious problems in any of the French territories. The expulsion of the French from Indochina was effected in the first instance by the Japanese occupation. Returning after the Second World War, the colonisers encountered a communist partisan movement that had grown up in the course of the struggle against the Japanese.

In India, a wave of nationalist agitation arose in 1942. But the slogan 'Quit India', advanced by the nationalists in the heat of the war, did not meet with universal approval even among the critics of British power. In April 1942 the leaders of the Indian National Congress bargained actively with the colonial authorities for participation in the government. The fall of Singapore had transformed the military situation in Asia. The need had arisen to defend India against a possible Japanese invasion, and this required political consolidation. After the nationalists had failed to reach an agreement with the colonialists on power-sharing, the call resounded for the British to get out of India. This demand was in clear contradiction with the need to defend the country from Japan. As a result, it could not win support from ruling-class circles in the United States who had earlier been inclined to encourage Indian nationalism. Nor did the Quit India movement receive support from the Muslims and Sikhs. Exacerbating the split between the religious and national communities, the movement prepared the way for the subsequent partitioning of the country. The Muslim League made use of the crisis to prove to its supporters the danger represented by the Congress.[18] At the same time, the leaders of the Muslim League pointed out to the British authorities their own loyalty and readiness to support the war effort, both in striking contrast with the irresponsible conduct of the Congress supporters. As a reward the League demanded firm guarantees that a separate state, Pakistan, would be established in the Islamic regions of India.

Also taking an extremely negative attitude to the demands of the nationalists was the leadership of the Soviet Union, whose lead was followed by the Communist Party of India. At a time when German armies were on the Volga, destabilising the rear areas of the British ally could not be interpreted except as treachery to the cause of the antifascist coalition. In circumstances where Indian armies were fighting Rommel in Africa and were holding off an offensive by the Japanese in Burma, on India's very border, the movement was objectively a stab in the back for the country's own soldiers – and was thus suppressed with relative ease.

Overall, the resistance encountered by the colonial regimes in Asia and Africa during the 1940s and 1950s was far less significant in its scope than in the late nineteenth century, at the height of the military expansion of Western imperialism. The British succeeded in crushing uprisings in Kenya and Malaya. The French colonial authorities were less successful; they were defeated in Indochina and became entangled in the conflict in Algeria. They were, however, able to put down a revolt by the Berbers in Morocco without difficulty. Meanwhile, troops from Senegal in Africa remained to the last among the most capable and reliable units of the French army. Little Portugal, with incomparably smaller resources than Britain or France, managed to hold onto its overseas possessions until the mid-1970s.

In the 1950s the Soviet Union was not yet playing an active role in Africa or in most regions of Asia. Moscow began to support anti-Western uprisings only in the second half of the 1960s, when it was drawn into the military-political struggle in Africa after the crisis of the new post-colonial regimes had become evident. In this period the inertia of decolonisation gave rise to a new wave of more radical liberation movements in countries which this process had not earlier affected, or where it had been blocked by local white elites – in Angola, Mozambique, Namibia, South Africa and Rhodesia.

The main reason for the rapid, and as it initially seemed, comparatively painless decolonisation was not the struggle of the masses, but the need to reconstruct the world capitalist system, and in the first instance to transfer hegemony from the British empire to the United States. At the beginning of the Second World War

Roosevelt had hinted clearly to his British ally that decolonisation was essential, calling on the British 'to recognize a world change which has taken deep root in India as well as in other countries'.[19]

The Anglo-Indian commentator Palme Dutt notes that between the nationalists and the colonial authorities in India on the eve of independence there existed 'a certain compromise alliance against the mass movement'.[20] The suppression of resistance from the masses during the social conflicts of the 1920s and 1930s was largely successful, but the price the British government had to pay for this was a steady strengthening of the political positions of the Indian bureaucracy and bourgeoisie, which in formal terms remained loyal to the crown. The problem lay in the fact that the price of their loyalty was steadily rising.

From official British documents it is abundantly clear that in 1946 and 1947 the authorities in London were less afraid of resistance from the Indian masses than they were of the discontent of the local bourgeoisie and bureaucracy, which with each passing year were becoming more and more nationalist-minded. A wave of mass anticolonial protests swept across the country in 1946, but did not grow into serious political resistance, not to speak of an armed uprising. The Indian army was true to its oath. But the moods of the educated middle class and of the bourgeoisie were no secret: these layers of society were thoroughly hostile to British rule. A paradoxical situation had arisen: the lower classes, in the view of the British leadership, were not particularly interested in the question of independence, but without the support of the local bureaucrats ruling these lower classes would be impossible, and the bureaucrats were demanding decolonisation.

After recognising the independence of India in 1947 in the form of a dominion, soon to be replaced by an independent republic, London for some time nourished the illusion that it could retain its colonial empire in Africa. Describing the attitude of the colonisers to the prospect of political self-rule on that continent, a British historian reported with touching imperial naivety: 'Africans were to be protected and a sincere sense of trusteeship characterised the British rulers; but no responsible person envisaged a time when Africans would share in the business of government.'[21]

In the 1930s British politicians had formulated the concept of 'imperial responsibility'. By that time the official doctrine included the 'obligation to promote the material welfare and general progress of colonial subjects'.[22] An illustration of this 'imperial responsibility' is provided by Indian finances during the Second World War. By 1947 Britain had run up a substantial debt to India. Despite its colonial status India, whose government was under British control, not only maintained an independent financial system, but like the USA and Canada was also able to issue credits to its own metropolis.

The slogans of 'imperial responsibility' were of course intended primarily to soothe liberal public opinion in Britain and in the most developed parts of the empire. But under conditions in which a direct and indissoluble bond existed between the political structures of the metropolis and of the colonies, it was impossible to radically alter the policies followed in the centre without at the same time affecting the periphery. This in turn meant enacting measures that were aimed, if only within the most modest bounds, at establishing a welfare state throughout the entire empire.

In London, Palme Dutt observed, supporters of retaining the empire devised 'grandiose schemes for colonial "development"'.[23] During the war the Colonial Development and Welfare Acts of 1940 and 1945 were drawn up and adopted, and a further, analogous document was published in 1950. The Labour Party, which by this time had come to power, promised in 1949 to organise a 'partnership to liquidate ignorance, poverty and disease' between Britain and its colonies.[24]

This approach would have signified an extension of the Keynesian redistributive model from the countries of the 'centre' to those of the 'periphery'. The problem, however, lay in the fact that the redistribution of resources between the 'centre' and 'periphery' of the capitalist world-system was a key condition for carrying out the shift, under way in the West, to a consumer society. To the degree to which the colonial system acquired progressive traits, it ceased to be included in the overall strategy for the progressive reforms under way in the countries of the 'metropolis'. Naturally enough, this contradiction was by no means always recognised, but it made its effects felt constantly when practical problems had to be resolved. As noted by the French historian Marc Ferro, the question of 'whether the colonies were profitable' had been the topic of sharp debates since the mid-eighteenth century, when the European powers had made the transition from establishing trading posts and settlements to outright conquest. 'Although this question had been posed long before, in the twentieth century it nevertheless became central.'[25] French legislation stipulated uncompromisingly that colonies and their administrative apparatus should be self-financing.[26] British authors state that retaining overseas possessions had become an expensive pleasure: 'With relatively reduced resources and a declining proportion of world trade, the costs for Britain of running and defending her empire were simply too great. Withdrawal enabled British governments to cut their losses.'[27]

By the mid-twentieth century it had become clear that the development of colonies required large-scale investments and the redistribution of resources, only this time from the 'centre' to the 'periphery'. In France as in Britain, the costs associated with maintaining a colonial empire had begun to outweigh the benefits. The main problem lay in the fact that the empire 'was paid for by the state, while the profits went to private capital'.[28] After the end of the Second World War, when capitalism made the shift from a regime of private enterprise to one of state regulation, the questions of state responsibility for social welfare, education, health care and employment came to the forefront.

Decolonisation proved to be the simplest, and importantly, the most conservative solution, since at the cost of losing the political sovereignty of the metropolises it made it possible to retain the economic status quo, the dominant position of the centre in relation to the periphery. Of course, the practical implementation of this policy had to contend with the cultural inertia of the old empires, meeting with resistance from the most conservative sectors of the Western European elites and also, at times, from elements of the old colonial elites themselves. But the local elites gained a historic chance to take the process of transformation into their own hands. Without them it would have been impossible to decolonise Africa and Asia, just as earlier it would have been impossible to maintain the colonial regime.

The breaking-point finally came after the Suez Crisis of 1956. When a military coup in Egypt brought Gamal Abdel Nasser to power, the question of nationalising the Suez Canal, which belonged to an Anglo-French consortium, came onto the agenda. The Western governments were indignant at the violation of property rights, and demanded compensation for the losses of the investors. Retribution was not long in coming. Israel, prompted to go to war by Paris and London, attacked Egypt. The United States did not hide its displeasure at what was occurring, moving a resolution in the United Nations demanding that Israel halt its military operations, but Britain and France exercised their vetos. The British and French then invaded the zone of the Suez Canal, explaining their actions on the basis of the need to defend navigation.

Prior to the Suez adventure, Britain's Conservative Foreign Minister Sir Anthony Eden declared that in the Near East Britain remained stronger and more influential than the United States, and that it should not fear 'to act without full American support. We should frame our own policy in the light of our interests in the area and get Americans to support it to the extent we could induce them to do so.'[29] Events showed how greatly the British government had erred. The resistance of the Egyptian army and navy was easily swept aside, but the USA and the USSR formed a common front in Egypt's support. American President Dwight Eisenhower mobilised the United Nations to oppose the British and French actions, and put economic pressure on Britain. Moreover, he dealt the empire a diplomatic blow to its very heart; as a British historian records, he 'took advantage of the hostility to the Suez operation in Commonwealth countries such as Canada, India and Pakistan'.[30]

The failure of the Suez adventure was followed, the *Economist* stated, by the 'demolition' of what remained of 'a special British position in the Eastern Mediterranean – ultimately, probably, in the whole Middle East'.[31] The decolonisation of the empire became a deliberate and consistently implemented policy of the British government. The slogan of curtailing the British presence 'to the east of Suez' was replaced by total evacuation. In Africa the first country to become self-governing was Ghana, which was proclaimed a dominion in 1957. Nigeria had received a constitution even earlier, in 1954. The only question now was the precise timing of independence.

The existence of the British empire had been indispensable as an element of the world capitalist system, providing a political and economic structure to the global market space. Under the new conditions the market lost its structural and organisational role, and hence ceased to be necessary either to British, American or international capital. After the Second World War the British Commonwealth of Nations still appeared to represent a renewed and somewhat democratised variant of the empire. But the idea of the Commonwealth as a democratic continuation of the empire proved another illusion. When Britain in 1962 declared its intention of entering the European Economic Community, it demonstrated clearly to its former dominions and colonies that it was 'running away from the Commonwealth'.[32]

The French elites had grasped the meaning of what was occurring earlier, and experienced it much more painfully. But they too were forced to reconcile themselves to the process under way. The last colonial power in Africa was Portugal, once the first to start seizing the territory of the continent. Portuguese colonialism collapsed in the mid-1970s.

The process of decolonisation was met with enthusiasm by the European left, in whose political philosophy the principle of the self-determination of nations had been a key idea since the time of the national revolutions of the nineteenth century. The question, however, was the degree to which established nations were involved, and especially, who in practice was carrying out decolonisation, in whose interests and with what goals. European left-radical consciousness lost sight of this class aspect of the question with astonishing ease, limiting itself to romantic raptures over the 'dawn of African freedom' or the 'awakening of the East'.

Decolonisation took place, on the whole, according to an imperialist scenario, exacerbating the dependency of the periphery on the centre. Contrary to the notion that had been generally accepted in the 1960s of the 'collapse of the colonial system of imperialism' in Africa and Asia, what occurred was not a retreat by imperialism, but a redistribution of power and a reconstruction of the system of control. In essence, decolonisation was yet another crime of imperialism, this time unrecognised. Western Europe twice brought the countries of the 'Third World' to ruin; the first time through colonial conquest, and the second time in the process of transition to independence.

Just as the supporters of free trade in the mid-nineteenth century managed the departure of the East India Company and the opening of the Indian market, so the national bourgeoisie born of colonialism or developing under its influence managed the departure of the colonisers a century later. Such was the dialectic of the development of capitalism. The imperial form of organisation of the periphery, characteristic of the nineteenth and of the first half of the twentieth century, was made to give way to a new system of independent states under the military-political and economic hegemony of the USA. Drawing up a balance-sheet of decolonisation a half-century later, many analysts found to their astonishment that the 'postcolonial situation was not very different from the colonial'.[33]

From the point of view of the practical results of independence for the peoples of Africa and Asia, decolonisation in many cases was a failure. The reasons for this should not be sought in particular errors or in the political collisions typical of newly independent states, nor even in their backwardness and the limited vision of the local elites (including the so-called radicals), but in the fact that colonialism from the first had simply been a means for implementing the global capitalist project. Decolonisation did not signify the defeat of this project but, to the contrary, marked its entry into a new phase. Since colonialism was merely a technical instrument of capitalist expansion, the form in which it developed *under the conditions of the nineteenth century*, ending it not only failed to resolve the problem in essence, but on the contrary, rendered the exploitation of the periphery more effective, cheaper for the Western 'centre', and better attuned to the new, altered conditions of development of the West itself.

Nationalism, as the ideology that triumphed predictably in the process of decolonisation, quickly took on a repressive and authoritarian form. Even so uncompromising and insightful a critic of imperialist culture as Edward Said was forced to state that the nationalist myths were in no way superior to the myths of Western 'orientalism', since they reduced the life of people and cultures to 'separation and distinctiveness'.[34]

Post-colonial nationalism, like any other nationalism, based its political claims on history reconfigured with hindsight in self-serving categories that allowed its adherents to present themselves as heirs to the national liberation movements of the colonial epoch. In some cases this reference to the past was 'technically' correct: the party of the Indian National Congress, as it existed in the early twenty-first century, was a continuation of the Congress to which Mahatma Gandhi and Jawaharlal Nehru had belonged, though its politics, social base and aims had changed repeatedly in the course of its existence. In exactly the same way the People's Movement for the Liberation of Angola (Movimento Popular de Libertação de Angola) which heads the government in Luanda is a formal continuation of the organisation that once led a guerrilla war against the Portuguese. But references to formal succession do not prove the main thing – the adherence of this or that party to the goal of liberating the masses.

Within the framework of the new dominant ideology any resistance to the colonial regime is interpreted as 'national'. The social dimension of history and the subtleties of the political process are totally ignored in this approach. Meanwhile, the mass protests that took place in British India and many other colonies during the period of European rule were directed not only at the colonial state but also at the existing social order, and the rejection of the colonial regime occurred not because it was imposed by a foreign power, but because it was a tool for maintaining and defending a social system hated by the lower classes of society. Only in a few cases, however, did anticolonial resistance turn into social revolution. To the contrary, the replacing of the colonial administration with 'national' authorities was very often a means of retaining, supporting and legitimising the existing order, and for preserving the positions of the local elites. Breaking the bond between the struggle of the workers in the 'centre' and 'periphery', the new nationalism undermined the basis of the internationalism and solidarity that are cardinal conditions for the success of social movements in a globalised world. National independence and decolonisation not only failed to weaken the positions of imperialism as a system, but breathed new life into peripheral capitalism where it survived the crisis. Edward Said complained justly that the energy of the mass movements that had protested against the colonial authorities was 'finally contained and extinguished by independence'.[35] It is not suprising that by the end of the twentieth century the political parties and organisations that came to power under slogans of radical nationalism in the former colonial countries had almost everywhere lost their radicalism, and had been transformed into administrators of a neo-colonial system that in many social respects was much harsher and far less responsible than the earlier imperial colonialism.

The colonial state not only arose when the logic of the development of capitalism required it, but also departed from the scene when it came to contradict this logic.

As always happens in periods when reconstruction takes place on a vast scale, the process of decolonisation was of course accompanied here and there by a loss of control, which at times provided opportunities for the development of serious revolutionary movements. The anticolonial struggles in the Portuguese colonies, where because of the drawn-out nature of the decolonisation process radical movements were able to gain mass support, in many ways resembled a revolution. In much the same fashion, the popular protests against the apartheid regime in South Africa showed that the potential existed for social transformation. But after the disintegration of the Soviet bloc and the departure of the USSR from Africa, such movements no longer set themselves any goal apart from achieving reconciliation with international capital, on any terms.

Notes

1 V.I. Dashichev, *Bankrotstvo strategii germanskogo fashizma* [Bankruptcy of the strategy of German fascism], Vol. 1, p. 30.
2 Ibid., p. 32.
3 For more detail see L. James, *The Rise and Fall of the British Empire*, London: Abacus, 2005, pp. 467–80.
4 A.G. Bol'nykh. Foreword to the book by P. Ch. Smit *Pyedestal* [Pedestal], Moscow: AST, 2006, p. 17.
5 See A. Isaev, *Kogda vnezapnosti uzhe ne bylo. Istoriya VOV, kotoruyu my ne znali* [When there was no longer the element of surprise. The unknown history of the Great Patriotic War], Moscow: EKSMO, 2007.
6 *Bankrotstvo strategii germanskogo fashizma*, Vol. 2, p. 309.
7 V. Zamulin, *Zasekrechennaya Kurskaya bitva. Neizvestnye dokumenty svidetel'stvuyut* [The secret battle of Kursk. Unknown documents bear witness], Moscow: Yauza, EKSMO, 2007, p. 569.
8 See E. Manshteyn, *Uteryannye pobedy* [Lost victories], Moscow: Voenizdat, 1957, pp. 447–8.
9 P. Clarke, *The Last Thousand Days of the British Empire*, New York: Bloomsbury Press, 2008, p. 33.
10 Quoted in P.B. Boyer, *Promises to Keep: The United States Since World War II*, Lexington/Toronto: D.C. Heath and Co., 1995, p. 32.
11 See Boyer, *Promises to Keep*, p. 37.
12 H. Patomäki, *The Political Economy of Global Security. War, Future Crises and Changes in Global Governance*, London and New York: Routledge, 2008, p. 100.
13 C. Lutz (ed.), *The Bases of Empire. The Global Struggle against U.S. Military Posts*, London: Pluto Press, 2009, p. ix.
14 *Korea Focus*, 12 (1): 6, January–February 2004.
15 See Lutz, *Bases of Empire*, p. 14.
16 J.R. Blaker, *United States Overseas Basing: An Anatomy of the Dilemma*, New York: Praeger, 1990, p. 28.
17 Lutz, *Bases of Empire*, p. 1.
18 See L. James, *Raj. The Making and Unmaking of British India*, London: Abacus, 2003. p. 570.
19 Clarke, *Last Thousand Days*, p. 19.

20 R. Palme Dutt, *The Crisis of Britain and the British Empire,* London: Lawrence & Wishart, 1957, p. 201.
21 P. Griffiths, *Empire into Commonwealth,* London: Ernest Benn Ltd., 1969, p. 292.
22 A.N. Porter and A.J. Stockwell (eds), *British Imperial Policy and Decolonization,* London: Macmillan, Vol. 1, p. 12.
23 Palme Dutt, *Crisis,* p. 287.
24 Cited in ibid., p. 274.
25 M. Ferro, *Histoire des colonisations. Dès conquêtes aux independences, XIII–XX siècle,* Paris: Seuil, 1994, p. 389.
26 C. Calhoun, F. Cooper and K.W. Moore (eds), *Lessons of Empire,* New York: New Press, p. 37
27 Porter and Stockwell, *British Imperial Policy,* Vol. 1, p. 5.
28 Ibid., p. 393.
29 Quoted in D. Reynolds, *Britannia Overruled. British Policy and World Power in the 20th Century,* London and New York: Longman, 1991, p. 207.
30 P. Brendon, *The Decline and Fall of the British Empire. 1781–1997,* London: Jonathan Cape, 2007, p. 496.
31 *The Economist,* 6 December 1956. Quoted in Palme Dutt, *Crisis,* p. 256.
32 A. Lower, *Colony to Nation. A History of Canada,* Don Mills, Ont.: Longmans Canada Ltd, 1964, p. xxiv.
33 G. Blue, M. Bunton and R. Croizier (eds), *Colonialism and the Modern World. Selected Studies,* Armonk/London: M.E. Sharpe, 2002, p. viii.
34 E. Said, *Culture and Imperialism,* London: Chatto & Windus, 1993, p. 408.
35 Ibid., p. 322.

12

IMPERIALISM WITHOUT AN EMPIRE: THE UNITED STATES

The distinguishing feature of American imperialism was the fact that the United States did not recognise itself as an empire. Of course, in the late eighteenth century when the young state won its independence from Britain, many people spoke of it as a future empire – to use Jefferson's expression, 'an empire of liberty'.[1] But even when formulated in this way, the idea of an 'American empire' did not catch on. 'Until a few years ago, most historians and commentators who wrote about empire angrily rejected any application of the concept to the United States as somehow un-American', the American historian Charles S. Maier wrote in the early 2000s.[2]

The success of American hegemony was linked to the fact that this was an imperial hegemony of a new type, with no need to impose territorial control over countries of the periphery. It became clear that decisive influence over governments could also be exercised without the annexing of territories. The hegemony of the USA involved a proclaimed but unrecognised responsibility for the entire world, unlike the case with Victorian Britain, where there was a recognised but unproclaimed global responsibility. In this sense the American world dominion that arose after 1945 has represented, in the words of a number of authors, 'organized hypocrisy', or an empire in denial.[3]

Despite the free-market ideology proclaimed by its leaders, the United States became a hegemon through the processes of regulated capitalism, and to an important degree, in the process of formation of this regulated economy. The ability of the ideological apparatus of the American elite to present the achievements of the state as those of the free market has been one of the main secrets of its success. Throughout the post-war period the system of American hegemony demonstrated its strength, sustaining and winning its struggle against the Soviet Union, restoring economic life and creating consumer societies in Western Europe and Japan, suppressing revolutions in Latin America, and undermining the global positions of the left and labour movements which were capable of posing a threat to capital in the period from 1940 through the 1960s. The system also survived the youth revolts of the new left in the late 1960s, along with counter-culture movements and the challenge of Islamic fundamentalism, which filled the vacuum in the East after the collapse of left-wing forces. But like any successful system, American hegemony was forced to deal not only with external challenges, but also with the consequences of its own successes.

Neoliberalism

The collapse of the Soviet Union not only transformed the United States into the sole global superpower, but also ended a political challenge to capitalism that had existed on a global scale. By the late 1960s the Soviet model had already ceased to be attractive as a systemic model for workers in the West, but for some time the rivalry between the two systems left open a political and ideological space which allowed the rise of new alternatives. Under the conditions of the Cold War the reformist wing of the labour movement achieved important successes in Western Europe, forcing capital to reconfigure its relations with the world of labour, to the advantage of the latter. But the decay and subsequent disintegration of the Soviet system was accompanied by a growing aspiration on the part of capital to revise the existing social contract.

Throughout its history capital has regularly made use of diverse social forms and relations, adapting them to its purposes. The regulated capitalism of the second half of the twentieth century was notable for the fact that it included elements of socialism. But the system could tolerate these socialist institutions only so long as they did not undermine the general, fundamental logic on which the system was constructed – in the first instance, the logic of the accumulation of capital. The socialist institutions and relations that penetrated the fabric of capitalist society in the course of the twentieth century had their own logic which constantly contradicted that of capitalism. In the mixed economy that was established after the Great Depression this contradiction was a life-saver, since public-sector enterprises, the institutions of the education, health care and pension systems, and the mass organisations of workers combined to complete the social and cultural work with which the market was unable to cope. But the development of these institutions and their growing strength made them potentially dangerous to capital. The post-war system of democratic regulation found itself in an impasse, demonstrating that the limits of the 'painless' integration permissible within the framework of capitalism had been reached.[4]

The neoliberal ideology that gradually gained ground among the ruling classes of the West, and then of the world as a whole, is reducible ultimately to a summons to liberate capitalism from its socialist elements. The mercantilist economics of Keynes and his followers gave way to a new order in which the logic of commercial-financial capital was once again paramount. The main tasks carried out by the systemic counter-reform were the lowering of the costs of production and the weakening of the position of labour in relation to capital.

The reduction of the cost of labour power in the countries of the centre has gone ahead as a result of the industrial development of the periphery. The technological changes that had occurred by the end of the twentieth century created the conditions for a counter-offensive by capital against labour. As in the time of the industrial revolution, rapid technological transformation had the initial effect of devaluing the skills and experience of qualified workers. The simultaneous abolition of social regulation and the rejection of the state policy of supporting employment levels brought an extremely sharp change in the relationship of forces on the labour market. The new information technologies permitted a dramatic improvement in the coordination of productive processes, allowing them to be dispersed in spatial terms. Large enterprises were replaced by smaller ones, in which the trade union organisations could more readily be smashed. Growing areas of production were shifted to countries where labour power was cheap. The mobility of capital increased, and along with it, the role of credit and of financial speculation. A new relationship of forces emerged between financial and industrial capital. While mercantilism had limited trade in order to encourage production, liberalism undermined the social base of production in order to encourage trade.

The purpose of the reforms implemented first in Britain and the USA in the early 1980s, and later reproduced with growing radicalism throughout the world, was to reduce wages while simultaneously creating new markets and increasing consumption. This aim, though seemingly impossible, was able to be realised on a global level. Opening up new territories for exploitation, capital transferred production to countries where labour power was cheap, while consumption as before was concentrated in the wealthy countries of the West. After 1989–91 the fall of the Communist regime in the USSR created ideal conditions for such an expansion. Not only had the markets of the former Soviet bloc opened up, but the vast resources of the formerly state-run economies were being stolen and sold off cheaply. After the victory of the West in the Cold War the countries of the 'Third World', lacking outside support, one after another began surrendering their positions. The international commercial-financial institutions – the World Bank, the International Monetary Fund and the World Trade Organisation – became transformed into a powerful force dictating the policies of sovereign states. Privatisation, deregulation and the commercialisation of all areas of life became the slogans of the day. China and Vietnam, which had maintained their communist façades, put their gigantic resources of labour on sale. A disciplined labour force, controlled by a harsh repressive apparatus established through the state infrastructure, permitted the rapid growth of the Chinese economy. China was transformed into the 'workshop of the world', while not as a result attaining a dominant position in the world capitalist hierarchy. The main centres of accumulation of capital remained in the countries of the West, and the levers setting the world economy in motion were still in Western hands.

Like a boomerang this process returned to the West, further weakening the remnants of the welfare state. The lowering of wages was accompanied by a systematic reduction of taxes and of the social requirements placed on business.

This was aimed at attracting mobile capital from abroad, and at aiding the growth of business activity. The British economist Harry Shutt explains:

> Inevitably this aspect of globalisation has led to a competitive lowering of taxation and other standards – commonly referred to by critics of the process as a 'race to the bottom'. It is striking that the global establishment – representing the obvious beneficiaries of this tendency (big business and the owners of capital) – has refused to recognise the ultimately unsustainable consequences of the resulting progressive damage to public services and human welfare. Perhaps still more remarkable is their collective failure to grasp that such anomie is quite as likely to deter investment as to encourage it, given the increased threat of unfair competition that it poses to entrepreneurs – not to mention the impact of deteriorating infrastructure.[5]

While the state as before implemented large transport projects, this was done at the cost of allowing secondary transport networks to deteriorate. This in turn led to the decline of the internal market and to the decay of small provincial centres – a process observed not only in Russia and other countries of the periphery, but in America as well.

The industrialisation of the peripheral countries of the 'global South' resulted in a number of leaders emerging from the pack (this was the case especially with China), while the situation elsewhere continued to deteriorate. The success of China and of the countries of East Asia worsened the position of the periphery as a whole. Taking part in a 'race to the bottom', these states lowered their taxes and collaborated in reducing wages. They were nevertheless to lose this race, with the painful and socially dangerous measures registering no positive effects.

Neoliberalism was perceived by many people in the 'Third World' as a return to colonialism, a second edition. But the principal difference lay in the fact that 'classical' colonialism was a policy that ensured the social and cultural progress of the West at the expense of the oppression and enslavement of the 'non-Western' world. Neoliberalism, by contrast, made use of the resources of the periphery to guarantee social regression in the Western world itself. While the exploitation of the periphery in the early twentieth century helped allay social contradictions in the West through a redistribution of the resources coming from the colonies, in the early twenty-first century this exploitation was becoming a means for cutting wages and undermining the social gains of working people. Similar means were employed to carry out diametrically opposite tasks. And while in the nineteenth and early twentieth century it had been possible to speak of the ambivalent and contradictory nature of the process, of the cruel and sometimes bloody price paid for the social progress of a small section of humanity, this time the contradiction was removed – along with the progress.

Against the background of the dismantling of the welfare state, Western consumer markets gradually ceased growing. Global labour resources were also limited – by the mid-2000s, the possibilities for expanding the Asian economies through the exploitation of cheap labour had mostly been exhausted. Attempts to make use of Africa as a 'new frontier' for industrial expansion were doomed by a lack of skilled workers and suitable infrastructure. Capital responded to these difficulties by maintaining Western consumption through vast credits. But this in turn brought about a redistribution of monetary resources; these were now categorically in short supply in the 'real sector', while on the financial markets wildly speculative 'bubbles' arose one after another.

As in the epoch of early capitalism, the rapidly growing state debt and its servicing acted as a mechanism for redistributing public funds to the advantage of financial capital. But unlike the situation in the seventeenth and eighteenth centuries, this debt was accumulating not against a background of the growth and development of the state, but of feverish and unavailing efforts to reduce its role in society and the economy, to strip it of its social obligations, to limit the expenses associated with it and to reduce its apparatus to a minimum. These attempts failed regularly; in other words, unlike the situation in the times of early commercial capitalism, the goals that were posed were not achieved. Private corporations followed the same trend as governments. Despite the gigantic redistribution of funds to the advantage of the private sector, private debt in most countries grew even more rapidly than state debt.

The divorcing of financial from commodity markets took place from the very moment when financial capital arose in its original form, in other words, from the fourteenth century. But while in earlier eras the disproportions accumulated gradually, by the early twenty-first century the problem no longer lay in finding ways to coordinate these processes, but in the fact that they did not converge at all. As two French scholars have noted, 'financial markets move their investments around at a pace that is out of all proportions to the commodity exchanges that not long ago underlay the basics of international financial fluctuations'.[6]

The myth of global democracy

The neoliberal ideological offensive took place beneath the slogans of the triumph of freedom and democracy, which in earlier times had been threatened not only by the 'totalitarianism' of regimes of the Soviet type but also by the bureaucratic apparatus of the Western state. The answer was the universal implanting of institutions of formal democracy on the Western model, and the no less universal privatising of public property. As the Finnish sociologist Teivo Teivainen notes, the greater the curtailing of the public sector and of the area of state responsibility for solving social and economic problems, the narrower the democratic space becomes, since specific decisions pass into the hands of private individuals and corporations that do not allow public debate.[7] Democratic discussion, when abstracted from social and economic questions, loses its content. Instead of democratic freedoms spreading throughout the world, they finish up discredited on a no less global scale.

Until about 1880 the old liberal politics in the countries of the West represented a limited democratic process within whose framework the masses had certain rights but were not admitted to decision-making. The crudest expression of this principle was to be found in the electoral qualifications that robbed workers of the right to vote, but it was also enforced through a multitude of other usages, laws and institutions. The civil war in the United States saw the first signs of the looming revolt of the masses which became the main content of politics in the years from 1880 to the 1930s. Universal suffrage became a reality. Legislation was enacted to set in place the civil equality of women, while racial segregation and restrictions on the rights of religious minorities were consigned to the past. Following the victory over fascism in 1945 the general principles of Western democracy would appear unshakeable, and their triumph – at least in the countries of the 'centre' – to be irreversible. Under the influence of reformist workers' parties, which had achieved a real participation in power, the political system expanded beyond the framework of a narrowly conceived 'bourgeois democracy', taking on the character of a broader class compromise. All this, however, had vanished into the past by the late twentieth century, when the decline and fall of the Soviet Union signified the beginning of a new, large-scale counter-offensive by capital.

In the political life of the years from 1990 to 2008 we may observe the open revenge of the elites – the exclusion of mass interests from politics without the formal removal of electoral rights.[8]

The social division did not correspond to the political one. In official politics the differences between left and right were effaced, transformed into the difference between brands in elections, treated as a variety of market competition in which the goods were policies and parties. Political scientists began speaking of the loss of the loyalty of the traditional voter, of an end to the bond between parties and the broad population. In reality it was not electors who showed disloyalty to the parties, but on the contrary, the party elites who displayed a demonstrative and aggressive disloyalty to the voters. It is not surprising that the spread of democracy in the countries of Eastern Europe, going hand in hand with neoliberal reform, led to civic demoralisation and the spread of apathy and cynicism. A similar 'reborn democracy' in Latin America replaced the dictatorial regimes of the 1970s and of the first half of the 1980s, but retained the economic order which the dictators had installed. The replacing of repressive regimes with elected governments in essence legitimised the results of the dictators' terrorist activity. Nor does the formal observance of the rules of the multi-party system, characteristic of Africa since the 1990s, testify to a profound democratisation of society, especially since election campaigns in the 2000s regularly culminated in inter-tribal massacres, even in countries such as Kenya and the Ivory Coast that were considered stable.

This new system has been described by a Brazilian scholar as 'passive democracy', established as a result of the fact that 'popular movements have suffered a historic defeat'.[9] The US researcher Bill Robinson denies altogether the right of the new regimes to call themselves 'democracies', characterising them as 'polyarchic', or as ruled by a plurality of oligarchies.[10] Meanwhile, Washington as the supreme arbiter on questions of democracy reserved for itself the right to recognise as free a country that observed the technical rules of parliamentary government, while refusing this recognition to other states on the basis that their formal observance of the procedures might have seemed insufficient. This ideological ruse was employed to justify the ideological rapprochement of the USA with states, by no means among the most democratic, that acted as strategic partners of Washington in Asia, Africa and Eastern Europe, as well as to explain US support for *coups d'état* that occurred in former communist countries in the early 2000s. Under this logic, the deposed regime was each time found with hindsight to have been insufficiently democratic. Such overturns, termed 'coloured revolutions' by the press, occurred in Serbia, Georgia, Ukraine and Kirghizia. Subsequent attempts to imitate them in Belarus, Moldavia and other countries were blocked by the local elites. It does not, however, by any means follow from this that the new regimes were more democratic than their predecessors, or that the old political elites against which the coups were directed had been fundamentally anti-American. The ideology of the 'progress of democracy' worked most successfully precisely when the need arose to replace one friendly regime with another – in line with considerations of tactics and political effectiveness.

The most important achievement of neoliberalism was the imposing of a universal ideological hegemony, without precedent at least since the end of the nineteenth century. This success was not ensured by the power and scale of the propaganda or by the effectiveness of its manipulative techniques, but by the defeat of the system's historical opponents and critics. Not only has left-wing ideology gone into deep crisis and lost ground, but the bourgeois progressive tradition as well has finished up in question. The critique of the heritage of the Enlightenment that began 'from the left' after the Second World War turned ultimately into the ideological basis for a whole series of reactionary utopias.

The Marxist dialectic has proceeded from the dual role of the Enlightenment tradition, which on the one hand embodies the universal human potential of emancipation, but on the other, bears the stamp of its bourgeois class limitations. The attempt by the enlighteners to present their own values as those of all humanity involved an obvious contradiction, since in a society divided into classes such values are either impossible, or amount to no more than banal commonplaces. A universal human consciousness is theoretically possible only in a classless society. Further, consciousness does not come into being in an empty space, but on the basis of the cultural and social experience of world history. For Marx, meanwhile, making a critique of the Enlightenment involved exposing its contradictions and class limitations, and not repudiating the Enlightenment itself. From the point of view of various twentieth-century thinkers, Marx in this instance was insufficiently radical; according to these thinkers, the Enlightenment should have been rejected as such, along with all its concepts of human rights and universal freedoms and as a consequence, the general historical logic of class struggle. This trend was expressed to perfection by Adorno and Horkheimer,[11] and then received a new and still more radical anti-Western interpretation in books by a number of authors who proclaimed as their goal the liberation of the Third World as such. The end-point of this ideological journey consisted of gloomy anti-Enlightenment ideologies of an openly right-wing cast.

This path was logical in its own fashion. Repudiating the Enlightenment tradition of universalism leads to the disappearance of an understanding of, or interest in, the differences between class interests and ideologies within the context of the general evolution of Western society; between liberalism (which restricts the Enlightenment to a bourgeois framework) and socialism (which strives to overcome this framework); between the strictly capitalist and the broadly 'Western'or 'modern', and so forth. A class critique of capitalism is replaced by a critique of Western civilisation, of the 'modern' or in the best case, of an 'industrialism' stripped of its specific social character. The rejection of a universalist understanding of freedom, of the rights of humanity and of social progress becomes ultimately a reversion to the medieval concept of social struggle, as a struggle for specific privileges and freedoms for distinct, self-sufficient groups. Within 'Western' society this may be the rights of Muslims or homosexuals, of women or blacks, of animals or of migrants. Outside of Western society, by exactly the same logic, we find proclaimed the sovereign right of diverse dictators to oppress and control their own peoples within the context of 'distinctive cultural traditions', and the right of traditionalist majorities to reject such 'Western' innovations as rights for women, homosexuals or blacks. In methodological terms there is no fundamental difference between these approaches, and they are constantly reinforced by mutual justification and ideological interchange. Hence rightists in the West refer to the threat of 'Islamic intolerance' or 'Russian nationalism' in order to justify a struggle to defend 'Western values', but themselves call for putting an end to the 'licentiousness' that results from showing excessive tolerance for the rights of minorities. Meanwhile traditionalists in the East and in Russia, repeating word for word the narratives of Western rightists concerning the 'licentiousness' of the West, demand a struggle on this basis against 'European' influence.

Since the universalist idea of class struggle is fundamentally denied in all the numerous variants of these ideologies, all of them are reduced ultimately to the defence of the existing order, regulated only in a certain fashion.

New contradictions

The triumph of neoliberalism does not by any means signify that the world, now integrated ideologically, has become homogeneous, harmonious and unified. In the early twenty-first century, the same unevenness of economic development that was undermining the positions of the British empire toward the end of the Victorian epoch was starting to create potential problems for the dominant world role of the United States.

Rivalry had appeared between several neoliberal projects, similar in their main outlines, but for this very reason also doomed inevitably to collide. In the 1950s and 1960s the more liberal socio-economic system of the US and the social democratic societies of Western Europe had complemented one another in their fashion. But from the 1990s, when Western Europe became just as neoliberal as America, the situation changed.

Initially, the European Economic Community had been supposed to do away with the causes of new conflicts, providing the revived German capitalism with extensive sales markets for its industrial products, but simultaneously taking account of the interests of the other Western powers. French industry became increasingly integrated with that of West Germany. Meanwhile, the continuing decline of Great Britain helped strengthen the position of financial capital in London. British capital, like French banking capital in earlier times, now had an interest in the development of American and German industry, to which it could provide credits and services. At the same time as the West German industrial centres, having restored their production after the Second World War, held the leading place in Europe, the Frankfurt stock exchange lagged far behind the City of London in its turnover and importance. The restructuring of European capitalism in the 1950s and 1960s ensured a new division of labour, creating the conditions for several decades of comparatively peaceful and 'harmonious' development.

The success of the European project also spurred growing ambitions. After the disintegration of the Soviet bloc the countries of Eastern Europe were formally integrated into the European Union, without, however, receiving a real weight comparable to the influence of the 'old Europe', the leading countries of the West. In essence the European Union, with its informal hierarchy of rich and poor countries, its undemocratic decision-making procedures, irresponsible bureaucracy and mutual guarantees for its elites became transformed into yet another imperial project. As in the case of the United States, this was an empire that refused to recognise itself as such.

Within the framework of the European West, the role of informal hegemon came in turn to be played by the unified Germany, which surpassed all its neighbours in the numbers of its population and in its industrial and financial might. Overcoming the psychological trauma connected with defeat in two world wars, the German ruling class began to lay claim to a growing share of influence in the world. Acting through the institutions of the European Union, the German leaders gained the ability to go on the offensive without setting loose the demon of nationalism, whose dangers were too well understood by the Germans themselves.

In similar fashion, the elites of Germany and the European Union saw neither the possibility of mounting a struggle to seize global hegemony from the USA nor the need to do so. Nevertheless, the strategic goal of the European neoliberal project was a review of the conditions under which American hegemony was exercised, and an enhancing of the European role within this system. While not taking issue with the Americans in the military arena, and avoiding the risks associated with confrontations and the arms race, the Western European leaders issued a challenge to the Americans in the sphere of finances, creating a unified currency – the euro. This project, however, turned out to be far more problematical than it initially appeared.

Combining countries with completely different types of economy in a single monetary system, the authors of the project made these countries hostages of one another, and subordinated the economy of the entire region to the interests and ambitions of German financial capital. The level of inflation in Spain could not be the same as in Germany, since for this to be the case the entire Spanish economy and society would have to resemble that of Germany. The magical transformation of Greece into Germany did not of course occur, and moreover, no-one even proposed such a goal, since the differences between the various European markets were actively exploited by mobile capital. As it turned out, the excessively expensive currency smothered development in Southern Europe, and the latter in turn exploited inflation to the North.

Through mechanically combining countries with different economic structures and levels of development within the framework of a single monetary system, the project of the euro did not work objectively to bring these societies closer together, but made the contradictions more acute. This situation made its effects felt in the mid-2000s, when the mass resistance of the lower orders of society and squabbles between the political elites of the European Union effectively paralysed the integration process. The growth of social and economic problems in both parts of the united Europe, and the reluctance of the ruling circles even to recognise these problems, let alone solve them, caused an increase in dissatisfaction. This, however, did not by any means always take on democratic and progressive forms.

Migration became a vexed topic of political debates, accompanied by a growth of ethnic and cultural tension. Compared with the epoch of more regulated capitalism, the nature of migration had changed radically. 'In the 1960s and early 1970s emigration from the former colonies to the West had been connected with a growing demand there for labour power, but from the late 1990s mass resettlement turned into an inertial process, driven by the social crisis of the South and by people's desire to gain access to the consumer society.'[12] The result was that the Third World finished up inside the 'first'.

The problems arising from this situation finished up providing a nutrient medium for the growth of neofascist movements, which became a real political force in Austria, Italy, Holland, some regions of France, and by the end of the 2000s in Britain as well. The lack of an influential left movement in most of the countries meant that in elections, the 'protest vote' went to the extreme right. Meanwhile, the dissatisfaction of the population with the deteriorating state of affairs meant that the 'protest vote' would keep increasing.

War and rivalry

In 2003 the accumulated problems and contradictions surfaced abruptly in relation to the US military operations in Iraq. The coming to power in Washington in the early 2000s of the extremely conservative administration of George Bush the younger sharply exacerbated relations between America and the rest of the world. When the Bush administration, referring to the need for struggle against the terrorist threat, invaded Iraq and overthrew the regime of Saddam Hussein, instead of the accustomed universal approval from its Western allies it met with harsh criticism from the leaders of France, Germany and Belgium, founding countries of the European Union. The contradictions between the east and west of the united Europe were superimposed on the conflict between Germany and the USA, but simultaneously, a lack of unity appeared within the European Union itself, where Britain, cleaving to its historical 'special relationship' with Washington, spoke out against its partners on the continent.

Meanwhile, the policies of Bush in and of themselves reflected the difficulties which American hegemony had encountered by the early twenty-first century. The growing aggressiveness of the neoconservatives who had come to power represented a sort of intuitive means of compensating for the relative weakening of the economic position of the United States, and also of its cultural and ideological attractiveness to the rest of the world. The economic and technical leadership of the USA, earlier beyond dispute, had ceased to be obvious. With the ending of the Cold War the importance of US military power also diminished, since it was no longer needed to defend Europe against a potential Soviet invasion. The size of the nuclear arsenals, which had been of huge significance in the epoch of mutual restraint by two superpowers, was no longer a decisive factor in the relationship of military forces. Meanwhile, new states – China and Israel, followed by India and Pakistan – had gained access to nuclear weapons. From being the basis of a global mechanism enforcing strategic restraint, nuclear bombs had been transformed into a factor in the regional balance of forces between secondary powers. The deregulation of world trade had sharpened the competition for markets. As in the early twentieth century, a struggle for resources flared up.

In the late twentieth century, the development of transnational corporations had created a sense that capital had finally lost its connection with national states, and that consequently the danger that market competition would be transformed into international conflict had disappeared as well. Subsequent events, however, showed this to be an illusion. The corporations counted endlessly on the power of the state to solve their problems, and using their influence on governments, provoked rivalry between them, winning for themselves the best possible conditions for their activity. The crisis that followed strengthened the dependency of the firms on state financing, finally burying the misconceptions of the 1990s.

Although the United States for two decades had been the major force promoting global market reforms, many elements of these reforms were ultimately to turn against it. The wealth of American corporations increased, but not the solvency of the American consumer on whose demand these corporations had mainly counted when they set up factories overseas. The ruling groups in Washington found themselves in a trap, unable to alter the economic course they were pursuing, but with an acute need to do something about the problems that course had created. Unable simply to reconcile themselves to a changing situation, they also lacked the means to alter it.

In such a situation, the use of force becomes especially attractive. Paradoxically, the less significant the military superiority of the leading power becomes, the greater the temptation to make use of it before it loses its significance completely. In many ways, the unilateral actions of the Bush administration in the early 2000s recalled the aggressive behaviour of the world powers of the sixteenth and seventeenth centuries, as they sought to turn a world-economy into a world-empire. The USA was acting not as a hegemon, but as a leader trying to issue orders to other countries and to punish them for non-fulfilment. This behaviour by a superpower reflected not only the incompetence and short-sightedness of its leadership, but also a crisis of hegemony. The ineffectiveness of the attempts by the Americans to impose their leadership on their partners, who were accustomed to a far more balanced system of relations, was obvious; during the Bush years the prestige and influence of the USA declined sharply, and this was reflected ultimately in American internal policy as well.

Strengthening its military presence in the Near and Middle East, the United States was clearly trying to place the extraction and transport of oil under its control, and simultaneously to create a new international situation in which armed force played a growing role. Occupying Iraq, American forces encountered armed resistance, aggravated by socio-political chaos, a vacuum of power and a civil war. Adding to the US dilemma were the results of the invasion of Afghanistan. The policy of the Americans in the occupied countries proved to be internally contradictory. On the one hand, the occupation forces in Iraq permitted a degree of self-organisation by the local society, allowing clans and religious communities whose influence had been suppressed by the earlier dictatorship to come to the surface. Both in Afghanistan and Iraq the Americans did everything possible to encourage the formation of a local administration and army. On the other hand, the representatives of the USA did not trust the local politicians and military commanders, and did not shrink from trying to exercise political control. Meanwhile the occupiers, with no possibility of constructing an authentic nineteenth-century-style colonial administration, were forced constantly to resort to indirect methods of imposing their informal authority, methods which just as constantly failed.

The attempt to rely on local structures did not bring about a flourishing of civil society, but a revival of clan, tribal and religious communities, archaic forces suppressed by the previous regime which the Americans had overthrown. In practice, the implanting of democracy and the encouraging of civil society resulted not in the modernisation of Iraqi political life but in its archaisation. As one researcher has noted, in this situation 'American policy analysts have expected a different result only by neglecting [Iraq's] history.'[13]

Unlike the practice of British colonialism or the Soviet model of 'fraternal assistance' to developing-world countries, the American project did not foresee systematic work to create socio-political institutions, productive capacity or transport infrastructure, or the planned training of the local administrative and technical personnel required if these were to arise and function. The Americans presumed that all these problems could either be solved through pouring money into the country, or that the market would solve them spontaneously.

The tactical failures suffered by the Americans in Iraq and Afghanistan were not, however, as important as the long-term consequences of the armed actions they initiated. As Patomäki notes, the war in Iraq, accompanied by a fierce polemic between supporters and opponents of the 'new imperialism', seemed to 'resemble the era of 1875–95'.[14] In the early twenty-first century, he concludes, the 'logic of violence and war' has returned to the core areas of global political economy.[15]

Nevertheless, the principal difference between the situation that arose in the early twenty-first century and the epoch of classical imperialism lay in the fact that there was no power prepared to assume the role of new global hegemon and actively laying claim to it. The United States was obliged to concern itself simultaneously with a multitude of distinct challenges from forces calling for a revision of the 'rules of the game', or demanding to take on particular functions that earlier had been a monopoly of the global leader.

The illusion of a 'new hegemony'

Theoreticians of the world-system school are inclined to believe that capitalism cannot in principle cope without a hegemonic power, and throughout the final two decades of the twentieth century and into the twenty-first discussed incessantly the question of who might replace America in this role. Their attention was concentrated on the countries of Asia, to which a significant portion of industrial production had been relocated from the West as neoliberal globalisation went ahead.

In Asia itself, the relationship of forces had changed. At the beginning of the 1990s the undisputed economic leader in the region had been Japan, with South Korea gradually gaining on it. But from the middle of the decade the logic of uneven development brought about a weakening of the positions of these two countries, and a strengthening of China.

Describing the redistribution of capital between states, Marx noted that Venetian credits had provided a hidden basis for the enrichment of Holland, that Holland later financed the rising power of England, and that the British later financed the United States, destined to become the next world leader.[16]

The prediction by the author of *Capital* was completely borne out; American capitalism inherited from that of Britain the dominant role within the world-system. But the better part of a century went by between the time when Marx observed the flow of capital from Britain to the USA and the moment when the USA genuinely replaced Britain as the leading world power. During this time the USA not only transformed itself into the world's leading economic power, but also used its resources systematically to support the declining British empire. In the early twentieth century, in other words, the financial current was already moving in the opposite direction. The recent history of the USA has showed that a different logic is also possible: the weaker the American economy became around the beginning of the twenty-first century, the more it came to depend on a financial influx from other countries, including Japan, China and Russia.

The rise of Japan in the 1970s, meanwhile, did not lead to a massive flow of funds from the USA to Asia. The Japanese bourgeoisie kept granting credits to American companies and investing in the US economy. The international financial and monetary system ensured that the American dollar would remain the most attractive instrument for global accumulation. Meanwhile, the neoliberal economic model made putting money into the financial sector more profitable than investing in production. The outcome was that the deindustrialisation of the USA and the growth of industry in the states of Asia not only failed to result in a redistribution of funds between America and the Asian countries, but to the contrary, helped set up a constant flow of resources in the opposite direction. The growth of Asian producers depended on American consumption, which the rising industrial giants were forced directly and indirectly to subsidise. By September 2008 China had become the main creditor to the United States, which owed it $85 billion.[17]

With the weakening of Japan in the 1990s, China was transformed into the leading industrial power in Asia and later, the world. The first consequence of this change was an influx of Chinese capital to the USA. Giovanni Arrighi explains this situation[18]on the basis of political circumstances, but the key elements were not only political but structural. For a state acting in the role of hegemon of the world capitalist system, it is not enough to be economically powerful, and to possess financial and material resources. Also essential is to create the corresponding structures – organisational, political, military and cultural. The economy of a hegemonic power must not simply be strong, but must also be organised in the corresponding fashion.

For much of the twentieth century the United States, for all its industrial and financial might, lacked a sufficient degree of structural 'maturity'. For this reason the American elites were forced to support and maintain Britain, paying it a sort of tribute.

Neither China nor India, despite the strengthening of their positions, has been able to lay claim to the global role belonging to the USA. But the United States, for its part, has not been able to play the role of leader effectively in relation to the countries on which it has in many ways been dependent.

The economic reforms begun in China under Deng Xiao-Ping following the death of Chairman Mao transformed the country, turning it into a world industrial leader. Initially, the reforms were pursued cautiously. Immediately following the effective abolition of the agricultural communes, market relations began to be instituted in industry, and foreign capital was attracted to 'special economic zones', though at first without the privatisation of state property.

A key question was the retention of political control, which was threatened both by the resistance of orthodox Maoists and by the demands of liberal dissidents. In 1989 mass protests by students demanding democratic changes were ruthlessly crushed, after which conditions became ripe for the next stage of the liberal reforms. Inspired by the successes of the 1980s and early 1990s, the new generation of Chinese leaders grew in boldness. The bureaucratic elite that had evolved in the changing conditions was now far more ready for privatisation and for the open restoration of capitalism. Integrating China into the global economy, the Chinese leaders not only sought to use the triumphant neoliberal order to their advantage, but also implanted its principles more and more consistently within their own country.

The wages of industrial workers were kept at a low level. Strikes and revolts were harshly suppressed, and attempts to establish free trade unions were nipped in the bud.[19] In this fashion, the 'Communist' regime in China created highly attractive conditions for transnational investors. The open transition to capitalism led to the rise among the intelligentsia and workers of a 'new left' opposition current. At its Sixteenth Congress in 2002 the Communist Party, declaring itself the expression of the interests of all strata of the population, granted permission for members of the bourgeoisie to enter its ranks.

Among adherents of the world-system school in the West, the industrial growth of the Celestial Empire aroused genuine euphoria. Giovanni Arrighi predicted that China would be transformed into a new global hegemon, replacing the decrepit United States. Extolling the successes of the capitalist China, the radical thinker acknowledged that the party had transformed itself into 'a committee for managing the common affairs of its national bourgeoisie',[20] but expressed the hope that the system installed as a result would be better than that in the West, by virtue of being infused with 'the Confucian ideal of social harmony'.[21]

Like Russia in the late nineteenth century, China had become an imperialist power without ceasing to be part of the periphery. The political organisation of post-Maoist China not only distinguished it from the Western countries that had earlier laid claim to world hegemony, but also placed the very possibility of its establishing and maintaining this hegemony in question. Within the capitalist world-system, the hegemonic powers have by no means always been models of liberal economies, but their political life has always been ordered on the basis of liberal democracy. The traditional Western hegemony, whether British or American, has presumed a combination of compromise and democratic principles of rule within its own country (and for the most part in relation to the 'centre') with the harsh application of authoritarian measures in relation to the 'periphery'. In China in the early twenty-first century, by contrast, the national territory itself was subject to a political authoritarianism that ruled out the possibility of social compromise with the lower strata of society.

Nor has post-Mao China shown any special regard for democracy in its relations with the outside world. In their search for cheap raw materials and labour power, Chinese corporations in the early twenty-first century were actively asserting their control in various regions of Africa, without paying the slightest consideration to human rights or civil liberties in the countries concerned. Chinese investment was also being directed to Burma, where in 2009 it accounted for 87 per cent of the foreign funds invested in the country, as well as to Iran.[22] Chinese companies were buying up the shares of enterprises in Kazakhstan and Central Asia, as well as expanding their influence vigorously in Latin America. This foreign expansion, however, does not point to radical change within Chinese society itself, and certainly not to the type of change sought by the ideologues and statesmen of late nineteenth-century Western colonialism, who saw in their policies of conquest a means for reducing class tensions within their own countries. To the contrary, China in the early twenty-first century needed foreign resources above all to maintain its cheap labour force, which Chinese firms relied upon in order to continue penetrating foreign markets with their products.

China's industrial growth took place on a basis of the ruthless exploitation of cheap labour power, with the situation bringing about a lowering of social standards on a world scale. In practice, what occurred was a return by capitalism to the savage forms of exploitation characteristic of the early industrial period. The number of people added to the labour market each year was so great that it affected the entire global relationship between labour and capital. 'At the present time,' a French newspaper reported in 2009, 'around twenty million Chinese peasants leave the countryside each year to look for work in the areas of industry and services. This is as if a country the size of France, where approximately as many people are employed in the economy, were added to the world market each year.'[23]

The new proletarians, who lacked experience of struggle and of class self-organisation, were deprived of the right to establish free trade unions, and who found themselves under harsh political and security-force control by the state, were used in what amounted to a vast labour dumping operation. The conquests of working people were eroded not only in Western Europe and the USA, but also in other countries of Asia, in the former Soviet bloc and in Latin America.

Here we find yet another crucial difference between China and previous claimants to hegemony. Both Britain and the USA during the epochs when they flourished were not only leaders in terms of production, but also scientific and technological leaders. It was this advantage that allowed them to maintain their superiority over many decades, while drawing other industrial countries up to their level. In China we see nothing of the kind, but find the opposite tendency. The presence in the early twenty-first century of many millions of cheap Chinese workers not only served to make the introduction of new labour-saving technology unprofitable, but even ruled out the use of many long-familiar mechanisms and techniques. On the world scale, the late twentieth and early twenty-first centuries were thus a period without precedent, when the technical progress of world industry was not only held back, but to a significant degree was reversed.

The Chinese model of exploitation, however, was already encountering growing difficulties and contradictions by the mid-2000s. Contrary to the widespread view, China in the early twenty-first century was not the new 'workshop of the world', but rather the 'assembly shop of the planet'. Unlike the case in Victorian Britain, goods were produced here to foreign designs, using foreign technology, and on the basis of investments of foreign capital. Moreover, a substantial portion of the components from which the goods bearing the mark 'Made in China' were assembled had been produced in other Asian countries.

The Chinese labour market, along with social relations in general within the country, also experienced growing difficulties. The demographic policy followed by Beijing for several decades had yielded results, bringing about a sharp reduction in birth rates. Meanwhile, the lack of an overall national pension system increased the burden on the younger generation, which was forced to use its income to support older relatives. The countryside was gradually ceasing to represent an inexhaustible reservoir of labour power. The consolidation of the working class, which in earlier times had constantly been diluted by newcomers from the villages, was becoming a real prospect despite the repression. The world capitalist crisis that began in 2007 exposed and sharply exacerbated all these contradictions, while naturally being accompanied by a powerful outburst of worker protests. Unemployment, which in the 1990s had already reached 10 per cent of the able-bodied population, approached 20 per cent. As described by a French journalist, Chinese society stood on the brink of 'social drama' and even 'social shock'.[24]

Crisis

The year 2008 saw the outbreak of a vast economic crisis, among the most massive and profound in world history. Assessing the significance of the crisis for the USA, the economist Doug Henwood noted that the figure for job losses in the first two years of the recession was the highest since the end of the Second World War: 'Not only has the recent job loss been without precedent in modern times – it comes after the weakest expansion on record.'[25] Unlike the usual periods of rise and decline in business activity, the first decade of the new century revealed a pattern in which investment in the USA lagged clearly behind profits even during the period of expansion, while the number of new jobs created was exceptionally small. The weak investment activity by American business was especially striking against the background of high profits. Although neoliberal policies had led to a restoration of profit rates after the recession that took place at the beginning of the 2000s, these additional funds had not been invested in production but in financial speculation.

The crisis of the late 2000s presented a balance-sheet of the two decades of 'reform from the right', an especially gloomy accounting against the background of the achievements of regulated capitalism, a critique of which had begun the process that saw the imposing of neoliberal hegemony in the West. The main result of deregulation proved to be a long-term decline of the growth rates for gross domestic product on a world scale. Harry Shutt notes 'deepening economic stagnation', going on to observe that 'instead of the promised revival of economic growth from the levels of the 1970s the rate of increase in global output (as reflected in average GDP growth) has continued to decline in each succeeding decade.'[26]

The expectation that the technological innovations of the late 1990s would provide the conditions for long-term expansion was not borne out. The problem was that the information revolution mainly affected management and consumption, not production. As a result, the potential for economic expansion on this basis proved extremely weak. All the disproportions, problems and contradictions that had accumulated over several decades, and that had been ignored, now made their effects felt simultaneously. A mere change of course was no longer enough to deal with the situation; the entire neoliberal economic model, constructed over the three preceding decades, had collapsed.

'As a result of the globalisation of 1975–2008, which represented a new stage in the development of the world economy,' wrote the economist Vasily Koltashov,

> whole regions of the planet were transformed from agrarian to industrial. Hundreds of millions of people were forced to leave their traditional natural economies and to become hired workers. A proletarianisation without

precedent in world history took place. The realm of market relations expanded, and labour power became cheaper than industrial technologies. In the 'old industrial countries' governments began implementing a policy of 'jettisoning ballast' – that is, of privatisation, liquidating social gains, and reducing spending on education and other areas of the social sector.

The neoliberal economic model had at its basis contradictions whose development meant an end to its existence. Goods produced in the countries of the periphery had to be sold in the centre, in the developed countries of Western Europe and North America. But as production was shifted out of these countries, consumer demand from the population diminished, compensated only to a very limited degree by the 'new economy', the area of services and information technology. The growth of consumer markets in the countries of the industrial periphery could not make up for the growing shortage of demand.[27]

When the crisis erupted, its first victims were American investment banks. One after another, five financial giants collapsed. The largest catastrophe was the crash of the bank Lehman Brothers. Following this bankruptcy, the government of the USA was forced to intervene and save the surviving structures through the help of a special agency designed to support the stricken companies of the financial sector. Over several days the shares of Morgan Stanley lost 49 per cent of their value, and over approximately the same period shares in Goldman Sachs fell from $175 to $86.[28] Carried out at government expense, the rescue amounted in effect to nationalisation. The Moscow business journal *Ekspert* stated: 'In 2008 the world witnessed the rapid disappearance of independent American investment banks.'[29] But having thrown the costs of saving the financial sector onto the government, the American elites did not allow direct public control over the banks' activity. The neoliberal nationalisation that had come to replace neoliberal privatisation pursued essentially the same goal: supporting private business and accumulation at the cost of public funds. In other words, the US administration along with the governments of other countries rejected any change of course, refusing either to carry out structural reforms or to mount a struggle against the main causes of the economic collapse. The replacing of the conservative administration of George Bush with the moderate-left administration of Barack Obama in Washington changed nothing.

The governments of the world's leading countries responded unanimously to the crisis by pumping money into the economy, in other words repeating the actions taken by the Federal Reserve System and the US administration in 1924 and 1929. This time, the torrent of funds pouring into the corporations and banks made it possible to stop the fall of share prices and prevent a collapse of the banking system, but only at the cost of worsening the problems in the areas of production and material consumption.

In Europe, the first victims of the crisis were in the traditional semi-peripheral zone of the continent – Poland, the countries of the former Austro-Hungarian empire, the Baltic states, and in the west, Ireland. By the summer of 2009 Latvia was effectively bankrupt, saved only by loans extended by the European Union and the International Monetary Fund. In the next stage of the crisis, contradictions were exacerbated within Western Europe itself. The economies in the northern countries withstood the slump far better than those in the countries of the Mediterranean. By the winter of 2009 the budgets of Spain and Greece were coming apart at the seams. The foreign debt of Greece reached 300 million euros, or about 125 per cent of the country's Gross Domestic Product.[30] As hostages of the Eurozone, these countries could not do what countries had done in such circumstances since the time of the English King Edward III; they could neither write off their debts unilaterally, nor debase their currencies (through 'resorting to the printing press'). By comparison the budgetary crisis in Britain, which remained outside the Eurozone, appeared quite mild. But this crisis too made a definite impression. According to experts, Britain's state debt in 2009 amounted to 13 per cent of Gross Domestic Product, and was rising rapidly.[31]

A crisis of hegemony?

The economic shocks of the late 2000s showed that the development of capitalism was in a structural impasse. Neither the attempted return to imperialist methods undertaken by the Bush administration, nor the transfer of production to countries with cheap labour power, nor massive infusions of state funds to private corporations under Barack Obama had created the conditions for a renewal of economic growth.

The system of American hegemony underwent an acute and obvious crisis, but clearly, it was not replaced. The situation reflected the historic crisis of capitalism, which had made itself felt for the first time in the early decades of the twentieth century. But the first impacts of that earlier crisis, contrary to the expectations of socialists, had been overcome through reforms, social concessions and restructuring of the world-system. The British empire, along with the French colonial system, had been sacrificed to allow the rebuilding of the world economic order.

In the early twenty-first century capitalism again encountered an acute systemic crisis. The question was posed of a global reconstruction on no less a scale than that which had taken place in the middle of the previous century. The lack of an influential socialist alternative meant that as before the search for a solution would be mounted essentially within the framework of capitalism, but the economic and social logic of the system had been placed in question, and this meant that changes could easily escape the bounds within which the dominant classes wished to keep them. So long as the hegemony of capital remained, the possibility of anti-bourgeois revolutions existed as well.

By the early twenty-first century the development of human civilisation had placed on the agenda the need to carry out directly coordinated actions on a global scale. But paradoxically, it was at precisely this moment that capitalism, which had achieved its greatest triumph in creating a global system not only on the economic but also on the political level, proved incapable of solving the dilemma that had become the main obstacle to its continued existence.

Throughout the modern era, at least since the mid-seventeenth century, European rationalist thought had been focused on conquering nature with the help of science and technology, and on transforming it through human activity. By the early twenty-first century civilisation had in fact become a decisive factor altering the shape of nature – though not consciously and in the interests of humanity, but haphazardly, and to a significant degree to the detriment of humankind.

This did not so much represent the collapse of European rationalism in the form in which it had become established by the beginning of the modern era, as the outcome of the evolution of global capitalism, which had transformed itself from a rationally organised system into an irrational and destructive force. The creative destruction extolled by Schumpeter had been replaced by simple destruction, devoid of creativity, and even where real creative and innovative initiatives were under way, they were maninfesting their destructive, irrational and antihuman aspects. This time, the crisis of political hegemony of capitalism was not an intermediate stage through which the system was passing while transforming and renewing itself, but the final result, a historical symptom of the fact that the system had entered the phase of its decline and irretrievable collapse.

The historic achievement of the market economy was that it ensured an interactive balance between production and consumption, maintaining a link between them where there was no direct contact between the people involved. In an epoch where global communications were lacking, the market served as the first, crucially important information network, functioning to a significant degree spontaneously. Without the development of the market there would not have been integration of the world economy, and accordingly, the unification of humanity would not have taken place.

But from the moment when the logic of the market finally became combined with the process of accumulation of capital, we are confronted not simply with a spontaneous process of the interaction of sellers with buyers, but with the planned and consistent creation of infrastructure, with a whole system of institutions. In the course of history the institutions of the market, like any other, have become con-solidated and have reproduced themselves, working out their own logic and their own specific interests, embodied above all in the self-aggrandisement of financial capital. Such processes would have been impossible without constant state regula-tion, with the government compelled to intervene in economic and social life, not restraining the market but working in its interests. By the late twentieth century, however, the propagation of the market and the spread of its associated institutions had far outgrown their historical and rational limits. In the epoch of late capitalism this system of institutions, instead of serving to unite producers with consumers, had become transformed into a barrier between them. The less direct the connec-tion between producers and consumers, the more quickly the market infrastructure spread and grew stronger.

Manipulating demand and supply, and strengthening itself at the expense both of consumers and producers, the intermediary structures arising out of the market became a factor of dissociation, disorganisation and of the breakdown of commu-nication within the world economy. The massive crisis that began in 2008 revealed this with the utmost clarity. The first, natural reaction to this crisis, as to previous ones, was to strengthen the role of the state, to reorient production toward local markets and to renew direct contact with the consumer, while bypassing the global market infrastructure. This, however, could not provide a definitive solution, since the tasks of global human development required the restoring of coordination on a new level and through new mechanisms. The return to earlier and simpler forms of market exchange signified a regression. History required a new economy, founded on democratic coordination.

The monopolisation of production was the outcome of the development of the free market, while oligopolistic competition was the sole global form in which the bourgeois order could exist in an epoch when the concentration of capital had reached planetary dimensions. The state once again concealed itself behind the market, providing capital with direct management of current processes – to the degree to which capital itself could not accomplish this efficiently and independently, and while avoiding the use of direct coercion.

By the early twenty-first century the resources of bourgeois self-regulation had been exhausted. The speed with which these resources were used up provides grounds for suspecting that the free market takes the form of a series of episodes within the framework of capitalism, rather than making up one of its normal elements. The crisis is now returning the state to the forefront of economic development, but just as occurred during the crises of the fourteenth and seventeenth centuries, and also those of the early twentieth century, this return will be accompanied by wars and revolutions. This time, more likely than not, the revolutions will be anti-bourgeois.

Notes

1 See P.S. Onuf, *Jefferson's Empire: The Language of American Nationhood*, Charlottesville: University of Virginia Press, 2000.
2 C. S. Maier, *Among Empires. American Ascendancy and Its Predecessors*, Cambridge, MA/ London: Harvard University Press, 2006, p. 2.
3 C. Calhoun, F. Cooper and K.W. Moore (eds), *Lessons of Empire*, New York: New Press, p. 37.
4 See I. Wallerstein, *After Liberalism*, New York: New Press, 1995.
5 H. Shutt, *The Decline of Capitalism. Can a Self-Regulated Profits System Survive?* London: Zed Books, 2005, pp. 21–2.
6 L. Boltanski and E. Chapello, *The New Spirit of Capitalism*, London/New York: Verso, 2005, p. 365.
7 See T. Teivainen, *Enter Economism, Exit Politics: Experts, Economic Policy and the Political*, London: Zed Books, 2002.
8 See C. Lasch, *The Revolt of the Elites and the Betrayal of Democracy*, New York: W.W. Norton, 1995.
9 R. M. Marini, *América Latina: dependência e integração*. São Paulo: Editora Brasil Urgente, 1992, p. 30.
10 See W. I. Robinson, *Promoting Polyarchy: Globalization, US Intervention, and Hegemony*, Cambridge: Cambridge University Press, 1998.
11 See M. Horkheimer and T. Adorno, *Dialektika prosveshcheniya. Filosofskie fragmenty* [The dialectics of enlightenment. Philosophical fragments], Moscow/St Petersburg: Medium, Yuventa, 1997.

12 IGSO report, 'Krizis global'noy ekonomiki i Rossiya' [The crisis of the global economy and Russia], *Levaya politika* [Left politics], 2008, 5: 21.

13 Calhoun *et al.*, *Lessons of Empire*, p. 111.

14 H. Patomäki, *The Political Economy of Global Security. War, Future Crises and Changes in Global Governance*, London and New York: Routledge, 2008, p. 125.

15 Ibid., p. 156.

16 K. Marx and F. Engel's, *Sochineniya* [Works], Vol. 23, pp. 765–6.

17 See *Inprecor*, 543–4: 13, Nov.–Dec. 2008.

18 See G. Arrighi and B.J. Silver (eds), *Chaos and Governance in the World System*, Minneapolis/London: University of Minnesota Press, 1999, pp. 266–8.

19 For more detail on social conflicts in China, see B. Astarian, *Luttes de classes dans la Chine des réformes (1978–2009)*, La Bussière: Les Éditions Acratie, 2009.

20 G. Arrighi, *Adam Smith in Beijing: Lineages of the Twenty-First Century*, London: Verso, 2007, p. 359.

21 Ibid., p. 329.

22 See *Ekspert*, 17: 26, 2009.

23 *Inprecor*, 543–4: 10, Nov.–Dec. 2008.

24 See *Inprecor*, 543–4: 13, 10, Nov.–Dec. 2008.

25 *Left Business Observer*, 121: 4, Sept. 2009.

26 Shutt, *Decline*, p. 2.

27 IGSO report, 'Krizis global'noy ekonomiki i Rossiya', *Levaya politika*, 2008, 5: 21.

28 See *Ekspert*, 'Luchshie materialy' [Better materials], 7: 90, 2009.

29 Ibid.

30 See http://www.newsru.com/finance/10dec2009/greece_debt.html.

31 See http://www.bfm.ru/articles/2009/12/12/grecija-i-irlandija-mogut-vyjti-iz-zony-evro.html.

CONCLUSION

In the course of its development, capital came to require a world economy. Meanwhile the world-system, for its part, required empires. If there had not been great discoveries and conquests, technical, social and cultural progress would not have occurred in the form in which we find it in history.

Capitalism is at the same time both a system and a mode of production. But the development of the bourgeois mode of production does not give rise automatically to the capitalist system, even if all the basic elements of this system are already present. Historical facts demonstrate clearly that it was the state that played the decisive role in the formation of capitalism as an economic and social system.

Government was not only the force preserving political order in the interests of capital, and not only enabled the establishing of the institutions and relations essential to the bourgeoisie, but was also an essential element in the everyday main-tenance of this economic system. By contrast, the power of private corporations, by giving rise to monopolism and corruption, posed a constant threat to the regime of free entrepreneurship in the form it had taken on by the early eighteenth century.

When this is the case, why have bourgeois commentators from the time of John Locke shown such a suspicious and hostile attitude to the state bureaucracy? The answer, it appears, is to be found in the dual nature of the state, which despite acting as a tool of the ruling class bases its existence on a claim to express the interests of all society. This ambiguity constantly creates opportunities for the formation of coalitions resting on broader social layers, as well as the constant 'danger' that the state will exceed the limits – indispensable, from the point of view of the bourgeoisie – on the concessions that can be made in the name of preserving the loyalty of the working population.

The same ambiguity is to be observed in the attitude of the bourgeoisie toward democratic institutions. Political freedoms and independent courts are legitimate and essential conditions for the existence of the bourgeois system, which is based on the coexistence of property-owners who are independent of one another. The same institutions, however, are liable to be used and 'captured' by political forces outside of bourgeois control, and to become tools of labour in its struggle against capital. Throughout the seventeenth and eighteenth centuries, and during the first half of the nineteenth, the bourgeoisie succeeded more or less in maintaining a balance between democracy and authoritarianism, between state intervention and the sovereignty of property-owners. But from the mid-nineteenth century the equilibrium began regularly to be disturbed, and the system of bourgeois hegemony to experience crisis after crisis. Capitalism entered a new phase of industrial growth, followed on the one hand by the self-organisation of the proletariat into a political class, and on the other, by a change in the relationship of forces between the leading centres of economic development.

The West came to exercise global hegemony because it was there that the state assumed a form in which it was capable, if not of maintaining equilibrium within a contradictory system, then at least of regularly restoring this balance. European political life, marked by open displays of class conflict, by civil wars and by fierce struggles between diverse forces, ultimately developed democratic mechanisms that allowed capital to be accumulated without social progress being blocked. But as the global positions of the West grew stronger, foreign expansion came increasingly to be used as a means of obtaining the resources that were essential for accelerating social progress and consolidating a free society.

The countries of the East lost to the West not because they were backward in their development, but because they did not manage to devise (or did not devise in time) state forms that were able to ensure bourgeois development. Europe outstripped the East in this respect, and for this reason became the centre of the nascent capitalist world-system. The European empires became a form of organisation corresponding to the global economic and social space, and imperialism was the result of the development of these empires. The American empire was the unique culmination of this process, denying its own imperial essence and implanting its hegemony under the slogan of 'spreading democracy'.

As capital became a global force, it subordinated local development to its logic in the most diverse areas of the planet, summoning bourgeois relations into life in these regions along with the corresponding ideologies. On this level, nationalism is entirely a product of imperial globalism, although this kinship is invariably denied. Global capitalism, however, has constantly suppressed national bourgeois projects and subordinated them to its own ends. Consequently, a bourgeois alternative to 'globalism' is impossible in principle; any serious attempt to break free of the world-system puts the logic of capitalist development in question.

Capitalism has carried through the unification of humanity, relying on the compulsion and violence that are linked indissolubly with the logic of accumulation – the logic to which the system ultimately subordinates any productive activity. Sooner or later, this principle must be replaced with the democratic coordination of economic processes. In terms of technology and information, the possibilities exist for achieving this. But realising such a principle in practice means bringing the history of capitalism to an end.

INDEX

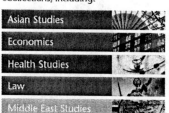